Comics: Anatomy of a Mass Medium

Comics
ANATOMY OF A MASS MEDIUM

REINHOLD REITBERGER · WOLFGANG FUCHS

Studio Vista London

Wolfgang J. Fuchs (left, born 1945) and Reinhold C. Reitberger
(right, born 1946) were brought up in the American-occupied zone
of Germany, and so they grew up with both German comic books
and their American originals. The years of uncritical reading were
followed by a period of collecting and sifting which eventually led to
a critical analysis of comics. Fuchs is an expert on mass media and
Reitberger has specialized in American studies. In this book the
knowledge acquired from a lifelong contact with comics is placed in
a social context and related to developments in the other mass media.
The authors are currently working on a new book on comics.
Reinhold C. Reitberger is editor of the comics magazine *Panel*.

Cover illustration
A drawing by Reinhold C. Reitberger, based on *The Anatomy
Lesson of Dr Tulp*

Frontispiece
Drawn by Herb Trimpe: a vision of himself at the mercy of the
characters he has created.
© 1970 Marvel Comics Group/Herb Trimpe

English translation © Studio Vista Publishers 1972
First published in Great Britain 1972 by Studio Vista
Blue Star House, Highgate Hill, London N19
Translated from the work published by Heinz Moos Verlag München
under the title *COMICS Anatomie eines Massenmediums*
© 1971

Set in Times 327 9 on 12 pt
Printed in Great Britain by Shenval Press, London and Harlow

ISBN 0 289 70319 0 (hardback)
ISBN 0 289 70266 6 (paperback)

Contents

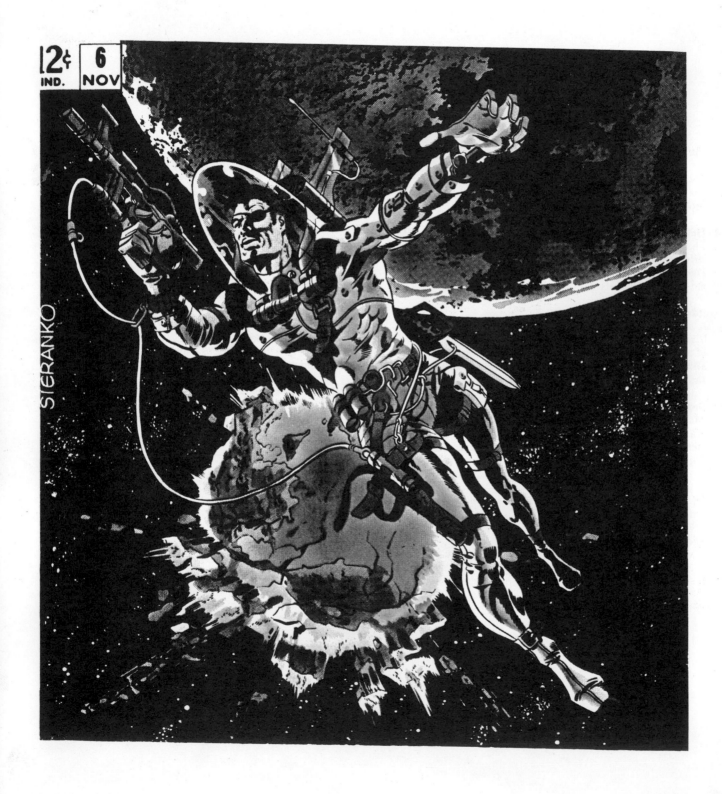

Introduction

Charges . . . that (the comics) were, in general a corrupting influence, glorifying crime and depravity can only, in all fairness be answered: 'But of course. Why else read them?'

Jules Feiffer *The Great Comic Book Heroes*

Comics have lost their innocence, for their secrets have been discovered. They have been subjected to investigation, dissected, analysed: the part they play in the orchestra of the mass media has at last been defined. Now that the veil hiding the true nature of their offerings has been lifted, the truth stands revealed: comics are essentially 'big business' and as such they help to perpetuate the system. The tempters of Madison Avenue, home of advertising, magazines and comics, have suffered the same fate as the glittering pseudo-magicians of Hollywood, for their mask has been torn away. We have realized that the creators are not the fatherly friends of their young readers. We have realized that their wicked motive is greed for money and profits.

'But of course' we are tempted to cry with Feiffer[1] who realized that it is the corrupting influence of comics which makes them attractive. What other reason would we have for reading them? Today we may admit without shame that we enjoy comics. An expert in the matter may even find himself admired by all and sundry. What a feeling of elation he gets from knowing about such avant-garde trends as Peanuts or the Donald Duck Revival! We have turned away from our more sophisticated pleasure in nudity and intellectual satire and we now behold with glee the flood of learned works on comics, which all confirm what we have known since our earliest childhood: comics are important because we love to read them!

Comics have existed for the last seventy-five years, and because newspaper strip cartoons were favourite reading matter for adults from the start, they became respectable long before comic books did. Paradoxically, it was not because of their fantastically high sales that people first began to investigate comic books. It was only in the fifties, when the hysterical cries of the guardians of our morals rose to a crescendo that the searchlight was turned on to the favourite literature of our innocent kiddies. People were blinded by the ghastliness of horror comics and for years they condemned all comics indiscriminately, declaring them a 'danger to youth'.

In the meantime comics have weathered the storm. Riding on the crest of the Peanuts and Asterix wave they have gradually overcome the 'danger to youth' stigma and have conquered new markets. In West Germany, for instance, approximately 144 million comic books are sold annually. Even highly respectable newspapers now carry comic strips. There are, of course, still people who regard them as a banal eyewash, but one glance at the readers' comments and the rising circulation figures of papers which carry comic strips dispels all doubt. Comic strips, by virtue of their immense popularity, strengthen the ties between readership and paper.

Even outside the United States, in Europe, for example—where despite the wealth of traditional folklore relatively few indigenous comics have appeared—people succumb to the fascination of comics, because they express so simply and directly the reader's fundamental wishes and inclinations. In comics we do not only meet the American archetypes, for the stereotyped figures of the American entertainment myth are not the only ones to satisfy the expectations of readers the world over. Comics are not just synthetic goods.

Comics, together with the other mass media, are a substitute for genuine folklore and culture and have developed into a self-perpetuating institution, an integral part of the American Way of Life. Of all the mass media, comics mirror the American Collective Subconscious most faithfully, and we know, without McLuhan having to tell us, that comics in turn manipulate and exploit the subconscious.

Several generations have already grown up with comics. Nostalgia sanctions and glorifies the fantastic dreams of youth, even dreams which are only rooted in the trivia of comics, penny dreadfuls and Hollywood films. All that remains of these dreams is a few well-preserved comic books—and also our memories, hallowed by time. For the vast numbers of comics which were in circulation have all been literally read to bits and thrown away. For some years now, old comic books and pages of Sunday paper comic strips have been selling at high prices. Exchange marts and specialized centres for the sale or purchase of old comics flourish in a big way. Rare early booklets have become collectors' items, or lie in the safes of millionaires who can afford to indulge their passion for comics.

But nostalgic collecting is not the only reason why old comics are in such great demand. They are useful reference material for sociological, historical or semantic research, or for research into advertising and publicity, as well as being of interest to museums. It is much more difficult to gain an overall picture of the growing diversity of comics, than of films, for instance. It is this massive output and this variety of ideas which make comics so fascinating.

Of course a large number of comics are of a very low standard, but the 'bad' comics are the most interesting from a sociological and psychological point of view. For in this mess of cheap entertainment unexpected pearls of beauty, hitherto undiscovered, suddenly appear. The same is true, incidentally, of Hollywood 'B' films.

We are, unfortunately, apt to be hypnotized by the popular strips that have 'made it', by the favourites of millions of readers the world over. True, Peanuts and Asterix are delightful, everybody agrees about that. But although more than sixty million book editions of *Peanuts* have been published this represents only one aspect of the situation. Figures like this tend to make us forget that—together with the whole of American society— comics, especially comic books, are on the lookout for new values. For this reason all comics, and particularly the great bulk of trivial comic books, are going to be presented and dissected in this *Anatomy of a Mass Medium*. The illustrations are intended to give the reader an overall impression and to let the comics speak for themselves.

And it has at last been accepted that a work dealing with comics does not need to begin by justifying its subject matter. For this reason we have dispensed with an 'archaeology of comics' that would try to relate them to Egyptian reliefs, the Bayeux tapestry or emblems of the Baroque period in an effort to raise them to a respectable level of research.

Their triviality is sufficient justification.

© 1970 Walt Disney Productions

1 The characteristics of comics

Zowie, bam, socko, grup, plop, wow, glug, oof, ulk, whap, bing, flooie and grr.

H. L. Mencken *The American Language*

Comics as an element in the communications media, satisfy in an exemplary way the longing of the reading masses to impose a pattern on psychological conflicts and the hero-worshipping of supra-maximal behaviour (the superman type, but also the comical, old, young, dare-devil, helpless, etc.).

(German) Dictionary of political journalism

Comics as a mass medium

When in 1970 Mort Walker searched for a name to give the little koala bear who was to appear in the series *Boner's Ark*—drawn by an artist with the pseudonym of Addison—49,329 children, parents and grandparents took part in the competition run by several newspapers to find a suitable name. Finally, the koala bear was christened Cubcake. The competition proved that today comic strips are still followed with the same enthusiasm as ever. Decades before, hundreds of thousands of suggestions had been sent in when Chic Young was looking for a name for the daughter of his world-famous comic strip figures Blondie and Dagwood; and when Al Capp requested drawings of Lena the Hyena, the ugliest woman in the world, one million ideas poured in from his readers.

But today even strips that have remained favourites for decades, whose readers protested furiously whenever newspapers omitted them for some technical reason, strips so popular that New York's mayor La Guardia read them over the air during a printing strike,[1] are no longer seen as old friends, simply to be enjoyed and admired without reflection. Al Capp, who since 1934 has castigated the American Way of Life with biting satire in his comic strip *Li'l Abner*, is to many of his eighty million readers, who devour his series every day, in thousands of newspapers the world over, a glowing example of the artistic heights to which comics can climb.

Capp has been euphorically praised and compared with Rabelais, Hogarth and Swift among others. Marshall McLuhan once described him as the only effective satirical power in the United States. And nobody who writes or talks about Capp ever forgets to mention that John Steinbeck once suggested him as candidate for the Nobel prize—Capp, of course, admires Steinbeck too much to doubt his literary sense of values. But in reaction to the deterioration in American standards, Capp's satire has become rather hysterical: long-haired students are now his favourite target for attack. He is in good company here—his political ally Spiro Agnew, who called the protesting students 'effete snobs', generally manages to put across the reactionary's hatred of the liberal and radical intelligentsia in succinct terms.

The droll koala bear Cubcake does not cause Captain Boner so much trouble as Rex, the tyrannosaur, or any of the other animals in the ark. Cubcake's name was chosen through a reader's competition. The enormous number of entries and the automatic success of *Boner's Ark* proved once again that comics are as popular as ever.
© 1970 King Features/Syndicate

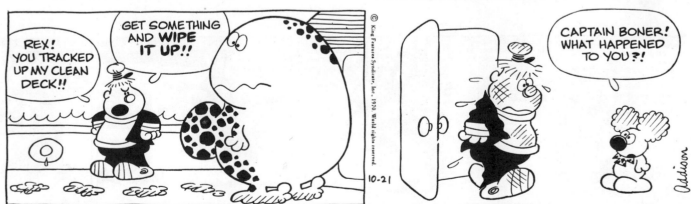

Chic Young's *Blondie*, the most successful comic strip in the world, has been coming out ever since 1930, which is the date of the first sequence shown on this page. On February 17, 1933 Blondie and Dagwood married. Dagwood's parents cut him off without a penny and so he began life as a typical American.

Although most of his ardent admirers do not realize it, Al Capp is no progressive satirical reformer, but a defender of the traditional virtues of the American Way of Life. *Li'l Abner* is only one example of the conservative strip, but he delivers his 'message' in a more forceful way than, for instance, *Little Orphan Annie*. In between *Li'l Abner* and the underground comics there is a whole spectrum of comics dealing with all manner of themes.

In principle comics are open to any theme or ideology. They can entertain, inform, or educate, just like any of the other mass media. Teamwork, expensive means of production and the high circulation necessary to cover the costs, impose restraints and taboos similar to those which radio, films and television have to accept. The specific means of production—line drawing—is time-consuming and in order to deliver a near-perfect product to as many consumers as possible, comics have to be prefabricated. This means they can only be called topical in so far as they show tendencies that stretch over longer periods of time: their topicality is latent, for their mere existence gives the reader the illusion of topicality. But they are more tyrannical than even Scherezade, and they oblige the reader to follow their stories.

Although comics can also be made to appeal to smaller groupings within a given society, mass appeal is a financial necessity for the comics syndicates and the publishers of comic books if they want to avoid a razor's edge existence on the borderline of profitability. Even if highly praised by its fans, the best comic strip becomes uninteresting to its producers if it can attain no more than a circulation of 100,000 copies. They also have to consider age groups: in the long run it is impossible to write for older readers without constantly going over the heads of younger readers. Indeed comic books like *Silver Surfer* and *Deadman* had to be abandoned because they were unwilling to lower their standards.

Comic strips are read by all classes of readers, because they offer almost any reader something on his own intellectual level. Their following is so great that new expressions like 'Let George do it', 'baloney', 'fall guy', 'got his goat' or 'Yes, we have no bananas' are taken into ordinary, everyday speech. Onomatopoeic words, too, like the ones quoted at the head of this chapter, are readily adopted.

But the language used in comics is not the main reason for their success. Comics have to be limited to non-controversial themes—humour, melodrama, action—because they are addressed to the masses. However, they incorporate the archetypal characters of fairy-tales, myths and American folklore and this is why their success was assured almost from the start.

Today anything that uses professional skill to appeal to mass audiences is called popular art: films, radio, television shows and television series, series of novels and, of course, comics. But individual works, performances or presentations are only rarely spoken of as popular art for it is a term reserved for the mass media. In his essay entitled 'Comic Strips and their Adult Readers' Leo Bogart defines the success of the popular arts as follows: 'The appeal of the popular arts stems from the fact that they express the fantasies, longings, and suppressed impulses of people living in a chaotic world. To lives burdened by frustration and monotony they bring a momentary release. Their heroes and heroines do all the things which the reading, listening or viewing public would like to do.'[2]

History of comics

The first exhibition to deal with comics, held in 1942 by the American Institute of Graphic Arts under the title 'The Comic Strip, its History and Significance', showed, as one of the earliest forerunners of comics, a Spanish cave-drawing dated approximately 3,000 BC. It is, of course, possible to trace the origins of stories told in pictures—humorous ones included—back to the very dawn of history; but cave-drawings, Egyptian hieroglyphs, Hokusai books, votive tablets and the Bayeux tapestry are only of interest inasmuch as they prove that comics are not an isolated phenomenon in the course of history. For the immediate forerunners of the comic strip had much more influence on its present shape and form than these earlier ancestors.

As the reader is probably familiar with the prominent figures in the history of comics—figures of the same stature as Méliès, Lumière and D. W. Griffith in the movie world—we shall mention only the most important milestones in the evolution of comics. Those who enjoy statistics and strict chronological order will find in the Appendix a chronological table ranging from 1894 to 1972.

The caricatures of the Middle Ages, drawn in a few sharp lines, can be taken as our point of departure. The great caricaturists of the eighteenth and nineteenth century, James Gillray (1737–1815), Thomas Rowlandson (1756–1827) and George Cruikshank (1792–1878), for instance, were quite familiar with the technique of a series of pictures. Rowlandson and other artists of his period already used 'speech balloons'. From political caricature to comic strip was but a short step.

This step was helped by the fact that in the nineteenth century American and European journals had already developed the basic elements of comic strips and comic books, in both humorous and serious picture series. Thus it was easy to adapt these techniques to newspaper printing techniques.

The American journals *Puck* (1877), *Judge* (1881) and *Life* (1883) carried contributions by Richard F. Outcault, James Swinnerton and Frederick Burr Opper, that were of paramount importance to the further development of the comic strip. In Europe the ground was prepared by artists like Gustave Doré, Wilhelm Busch and Rudolphe Töpffer, and by journals like the German *Fliegende Blatter* and *Neuruppiner Bilderbögen*, the French *Images d'Epinal* and the English *Comic Cuts, Ally Sliper's Half Holiday, The Illustrated Chips* and *Butterfly*. Many journals of that period catered quite intentionally for the more vulgar public tastes and so, together with dime novels and penny dreadfuls, cleared the way for comic strips and comic books.

One of the first illustrators whose work came close to our modern comic strips was Richard Felton Outcault (1863–1928). In 1894 he created a humorous cartoon composed of six coloured pictures entitled *The Origin of a New Species, or the Evolution of the Crocodile Explained*, for the *New York World*. The translation into newspapers had been made.

The comic's first wave of success came with the bitter war of competition between the various factions of New York's gutter press. Even in those early days it was recognized that next to sensational headlines comic strips were the most effective sales gimmick a newspaper could employ. There were two giants locked in a particularly keen battle for readers: Joseph Pulitzer's *New York World* and William Randolph Hearst's *New York Journal*. Each tried to beat its rival with sensational journalistic feats as well as with entertaining features in its Sunday editions.

Colour printing, which was to give a paper the edge over its rivals, was tested and found most promising; after some difficulties in producing the colour yellow had been overcome, Pulitzer tried out the new technique in the *New York World*. Outcault had been working for this paper since July 1895 and his regular contribution was called *Down Hogan's Alley*. This strip showed a small boy with sticking-out ears clad in a nightshirt which reached down to the floor. On 16 February 1896 this little boy became the main figure in a new large-format drawing, and as his nightie was now bright yellow the series became known as *The Yellow Kid*. The Yellow Kid's comments were printed on his nightie, but when he started to give voice to the crudest of jokes, whilst roaming the New York slums, he quickly lost the sympathy of his readers. But although this comic strip only had a short life the Yellow Kid lives on to this day in the expression 'yellow journalism' used to describe sensational journalism. In fact the Yellow Kid was himself a child of sensational journalism, for he was created to promote the sale of a paper.

On 12 December 1897, at a time when newspapers were engaged in full-scale war, the first pictures of a series that can be called a comic strip in the fullest sense of the word appeared in Hearst's *New York Journal*. Page 8 of that day's issue carried the first instalment of *The Katzenjammer Kids* created by the nineteen-year-old artist Rudolph Dirks of German descent. Hearst had seen Busch's *Max and Moritz*, and he wanted something similar for his own paper. Originally *The Katzenjammer Kids* had no dialogue, but the characters were soon speaking a strange sort of American-English with a strong German accent; their adventures took place in some fantastic, imaginary African country.

The Origin of a New Species, or the Evolution of the Crocodile Explained was one of the first strip cartoons drawn by Richard Felton Outcault, a pioneer of the comic strip, for the *New York World* in 1894.

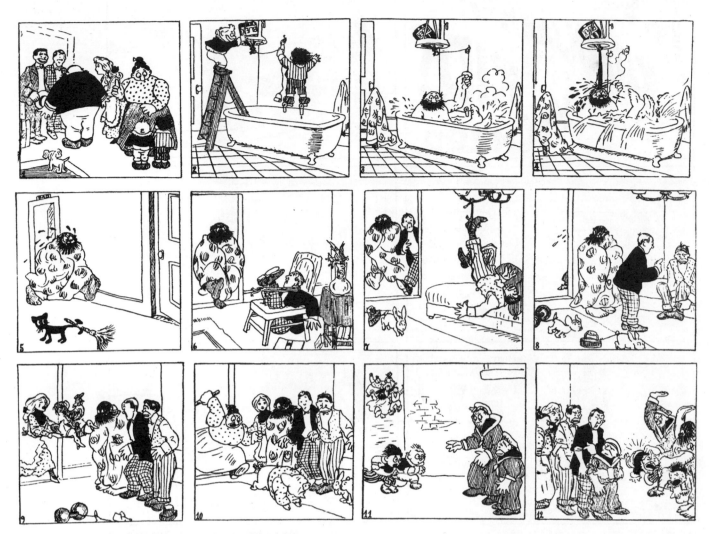

The Katzenjammer Kids by Rudolph Dirks was the first genuine
comic strip. In this early sequence which was also the first to be
reproduced in Europe (in 1908) Hans and Fritz are not satisfied with
playing just one prank—but eventually we see that their punishment
fits their crimes.
From: *Hjemmet* No. 39, 30 September 1958.
© King Features Syndicate/Bulls Pressedienst

It is in no way surprising that the first comic strips appeared
at a time of economic unrest. During the last decade of the nineteenth century the political tensions at home could only be side-
tracked by drawing attention to developments in foreign politics.
Then in 1900 the choice between 'Imperialism' and 'Isolationism'
was decided by the Presidential elections, when the votes cast for
President McKinley, who stood for Imperialism, showed a
greater majority than four years earlier. However at the end of
the Spanish War it became obvious that nothing could prevent
the United States from becoming a world power. Comics,
together with the first 'moving pictures', were a welcome means
of entertaining the masses and making them forget the troubles of
everyday life.

The Katzenjammer Kids is the oldest strip which is still producing new episodes today. It was also the first to become involved in
copyright wrangles, for when Dirks left the *Journal* he wanted to
take his creation *The Katzenjammer Kids* with him. In a court
case he lost the right to retain the title, but was granted the
copyright of his characters. Taking them to his new employer, he
first used them under the title *Hans and Fritz*, but when the
United States entered the First World War, the unmistakable
German origin of Hans and Fritz became an embarrassment and
the title was changed to *The Captain and the Kids*. This series was
not always located in Africa, but changed scene. However the
strip called *The Katzenjammer Kids* still follows the original
idea closely.

14

The pranks of Hans and Fritz became increasingly wilder under H. H. Knerr and the popularity of *The Katzenjammer Kids* grew, even after Dirks had left Hearst's *New York Journal*. The Kids' devilish tricks are punished with equal sadism.
© 1938 King Features Syndicate

In 1912, after leaving Hearst, Dirks continued his series centred around Hans and Fritz under the title *The Captain and the Kids*. Less pranks now and more adventures.
© 1962 United Feature Syndicate/UPI

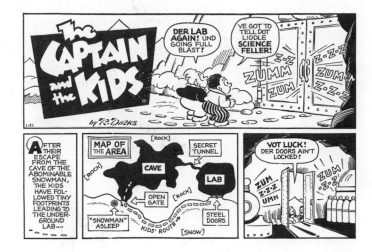

The issue of the *New York Journal* dated 12 December 1897, in which The Katzenjammer Kids made their debut, also carried James Swinnerton's *Little Tiger*, which had evolved from *Little Bears and Tigers*, a series drawn in 1892 for the *San Francisco Chronicle*. Under the influence of *The Katzenjammer Kids*, *Little Tiger* became a genuine comic strip with speech balloons and with the necessary continuity in the characters, and indeed it may be regarded as one of the ancestors of all our animal comics.

One of the most interesting early Sunday series was *Buster Brown*, created by Outcault after he left the *New York Journal* for the *New York Herald* in 1902. Buster Brown was an upper-class Yellow Kid—a little boy in a velvet suit. He and his dog created chaos wherever they went. This series alone would suffice to illustrate the enormous appeal and fascination of comics. *Buster Brown* influenced children's fashions and publicity campaigns for toys, whisky, shoes and cigars. The commercial exploitations of this series grew to such proportions that the results filled the Buster Brown Museum in New York (119 East 36th Street).

In 1907, when Sunday comics were already an established feature, there was a fresh development: on 15 November Harry Conway ('Bud') Fisher created the first successful strip to appear in daily instalments: *Mr. A. Mutt.*[3] Like Swinnerton's work, it was first published in the *San Francisco Chronicle*. Later, Hearst bought the series for his *Examiner*. In March 1908 the principal character, tall, lanky 'Augustus Mutt', met 'Jeffries', a squat little man wearing a top hat, in a lunatic asylum, and at this historic encounter Mutt pronounced the immortal words: 'This is gonna be a scream.' Since then the strip has been called *Mutt and Jeff*. Today it is drawn by Al Smith, who was Fisher's assistant until his death in 1932.

Thus it was possible, almost from the very beginning, for a comic strip to appear either on Sundays, or weekdays, or on all seven days of the week. Some of the strips are drawn by the same artist every day of the week, while others are drawn by different people on weekdays and Sundays.

As well as those which mark an important development in the history of comics, some comics—especially some of the very early ones—are graphic masterpieces. The drawings for *Kin-der-Kids* which Lyonel Feininger used to send to the United States from Munich have an expressionistic style. Winsor McCay's *Little Nemo in Slumberland* (1905–1911 and 1924–1927) and George McManus' *The Newlyweds* (a forerunner of *Blondie*) and *Bringing up Father* remind us of art nouveau.

Frederick Burr Opper gave human attitudes and reactions to the donkey Maud. Maud was one of the first anthropomorphic animals in comic strips.
© King Features Syndicate

One of the most imaginative series of comics was *Krazy Kat and Ignatz* created by George Harriman in 1911. It appeared under its final title *Krazy Kat* from 1913 to 1944 and entranced readers from all walks of life—even intellectuals. But the dadaist world of *Krazy Kat* was so strongly marked by the genius of its creator that the series had to be discontinued when Harriman died. This was one of the rare instances when a distributing syndicate was unable to find a new artist to continue an existing series.

In the beginning comic strips contained only funny stories or grotesque stories, or amusing caricatures. This is how they got the name 'comic' and this name was never changed, although they later widened their field to take in adventure and social problems.

In the early days there was much ethnic humour: humour aimed at a particular group of immigrants. Apart from the *Katzenjammer Kids,* there was *Alphonse and Gaston* with French characters drawn by Frederick Burr Opper, the artist who created *And Her Name Was Maud* and *Happy Hooligans* for the Hearst papers. Harry Hershfield's *Abie the Agent,* the first series to be

Happy Hooligan is an early example of Opper's particular type of humour. The warm-hearted clown with the tomato soup tin perched on top of his head is more compassionate than any of his associates.
© King Features Syndicate

known as an 'adult' comic, did not make fun of its Jewish hero but drew its humour from Abie's confrontation with his environment. *The Gumps*, created in 1917 by Joseph Medill Patterson, founder of the *New York Daily News*, became a faithful portrait of the 'American family' whose members, though poor, were proud and ambitious. Americans loved to identify with these lovable characters and *The Gumps* soon became their special darlings. This series was so successful that it brought its inventor the first contract worth a million—one million dollars for ten years—and for ten years he produced instalments of *The Gumps*. In 1935, just when his contract had been renewed for another five years at $150,000 a year, he was killed in a motor accident—and so the first chapter in the long history of this cheerful series ended.

But these amusing comics were not simply designed to entertain their readers. We can see from their history that comics were the tool of a few newspaper publishers who wanted to extend their power and their control of the market. Eventually big distribution syndicates were established, to prevent any single newspaper from reaping all the profits when a comic strip helped to promote their sales. They made strips available to smaller newspapers at fees they could afford to pay. Out of Hearst's International Feature Service, which started in 1912, the King Features Syndicate evolved in 1913–14. It took its name from Moses Koenigsberg (the German word Koenig means king!), the Hearst editor who had first included comics among the

features distributed by the syndicate. From then on comics were distributed throughout the American continent and eventually throughout the world. After 1915 the syndicate became 'big business' and comics were regarded as indispensable by all the daily papers—except the *New York Times* and the *Wall Street Journal*. Mass distribution started between 1919 and 1925 when strips such as *The Gumps, Harold Teen, Little Orphan Annie, Gasoline Alley, Moon Mullins* and *Barney Google* contributed to the comic's national success. Today there are twelve large and roughly 200 smaller syndicates in the USA, some of which only distribute a single comic strip. There are also syndicates abroad, as well as branches of the big American firms, and they guarantee a world-wide distribution.

The emergence of comic books can also be traced back to the profit motive. There was a forerunner as early as 1843, when Wilson and Company, a firm specializing in the popular paperback romances of that time, published a type of comic book called *The Adventures of Obidiah*. The drawings were not as artistic as they are today, and they had no speech balloons. Obidiah Oldbuck is an ancestor of today's comic book heroes, but he remains an isolated figure in the history of American popular literature. More than half a century passed before the idea of comic books was revived.

The best known early comic book that contained real 'comics' was a collection of Bud Fisher's *Mutt and Jeff* series, published by the *Chicago American* in 1911; but other series, including *The*

Yellow Kid, also appeared in cheap 75 cent volumes, as early as 1904. *Mutt and Jeff* was sent out on receipt of coupons and this proved to be a successful sales promotion gimmick for the newspaper, for the booklet reached a circulation of 45,000. But despite the great demand, the production of these booklets was eventually discontinued.

In 1929 George Delacorte, owner of the Dell Publishing Company, hit upon the idea of publishing a magazine in tabloid format,[4] printed on newspaper: a Sunday comics supplement with no accompanying news sections. The magazine contained original stories, not reprints of series, but after thirteen editions the experiment had to be abandoned. It probably failed because the magazine looked too much like part of a newspaper.

The Whitman Publishing Company was more successful when it published 'Big Little Books', handy booklets (10 cm. × 12.5 cm.) of 260 pages, half of them showing full-page pictures, the other half giving the consecutive text. They were very popular in the thirties, but lost appeal when the comic books appeared on the scene.

At that time various firms gave comic books with reprints of popular series as publicity gifts to their customers. Harry I. Wildenberg and M. C. Gaines, the pioneers of comic books, stuck 10 cent stickers on the free issues of the *Famous Funnies* series, and the vendors whom they persuaded to display the booklets in their kiosks sold them all within a few days.

The next noteworthy experiment was made by Delacorte with an edition of 35,000 booklets of reprints, which sold rapidly through a chain of stores; but the experts remained sceptical. In 1934 the *New York Daily News* emphasized the importance of comics for newspapers in an advertisement. The Eastern Color Printing Company, which had produced the earlier experimental comic books, decided to try again. *Famous Funnies* were printed, sold for ten cents a copy and—the first issue was a flop. After the fifth book the venture began to climb out of the red. Comic books had arrived.

In 1935 Delacorte published the *Popular Comics* produced by Gaines. United Feature Syndicates' *Tip Top Comics* and the

In the twenties and thirties pantomine strips were very popular. Many of the favourite strips in Sunday papers carried a smaller top strip above them. Chic Young's *Colonel Potterby and the Duchess* (a pantomime strip) was the top strip to *Blondie*.
© 1949 King Features Syndicate

McKay Company's *King Comics* (with strips taken over under licence from King Features) appeared the following year. Still in 1935, Major Malcolm Wheeler-Nicholson, a former pulp-writer, started his comics publishing company. It was soon taken over by Harry Donenfeld who, in March 1937, presented the public with the first comic book featuring original stories instead of reprints of strips: *Detective Comics*. It bore the stamp of success from the start and this series is often regarded as the first true comic book. The initial letters of its title still feature on the title pages of National Comics issues and the imprint 'DC-Comics' has become more popular than the publishing firm's full name.

The type of stories that were to be published in these new comic books, of original stories,[5] was determined by *Action Comics* which appeared in 1938 featuring *Superman* for the first time, and by issue 27 of *Detective Comics* which appeared in 1939 with the first *Batman* story. By 1939–40 there were already 60 different series of comic books and by the end of 1941 the number had risen to 168; by 1950 there were approximately 300, and by 1954, before the introduction of the Comics Code, there were roughly 650. Under the supervision of the Code Authority exactly 18,125 issues of comic books appeared up to the end of 1969, of which 1,110 issues were published in 1969. The number of titles published in 1969 came to 250, of which about 175 were published under the supervision of the code.

Side by side with the adventure stories of the forties, stories of anthropomorphic animals, like Paul Terry's *Terrytoons Comics* and *Walt Disney's Comics and Stories,* boomed; and after the rip-roaring characters of the adventure story comic books came the first 'informative' comic books: George Hecky's *True Comics*, the *Classics Illustrated* of the Gilberton Company and M.C. Gaines' *Educational Comics*.[6]

The Second World War had a brutalizing effect on the output of all the mass media, including comics. Things that would have been judged sadistic in 1940 were deemed accurate reporting in 1945; but later some comics went too far and what weighed most heavily against them was the fact that they could be bought by anybody, including children. For many kids comics were, because of their low price, the only literature they could afford to buy. In the end the inevitable happened: because of the excesses of some comics, all comics were attacked and denounced. Like the makers of films and the producers of other mass media presentations, the producers of comics were obliged to lay down certain rules regarding the content of comics, and the Comics Code Authority came into being. The most beneficial effect of this was that the bloated comic book market shrank to a healthy size.

The critics of comics made no distinction between newspaper strips and comic books, but the newspaper comics escaped the worst of the comics debacle, because, as the National Cartoonists' Society (created 1946) pointed out, newspaper comic strips had long since observed their own code. To boost the prestige of comic strips after the cleaning operation and make them more 'respectable', a Newspaper Comics Council was created in 1955.

The advent of the Comics Code is a good point at which to end this survey of the history of comics, for it set the final seal on the character of comic books. All later developments and the series that evolved after the syndicates had taken over distribution, will be treated in the following chapters according to their importance.

The first *Superman* comic book, published in 1939, gave a reprint of the story in *Action Comics* No. 1.
© 1939 National Periodical Publications, Inc.

Sappo, top strip to Elzie Segar's *Thimble Theatre*, bases the imaginative and fantastic humour of its series on the confrontation between man and intelligent plant-beings on another planet. The main character Sappo acts as befits his name.
© 1937 King Features Syndicate

Picture from Al Williamson's *Secret Agent X-9*. Original size. Most of the daily strips are drawn in this format. © 1967 King Features Syndicate

Methods of production

In Richard Quine's film *How to Murder Your Wife*, Jack Lemmon gives a hilarious performance as a comics designer suspected of wanting to murder his wife. With terrifying realism this character acts out the wild adventures of the hero of his comics and, in order to get the pictures he thinks he needs for a highly realistic strip, he madly photographs everything as he goes along. But the profession of a comics designer serves only as a peg on which to hang the crazy exploits shown in the film. Lemmon's Stanley Ford is a playboy who lives exclusively for pleasure. Work is done in a jiffy, shortly after midnight. The drawings thus produced give him power over a nation thirsting for his strips: Lemmon's performance gives the profession of designer the sort of glamour usually reserved for film stars.

The only thing in this film that vaguely resembles reality is the prize a top comics designer may win—the takings can be enormous. In real life the comics world is even more hectic than the film, and a great deal more prosaic. The efforts that went into producing the first comic book to feature the joint appearance of *Sub-Mariner* and *Human Torch*, for instance, must have been more frantic than anything a film could show. The drawings were planned and executed in three days by a dozen designers, because the publisher wanted the booklet immediately after the idea had been discussed. And this was no isolated case. There is always a deadline lurking in the background and holidays are only possible after a great deal of preparatory work has been finished. Much more prosaic than the work shown in the film is the continuous work in archives, ferreting for references, or the search for material that can guarantee the accuracy of facts.

Though comic strips and comic books have much in common, there are some fundamental differences in the methods of production. Strips are serials, prepared for distribution among newspapers, and they have to ensure the continuity of each instalment. Comic books can deal with a wider context and their stories can have conclusions and sequels. The stories of some comic strips are created entirely by the designer himself. In other cases the designer invents the main theme and then engages a ghost writer to supply the following instalments but there are also comics which feature stories written by known authors—*Phantom* and *Mandrake*, written by Lee Falk, for instance—with pictures drawn by an artist working for the syndicate.

Hal Foster's *Prince Valiant* may serve as an example of how a comic strip is produced. To start with, the story is shaped and written like a novel, then edited and checked for accuracy. Correct historical detail, a much appreciated feature of this series, demands painstaking research into illustrations of the period. When the 'novel' has been completed, pencil sketches are made of the individual pages which contain the weekly instalments. Each sequence takes up the thread of the story and carries it towards the next climax. The 'novel' is cut by two-thirds, so as to achieve the shortest possible text to go with the illustrations. Then the pictures are executed in drawing ink on the 73 × 38 cm. pages and photocopied. The photocopies are subsequently coloured and from these the engraving plates are made.

During the inking process the assistant had to adapt himself one hundred per cent to Foster's style. Tex Blaisdell, who was left-handed, had to turn Foster's drawings upside down when he was asked to hatch in the background, so that the drawings would retain the overall impression of having been executed by a right-handed artist. The syndicates also expect this kind of perfectionism when a well established series is taken over by a new artist.

Al Williamson, John Prentice's assistant on the strip *Rip Kirby* in 1960, described the co-operation between a designer and his assistant:

> I would lay out a strip and then pencil and ink the backgrounds. Later on I would lay out a strip and then John would tighten the penciling on the main figures. Next I'd tighten up the backgrounds and then John would ink the whole thing—figures and backgrounds. I didn't think my inking was very good but once in a while, if I felt brave enough, I'd ink the backgrounds. This always scared me, however, I worked like this for John for two or three years

and then he gave me a chance to do the whole thing on occasion. . . . John would ink the heads of the main characters, when he first started me on my own, and then finally I graduated to being able to do the whole strip from time to time. At that time I was doing some other ghosting for other artists. [7]

'Ghosting'—anonymous work—is by no means rare on comics. Assistants relieve the designer of time-consuming research, or specialize in details like background, costumes, etc. The lettering for the text is nearly always drawn by an expert calligrapher.

Charles M. Schulz belongs to the few artists who do all the work themselves; they feel that only thus can the finished product really reflect what they have envisaged. It is probably the style of drawing which Schulz has chosen which enables him to keep the murderous deadlines necessary for a comic strip appearing seven days a week.

The finished drawings are submitted to the syndicate and corrections or alterations made if necessary. Usually they are only minor modifications, for the syndicate always knows the content of stories from the synopsis submitted by the author before the work is put in hand. At the syndicate screens are usually placed on the drawings where the designer has indicated

Rip Kirby by John Prentice is an excellent example of how a strip can be continued after the death of the original artist (in this case Alex Raymond), without a break in style.
© King Features Syndicate

light blue, because in the photographic process applied later the colour blue is not reproduced.

Sunday pages often differ from daily strips in that they tend to use less black drawing ink and do not draw the shadows quite so deeply, in order to exploit all the possibilities offered by colour; also Sunday pictures must be arranged in such a way that they fill a whole newspaper page lengthwise, but could equally well be used, when re-arranged and reduced in size, to spread across the width of half the page. Furthermore, either because of scarcity of space, or to present more comics, the editor must be able to dispense with the first row of pictures, so that the entire series, originally planned for a whole page, can be placed on a third of that page.

This means that in humorous comics the first row of pictures contains the title and then a gag that has some connection with the rest of the strip, but is not essential to the story. Adventure strips use the first row to refresh the readers' memory. Comic strips and comic books are produced up to six months in advance, but whilst comic strips in America always appear on the date marked on the picture, comic books are pre-dated. Nearly all periodicals have to be pre-dated because of delivery terms, but none go to such extremes as American comic books.

In the 'Golden Age' of comics many budding designers did no more to begin with than ink in the lines surrounding a picture with the help of a ruler. Many a great artist's career started in that lowly fashion. The production process of a comic book, however, generally starts with the editors hatching out the ideas; an author is engaged to write up the stories and a graphic artist to design the drawings. A pencil sketch is then made of each picture, framed by drawing-ink lines, and the letterer puts in the text. Sometimes the text is written or pasted in at a later stage. Finally a second artist inks in the whole design, or the 'penciller' does the inking himself. When the pencil lines have been removed, each completed page is sent to the Comics Code Authority in New York. If there are no complaints, the page receives the Code Authority's stamp and is sent back to be photocopied and colour processed. Stan Lee of Marvel Comics has modified the first step in the production of a comic book in a rational and imaginative way; the basic idea of a story is discussed with the artist, who then works out his design. When he submits his pencil sketch, the text is written and placed in the picture before the final inking is done. This is the secret of the famous 'Marvel Touch'.

Rick O'Shay, by Stan Lynde. This Western comic is designed for a third of a page. If (as shown here) it appears in half-page format, two pictures on the left are left out.
© 1968 Chicago Tribune—New York News Syndicate

Forms and features

Comics tell their stories by correlating picture and text. Artistic value is not of primary importance, as comics are made for everyday use and not for display in museums.

Some comic strips, like *Cisco Kid*, appear on weekdays only; others, *Prince Valiant,* for instance, only on Sundays; then there are those, like *Dick Tracy*, that can be read seven days a week. Adventure strips appearing throughout the week, including Sundays, bring either two adventure stories running parallel as, for instance, *Phantom*, or one story with linked weekday and Sunday instalments, such as *Terry and the Pirates*. This often necessitates a complicated distribution of the action, which must avoid too much repetition, offering the seven-days reader something new every day, yet making sure that the 'weekday only' or the 'Sunday only' reader does not lose the thread of the action.

The first daily strips used to span the whole width of a newspaper, but during the Second World War paper became scarce and had to be used economically. Comics shrank, first from eight columns to six columns, then from six columns to four columns. But the number of pictures in each daily instalment—between one and four—was retained. Sunday strips have at least four rows of pictures if they spread over the whole page lengthwise—like *Mary Perkins on Stage*—or they can have six rows, like *Blondie*. A half page usually has three rows (*Peanuts*), or two (*Rick O'Shay*). The various formats for the series are supplied by the syndicates in tabloid or newspaper format in the required sizes and page divisions. Syndicates can also supply ready made comic sections to newspapers, complete with the name of the paper in question; these are then added to the Sunday edition. In Europe comparable comic supplements to newspapers were introduced only a few years ago. France was the first country to adopt them. Before then only the European editions of the American army's newspaper *Stars and Stripes* and such weeklies as *Overseas Weekly* and *Overseas Family Weekly* carried them, so that American soldiers and their families were not deprived of their favourite comic strips.

Up to the early fifties comic books in the USA, such as *Super Comics* and *King Comics*, reproduced newspaper strips. But comic books containing original series, such as DC's *Flash Comics* shown below already constituted the main output of production.
© 1947 Chicago Tribune—New York News Syndicate (left)
© 1948 King Features Syndicate (centre)
© 1948 National Periodical Publications Inc. (right)

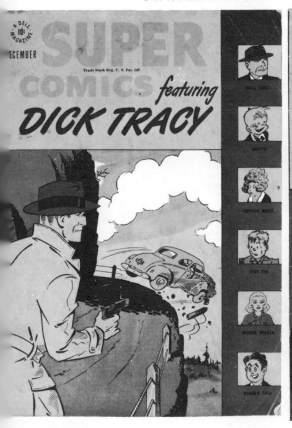  

Comic books have, generally speaking, a format of roughly half-tabloid size. Originally American comic books of sixty-four pages of newspaper print, bound in slightly heavier, smooth paper, cost 10 cents. They shrunk to fifty-two and forty pages, and today they offer only thirty-two pages, plus a cover. The price first rose to 12 cents, then to 15 cents, and it is now 20 cents. Special comic books called 'annuals' comprising ninety-six pages plus a cover, were sold for 25 cents up to 1962. Then in 1971 DC changed all its titles to fifty-two page books sold for 25 cents.

In contrast to newspaper strips, comic books offer opportunities for the publication of complete, conclusive stories, and the distribution of pictures within the rectangle of a page can be planned on a freer and more imaginative scale than in the Sunday newspaper strips. The style of comic books in the thirties and forties was much simpler and much cruder than that of the comic strips of the same period, but that was, in a way, their special attraction. The appeal to the reader—usually young—was more direct, and the drawings looked as if one could almost draw them oneself, given just a little talent. Since the early days of comic books, often described as the 'Golden Age of Comics', techniques of reproduction have been vastly improved, more is expected of the graphic artist working in the medium, and the quality of comic books has risen to a considerable degree.

Side by side with 'American style' comic books imported from the USA, or produced locally, European countries now present their youth with comic periodicals containing a plethora of adventurous or humorous stories, usually in serial form; they also bring, for full measure, articles on all kinds of subjects of interest to the young. Such periodicals evolved from picture series like *Images d'Epinal*. Examples of this type of magazine, designed especially for the youthful reader, are the Italian *Corriere dei Piccoli*, which started in 1908, the Belgian *Tintin*, 1946, and the French *Pilote*, 1959. They are weeklies and therefore better suited to the publication of serialized stories than the American comic books which are published monthly, bi-monthly or quarterly. Some of the European comics appeared in illustrated magazines or in newspapers long before they were published in specialized periodicals; *Tintin*, for instance, has existed as a comic strip since 1929. The habit of publishing stories in serialized form was inherited from these magazines and newspapers and the gradual swing away from serialization started only quite recently. These European comic weeklies are usually published in a format of 21×29 cm.

The range of German comic book publications extends from weeklies to quarterlies. Books in classic comic book format, uniting several series under one title, were first introduced after the Second World War. To start with they were monthlies, but now they are weeklies and they have the highest sales figures in the German comic market. *Micky Maus (Mickey Mouse)* has the lion's share of the market: 1·4 million copies out of the 12 million comic books sold in Germany every month.

At first, comic series appealed to their readership on national or ethnic lines, but soon the comics scene became more international and today the most popular series can be read in all continents and sometimes even in the politically opposing camps of East and West.[8]

Much as comic strips and comic books may differ from each other in their style of presentation, they resemble each other closely in the vocabulary used and the way in which the pictures express ideas. The most important rule for any comic is that the text must be contained within the picture. Strips like Hal Foster's first *Tarzan* series, which still had the text written outside the picture, are counted as comics because their stories appeared in instalments of similar dramatic construction, and then gradually adopted the same forms as other comics. If a text is able to stand by itself—that is, if it is not related to both picture and dialogue—then this is an illustrated story or a picture book, but it cannot be described as a comic strip or comic book. The text of a comic is usually based on dialogue: narrative is given in short sentences and confined in squares framed by black lines. Dialogue is placed in balloons of various shapes and sizes, with tails pointing to the character speaking the words. These balloons obey certain rules which all comics have adopted.

Normal dialogue appears in balloons with an unbroken outline, with the tail pointing to the speaker. A perforated line indicates whispering. If the words are written in very small letters within a big balloon, it means the speaker is astonished or ashamed. A cry has a spiky outline, and the famous 'telephone voice' has a zig-zag shape, with a zig-zag arrow disappearing into the telephone. Balloons indicating cold or conceited voices have little icicles sprouting from their undersides. Thought balloons are connected with the thinker by a series of small circles which look like bubbles, and if a speech balloon has a little arrow pointing outside the picture, the speaker is 'off'.

This very effective pictorial language expresses all manner of exclamations, feelings and moods. Curses can be expressed by stars, exclamation marks or various other signs. Someone who has had a sudden inspiration, or whose dense mind has been penetrated by an understanding thought, will see a lighted candle, lamp, bulb or chandelier appearing in his thought balloon. Depression shows itself in dark clouds inscribed with a single succinct word like 'Gloom!', but at the height of utter despair the unfortunate victim may even be drenched with rain—from his own black thought balloon.

'ZZZ' or 'CHRRR' or the picture of a sawing-trestle stand for snoring. A wealth of onomatopoeia is used to express different sounds. Someone groans 'GNNN'; a racing car moves off with 'VRRROAAAAW', and after years of searching for novelties, Marvel Comics came up with such onomatopoeiac pearls as 'THTUP!', 'FZOPPP!', 'SKIAK!' and 'PTOOM!'. Still, comics will never be able to compete with film and television as far as speech and sound are concerned. SPROIIINNNG-NNG-NG!

In this sequence from *The Born Loser* by Art Samson the thought balloon is used most effectively to put over a gag.
© 1970 Newspaper Enterprise Association Inc/UPI

The passage of time can be most effectively illustrated by means of a split panel, without using text like 'minutes later' to make the transition. Two or more pictures are united by a common background and the action moves in pictures from left to right in front of this communal background. Something similar happens in films when the camera takes a stationary longshot. This can convey the extreme isolation or loneliness of the characters moving across the scene. The split panel can also have symbolic significance. 'All men are equal', for instance, can be expressed by bringing together half a black man's head and half a white man's head as one head, in a split panel.

Countless emblematic devices are used in comics, but the few examples we have mentioned may suffice. They are not used rigidly and can be varied in many ways: their choice often depends on the genre chosen by a particular comic.

Donald Duck, trailing speed lines, races round a corner. From *Walt Disney's Comics and Stories*, No. 303 (reprint).
Drawn by Carl Barks.
© 1944 Walt Disney Productions

Speed lines may also serve to veil violence. The star in the right-hand picture indicates pain. Donald Duck is saying: 'The just must suffer'.
Drawn by Carl Barks.
© Walt Disney Productions/Ehapa Verlag, Stuttgart

Musical notes, sometimes whole musical phrases, appear when music is being played, or when somebody whistles or speaks in particularly dulcet tones, and comics have even devised formulas to express movement or the passage of time. Speed lines or action lines are used to show the direction of movement, and if the movement of a fist ends in a punch on the jaw, dashes emanating from the point of impact explode in all directions. Speed lines also follow the direction in which a person or an object is travelling. Sometimes the contours of a person or an object appear behind them and this serves the same purpose: it indicates movement.

Characteristic example of the split panel technique. The passage of time is conveyed without the use of narrative text. From: *Our Army at War* No. 218, drawn by Russ Heath.
© 1970 National Periodical Publications Inc.

Howie Schneider also uses the split panel technique quite frequently in his *Eek and Meek*. Eek is the mouse with the black hat.
© 1970 Newspaper Enterprise Association Inc/UPI

Like any entertainment geared to serialization, comics have their main characters or main themes. The adventures of the main character may be told in instalments or in a series of conclusive stories. A new humorous situation may be shown each day, as in *Blondie* or *Henry*. Some instalments lead daily from one climax of excitement to the next. Other series appear during the week as cartoon panels and on Sundays as a real comic strip *(Dennis the Menace)*. Adventures in comic books can be brought to a conclusion in one issue, but they may at the same time contain sub-plots that lead to new adventures and lend a feeling of continuity. Comics can tackle any given theme in all sorts of different ways and there are so many series in existence that we may wonder how we should categorize them.

The contents of comics have up to now been divided into two to eight main groups. The division into two main groups seems to be the most logical one from the point of view of historical development. It is, roughly condensed, as follows:

1900 to 1930 Funnies
1930 to 1940 Adventures
1940 to 1954 Super-heroes
Autumn 1954 Comics Code
1955 to 1962 Recession
1962 to 1970 New boom in comics
Spring 1971 Change in Comics Code. New contents in comics.

The period up to the introduction of the Comics Code shows that humorous and adventurous comics developed at different times. Within these historically motivated categories various genres gradually evolved. As the emergence of the adventurous super-hero coincides with the introduction of comic books and as the super-hero appears almost exclusively in comic books, he seems isolated and important enough to be looked at separately. The other types will be introduced within the framework of the two main categories of humour and adventure. The distinction between humour or comedy and adventure or drama is based on criteria of theme and form. If the intention of a given theme is primarily to entertain—with humorous situations from everyday life, or with the adventures of the 'little man'—and if the drawings support this intention with an amusing caricaturistic style, then the series can be classed as humour or comedy.

If adventure is the point of departure—deadly serious, melodramatic, or only slightly tinged with humour—and if realism is maintained, whatever the style chosen, then the series falls into the category of adventure and melodrama, or drama.

Japanese version of *Peanuts*. The onomatopaeiac word 'Swoop!', which accompanies Snoopy in the original, is very effectively represented.
© 1970 United Feature Syndicate/UPI

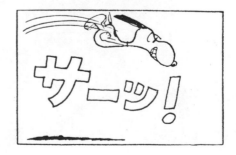

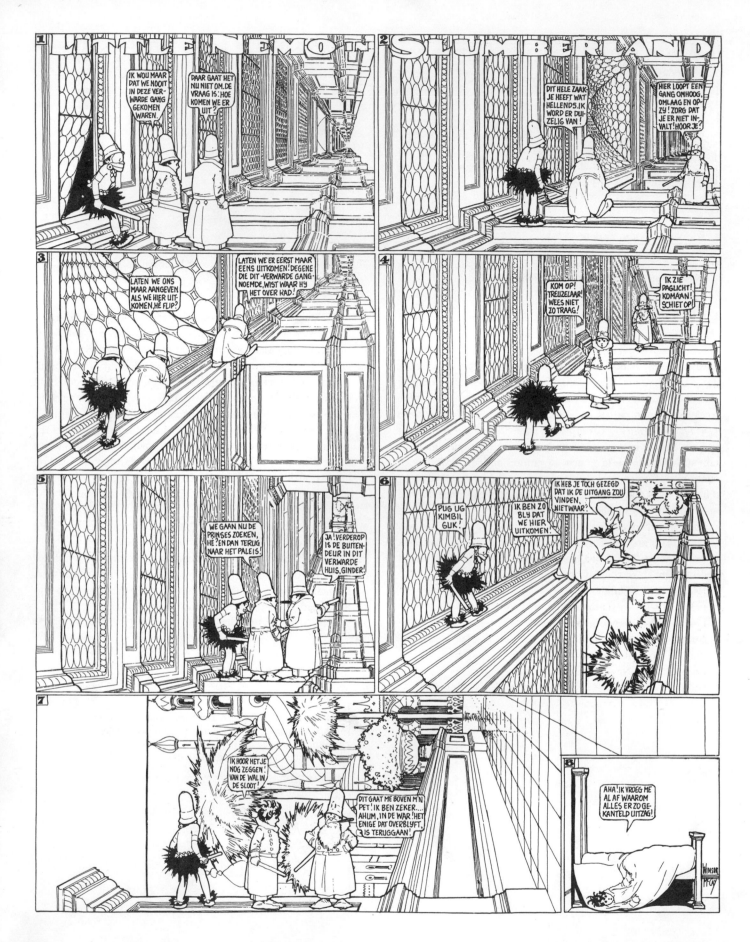

2 Humour and everyday life

American humour, as shown in the works of Mark Twain, or in first-class slapstick of the Mack Sennett and Jerry Lewis variety, is of a very particular and unmistakable brand. It is the tall tale, the outrageous exaggeration, the gags and nonsensical chat produced in shows like *Rowan and Martin's Laugh In*[1] on television. Most Americans fondly believe that they possess an abundance of that precious Anglo-American characteristic called a sense of humour. And this despite the fact that canned laughter —laughter recorded on tapes—had to be introduced into their radio and television shows to tell them at what point to laugh 'spontaneously'.

'Funnies' do not need similar crutches. Their humour also depends on the gag, the insubstantial joke, but the secret of their riveting effect lies in the very nature of comics: the correlation between the gag expressed in words and the point made by the drawing. Comics obey the precept 'brevity is the soul of wit', and come to the point quickly in just a few pictures.

Life is serious, the art of comics lighthearted. This concept held good up to roughly 1930; before the adventure strip came along, the comic sections of newspapers contained nothing but grotesque or burlesque humour of great variety, which is the reason why comics are still widely known as 'The Funnies'.

In the beginning, before comics spread through all the newspapers in the land and before the big syndicates turned them into a money-spinning commodity, funnies could experiment freely. In those days they were still farcical, based on comic situations and bringing ludicrous nonsense and way-out slapstick to their readers. It was humour that depended mainly on delight in others' misfortunes. Humour in early, silent films was largely based on tastes created by the funnies.

When the syndicates entered the scene, self-criticism started and provocative humour was (and remains) outlawed; feeble attempts at ethnic jokes soon petered out, while 'black humour', the 'sick joke', never existed in comics. Humour was then limited to the highlighting of minor human weaknesses of a universal nature. Satire or indirect comment on social conditions lost its bite; although a form of self-criticism of the masses, it was not allowed to hurt anybody. The white lower middle class, which has the highest percentage of comics readers, found itself mildly caricatured, but never really provoked by satire.

With the spoken gag becoming increasingly popular in comics, the jokes in some strips became wittier and more ingenious. Semantic misinterpretation, humour based on taking a symbolic meaning literally, and used at times with a typically Anglo-Saxon delight in sheer nonsense, gave a new direction to some comics.

These more sophisticated strips are often based on incongruous misunderstandings and absurdities and the charm of anthropomorphic animals also stems largely from this type of nonsensical humour. But despite the successes of *Pogo* (1948–49) and *Peanuts* (1950), sophisticated humour, especially when coupled with social comment, gained ground only very slowly. It was not until after 1955 that the flood of new comic strips began to pour in— a flood that continues to this day.

Of the thirty-nine strips introduced between 1956 and 1960, thirty-two are of a humorous nature and belong, when judged by the style of their drawings, to the funnies. Since 1960 more than thirty new humorous strips have been added: double the number of realistically drawn adventure series—and it must be borne in mind that usually an old strip has to be pushed out before a new one can establish itself. By definition (style of drawing and content) sixty to eighty per cent of today's comic strips are funnies.

Little Nemo in Slumberland by Winsor McCay. The fascination of Little Nemo's dream world lies in McCay's mastery of perspective. In Europe too reproductions, like this Dutch example, delight enthusiastic fans.
© 1945 McCay Features Syndicate, by permission of Woody Gelman

Most successful funnies have also been published as comic books, as have the popular adventure series—first as reprints of newspaper strips and later in special series designed by 'ghost' artists. In contrast to the funnies in newspapers, the funny comic books are read by and designed for children, although this does not deter the addicted adult from enjoying his favourite Walt Disney comic book.

The 'fall guy' and the grotesque

In order to be readily understood by everyone, the funnies drew on humorous folklore and borrowed a popular figure: the eternal loser, the unintentional clown, the underdog; and with the adoption of this figure began the social function of the comic strip. With increasing prosperity however, the bulk of the readership soon tired of clumsy criticism of social conditions, as expressed in Outcault's *Yellow Kid* and demanded lighter fare that would make them laugh in a joyous, liberating way. In silent films, too, social criticism was to be smuggled in only occasionally, as in Charlie Chaplin's portrayal of the irrepressible tramp.

The first of the witty clowns—so much more effective than the clownish wits—was *Happy Hooligan*, the clown with the tomato soup tin on his head, who made his first appearance in 1899. But his compassionate and goodhumoured nature, shown in the face of all the misfortunes and formidable hang-ups he suffers, either by accident or bad luck, and the patience and forbearance with which he endures undeserved beatings and cruelties, awaken in today's readers only cynicism, together with a *Schadenfreude* (malicious delight in someone else's discomfort) tinged with bitterness.

Frederick Burr Opper, who invented this endearing eternal loser, was one of the great innovators—a genius in the art of the comic strip. Like George McManus *(Bringing up Father)* and Herriman *(Krazy Kat)* he became immortal through one strip, despite the fact that he, just as his two great colleagues, had opened up a wide field of new possibilities with many other strips. He created, for instance, *Alphonse and Gaston,* a series which caricatured excessive politeness ('After you, Alphonse'—'No, after you, Gaston') and *And Her Name was Maud,* the gay adventures of a mule, one of the most popular animal strips of the funnies and the forerunner of a multitude of animal series.

Opper also influenced other artists. The broad mouth and large ape-like upper lip of his characters reappear in early strips by Herriman; George McManus, and Rube Goldberg and Milt Gross drew much of their inspiration from Opper.

The funnies invented the name by which the eternal loser is known today: 'fall guy', one of the most important neologisms the comics have coined. It was first used in Bud Fisher's *Mutt and Jeff.* The humble, anonymous man of the masses, whom the French call 'l'homme moyen sensuel', was given a face in the fall guy and became articulate through Happy Hooligan, Augustus Mutt, Barney Google, Dagwood, Donald Duck, Beatle Bailey, Archie, or characters like Mr. Mitchell, the father of Dennis the Menace.

The fall guy must drink the cup of misfortune down to the very dregs, so that the reader may find a momentary release from his own frustrations.

Mutt and Jeff (see also page 17) have won a more prominent

Snuffy Smith by Fred Lasswell. Snuffy follows his usual occupation: he rests, next to him is the 'moonshine'. His hill-billy, back-of-the-woods dialect has repeatedly enriched the American language.
© 1965 King Features Syndicate

Popeye, by Bud Sagendorf. For decades Olive Oyl has tried to persuade Popeye into marriage—in vain. Here Popeye uses his typical 'I yam'. Wimpy has, as always, nothing but food on his mind.
© 1970 King Features Syndicate

place in American folklore than, for instance, Stan Laurel and Oliver Hardy, and the expression 'fall guy' has become part of the American language, for Mutt typifies the unfortunate individual on whom fortune has turned her back—permanently. In Mutt's case, in view of his addiction to gambling, particularly galling. After he had teamed up with Jeff, Mutt's passion for gambling began to lose its gag-potential, and Mutt and Jeff turned into modern versions of Everyman (referred to as 'Mute' and 'Jute' in *Finnegan's Wake*), poor in spirit as well as in material goods.

In *Mutt and Jeff* the appeal of the fall guy was combined with the grotesque to begin with. In the early days it did not matter to Bud Fisher that Mutt sometimes had six or seven fingers, for the emphasis was entirely on the gag. Mutt and Jeff, like the Happy Hooligan and all the other main characters in grotesque strips, used to do something that has now gone out of fashion in comics: in order to stress a point or underline a joke, they used to faint. They fainted with such enthusiasm and alacrity that they often tumbled backwards and right out of the picture—leaving only their legs and a few speed lines behind. This method of expressing exaggerated emotional outbursts, signifying horror or extreme astonishment, was gradually abandoned in the course of a few decades. Together with a more sophisticated approach to gags the drawings too became subtler.

Barney Google, drawn by Billy de Beck (from 1919), is a fall guy like Mutt. One day Barney, the little guy who was pushed around by everybody and who could never hold a job down for any length of time, was given a racehorse. Spark Plug was the name of this gallant quadruped, never to be seen without a horse blanket reaching down to its hooves. To see the 'goo-goo-googly eyed' Barney, always sporting his bowler hat, careering away on Spark Plug was a sight for the gods.

But one fine day Spark Plug won a race and suddenly Barney

was made, and no longer quite such a fall guy. Perhaps this is why Snuffy Smith and his wife Loweezy, introduced into the strip in 1934, won popularity so rapidly that they soon became the main characters and almost pushed Barney Google out of the title of the strip. In contrast to the Snuffy Smith family, hillbillies from the back of beyond, Barney now appears as a city slicker. Snuffy sleeps most of the time unless he is busy playing poker or distilling 'moonshine' (dark whisky), whilst Loweezy does the work. Barney only becomes active when he joins battle with the 'revenooers' (tax collectors). Barney Google and Snuffy Smith have enriched the American language with such poignant phrases as 'the heebie-jeebies', 'fiddlin' around' and 'times a wastin''—to mention but a few.

The Thimble Theatre drawn by Elzie Crisler Segar is a pure 'gag-strip'. Like *Barney Google* it started in 1919. It centres round the Oyl family; then in 1929 'Popeye the Sailor' was introduced. Popeye was the first superman of the grotesque strip but for a long time his main efforts were concentrated on escaping from Olive Oyl's marriage plans.

Whenever Popeye eats spinach the impossible becomes possible. In 1937 the grateful spinach farmers of Crystal City, Texas, erected a memorial to the eternal memory of this sales-promoting comic strip figure. Another character who influenced the nation's eating habits is Popeye's friend 'Wimpy'. He is mad about hamburgers, and although originally his name had nothing to do with the chain of restaurants known as Wimpy Bars, his undisputed fame had a strong beneficial effect on both hamburgers and on the famous restaurants. Popeye, equally successful in Max Fleischer's cartoon films and since 1961 raised to fresh heights of glory in a new television series, was continued in comic strips after the death of Segar, first by Bela Zaboly, then by Ralph Stern and finally by Bud Sagendorf.

Boob McNutt by Rube Goldberg (1918) and *Count Screwloose of Toulouse* by Milt Gross (1919) betrayed in their titles the kind of gags and semantic experiments the reader could expect. True to their early promise, Goldberg and Milt Gross gave their readers many a new expression: 'banana oil' (Milt Gross), and *'Mike and Ike—They Look Alike'* (Goldberg) were taken into everyday usage.

Boob McNutt was the epitome of the blockhead, the eternal clod, always at a disadvantage and helplessly buffeted about by life. The bizarre mechanisms which characterized Boob McNutt's particular craziness, became one of the most famous features of Goldberg's work.

Goldberg died in 1970, but the special brand of Goldberg's humour left a lasting impression on the art of comic strips. He also designed the 'Reuben', the Oscar of the comic strip, awarded annually (since 1946) to the best cartoonist.

Bill Holman became the worthy successor of the two great pioneers, Goldberg and Gross. He has produced panel gags and strips for the funnies since 1924. Holman is the king of the pun and the greatest manipulator of words in the American language.

Smokey Stover, a strip Holman started to draw in 1935, is as 'nutty as a fruit cake'. Nobody, probably not even Holman him-

Smitty, by Walter Berndt, is one of the early 'kid' strips. © 1928 Chicago Tribune—New York News Syndicate

self, knows what 'Notary Sojac', an expression used somewhere in each sequence, really means. To describe Smokey Stover is impossible and it is best to let an example from the strip speak for itself.

At times a picture can say more than a thousand words. The forerunners of comics and the early comic strips had no speech balloons. Some had text written beneath the illustrations, but in the main they let the pictures make their point unaided. A few strips still follow this pantomime tradition. Cartoons and caricatures can express volumes in one drawing, the pantomime strip relies on a row of pictures and comes to the point of the illustrated gag in the last picture.

Smokey Stover, by Bill Holman. The most important facet of *Smokey Stover* is the illustrated pun. The last picture shows the strange 'Notary Sojac', over which readers have puzzled for decades. © 1971 Chicago Tribune—New York News Syndicate

Henry by Carl Anderson. Henry shows that a comic strip can succeed without words.
© 1970 King Features Syndicate

To this category belong *Henry,* drawn by Carl Anderson in 1932 for *The Saturday Evening Post* and adopted by the Funnies in 1935, and *The Little King,* by Otto Soglow, a strip taken in 1934 from the *New Yorker,* where it caricatured the customer as king. Other pantomime strips are Chic Young's *Colonel Potterby* and the Duchess, Hapless Harry by George Eatley, and the Sunday strip *Mr. Mum,* which appears on weekdays as a one panel gag; but the most important strip of that kind today is *Louie,* by Harry Hanan, which describes the martyrdom of a fall guy under the tyrannical rule of his wife.

The Little King by Otto Soglow. This strip started as a caricature of the customer as king.
© 1970 King Features Syndicate

'Kid' strips

During the early days of comics children were in the main protagonists and the 'kid' strip genre is still strongly represented in the funnies of today. Children in comic strips are by no means little angels and this is not only because The Katzenjammer Kids are an American version of Wilhelm Busch's wicked Max und Moritz.

Comic strips appeared in an era when the practical joke, the prank, the hoax, had become a cult.

Good examples of the popularity of *Schadenfreude* in that period are the practical jokes exercised by famous personalities,[2] which can be verified historically; and also George W. Peck's book *Peck's Bad Boy and His Pa*, which was published in 1883 and became a best seller. From 1871 episodes from this and many other books appeared with tremendous success as a regular feature in many newspapers.[3] The tricks played by Hennery, the bad boy, on his father are, judged by modern standards, incredibly clumsy, vulgar and cruel. Walt McDougall started to draw *Peck's Bad Boy* for comics in 1906 and other funnies also reflected the popularity of the practical joke.

In addition to *The Katzenjammer Kids* a number of other strips presented a selection of kids' varying degrees of maliciousness: 1902 *Buster Brown* (Richard Outcault); 1905 *Little Jimmy* (James Swinnerton); 1905 *Tim and Tom the Terrible Twins* (C. W. Kahles); 1906 *Hairbreadth Harry* (C. W. Kahles); and in 1912 the second edition of *The Katzenjammer Kids, The Captain and The Kids.*

The obsession, in early comics, with youth and with boys in particular, stemmed from a trend in literature which had produced Huck Finn, Tom Sawyer, the boys of Horatio Alger Jr. and, in the 1920s, Booth Parkington's Penrod. At the beginning of the twenties a new wave of 'kid' strips rose on the tide of successful child characters in silent films. *Skippy*, by Percy Crosby, was one of many boys resembling Jacky Coogan in *The Kid* (1921). Skippy, who reached film and Oscar fame in 1930, and another boy, called Smitty, seem to have stepped straight out of a Horatio Alger Jr. book.

Smitty, drawn by Walter Berndt from 1922 to 1971, was like many of his colleagues' boy characters a 'ragged Dick' on his way from rags to riches. Since he started on his career with the job of messenger in a respectable firm, he began at a comparatively high rung of the social ladder and so did not appear in tattered clothes, like Skippy, for instance. Smitty eventually grew up and his little brother Herby had to provide the 'tiny tot' humour. Smitty has not yet climbed the pinnacle of fame and fortune, but he married Ginny, his employer's secretary and finally became the proud father of his own little Herby.

Ad Carter's *Just Kids* (1921), or Gene Byrnes' *Reg'lar Fellers*, were gay, bright kids, with a developed sense of social justice, definitely a joy to their parents. This type of child humour has remained popular to this day. Boys in comics, as well as the girl *Little Iodine* by Jimmy Hatlo, were brats, at times veritable little devils, but they kept their childish charm and remained lovable. Comic kids of today, such as *Winthrop* (Dick Cavalli, 1956), *Nubbin* (Sam Burnett and George Crandall, 1956) or *Tiger* (Bud

Blake, 1965), also behave like kids, act according to their age and do the things one expects of them. In sharp contrast to these 'nice' children stand characters like those in *Peanuts* or *Miss Peach*, who talk, behave and act like grown ups. Here the humour is based on the discrepancy between their childlike appearance and their adult behaviour.

Neither are the *Katzenjammer Kids* really children, for Hans and Fritz get up to no ordinary pranks, no simple childish fun; it is fiendish mischief. With the battlecry 'Society iss nix' they declare total war on all representatives of social order and launch their outrageous plots against authority in any shape, be it 'der Captain', 'dir Mama', or 'der Inspector'.

One of the most successful descendants of these two young devils is *Dennis the Menace* (1951), drawn by Hank Ketcham. This strip appears on weekdays as a panel cartoon and on Sundays as a comic strip. Dennis romps through 700 newspapers in 43 countries around the globe, and the reprints of his weekly exploits, in pocket book form, sell extremely well. And *Dennis the Menace* is equally successful as a comic book, because—oh dreadful thought—children love to identify with him. A special treat are the *Dennis the Menace* annuals which are published at regular intervals, which show this household hurricane on holiday travel with his parents. To get the correct feel of the environment, a writer-artist team first visits the places chosen.

Perhaps *Dennis'* success lies partly in the fact that parents can draw a breath of relief when they see this small dynamo of destruction, because, in comparison, their own offspring are models of exemplary behaviour. Unlike Hans and Fritz, the Katzenjammer Kids, Dennis is not intentionally wicked, he simply acts so spontaneously and so completely without thought that he leaves a trail of destruction in his wake, plus an army of enraged policemen, bus drivers and shopkeepers turned kid-haters on the spot; because of Dennis, nursery school teachers begin to doubt their vocation and babysitters, if they come near the Mitchell's home at all, come dressed for near-combat.

Dennis is so successful because the Mitchells have average family appeal. They are like a toned-down version of the Bumstead family in *Blondie* except that Mr. Mitchell has less to suffer under his wife's whims and that the reason for the slightly (but permanently) worried look on Mrs. Mitchell's face is not hard

Little Jimmy by James Swinnerton, was one of the most popular 'kid strips'. Quite early in his career, Swinnerton introduced a clear, simple technique of line drawing into his work. © 1949 King Features/ Syndicate

to guess. Dennis' Christmas wishes include, as befits a television-conscious child trying to emulate Cowboy Bob, a pony and, more ambitiously, a submarine and an elephant.

Harvey Publications publishes comic books with strips especially designed for children. Very young readers do not require characters with super-heroic traits in order to boost their egos and so they are given the type of stories children prefer, but with an added 'message' or 'moral'. The most perfidious strip of that kind is *Richie Rich*, the good little rich boy who can make it so abundantly clear how very pleasant it is to be immensely rich (Uncle Scrooge is poor compared with Richie's father) and how beautiful and benevolently noble the people are who possess such riches.

The best of the Harvey Publications, and this includes the drawings, is probably *Casper, the Friendly Ghost* (imitated without success by Charlton in *Timmy the Timid Ghost*). The fairytale character of the little ghost, who frightens people but does no harm and always makes good the damage caused by his wicked relatives—also ghosts—delights children. Harvey Publications has cashed in on their success with *Casper* by publishing several booklets with similar characters, among them *Hot Stuff*, an endearing little devil straight from hell.

'HEY! LOOK WHAT I FOUND!'
Dennis the Menace by Hank Ketcham. In the daily sequences Dennis has just a single cartoon panel for his tricks: only on Sundays is he allowed a full comic strip. His parents have retreated into an attitude of silent martyrdom.
© 1970 Publishers-Hall Syndicate

Tillie the Toiler by Rush Westover. The capricious, flirty little Tillie, like all secretaries, marries her boss in the end.
© 1949 King Features Syndicate

Playful Little Audrey, Little Dot and a few other booklets of that type cater for the otherwise largely neglected girls, for among the whole wealth of children's strips in funnies there are hardly any that are designed for girls. Ernie Bushmiller's *Nancy* and Marge's (= Marjorie Henderson Buell) *Little Lulu* are among the few exceptions.

The family strip—mirror of life
The most successful strips are still those that have vulgar appeal and show characters with which the greatest number of people can identify. They hold up a (distorting) mirror to the readers of *Reader's Digest, The Saturday Evening Post* and of the various book clubs. These strips prove that the things people laugh at can reveal a great deal about their character. Gilbert Seldes (1926) calls this particular category of funnies 'vulgar comic strips'. They are commentaries on the way of life of their readers, mainly lower middle class, and this is the reason why they do not reflect the 'Jazz Age' of F. Scott Fitzgerald in any significant way; for the 'Jazz Age' concept implied a life-style belonging to the more well-to-do strata of society. *Polly and Her Pals* (1912), by Cliff Sterret, made some concession to that concept, but as Polly's

father and mother—both horrified at their daughter's 'flirty ways' and 'scandalous little frocks'—play major parts in the strip, we can assume that its success was due to the domestic interest in it. *Tillie the Toiler* by Rush Westover (1921) also tried to be fashionable, but more interesting than Tillie herself was her boyfriend Mac, who belonged to the 'loser' type of character shown in earlier strips. *Tillie the Toiler* came to an end in 1958 (having been transferred to a new artist) with Tillie and Mac's wedding.

After roughly ten years of experimenting, with strips like *The Newlyweds* (1904), among others, George McManus found in *Bringing up Father* the right formula for a character with which a broad readership could identify. This strip about Maggie and Jiggs, the Irish immigrants who have made it in the first generation and suddenly find themselves classed as 'newly rich upstarts', began in 1913.

Whilst Maggie, the one-time washerwoman, climbs the social ladder with gusto in order to join the class of society to which her daughter Nora already effortlessly belongs, Jiggs is always trying to find refuge in Dinty Moore's Saloon; there, enjoying his favourite meal of corned beef and cabbage, and a game of billiards, he can escape from the tyranny of his starched life at home.

Bringing Up Father by George McManus. Maggie's love of pompous decor gives McManus opportunity to exercise his genius by drawing the stylized interiors in all their baroque glory. As always, Maggie is portrayed in appearance as well as in her actions as a highly unpleasant character—in contrast to her beautiful daughter Nora.
© 1941 King Features Syndicate

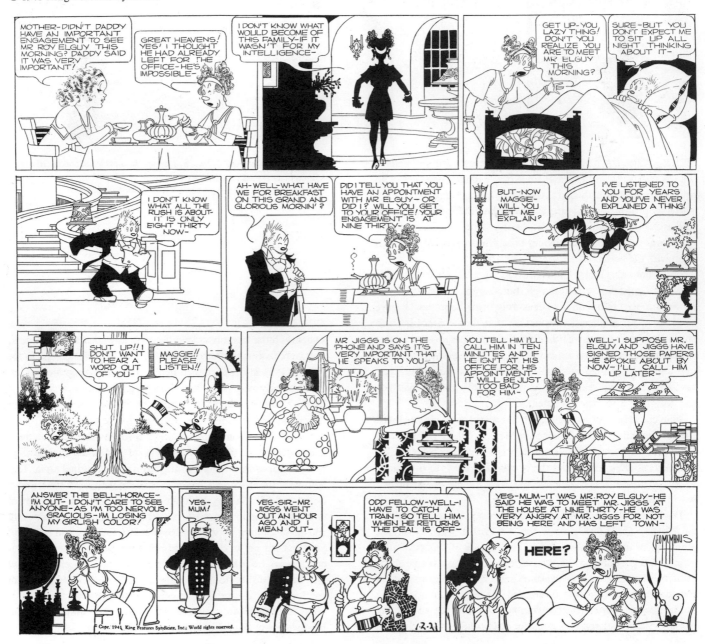

In the short, squat Jiggs, McManus has drawn himself, and his wife is portrayed in the beautiful Nora. Maggie, however, who apes even the silliest fashion, was given an ugly face to top her perfectly proportioned figure, as a punishment for the brutal and aggressive way in which she treats her husband. Maggie, with her ridiculous snobbishness, provides misogynists who identify with Jiggs with the perfect outlet for their hatred.

It was not only George McManus' genius as an artist that made *Bringing Up Father* such a success, but also the lesson contained in the strip that riches do not necessarily bring happiness. It gave millions of readers great satisfaction that they did not have to share Jiggs' burden of wealth: they did not have to wear an uncomfortable top hat and ridiculous spats, like Jiggs. Corned beef and cabbage acquired heightened prestige because it was Jiggs' favourite meal and readers could persuade themselves that they too preferred it to expensive steaks.

Jiggs could be understood by men the world over. He was loved under the name of 'Don Pancho' in Mexico, 'Illico' in France or 'Herr Schmerbauch' in Germany. Stage and film reflected his fame successfully, and so did the bombers of the 11th Bombardment Squadron which were decorated with his image in two world wars.

The Gumps (1917), by Sidney Smith, became at least as popular as *Bringing up Father*, despite the fact that it was not half as amusing, or as well drawn. It was the success of this particular strip which encouraged the syndicates to distribute comic strips to all the newspapers in the country, and this in turn resulted in the content of strips being orientated towards 'mass appeal'.

The subject matter for *The Gumps* story was the gossip, the trivialities and the problems of a poor but proud family, related in

Moon Mullins by Ferd Johnson. Despite his subtle methods, Moon Mullins has no success with women.
© 1966 Chicago Tribune—New York News Syndicate

a slightly bitter humorous vein. But this appealed to the readers; they were familiar with the type of life the Gumps lived and in the intentionally ill-proportioned figure of Andy Gump and his incredibly ugly wife Min they recognized themselves. The time came, however, when the popularity of *The Gumps* began to slump and in 1959 they were relegated to the archives.

Moon Mullins, on the other hand, is still as cherished as ever. It was started in 1923 by Frank Willard and taken over in 1957 by Ferd Johnson, who has continued it in its original style. This strip tells the story of a bunch of loafers who have inherited a house and live a happy-go-lucky, if chaotic, life. Though all are ambitious none like to work, and they only do it intermittently and never for long. Moon Mullins dreams of money and beautiful girls, but has no luck at cards nor at dice and because of his uncouth ways he makes no impression on the girls either. Lord and Lady Plushbottom, the latter as ugly as Maggie and Min combined, have somehow or other landed in that community and their ridiculously 'refined' behaviour only emphasizes the boorishness of the other occupants of the house.

Gasoline Alley (1919) describes the basically uneventful life of a middle class family. The story of the Wallets, of which Coulton Waugh wrote that it was not just a facet of life, but life itself, stands out mainly because its characters, unlike those of other strips, age naturally.

To start with, *Gasoline Alley* was a cartoon panel and its subjects were a garage and cars, hence the name. It was later turned into a strip. On 14 February 1921 Walt Wallet, owner of the garage, found a baby on his doorstep. This foundling, named Skeezix, celebrated his fiftieth birthday on St. Valentine's Day 1971. Frank King's *Gasoline Alley* is really a generations novel, for it relates with homespun frolic not only the adventures of Skeezix since his arrival, but also the life stories of his relatives. The happy reader is allowed to share Skeezix's childhood, his joining the army during World War Two as a humble G.I., his return home and (of course) his marriage to his childhood sweetheart Nina. Skeezix in due course becomes a father and Uncle Walt's joy on becoming (several times over) a grandfather knows no bounds; all these and many more family events the reader shares.

The quiet, unobtrusive humour of *Gasoline Alley* offers its readers instruction on how to tackle the simple problems of everyday life with a cheerful smile. For this reason comic strips of that type—which include *The Gumps, Moon Mullins* and *Blondie*—became an American institution and played a major role in establishing the funnies in the American Way of Life.

Blondie, a strip started in 1930 by Chic Young, is very much an institution. It has long since reached saturation point in the US and appears in 1,200 newspapers all over the world. For decades now, *Blondie* has been the favourite strip anywhere and everywhere and this is mainly due to the fact that the character of Dagwood Bumstead combines the appeal of the fall guy with that of the henpecked husband. Marshal McLuhan thinks that the strip should really be called *Dagwood*—and in fact there is a strip dedicated entirely to Dagwood, as well as the comic book series called *Blondie*.

Chic Young explains the success of his strip as follows: 'I . . . use the greatest, simplest, and most interesting continuity of all, the continuity of life itself, and add a little humour, the spice of life!'[4]

Gasoline Alley by Bill Perry. Two weeks before Skeezix's birthday Uncle Walt Wallet gathered together the different threads in this story and presented the most important episodes in the life of the foundling he had originally found on his doorstep.
© 1971 Chicago Tribune—New York News Syndicate

Dagwood Bumstead, sporting a hair style that looks as if horns were growing out of his head, typifies and at the same time caricatures the average American. Dagwood is a fall guy who can rarely—if ever—cope with a given situation. Every morning he has to beat the clock. He wins only by the famous jump on to the already moving bus. At Mr. Dither's office, where he works as a faceless zero in the ranks of the white collar proletariat, he stands out only because he has been given the sack over and over again for his unbelievable incompetence.

Exhausted by the office routine, incapable of lending a hand in the simplest household chore, receptive only to the passive joys of his television set, his spare time is one long battle against salesmen, the neighbours' kids and other intruders. Dagwood's main pleasures consist in a comfortable snooze on the sofa, or a long-drawn-out hot bath. Both are invariably interrupted. To compensate for all his frustrations, Dagwood, for whom the reader's heart beats in compassion, creeps down to the fridge at the dead of night to feast on the famous, several feet high 'Dagwood sandwich'.

Before her marriage Blondie was a typist in the firm of Dagwood's millionaire father. But she was no gold-digger, like Dumb Dora, a character Chic Young drew previously; she was an empty-headed little thing, pretty and—as her name indicates—blonde. After her marriage to Dagwood, who was consequently disinherited, Blondie took command. Now Dagwood is utterly subservient to her. His pathetic little revolts are never even registered. A new dress or a good bargain sale represent Blondie's idea of heaven and Dagwood's purse is mercilessly rifled to satisfy her whims.

Among the many family strips that existed before 1930, was *Toots and Casper* by Jimmy Murphy, a direct forerunner of *Blondie*. It presented, in 1919, the unprepossessing and clumsy Casper, who constantly asks himself how he could possibly have merited the love of his beautiful wife. Toots is in looks and behaviour quite clearly the model for Blondie. *Toots and Casper* also shows Murphy's special technique of sometimes drawing the speech balloons three-dimensionally as real clouds in the sky.

Blondie by Chic Young. A typical day in Dagwood's life. Poor Dagwood can't even have a bath in peace.
(German version)
© King Features Syndicate/Bulls

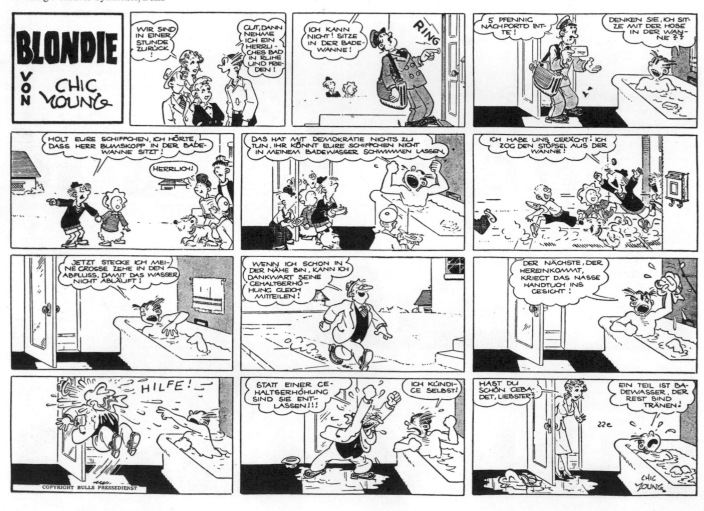

Dagwood Bumstead, prototype of the average middle class American, returning from a midnight raid on the larder.
© 1958 King Features Syndicate

Hubert by Dick Wingert. The nightmare of a visit from the mother-in-law has become a permanent reality.
© 1969 King Features Syndicate

Hi and Lois by Dik Brown and Mort Walker (German version). This family is lovable and objectionable at the same time, because of its 'normalcy' and its appeal to the average citizen. Mort Walker (*Beetle Bailey, Boner's Ark*) supplies the text to Dik Browne's drawings.
© 1970 King Features Syndicate/Bulls

All the family strips that came into being after 1930 were influenced by *Blondie*'s fantastic success. *The Born Loser*, by Art Samson, carries the fall guy motif to the extreme in the Dagwood-like figure of Brutus Thornapple, and the *Flop Family* series betrays its theme in the very title.

The gentle humour of *Hi and Lois*, written by Mort Walker (*Beetle Bailey*) and drawn by Dik Browne, is based on another middle class family's daily struggles, in which the reader can recognize many of his own everyday hang-ups. The strip *Hubert*, by Wingert, shows how the portly, good-natured head of the family, though tyrannized by wife and mother-in-law, nevertheless manages to assert himself from time to time.

Lancelot by Penn/Coker. Here the successful stereotype of the tyrannical wife is turned upside down and the husband is given the dominant role. The artist Phil Coker Jr became famous through his contributions to the magazine *MAD*.
© 1970 Newspaper Enterprise Association Inc./UPI

It's wonderful to be a teenager

Archie, with red hair, indicated by a simple criss-cross of lines above his ears, wearing orange chequered pants—they used to be knickerbockers at one time—and a black, sleeveless pullover, is the archetype of the American teenager as he appeared after World War Two.

Bob Montana created him for MLJ-Comics and the unprecedented success of the comic books soon prompted MLJ to concentrate on *Archie*; they suspended their super-hero books almost completely and changed their name to Archie Comics.

Whilst the term 'head of the family' is used only sarcastically in the strips just mentioned, in *Lancelot* by Penn and Coker junior, the boot is on the other foot and the wife is the subservient party.

Two episodes from the life of Archie, the typical American teenager who feels compelled to follow each and every modern trend. Drawn by Dan de Carlo.
© 1970 Archie Comic Publications Inc.

Since the end of the war Bob Montana has been drawing the *Archie* newspaper strip, whilst other, no less competent artists produce the comic books; the latter sell at a rate of over fifty million a year (roughly the same as the Marvel output). Not all, but most of the comic books show the exploits of Archie and his pals. *Archie, Archie's Jokes, Archie and his Friends, Betty and Veronika, Reggie, Jughead,* are but a few from this money-making series.

Innocently pure are the pleasures of the typical American teenager! His activities are centred mainly round the 'dating game'; the rest is the 'clean innocent fun' all growing youngsters the world over enjoy.

Archie's friends are a motley crew of diverse characters: Jughead, the misogynist, whose main interests in life are food (a budding 'Wimpy', he loves hamburgers best) and sleep; Reggie, Archie's conceited, unsympathetic antagonist, Moose, physically strong as a bull, but mentally not very bright; and Dilton Doily, the physically weak scientific genius.

Archie's only great love is the raven-haired Veronica, daughter of a multi-millionaire. Veronica's rival is blonde Betty, poor but sweet-natured and always willing to help, whilst Veronica's arrogance and selfishness indicate that too much money in the background is not always good for the character.

The teachers coping with Archie and his friends are all droll, slightly eccentric characters who have not forgotten that they, too, were once young. Despite all their basic strictness they have a warmhearted understanding for the innocent pranks played by their pupils. The fat rector Weatherbee's toupee is the target of many ingenious tricks; Miss Grundy, an old maid, always wears the same tube-like dress with frills, and Professor Noodle is absent-minded to a degree.

For roughly fifteen years the characters in *Archie* did not alter by a hair's breadth. Veronica's hair-style remained unchanged and so did Betty's pony tail. But now both have become more versatile and Reggie no longer sports the Rudolph Valentino type of middle-parting; Archie's hair is still very short and like any self-respecting teenager he still drives an ancient car in its last stages of decay, but he has started to dress differently and now follows the latest fashions.

Archie Comics reflect the fads and fashions of modern commercialism and they see to it that adolescents accept them as 'in'. During the *James Bond* and *Man from U.N.C.L.E.* fever Archie acted as 'Man from R.I.V.E.R.D.A.L.E.' and recently he even tacked on to the super-hero boom as 'Super-Archie'.

At the time of the great rock and roll craze Archie had his own cartoon television show featuring his rock and roll group called The Archies. Its fame spread beyond national frontiers and The Archies were much more popular than The Monkees—the group they had originally copied.

Archie Comics, who also produce *Josie,* a rather more modern, but equally stereotyped copy of *Archie,* are not the only ones to profit from the teenage market. Employees of Marvel Comics, for instance, jokingly refer to the fact that *Millie the Model* sells better than their super-hero series. Most of these jolly teenage strips follow the *Archie* recipes closely and it is almost impossible to distinguish between *Binky, Binky's Buddies* (revived after a lengthy absence) and *Scooter,* all published by DC; *Bunny,* by Harvey, or *Tippy,* a Tower publication. A variant was DC's *Dobie Gillis,* adapted from a TV series, but this did not survive for very long.

Before the advent of *Archie*, a comic series called *Etta Kett* (Paul Robinson, 1925) was instructing America's youth in etiquette (get it?): Youth portrayed in this strip acted as innocently, and with the same blank facial expressions, as in *Teena,* by Hilda Terry, *Penny* by Harry Haenigsen, *Ponytail* by Lee Holley, *Aggie* (male counterpart to Ponytail) by Roy Fox and *Emmy Lou* by Mary Lind. Today *Teen Wise* by Berrill has been added to strips that try, in their own sweet way, to advise youth on its problems and to smooth over difficulties vis-à-vis the older generation.

Typical teenage humour. Artist: Henry Scarpelli.
© 1970 National Periodical Publications Inc.

Donald Duck & Co.

Ever since Aesop's fables animals have had to act out human weaknesses in order to teach us our lessons, and since we have read Swift's biting satires we know that animals are the better human beings. But not only in fables and fairy-tales, in art too anthropomorphic animals abound. The Japanese artists Kiosai and Hokusai of the eighteenth and nineteenth centuries commented on the world in satirical animal pictures, and Grandville, a contemporary of Daumier, caricatured human beings mercilessly under the guise of animals.

In comics the only artist who has so far continued the old tradition of animal satire is Walt Kelly, with *Pogo*. The first animals in comic strips, like Swinnerton's *Little Bears and Tigers* (1892), Opper's *Maud* (1905) and on a higher level Herriman's *Krazy Kat*, were anthropomorphic like all their successors, but their purpose was to provide humour, not satire.

All comic books and strips featuring animals taken from cartoon films, such as Bugs Bunny, Tom and Jerry or the Big Bad Wolf, always treat the same theme in never-ending variations: some clever little David of the animal world succeeds in winning victory over his much bigger, much stronger antagonist. It all started with Walt Disney's Big Bad Wolf and the three little pigs. Tom and Jerry, Tweety and Sylvester, Bugs Bunny, Elmer Fudd, Woody Woodpecker, Buzz Buzzard and many others carry on the tradition.

In Donald Duck, the anthropomorphic fall guy, a figure was created which fascinated children and grown-ups alike. A controversy, which blew up recently in Bavaria over the ideological content of Donald Duck comics, has given tremendous impetus to Donald Duck research. Two diametrically opposed theories confront each other: exponents of one state with utmost conviction that according to the results of their research Donald Duck belongs ideologically to the left; whilst the others are equally certain they have discovered that Donald Duck is a petty bourgeois with fascist inclinations.[5]

The truth of the matter is that Donald Duck has managed to make a deeper impression on the grown-up mind than any other Walt Disney animal. American newspapers have carried a Mickey Mouse strip since 1930 and since 1938 also a Donald Duck strip.

In 1940 Walt Disney started to publish his comic strip series in booklets like *Walt Disney's Comics and Stories*. Above is issue No. 90 (1948) published when Donald was already the favourite Disney character. At this time reprints of daily newspaper strips appeared on a few pages only.
© 1948 Walt Disney Productions

Bugs Bunny by Ralph Heimdahl and Al Stoffel. In cartoon films, as in comics, Bugsy always gets the lisping Elmer Fudd into uncomfortable situations.
© 1970 Warner Brothers Inc./NEA/UPI

Both animals have enlivened *Walt Disney's Comics and Stories* since October 1940, but up to April 1943 these booklets contained only reprints of newspaper strips. In 1947 Uncle Scrooge joined the cast of *Comics and Stories*. Mickey, Donald and the other Walt Disney stars appear in a multitude of comic books, each bearing as its title the name of the main animal character featured. The most successful and long-lived of these comic books are *Donald Duck*, *Mickey Mouse* and *Uncle Scrooge*. In *Walt Disney's Comics and Stories* Donald occupies the first ten pages of the booklet, whilst Mickey Mouse has to be content with appearing at the end, and it is Donald's image that greets the reader on the title page. In comic books as well as in cartoon films Donald has overtaken Mickey long ago in popularity, and in many countries of the world Walt Disney's booklets appear under Donald's, not Mickey's name.

The duck's incredible popularity is largely due to the genius of Carl Barks, the artist who drew the pictures for *Uncle Scrooge* and *Walt Disney's Comics and Stories*. Unfortunately Carl Barks stopped drawing in 1968 and since then Donald has not been the same. But at least Carl Barks has since then emerged from the anonymity under which he had worked for almost thirty years. Up to then he had only been known as 'the good artist' to readers the world over. Reprints of Barks' work—and there is a large fund stretching back over two decades—are some consolation for this loss.

Carl Barks made *Uncle Scrooge* so popular that the number of its editions reached more than a million at times. But Scrooge McDuck's success is not only based on the humorous potential which lies in the fact that he is the wealthiest imaginary fantasticatrillionaire in the world and that he lives up to his name in a way that would impress even Charles Dickens.

A special fascination attaches to the Uncle Scrooge stories, because Scrooge leads Donald and his young nephews, Huey, Dewey and Louie in a fantastic search for hidden treasure. Their adventures take them to the far corners of the earth, and wherever Uncle Scrooge seeks he finds new riches; whether on the trail of Ponce de Leon, or discovering El Dorado, Ophir or the mythical Seven Cities of Cibola, Scrooge never seeks in vain. He finds Montezuma's hoard, King Solomon's treasure, and the philosopher's stone. In this way Uncle Scrooge and his intrepid followers re-live practically every myth and legend. Robert Louis Stevenson and Enid Blyton mingle happily with the Disney touch and to top it all, every known adventure cliché ever used to dazzle the public is cleverly caricatured.

The 'from rags to riches' philosophy and the glorification of free enterprise are combined in Uncle Scrooge, who once stood penniless on the gold-fields of the Klondike and, steeled in this the hardest of all social Darwinistic schools, can now detect the smell of gold or money from miles away.

The hoarding of Scrooge's fantasticatrillions in an enormous 'money silo' runs contrary to the most elementary principles of capitalist investment policy. Why then this mountain of gold? Because Scrooge loves to plunge into it like a porpoise into water, because he likes to burrow through the coins like a gopher, tossing them high up into the air and letting them hit him on his bald plate like beneficent rain.

This is rampant money fetishism, an apotheosis of Mammon—it is making fun of wealth in an absurd and at the same time most fetching way. Uncle Scrooge could never even contemplate parting with any of his riches for altruistic reasons; a Scrooge McDuck Foundation on the lines of Ford or Rockefeller is unthinkable. Scrooge simply rejects the whole credo of the American 'gospel of wealth' and acts in an entirely un-American way. But then, of course, there is no time for him to play the part of patron, for day and night he has to protect his hoard against the thievish intentions of the Beagle Boys—a task he accomplishes with the freely given help of Huey, Dewey, Louie and Donald.

Poor Donald! He will never be able to follow in Uncle Scrooge's footsteps; as the eternal fall guy he is destined to remain the poor, unlucky feller with whom the readers love to identify. This never varying function is the reason for his popularity with older readers, for Donald is Dagwood, Happy Hooligan or Augustus Mutt in the shape of a duck. Those who feel drawn to him, who sympathize with him and pity him see themselves—the fall guy—in the duck's pathetic image.

Donald is always battling with malevolent objects, always prey to the most ridiculous mishaps. But not only the 'slings and arrows of outrageous fortune' bar the way to lasting happiness and success: Donald attempts the possible and the impossible alike and can show incredible ingenuity in overcoming ever-mounting obstacles; but as the smallest accomplishment leads him to swaggering over-confidence, he stumbles immediately into the next mishap and is back where he started.

Standing on top of his mountain of money, Uncle Scrooge preaches his own capitalist credo to Huey, Dewey and Louie.
From *Uncle Scrooge* No. 41, drawn by Carl Barks.
© 1959 Walt Disney Productions

Gladstone Gander is almost always favoured by luck—at the expense of Donald. From *Walt Disney's Comics and Stories* No. 342; drawn by Carl Barks.
© 1951 Walt Disney Productions

In contrast to the ill-fated Donald, Gladstone Gander, Donald's antagonist and rival for the affections of Daisy Duck, enjoys uninterrupted good fortune wherever he goes; but we love Donald, and so Gladstone, the darling of the gods, appears to us in a highly unfavourable light. Not even the flicker of a wish to identify with him stirs in our hearts.

Gyro Gearloose is the harmless mad scientist of the anthropomorphic Disney world and a perfect example of the unrivalled way in which Walt Disney's comics can caricature clichés and stereotyped ideas.

Malicious joy over Donald's misfortunes may serve young readers as an outlet for their more aggressive tendencies, but they will always like to identify with Huey, Dewey and Louie, because those three are all a child could wish to be himself. They are much more clever than grown-ups and, serving Uncle Scrooge as 'trouble shooters', they experience all the adventures children dream of, they are members of the Junior Woodchucks of Duckburg and thanks to the Junior Woodchuck Handbook, they know exactly what to do in any given circumstance.

They educate themselves and, realizing Donald's hopeless position in life, they do not look up to him—on the contrary, it is Donald who would be completely lost without the help of his little nephews. Love of adventure and love-hate for the washing-up keeps the Duck family together.

Disney comics for children are, like all American children's comics, strictly censored with regard to family relationships. So that childish minds may not begin to ponder on sexual matters, no parents appear in the stories. Relations are confined to uncles, aunts, nephews and cousins—which means that the doors are opened wide (and not only in Donald Duck comics) to all manner of repressed sexual interpretations.

Mickey Mouse accompanied by Goofy experiences similar adventures with his nephews; Mickey, however, in contrast to Donald, has both feet on terra firma. To add interest to the stories, Goofy was cast as the fall guy, and recently Goofy—in the shape of 'Super-Goof'—has started to make fun of the super-hero cult.

The Disney Studios have seized on the commercial potential of their film characters by issuing, together with each new cartoon film, parallel movie comic books or comic strips, from which in turn whole series of comic books have often evolved. To give old ideas a new twist, a minor film character is often placed in the limelight. From the cartoon film *The Three Little Pigs* emerged the comic *L'il Bad Wolf* (the little bad wolf who isn't really all that bad). *Lady and the Tramp* became *Scamp, Jungle Book* became *Mowgli,* and *The Sword in the Stone* became *Madam Mim*.

European demand for Disney comics is so great that in Italy Walt Disney stories are drawn locally under licence; but the Italian versions of Donald Duck (Paperino) and Mickey Mouse (Topolino) are inferior to their American originals in the quality of drawing and in the story content, which is much simpler and often clumsily schematic.

On Grandma Duck's farm the States are still what they used to be: apple pie, Grandma's electromobil and the absence of modern tools, reminding us of the good old days. Donald's grandma has not yet sacked the lazy farmhand Gus Goose, because he happens to be her nephew. From Walt Disney's *Vacation Parade,* drawn by Carl Barks.
© 1950 Walt Disney Productions

Mickey Mouse and Goofy, the anthropomorphic Mutt and Jeff characters, tumble from one excitement into the next. From *Walt Disney's Comics and Stories* No. 335, drawn by Paul Murry. © 1968 Walt Disney Productions

High-flying imagination

The surrealist dream world of a small boy is caught in *Little Nemo in Slumberland,* a comic strip which to this day appeals especially to adult readers. Each sequence is an excursion into the realm of King Morpheus and usually ends with Little Nemo waking suddenly because he has fallen out of bed.

This strip, drawn by Winsor McCay in 1905, appeared in the first instance for six years only, because its innovator became interested in the idea of trick films and helped to produce the first commercially successful cartoon film, *Gertie the Dinosaur.* In 1911 he also undertook the drawing of another comic strip, *Dreams of a Rarebit Fiend,* under the pseudonym of Silas. Then in 1924 McCay returned to *Little Nemo in Slumberland* and continued to draw it until 1927. When, after McCay's death in 1947 *Little Nemo* was once again distributed, there appeared a rival strip entitled *Dick's Adventures in Dreamland,* drawn by Neil O'Keeffe. Even today people are entranced by *Little Nemo in Slumberland's* poetic charm and by the unreal, dreamlike quality of McCay's drawings. Nemo is usually accompanied by Flip, a kind of perverted, cigar-smoking little Irish leprechaun. Nemo, Flip and their various playmates drift quietly through the magic atmosphere of Slumberland in their airship, or run into various difficulties with strange metamorphoses of their surroundings.

In Winsor McCay's drawings dimensions dissolve into the weirdest perspectives. This together with the opulent *fin de siècle* architecture he chose for the interior as well as the exterior of buildings, makes each one of his pictures a gem of artistry.

In the middle sixties, encouraged by strips like *Peanuts, Pogo* and *Beetle Bailey,* comics of a more sophisticated nature began to pour on to the market. It all started with George Herriman's *Krazy Kat* creating a new genre of funnies, which aimed at offering more to their readers than just escapist laughter; a genre with its own, special and very subtle mystique—closed to those who have no feeling for it.

These strips, with their bitter-sweet, sophisticated humour, also reflect in their human comedies the human condition—and their comment often goes right to the heart of the matter.

Many readers still consider *Krazy Kat* to be the best strip ever produced. In his book *The Seven Lively Arts* (1924) Gilbert Seldes devoted a whole chapter entitled 'The Highest Praise', to *Krazy Kat* and declared that this strip was art indeed. *Krazy Kat* was read by people from every social strata and was the first comic strip to appeal particularly to intellectuals.

Krazy Kat started in 1910 as additional strip to Herriman's *The Family Upstairs*, but it soon became independent and from 1911 appeared under the title *Krazy Kat and Ignatz*; by 1913 *Krazy Kat* had supplanted *The Family Upstairs* and from then on it was published under the title that was to make it famous. The intriguing flavour and special magic of Herriman's sense of humour was unique and quite irreplaceable, and when the artist died in 1944 Krazy Kat had to be abandoned.

The basic theme was a wildly unnatural *ménage à trois*: Krazy Kat, the cat of uncertain sex, desperately loves Ignatz, the mouse, and Offissa Pup, the dog, loves Krazy Kat. Deeply offended by the love of Krazy Kat, Ignatz bombards the unfortunate Krazy with bricks (especially made for this purpose by Kolin Kelley's brick factory) for well on 34 years. Krazy, however, takes the bricks as signs of an affection that cannot express itself in any other way. Offissa B. Pup, guardian of the law, sees in the whizzing bricks a serious breach of law and, of course, he also wants to protect the beloved Krazy and shield her (him?) from Ignatz's well aimed missiles. And so, after many sequences, Ignatz lands in jail.

Herriman freely varies this theme in dialogues full of absurdities and Joyceian fancies, without the slightest regard for grammatical or semantic rules. Characteristic are the metamorphoses which things in the background, or heavenly bodies in the sky, undergo from one picture to the next.

John Alden Carpenter, who made a ballet of *Krazy Kat* in 1922, described Krazy as a combination of Parsifal, the purest of all fools and Don Quixote, the perfect knight. Sure, if so inclined, one can see in Krazy the incarnation of the wisest of all fools, who sits waiting for the brickbats, with a masochism generated by frustrated love; but Krazy could equally well be regarded as the silliest animal ever to wander through a comic strip.

Herriman, who is said to have once begged Hearst to cut his salary, started drawing in 1903 and had several strips to his credit before he invented *Krazy Kat*. One of his early series was *Don Kiyoti and Sancho Pansy*, which reflects his fascination with Cervantes. In *Krazy Kat* there is a minor character who is also called Don Kiyoti.

But Krazy is usually interpreted as a symbol of pure all-embracing love which succeeds in the end. Seen in that light, Offissa Pup also appears as an allegorical figure representing the law, the moral code itself, the rock against which anarchy, in the shape of Ignatz, must always founder.

Herriman's art was that of an abstract, potential Lewis Carroll, and Robert Warshow wrote in praise of *Krazy Kat*: 'Krazy Kat is "pointless" and "silly", it comes from the peripheral world where the aims and pretensions of society are not regarded.'[6] And this was probably the very reason for *Krazy Kat*'s success.

An immediate successor to *Krazy Kat* was *Felix the Cat*. Felix, created by Pat Sullivan for a cartoon film, appeared as a comic in 1923. Today *Felix the Cat* no longer has the sophistication of its earlier years. It has lost that fantastic element that for decades attracted adults as much as children. Felix was then a lonely cat who stalked through a grotesque landscape filled with bizarre figures which defied all the laws of nature, with houses standing on their roofs and all sorts of other abstruse objects; but gradually *Felix the Cat* lost this marvellous, magic quality, so akin to that of *Krazy Kat*, and dwindled into an ordinary strip without distinction.

Krazy Kat by George Herriman. Krazy Kat, Ignatz Mouse, the brickbat—and Offissa B. Pup. They lasted over 35 years.
© 1938 King Features Syndicate

Pogofenokee

It was several years after Herriman's death before a worthy successor—Walt Kelly—appeared on the scene and Pogo stepped into Krazy's shoes. Since 1949 *Pogo* has been the strip worthy of the highest praise. Walt Kelly, not Al Capp, is the Swift of comics. His varied range of 'Houyhnhnms' awaken strange echoes in us and an unknown 'Yahoo' being stirs within our soul.

In the Okefenokee swamps of Georgia, Kelly creates his apparently pastoral land of Pogofenokee, a kind of allegorical America, reminiscent perhaps of Faulkner's Yoknapatawpha County. The inhabitants of this swampy domain speak a language spiced with Freudian slips of the tongue and Joycean phrases and flights of fancy. Reuel Denney[7] calls this tongue 'Pogo-Latin' or 'Okefenokese'.

Continuous semantic and phonetic mutilation of words, metaphors taken literally and malapropisms galore result in communication without comprehension and against the background of this verbal foliage the phobias and neuroses of each individual swamp dweller stand out all the more clearly.

In *Pogo* Walt Kelly treats the American language in a completely free and easy manner. Even the lines framing the pictures, which are drawn without a ruler, fall away whenever the occasion demands and help to underline the absence of any hard and fast rules. The speech-balloons are not just a stylistic convention, they are often drawn into the story as objects in their own right—and how delightful their content!

Each of *Pogo*'s main characters—there are over 150(!) additional ones—is gifted with golden eloquence and each one speaks in a complicated style or dialect all his own. Moreover, the flood of words issuing from some of the animals is expressed in highly artificial script within their speech balloons. Deacon Mushrat, for instance, speaks only in Gothic letters—which emphasizes his pharisaic character; but the best example for Kelly's unique speech technique is the bear P. T. Bridgeport, who is an amalgam of the circus magnate P. T. Barnum and W. C. Fields. Phineas T. Bridgeport's speech balloons are small circus placards. *Pogo* is certainly not easy to read.

The swamp dwellers' rhetoric and their love of demagogy is also the reason why this, the best of all American strips, remains incomprehensible to most European readers. Exceptions are, of course, comics fans who read reprints in specialized magazines. When told about this Kelly commented laconically: 'Pogo language does not improve in translation.' How true!

From 1935 to 1941, before he came into comics, Walt (Walter Crawford) Kelly worked for Walt Disney Studio and the (positive) influence of Walt Disney is clearly visible in the technique of Kelly's drawing, which gives his animals unsurpassed powers of mimicry.

For children, as for adults, *Pogo* has all the appeal of anthropomorphic animals; in contrast to their complicated 'adult' way of speaking, the inhabitants of Pogofenokee are most endearing to look at. Some, like the small alligator Alabaster, are the cutest little creatures imaginable and Chug-Chug, the simple-minded postman, has a Donald Duck touch about him.

Pogo can therefore be enjoyed on different levels: as an amusing animal strip, Walt Disney style, or as pungent satire, and sometimes *Pogo* takes his reader from one level to the next. In 1942 a five page story entitled *Albert the Alligator* was published by Dell's *Animal Comics*, and alligator Albert was supposed to remain the chief character in Okefenokee; but in 1943 the opossum called 'Pogo'—looking, as yet, quite un-Pogo-like—made his first appearance in *Bumbazine and Albert the Alligator*. The success was such that *Animal Comics* were re-named *Albert and Pogo*. In 1949 they changed to *Pogo Comics* and up to 1951 eight different booklets appeared. Dell's comic books sold very well, and today they are rarities and precious collector's pieces.

After several false starts and after the New York *Star*, in which *Pogo* appeared as a comic strip in 1948, had folded in January 1949, *Pogo* was taken on by the Hall Syndicate, and after a rather slow start rocketed to success. Since 1951 *Pogo* has also been published in books, carrying reprints and original stories.

In the isolated region of its swamp, Okefenokee seems far removed from the modern urban jungle, yet Kelly manages to set within that unlikely environment the most telling satire of modern society produced in comics today. Complaints were heard from Republicans as far back as 1948, because Kelly had portrayed Dewey, their candidate, as a mechanical doll. *Life* wrote in 1952 that Kelly's satire could never be biting, the swamp inhabitants were too naïve for that sort of thing. Whoever wrote that cannot have looked very closely; or perhaps *Life* did not want to admit that in the Audible Boy Bird Watchers Society Kelly denounced the ultra right-wing John Birch Society.

Mushrat Deacon (note the subtle symbolism of names!), the Protestant hypocrite, whose pompous waffle oozes out in Gothic letters, is the Head Bird Watcher. Molester Mole MacCarony is another member of the society which (just as the real John Birch Society in America) wants to protect the swamp society from 'undesirable' immigrants. A third one is Wiley Catt who sees in lynch-justice the only panacea.

In 1953 Kelly introduced the witch-hunting Senator Joseph McCarthy into *Pogo*. He gave him the name of Simple J. Malarkey and drew him in the shape of a lynx, a wild cat, because he entered the strip as a cousin of Wiley Catt, the lyncher.

Simple J. Malarkey, a devilish expression permanently fixed on his face, immediately usurps the leadership of the Okefenokee John Birch Society, whose members, having called the troublesome spirit, now dearly want to be rid of it. Not for the first, nor for the last time, *Pogo* was suspended from the comics sections of some newspapers.

Much of Kelly's work is closely related to political caricature and he returned more than once to his attack on certain illiberal elements in American politics. Later, his satire warns once more against the danger from the right: in 1970 Spiro Agnew (a hyena!) agitates the pages of *Pogo* and once again the Boy Bird Watchers prepare the ground for fascism in Okefenokee.

Characters from Harold Gray's highly conservative and highly popular strip *Little Orphan Annie* were repeatedly caricatured in *Pogo*. It was no coincidence that in the McCarthy sequences Beauregard appeared as 'lorn Orphan', and even earlier, in 1952,

Pogo by Walt Kelly. Preparation for America's National Holiday on the Fourth of July. A political satire in which Spiro T. Agnew appears as a hyena, spouting alliterations. Deacon Mushrat's pomposities appear in Gothic lettering. The jail is slowly filling up.
© 1970 Walt Kelly

Pogo and Beauregard had been active as 'Li'l Arf An Nonney', running around with white buttons in their heads instead of eyes and consequently falling into the water. In 1958 Albert put in an appearance as 'Lulu Arfin' Nanny'. Harold Gray was not amused.

At four-yearly intervals elections are held in the swamp. This is when Tammananny Tiger, the master of ceremonies, comes on to the scene. The tiger is the personification of New York's Tammany Hall, seat of the democratic party machinery; with these and other topicalities the everyday lunacy of Okefenokee is interrupted from time to time and brought up to scratch.

The animal inhabitants of the swamp are the great actors of the comic scene. They are free of all stereotyped classifications. The whole of Okefenokee is their stage and some of the parts they play are sad or even tragic. Only Pogo Possum is never tempted into a lunatic swapping of roles. He remains placid and matter-of-fact; uncomplicated and slightly simple-minded, he is a splendid contrast to the other characters. *Pogo* is Kelly's great satire on the unnatural behaviour of human beings who live like marionettes—slaves to the repressions of their society. Pogo Possum, however, does not accept to play a part in society, partly, perhaps, because he is too stupid or because, like any other opossum, he can close his mind to depressing realities.

What stage ever had more brilliant actors? There is Seminole Sam, the mealy-mouthed fox, the only one to carry on the part assigned to him by fable. He is the cheating sales representative with the horse-dealer mentality, akin to Snopes in Faulkner's *The Hamlet*. Then there is Sarcophagus McAbre, the vulture, whose speech-balloons sometimes look like death-announcements, Houn'dog Beauregard, the dog with the less than efficient sense of smell, is another great Okefenokee orator with a tendency to self-deception; Porkypine, the porcupine, is the misanthropist with an ever-clouded brow; Churchy La Femme, the tortoise with the pirate's hat, is the silliest of all the animals. He often assists Prof. Howland Owl in his lunatic experiments. Howland Owl, often sporting his Merlin hat, is the irresponsible scientist who couldn't care less about the implications of his inventions. There is also Miss Ma'm'selle Hepzibah, the vamp in the shape of a skunk (!) who brings romance to the swamp.

But Albert, the alligator, is the greatest of all the Okefenokee actors. 'Why do dogs get all the good parts?' he asks once. 'Alligators can out-dog dogs the worst day they ever crawlt.' Albert suffers from subconscious cannibalistic tendencies. Reuel Denney sees in Albert's cigar—he is never without it—a substitute for the satisfaction of such tendencies which are, after all, quite natural for a carnivorous animal.

Once again Albert the Alligator, great actor and chief character in *Pogo*, has not been able to resist his compulsion to eat whatever comes his way.
© 1970 Walt Kelly

Li'l Abner by Al Capp. The Yokums.
© 1970 Chicago Tribune—New York News Syndicate

Dogpatch, USA

Ask any American which comic strip he considers to be the most typically American, and he will answer: *Li'l Abner*! 'Dogpatch', the hillbilly village, represents the whole of the USA and Li'l Abner stands for the typical 'true American boy', while at the same time caricaturing him.

But do Americans really like to identify themselves with Li'l Abner, the innocent fool with the slightly idiotic facial expression? Al Capp (Alfred Gerald Caplin)[8] had previously worked on Ham Fisher's *Joe Palooka*. When he started *Li'l Abner* in 1934, Li'l Abner's parents, Mammy and Pappy Yokum, were of normal size; but in the early days of the strip they began to shrink, then grew again, and after some dithering stabilized themselves at a midget's height, thus symbolizing the American parent–son relationship.

Mammy Yokum is undisputed ruler, not only over the Yokums but over the whole of Dogpatch. She is the incarnation of American matriarchy; with her voice: 'Goodness is stronger than evil because it is nicer.' She triumphs over everybody and everything. She is invincible. Her eyes radiate such heavenly and omnipotent goodness that she defeats all evil, including the wicked machinations of 'Evil Eye Fleegle', the powerful 'Master of the Whammy'. 'Good' always wins, 'evil' never; and somehow the suspicion arises that Capp really means it, that this is no part of his satire.

Mammy's husband, Lucifer Yokum, is an utterly useless little man with only one interest in life: food. Son Abner also likes his creature comforts and is usually seen munching something.

In the course of time a gallery of grotesque characters assembled round the Yokums—all suffering from acute symbolism of names. In contrast to the males, such as Big Barnsmell, Hairless Joe, Clark Raspuntigable, Robin Hoodlum or Senator Jack S. Phogbound, the girls all look like 'you know how'.[9] Moonbeam McSwine and Stupefying Jones represent the ideal 'farmer's daughter' and Daisy Mae, Abner's wife, is reminiscent of Marilyn Monroe or Mae West.

Capp has a very simple basic guideline: 'My formula is to throw comedy characters into melodramatic situations and to show them solving the monstrous tribulations in a simple-minded way.'[10]

Li'l Abner does not age, but public opinion forced him into marriage and his and Daisy Mae's wedding was a national event broadcast and presented in detail on all the media. It was the culmination point of Capp's satire on the ultimate aspiration of every American girl: to get married. In 1946 a 'Sadie Hawkins Day' was introduced into the Dogpatch way of life, and annually on 15 November, all bachelors become fair game and may be hunted by all as yet unmarried females. He who gets caught must marry. This Dogpatch innovation caught on and many a university campus introduced its 'Sadie Hawkins Day'.

But what Americans appreciate most are the things that can be commercially exploited as, for instance, the miraculous Kickapoo Joy Juice, which eventually gave its name to one of the many lemonades available on the American market. The biggest success, however, was reserved for the Shmoo; they were small, delectable animals who possessed the gift of fulfilling any materialistic wish a human heart could harbour and who dropped dead with joy if a human being looked at them hungrily. As always in life there was a flaw: the Shmoos endangered the productivity of the capitalist system—they made things too easy—and had to be eliminated.

Capp was accused of 'Shmoocialism' and the question: 'Does Capitalism Meet the Need of Modern Man?' was everywhere seriously discussed, even in a radio programme in which Al Capp himself took part. The answer in the end was decidedly: 'Yes'.

A little less fuss was made over the creation of the Kygmies (kick me), scapegoats everybody was welcome to kick in order to get rid of his or her frustrations. 'What this country needs is a good five-cent masochist,' Capp declared when asked why he had invented these creatures.[11]

When America's glory began to diminish and all the old-fashioned ideals were beginning to totter, Capp's popularity waned in proportion. The hymns in praise of Al Capp as the greatest of all comic strip designers grew less and less loud, and this despite the fact that *Time* had called him the D. W. Griffith and the Gershwin of the comics; others had compared him with Voltaire, Dante or Mark Twain. Many critics thought that *Li'l Abner* showed complexities of plot, motive and construction akin to the novels of Henry James.[12] If literature could not do it, then at least a comic strip should be able to present the world with the Great American Novel. No wonder that John Steinbeck proposed Al Capp for the Nobel Prize! But then, not only because of his engagement in the Vietnam War,[13] people, particularly the young, began to look more closely at Steinbeck's work and doubts about the value of his judgement of Capp's excellence began to creep in.

With the emergence of Civil Rights and other movements in the early sixties, some sections of American youth were suddenly preoccupied with quite different things from the furtherance of all-American ideals and aspirations. Al Capp felt the ground being pulled from under his feet, and as a staunch conservative he began to defend his position.

He now went for longhaired hippies and students and lamented the inability of the police to enforce law and order. Still, in 1970, Capp did give Li'l Abner a hairstyle trimmed to modern fashion!

Al Capp still determines the basic ideas of his satires, but he no longer draws the whole of the *Li'l Abner* pictures, only the heads. This leaves him free to expound his point of view in television and

This is how the 'great American satirist' sees protesting youth.
© 1970 Chicago Tribune—New York News Syndicate

radio interviews and, above all, in his newspaper column 'Al Capp here'. This column shows even more clearly than the comic strip that this great American satirist is anything but progressive. As far back as 1965, after Al Capp had praised Jules Feiffer in a character-revealing interview,[14] Feiffer said that in view of Capp's opinions on social matters his praise was a doubtful compliment; and farther back in time, in 1964, Robert Warshow stated that he found most of Capp's satire mechanical and in rather bad taste. Up to a point Capp may even agree, for he knows very well that his incredible success—Li'l Abner appears in over one thousand newspapers and reaches roughly eighty million readers—rests on the lack of real wit and on the fact that his satire does not attempt to remedy social evils, but only tries to protect the traditional American virtues.

Al Capp does, however, poke fun at the American national character. Dogpatch stands for the USA, and the Yokums, as representatives of the American people, do not present themselves in a very favourable light; but the types Capp has in mind when he draws a very telling picture of their foibles only laugh indulgently, for nobody is willing to compare himself with these uncouth creatures from the back of beyond.

Very often there is a strip within the strip in Li'l Abner: Fearless Fosdick, for instance, a parody of Chester Gould's Dick Tracy. Police-detective Fearless Fosdick earns but 10 to 20 dollars a week, but time and time again some dreadful misfortune loses him the rise in salary he has earned in years of painful slogging. It is Fosdick's speciality to shoot holes into the heads of countless innocent bystanders when arresting a criminal. Once, pursuing a balloon vendor who had no licence, he achieved the grand total of forty-two innocents—the balloon vendor, needless to say, escaped.

Al Capp also likes to incorporate a colleague or two into his strip and at one time he gave Allen Flounder (Allen Saunders) together with his creation Mary Worm—that 'idol of the comics page, America's most beloved busy-body'—an airing in Li'l Abner. Allen Saunders, writer of Mary Worth, reacted like Queen Victoria: he was 'not amused' (unlike Chester Gould who had enjoyed Fearless Fosdick) and in revenge he conjured up a drunken lout of a comics designer in his strip and called him Hal Rapp. At this point the syndicates stepped in and forbade private feuds.

But in three Sunday editions of Li'l Abner, from 13 to 27 October 1968, Capp made fun of yet another designer, whom he called Bedley Damp and his strip Peewee. Bedley Damp's offerings were full of Freudian wisdom, Krafft-Ebbing, Jung and Adler sayings, and 'Dear Abby'. Croopy, the dog in this strip, acted like Eddie Rickenbacker, the American air-ace. But Bedley Damp got all his ideas for the strip from a psychiatrist, his neighbour, and when the psychiatrist moved from the district the children and the dog in Peewee suddenly became normal, whereupon the syndicate fired Bedley Damp and engaged the psychiatrist. Moreover, the syndicate was delighted to find in the person of Li'l Abner the ideal designer, whose scratchings admirably partnered the incongruities issuing from the mouths of the Peewees.

It is significant that this 'satire' appeared in the Sunday editions. Al Capp himself once said that of two ideas he always relegated the less promising one to the Sunday series.

Long Sam by Bob Lubbers. Al Capp's particular kind of humour can also be seen in the dialogue he wrote for the strip Long Sam (drawn by Bob Lubbers), a melodrama about a hillbilly girl.
© 1962 United Feature Syndicate/UPI

Peanuts

It is easy to see the grain of truth in Capp's caricature of *Peanuts*. That Charles M. Schulz, the creator of *Peanuts*, is a lay preacher in the 'Church of God', a conservative, biblically orientated Protestant sect, is today common knowledge; and books like *The Gospel According to Peanuts* and *The Parables of Peanuts*, both by Robert L. Short, have made it clear that Peanuts has a metaphysical background. Short's biblical paraphrase of the human condition is illustrated by sequences from *Peanuts* and it is evident that Schulz, in his own way, gives a much clearer picture of humanity's malaise than Short's often cited favourite authors Kierkegaard, Barth and Tillich.

Peanuts, the most successful strip up to date, began in 1950, after several syndicates had rejected Schulz's strip, then called *Li'l Folk*. United Features Syndicate finally bought it, but changed its title to *Peanuts* because a strip called *Little Folk* already existed. The author was never asked whether he agreed to the new name. In fact, he did not. He wanted to call it *Good Ol' Charlie Brown*; but he had to wait nearly twenty years before he was allowed to use this name as a subtitle to the *Peanuts* Sunday series.

Schulz is one of the few cartoonists who do all the work on the strip themselves—from the first idea to the final execution. He needs roughly a day to do the Sunday strip, the six weekday strips he often manages in an afternoon. His style of drawing is ingenious and does not cost him much time. He finds Charlie Brown's head the most difficult bit to draw and the dog Snoopy the easiest.

The title, which Schulz had found so unacceptable, nevertheless helped to establish the strip not only in all the American newspapers but in papers the world over. The number of paperback reprint editions is so high—above the sixty million mark—that Schulz can rank with best-selling authors like Erle Stanley Gardner and Mickey Spillane; but this is only a small part of the picture and a commercial undertaking of gigantic proportions has grown out of the once rejected comic strip. In 1967 *Life* called it a fifteen million dollar business. In 1971 the Peanuts industry grossed 150 million dollars according to *Newsweek*. Television shows, films, records, dolls and gimmicks of every description have made of *Peanuts* a highly lucrative venture, but they have also robbed it of much of its original charm. Walt Kelly, who could have made an equally successful business out of *Pogo*, has refused to let his character be exploited.

The Peanuts children have aged only about two or three years since 1950, but spiritually they have undergone much greater changes. Right at the beginning Charlie Brown and his friends acted like any other normal children. Sally liked Charlie better than Shermy and even quarrelled with Violet, who insisted she loved him even more.

Those were happy days for Charlie Brown; but soon his balloon-shaped head became a target for malicious personal remarks, and whilst the other kids developed more and more odd traits and even phobias, which they paraded quite openly, Charlie Brown remained normal and human and consequently became the outsider. The time of childish innocence had passed. Schulz is always at his best when he portrays the inability of the naïvely simple and humane Charlie Brown to integrate into the community, in contrast to all the other Peanuts characters who find no difficulty in doing so. He shows how society attaches a stigma to the lone wolf, the individualist who wishes to remain himself. Whilst the other Peanut kids splash about together in a plastic swimming pool, Charlie Brown sits in a bucket on the other side of the fence, heaving a lonely sigh, and whilst the others play astronauts Charlie Brown acts the lonesome cowboy. Lucy and the other Peanuts, integrated conformists, slaughter Charlie Brown emotionally and the latter's inability to defend himself stems from the fact that he is a vulnerable character, quite untypical for this day and age. He is sensitive, warmhearted,

Peanuts by Charles M. Schulz. German version. Charlie Brown ponders on the theological implications of 'never having been born'. 'Good grief! The theological implications alone are staggering!'
© United Features Syndicate/UPI

compassionate, constantly troubled. His tortured nervous system never finds peace. Charlie Brown is not as intellectual as his interpreters: he does not indulge in vast metaphysical questioning or deep theological suffering, for he simply wants to be a human being.

Charlie Brown elicits the admiration of the reader, because he refuses to take refuge in neurosis. He never gives up, even if he is the loser in every game and none of his kites ever fly. He does not quit, though his baseball team is always beaten (once 123:0) and the fault is always his. When this happens everybody blames him; he is the 'goat', the 'blockhead', the ass who is ridiculed and shunned by all.

Yet, Charlie Brown does not want to be alone; his efforts at integration, doomed to failure because of his separateness, are mute demonstrations of John Donne's 'no man is an island' thesis. The only person to whom he can sometimes open his heart is his 'pencil-pal' (he does not yet write well enough to have a 'pen-pal'!). When will Schulz, his creator, let a little sunshine into his life? When will Charlie's unrequited love for the little red-haired girl be returned—at least to the degree of allowing him to eat his sandwiches in her company during recreation time?

Schulz reflects the literary tendencies of the day most accurately in *Peanuts*. In the fifties it was psychoanalysis (Lucy); in the sixties Charlie Brown showed traits of Herzog, the title hero of a psychological–philosophical novel by Saul Bellow (bestseller 1964–65), and the inclination towards pure fantasy which followed equally paralleled the literary scene.

Charlie Brown is another fall guy with whom everyone can identify. He is the son of a hairdresser (like Charles M. Schulz) and dreams, like all American children, of becoming a baseball hero, perhaps even President of the USA. The other Peanuts, adjusting and conforming to society, have an easier time ahead of them; they will not find it so difficult to accept their stereotyped roles in the adult world of American suburbia. They have already chosen their spiritual crutches.

There is, for instance, Lucy Van Pelt, Charlie Brown's chief antagonist. She is a one hundred per cent materialist, self-centred and egotistical to a degree and without a trace of pity or compassion for man or beast. She is so penetratingly domineering that even the reader suffers under her tyranny. The one-time lemonade kiosk for children has been taken over by Lucy as an office for psychiatric treatment. Her diagnoses, at 5 cents a piece, are devastatingly cruel but true, and her brother Linus is forced to conclude: 'Big sisters are the crab-grass in the lawn of life.' But Linus has his flannel blanket which absorbs all his fears and frustrations. Charlie Brown comments: 'I think most of life's problems are too complicated to be solved with a spiritual blotter.'

Charlie Brown showed Schroeder a toy piano and Schroeder immediately began to play brilliantly on it. A little later he composed a rhapsody and was given a contract with the 'New York Philip Harmonic'. Asked how this was possible, since the toy piano's black notes were only painted ones, he answered: 'I practise a lot.'

Schroeder is a monomaniac virtuoso with a Beethoven complex. His whole life is dedicated to his art and he is comfortably established in his paranoia. Schulz himself seems to prefer Brahms and Dvorák, but Schroeder has a fixation on Beethoven. His repertoire includes all other classic composers, but only when playing Beethoven's Ninth Symphony are the shivers that run down his spine so cold that he has to wear a coat.

There are other Peanut characters with equally peculiar habits, like Frieda, the girl with the 'natural curled hair', or Pig-pen, to whom the dirt of centuries clings. Sally, Violet and Shermy are more 'normal', but their normalcy makes them much less interesting and they appear only on rare occasions.

The beagle hound Snoopy, on the other hand, gradually pushed himself into the foreground until he became the centre of attraction and the main character of the strip. During the

The loneliness of Charlie Brown.
© 1959 United Features Syndicate/UPI

55

Peanuts' philosophical phase Snoopy was just an ordinary dog, the perfect hedonist who did nothing but dream away the hours sitting on top of his kennel. If he had one of his rare doggy hangups, he simply put his head into his water-bowl.

In the beginning Snoopy's main interest was food and apart from a few minor attacks of claustrophobia whilst lost in high grass, he acted natural; but after a while he began to outgrow his dogginess.

Soon his kennel was fitted with air-conditioning, a billiard table, carpets, tapestries, a record player and a painting by Van Gogh which was later replaced by an Andrew Wyatt after there had been a fire in the kennel. A Walter Mitty of the canine world, Snoopy dreamed himself into all sorts of situations. He imitated vultures, gorillas, dinosaurs and became a real menace as 'The Mad Punter'. Frieda's cat had to disappear from the strip,

Peanuts by Charles M. Schulz. German version. Lucy asks what the boys can see in the passing clouds. Whilst Linus sees Michelangelo, St Stephen, The Apostle Paul, as well as a map of British Honduras, Charlie Brown sees only a 'horsie' and a little 'ducky'. This episode also served as opening to the film *A Boy Named Charlie Brown* 1969–70.
© 1970 United Features Syndicate Inc./UPI

Snoopy, 'man's best friend', in his 'Sopwith Camel' plane, looking for the Red Baron.
© 1966 United Features Syndicate Inc./UPI

because contrasted with her Snoopy would have given the impression of being a normal dog. Schulz commented jokingly that apart from anything else, he couldn't really draw a cat.

Snoopy's imagination soon ran amuck, dream and reality became indistinguishable. He developed a weakness for the air aces of the First World War (the film *The Blue Max* had unleashed a wave of First World War enthusiasm in the USA). Perched on top of his dog-kennel, his 'Sopwith Camel' plane, he flew against the 'Red Baron' (Richthofen) until the German air ace muttered: 'Happiness ist eine kleine kaput beagle.' (According to the *MAD* version.) Snoopy was shot down in flames behind enemy lines more than once and had to limp back to his kennel in front of Charlie Brown's house.

But the charm of *Peanuts* does not depend on the daydreams of Walter Mitty Snoopy, it lies in the metaphysical content; the whole point of Snoopy's activities as author, ice hockey player, or 'world-famous check-out man in a grocery store' lies in the fact that—in appearance at least—he is a dog and this is neither funny nor ludicrous in the long run, but becomes a symbolic formula. Charles Schulz has shown however, that he wants to get back to his old formula, to the type of content which will make him immortal in the world of comics.

Beetle Bailey

Mort Walker's *Beetle Bailey*, which started in the same year as *Peanuts* (1950), was to become almost as famous. *Beetle Bailey* is published in 1,100 newspapers throughout forty-three countries. Like Schulz, Mort Walker won most of the honours, distinctions and prizes a comic strip could win—but although *Beetle Bailey* has a humorous military motif, no honours have been bestowed on Walker by the military pundits. The Air Force has *Steve Canyon* and *Terry and the Pirates*, the Navy has *Buz Sawyer Thorn McBride*—and the Army? The Army had *Sad Sack* and *Beetle Bailey*! And these two are no conquering heroes who could boost the troops' morale or in whose reflected glory the soldiers' friends and relations could bask.

During the Second World War, before *Beetle Bailey* came on the scene, several humorous soldiers' strips existed: Clyde Lewis' *Private Buck*, the much appreciated *Private Breger* and George Baker's *Sad Sack*. Sad Sack, the fall guy of the Army, was introduced into *Yank* (an army publication) during the war, but later it failed to make its mark in comics. It was, however, accepted as a comic book by Harvey Publications and reached a high number of editions, because the Army distributes it as a complimentary issue to soldiers.

Beetle Bailey by Mort Walker. Beetle will never learn that the Sarge always comes off best.
© 1970 King Features Syndicate

Boner's Ark by Addison. The captain made his first 'boner' when he took only one specimen of each animal species into the ark. Mort Walker signs the strip with his first name, Addison.
© 1970 King Features Syndicate

Beetle Bailey is no fall guy and though he never wins promotion (he can't because the strip would lose its *raison d'être*), he does manage to get some perks out of army life; besides it is peace time and life at Camp Swampy isn't all that bad.

Beetle Bailey is a genuine satire on army life. Beetle himself is a civilian in uniform and therefore ceaselessly occupied with the avoidance of a soldier's duties, particularly kitchen or latrine duty. Sergeant Snorkel, with whom he always crosses swords, is fat and greedy; but he is competent, which is more than can be said for General Halftrack. Cookie, the cook, has never yet managed to satisfy a single soldier with his cuisine.

Probably inspired by *Peanuts'* Snoopy, Mort Walker introduced a dog named Otto into *Beetle Bailey*. Otto is the mascot, wears a uniform and walks on his hind legs; he has his own thoughts about military life. Mort Walker likes to caricature trendy ideas of the moment in his strip. On 28 November 1965, Sgt. Snorkel dreamt of being Super Sarge and on 22 January 1967, the doughty Sergeant appeared as Haws Snorkwright of Bananza, together with General Halftrack as 'Ben Snorkwright, owner of the Mama Rosa Ranch', and Beetle as 'Little Joke'.

The New Wave

Mel Lazarus uses for his strip *Miss Peach* (1957) a technique similar to that of Charles Schulz; not only are his children—just like the Peanuts—no real children, he also uses a very similar

drawing technique. His style is such that at first glance his 'children' seem to consist entirely of head; moreover, in profile both eyes are placed on the same side of the face. Lazarus' strip also has grown-ups, but they are of such naïve stupidity that they are the ones who appear to be childish. They are really only there to highlight by contrast the appalling intellectual precociousness of the so-called kiddies.

Lacking even the rudiments of childish innocence and charm, these little devils in their classroom at Kelly's School are object lessons for psychiatrists. Miss Peach and Miss Crystal, the teachers, watch their antics with a slightly vacant air and are as incapable of restraining or influencing their so-called charges, as is the hopelessly incompetent Mr Grimmis, principal of Kelly's School.

Friendship or comradeship are unknown words in this diabolical school, where all activities are concerned with clubs, organizations, excursions, or discussions in depth—anything but lessons. The Kelly School can be said to mirror American society.

Typical characters among these bundles of joy are Marcia, who strongly resembles *Peanuts'* Lucy Van Pelt in that she tyrannizes her mates; Freddy, the cynic, who sits at the back of the class and therefore always automatically has the last word; the greedy and cowardly Ira, who fatalistically confesses his misdemeanours, and other little monsters like Arthur, Lester and Francine. Certainly not a class to attract sorely needed new teachers.

Many funnies of the *Peanuts, Pogo* and *Beetle Bailey* era took

Miss Peach by Mel Lazarus. Lessons at Kelly's School: a comment on American culture. Miss Peach and Miss Crystal do not seem to know exactly what is going on.
© 1958 New York Herald Tribune Inc/Publishers—Hall Syndicate

The Small Society by Brickman. A comment on the political scene, this strip comes near to political satire. One of many examples of the growing sophistication of funnies in the sixties.
© 1970 Washington Star Syndicate/King Features Syndicate

Redeye by Gordon Bess. A German version of the strip. Redeye promises double ration of fire-water to anyone who volunteers for a death-mission, and he sends a messenger to tell the members of the tribe. But the lure of fire-water is too strong, and Redeye himself snatches the message to be taken to the pale-face camp and rides off.
© 1970 King Features/Bulls

note of a new approach, a new awareness among readers, and the emphasis on the fall guy and other lower middle class identification-figures grew less strong.

One of the truest and most sincere followers of George Herriman's style is Johnny Hart, the creator of *B.C.* (which appeared first in 1958), a strip of delightful off-beat humour set in the Stone Age—to be precise, in the pleistocene era.

John Hart's cave-men behave in a completely anachronistic manner. Clumsy Carp, awkward and butter-fingered, wears spectacles; Whiley, the poet, has a wooden leg; Thor, the ingenious speedster, tears about on a bicycle; Peter Curls, the sophist, is much further advanced in evolutionary development than Grog who looks like a hairy ball on two legs. Two girls and an anthropomorphic menagerie complete the cast of *B.C.* Their actions represent in stone age terms the human comedy in general and modern society in particular. When the terror cry 'The Midnight Ecologist skulks again!!' echoes across the stone age plane, it is but the super-hero boom reflected in the pleistocene era.

Johnny Hart also wrote the gags for *Wizard of Id*, a strip drawn by Brant Parker (1964). Here the humour is, if possible, even more way out. The action is set in the Dark Ages; the king, because of his dwarf-like appearance, is plagued by neuroses and complexes of varying shades; this prompts him to torture and tyrannize Sir Rodney, his knight, the eternally drunk court jester, diverse peasants, serfs and the prisoner in the dungeon, whose fate is not half as terrible as that of his warder. The wizard is punished enough by his own—always misfiring—magic spells and his scold of a wife.

The dragons in *The Wizard of Id* do not hinder the sudden appearance of the Lone Ranger or an Apollo Moonship, and so both strips, *B.C.* and *The Wizard of Id*, make their readers laugh simply by letting people of the Stone Age of the Middle Ages act and react like modern man. Similar methods are used in two Western strips, Tom K. Ryan's *Tumbleweeds* (September 1965) and Gordon Bess' *Redeye* (1967). *Tumbleweeds'* style is entirely that of a mock Western. Tumbleweeds, the cowboy, riding his sleepy horse Blossom, meanders through the countryside and the town of Grimy Gulch in the Wild West. Tom Ryan pokes gentle fun at Cowboy-Red-Indian-cavalry clichés, but does not break out of the genre by using anachronisms. Gordon Bess takes many more liberties in his *Redeye*, the humorous satire concerning Red Indian Chief Redeye. In this series all the characters belong to the same tribe. White or Red adversaries sometimes affect the course of the story, but they always act off stage. *Redeye* does not make fun of Red Indians, it is a sharp, humorous, hard-hitting satirical sketch of American society; the medicine man is a golf-playing medical practitioner and psychiatrist; Redeye's wife, sick and tired of sitting in her wigwam, intentionally spoils her husband's appetite for her own cooking, so that he may take her out to dine; Redeye himself drowns his sorrows in alcohol (hence his name); and Tanglefoot, clumsiest Red Indian ever born, courts Redeye's daughter forever in vain. Past and present mingle in the absurdest fashion: the thoughts and deeds of the protagonists caricature modern man, and it becomes easy to see what Marshall McLuhan meant when he maintained that modern society tried to look at itself through the rear mirror of its past (in America particularly through the 'Wild West').

3 Adventure and melodrama

Tired with the everyday routine?...
Wanna get away from it all?...
We offer you ... ESCAPE.
Introduction to the American radio programme 'Escape'

The title *Wash Tubbs* does not conjure up images of high adventure, but this comic strip by Roy Crane (1924) was the first to take its readers on adventurous excursions. The majority of Americans still enjoyed the humorous strips churned out by the syndicates and did not clamour for adventure. It was not so long ago that the First World War had ended and the urge to fulfil a mission had given way to disillusioned cynicism. The twenties was a period of intellectual negation and passivity.

Most people wanted to make up for lost time. Everybody sought to get rich quickly; all classes of society strove to get as large a slice of the national cake as possible and as the wealth of the nation grew so money became a cult, the golden calf to be worshipped above all else. Traditional ideas of thirft were forgotten and spending orgies encouraged. Customers were urged to buy on the 'never never', and to speculate on the Stock Exchange became a fashionable and respectable business. The motor car began to rule and it brought a mock mobility which blinded people to the fact that the time of the 'frontier', when it had been possible to move, to expand, to find fresh fields, had gone forever. The great disenchantment came one black Friday morning in October 1929. Corruption, mismanagement and the unbearable social conditions of the depression created by the *laissez-faire* policies of the Republican Party rocked American society and made the rest of the capitalist world tremble. At this time of social upheaval the average American could find escape from his unending worries only in sport (and even here he was being pushed out of active participation into the role of a mere spectator) in the funnies, in penny dreadfuls and in films. The film industry had been using adventure as a theme for some time now and so the comics decided at last to take the plunge into adventure.

A successful double event

On 7 January 1929 two new comic strips started in American newspapers. That both appeared on the same day was mere coincidence and so was the fact that both introduced new worlds of adventure into comics. Both, however, had been carefully planned and prepared over a period of time. One was *Tarzan of the Apes*, the other *Buck Rogers*. Tarzan took his readers into the steaming jungle, Buck took his into the twenty-fifth century. What was the story behind the appearance of these two new strips?

On a trip to Los Angeles in 1928, Joseph H. Neebe, one of the directors of the Campbell-Ewald Advertising Agency, Detroit, had met Edgar Rice Burroughs, a writer he greatly admired. He suggested that Burroughs should give permission for his story of Tarzan, a young man who had been reared by apes in the jungle, to appear as a comic series. This, Neebe urged, would surely become as great a success as the Tarzan novels which had been appearing since 1912 and the Tarzan films which had been appearing since 1918. Burroughs agreed.

To cope with the sale and distribution of the Tarzan strip Neebe started a small syndicate, Famous Books and Plays, Inc. as an offshoot of the Campbell-Ewald Agency. He then negotiated with the famous illustrator of the Tarzan books, Allen St John. But the two men could not agree on the production timetable and so Neebe entrusted the drawings for the strip, for which the novel had been condensed to 30,000 words, to one of the designers in his advertising agency. It was Neebe's good luck that the designer happened to be Harold R. Foster and that Foster accepted the offer.

Though the Campbell-Ewald Advertising Agency had a good name in the advertising world, it had no experience in the distribution of comics and consequently newspapers had little confidence in this new venture and would not buy the Tarzan strip. Only after the agency's small syndicate had amalgamated with one of the big New York distributors, were some papers prepared to give Tarzan a chance. The first trial series kept strictly to the original novel and appeared in sixty weekday instalments of five pictures each. The text was placed outside the illustrations but each section belonged exclusively to a particular picture. By the time the last instalment appeared, on 16 March 1929, it was clear that the series was a resounding success and would have to be continued.

Despite high praise, however, Foster returned to drawing advertisements and the second episode, *Tarzan's Return*, which

Tarzan

by EDGAR RICE BURROUGHS

THE LONE AVENGER

AS TARZAN REACHED THE GAP IN THE CIRCLE, SHE CALLED IMPULSIVELY: "GO BACK! HE MEANS TO TRICK YOU!"

PRINCE JAGURT TREACHEROUSLY MADE THE SIGN OF PEACE ONLY TO DRAW TARZAN WITHIN THE CIRCLE OF GUARDS, THEN SEIZE HIM. LEECIA WAS SHOCKED BY HER FIANCE'S COWARDLY DECEIT, AND SHE SYMPATHIZED WITH HIS HANDSOME VICTIM.

NOW THAT HIS RUSE HAD FAILED, JAGURT COMMANDED: "ATTACK! TAKE HIM ALIVE IF YOU CAN—DEAD IF YOU MUST!"

AS THE GUARDS DASHED FORWARD, TARZAN TURNED AND RAN.

THEN—TO THE ASTONISHMENT OF THE ONLOOKERS HE SPRANG LIGHTLY INTO THE TREES.

JAGURT TURNED TO LEECIA. "YOU'VE ROBBED US OF A CAPTIVE. YOU'RE A TRAITOR TO ME AND THE PEOPLE!"

IN HIS FRENZY OF ANGER, HIS BIG HAND FLEW OUT AND STRUCK THE SLENDER GIRL. SHE FELL.

THEN A GRIM VOICE BOOMED DOWN FROM THE TREES. "SHE IS MY FRIEND. FOR STRIKING HER, I'LL PUNISH YOU!"

Tarzan drawn by Burne Hogarth. Hogarth's Tarzan, dynamic, lithe and agile, explores ancient civilizations. To heighten the effect of the picture and intensify its meaning, Hogarth toned the colour of his pictures in with their mood.
© 1939 United Features Syndicate Inc/UPI

TARZAN DROPPED TO THE GROUND AND STRODE FORWARD.

"PROTECT ME!" THE COWARDLY PRINCE QUAVERED. THE GUARDS WHEELED INTO A CIRCLE OF DEFENSE.

BUT TARZAN, THE LONE WARRIOR, ADVANCED STRAIGHT TOWARD THE BRISTLING BARRIER OF SPEARS!

HOGARTH—

Tarzan
by Edgar Rice Burroughs

THE SPY

Tarzan drawn by Harold Foster. Foster brought realism into the technique of drawing comic strips. Tarzan's designers had to know a great deal about anatomy.

started to appear 17 June 1929, was drawn by Rex Maxon. That same year Foster's Tarzan was published in book form by Grosset and Dunlap. In 1930 United Features Syndicate bought the Metropolitan Newspaper Service and Famous Books and Plays, Inc., together with the Tarzan strip they were distributing. On 15 March 1931 Maxon had to start drawing a coloured Sunday page in addition to the weekday strip. This proved to be more than one artist alone could tackle and on 27 September of the same year Hal Foster undertook to draw the Sunday pages whilst Rex Maxon continued the weekday strip.

These two artists were the first of many *Tarzan* designers who tried their luck with this famous strip: among them William Juhré, Dan Barry, John Lehti, Paul Reinmann, Nick Cardy (= Nicholas Viskardy), Bob Lubbers, Rubimor (= Ruben

Moreira), and John Celardo, but apart from Hal Foster it was above all Burne Hogarth who became famous for *Tarzan* strip drawings. Today, after many years of mediocrity, it is Russ Manning who has revived the tradition of Foster's and Hogarth's concept of Tarzan.

Tarzan was not an original comics idea, for it was taken from a highly successful area of trivial literature. *Buck Rogers* on the other hand, was created for the comics from the start. However, even he had his forerunner in the world of literature for the idea for a story set in the twenty-fifth century came from John F. Dille. He persuaded Dick Calkins to write the series and Phil Nowlan to do the drawings.

To bridge the time lag and make identification easier, it was decided that Buck Rogers should be a modern Rip van Winkle, a twentieth century man who falls asleep for five hundred years and wakes up to start a new life and a fresh career.

Due to the success of these two strips adventure strips became increasingly popular in the years that followed. The New Deal era necessitated a certain amount of economic and social regimentation, and man's imagination had to find new worlds of fantasy to which he could escape. Comic strips of adventure catered mainly for adults, offering refuge from repression, but soon comic books appeared which gave children their share of imaginary exploits. Within a decade adventure and melodrama had taken possession of half of the entire comics output—today their share has shrunk to a generous third—and a great variety of genres developed rapidly.

Back to nature

A decadent, technological society will always be fascinated by stories set in a wilderness or in primeval forests. Tarzan became a symbol of the 'noble savage', as described by Rousseau, and by identifying with him modern man was enabled to give expression to his own disdain of the blessings of civilization, without giving up his love–hate for the comforts they bring. He could now withdraw for a few minutes to the steaming jungle and watch his hero swinging his agile body through the treetops. rushing across the forest to his next heroic deed. And after each victory, as Tarzan's cry of triumph made every creature in the jungle tremble,[1] even the feeblest of modern men would feel—for a few seconds—as elated as Tarzan himself.

Tarzan succeeded as a comic strip not only because of Hal Foster's splendid illustrations, but also because Tarzan, the jungle man, had already captured the public's imagination through his appearance in literature and film. Not all the novels of Edgar Rice Burroughs are of the same quality, but generally speaking his work has been underestimated. Burroughs is the Jules Verne of the pulps, a riveting story-teller, with the gift of making even the most unlikely localities and events credible to his readers. He takes great care to give a clean account of the happenings and it does not matter one little bit that blood is shed by the bucketful, because good and bad are so clearly defined that all action must perforce end with a moral victory. Criticism of Burroughs' work stems mainly from the fact that film versions of Tarzan distorted and simplified the hero's image to such an extent that Burroughs' original figure was no longer recognizable. Burroughs realized this only too well and in his book *Tarzan and the Lion Man* he pokes fun at Hollywood's clichés: in this novel a film director gives the part of Tarzan to a dancer, and the film's producer can visualize Mr Clayton, who is the true Tarzan, at best only in the very minor part of a hunter fleeing from a lion.

Comic strips kept much closer to Burroughs' original conception of Tarzan; they either transposed Burroughs' novels faithfully into pictorial series, or told new Tarzan adventures which were true to Burroughs' own style. Naturally, the figure of Tarzan always reflects something of the personality and imagination of his designer. Hal Foster's Tarzan looked much like the film versions of Tarzan—Elmo Lincoln, the first screen Tarzan, for instance—but he did not copy Hollywood's cheap, sensational sentimentalism. The comic strip Tarzan is drawn clearly and strongly and there is no hint of a spare tyre round his middle; in contrast to Johnny Weissmuller, he can speak articulately, not only in ape-language but also in French, English, German, Swahili or Arabic—in fact he speaks as well as the Tarzan of the novels. Tarzan is not only self-taught as far as the art of reading goes, he is also a polyglot genius!

Rex Maxon's weekday strip Tarzan could not attain quite the same high level of excellence as Foster's Sunday page hero; he seemed a little wooden in comparison, less vigorous and less agile. Foster's Tarzan was regarded as a masterpiece of graphic art from the start, but he eventually turned to a new genre. A *Tarzan* adventure in which Vikings appeared gave the first hint of his plans: he wanted to draw adventures set in England at the time of King Arthur. When he terminated his Tarzan contract in 1936 United Features ran a competition for graphic designers to find a successor. The competition was won by Burne Hogarth, who took over the Sunday strip on 5 May 1937, stepping straight into the current adventure, *Tarzan and the City of Gold*. At first he kept very close to Foster's idea of Tarzan, but he gradually developed his own unmistakable, forceful style.[2]

Hogarth wanted to draw an intelligent rather than a primitively naïve Tarzan but all he achieved was a hero who was less like the film Tarzan. The adventure stories Hogarth had to draw were very typically of the Edgar Rice Burroughs brand and involved Tarzan roaming through ancient and long forgotten civilizations, which living man had never seen or heard.

But the great adventures of Hogarth's era came to an end. After bickering and quarrels over his creative freedom, Hogarth suspended his work on the strip for two years and then, on 16 July 1950, he gave it up completely. Hogarth's refusal to continue to work under the stringent censorship of the syndicate dealt the 'Lord of the Jungle' a serious blow. Hogarth went to teach at the New York School of Visual Arts where he later became the director and a number of comics artists tried their luck with Tarzan. The strip remained average in quality, an adventure series among many, until Russ Manning rescued it from mediocrity in 1968 and gave it back the imaginative spirit it had lost.

Manning was a pupil of Hogarth and by the time he took over

the Tarzan Sunday strip he had had fifteen years experience of drawing for comic books. He had also drawn the film and television comics versions of *Ben Hur,* Walt Disney's *Summer Magic, Wyatt Earp, 77 Sunset Strip* and many others for the Western Printing and Lithographing Company. He had been connected since the fifties with a Tarzan comic book which had started to appear with tryout issues featuring reprints of Foster's *Tarzan* in April 1938, and had been put on a regular basis by Dell in 1947; he had also drawn the 'fill in' series *Brothers of the Spear.*

Such 'fill in' series, consisting of four to eight picture pages plus one or two pages of text, were necessary so that comic books could be sent by post at the reduced rate, as second class mail. Apart from *Brothers of the Spear,* Manning had also drawn some of the stories for the quarterly Tarzan annuals.

The comic book Tarzan was as different from the hero of Burroughs' romantic novels as the film Tarzan was. He was, in fact, a combination of both the film and the literary version. In the comic books Tarzan was married and spoke several languages, but he lived in a tree-house, just as he did in films, and had a son named Boy. The stories in these issues were drawn from 1947 to 1965 by Jesse Marsh who had learned his craft in the Disney Studios where he had worked on such feature-length animated cartoons as *Fantasia* and *Pinocchio.*

In 1965 Russ Manning brought the comic book version back to the original Burroughs formula. The Tarzan novels were specially edited for the comic books market—authorized by Hulbert Burroughs who, together with his brother Coleman had worked on the Tarzan comics for many years. The publishers declared that these Tarzan booklets, which were faithful replicas of the original novels, were collectors' editions. Indeed Manning's drawings in *Tarzan of the Apes* and *Korak, Son of Tarzan* were so good that United Features Syndicate had no further difficulty in deciding who should be the artist for the Tarzan newspaper strip.

In 1968 Russ Manning started to draw Tarzan. His version brings out more of the true spirit of Edgar Rice Burroughs' novels. He even uses 'ape language'.
© 1969 United Features Syndicate Inc./UPI

Elements of myth and legend easily find their way into comic strips. Here the eagle's head worn by the villain Auric expresses the idea of a god in animal disguise.

Dyed-in-the-wool admirers of Hogarth's Tarzan will remain loyal in their devotion to this particular artist, but new readers will be able to see through the eyes of the Manning Tarzan that marvellous world of fantasy and heroic deeds that Burroughs created more than half a century ago in order to improve his financial position. The comic strip reader's gain is, of course, the comic book reader's loss, for no comparable artist has been found to take Manning's place as designer of the Tarzan books.

Of the three main Tarzan designers, Russ Manning is the one who has kept most faithfully to Burroughs' original image of his hero. He sees Tarzan like this:

> The Tarzan of the original novels, and now in the comic strip, is truly the Lord of his jungle, as we all dream of being; committed in the purest, most instinctual way possible to the protection of his territory, his 'nest' and his family. Deep within him lurks the savage beast that is also in all of us; the raging, tearing, fury-blind creature that smashes at adversity, when all other methods fail. He is an outdoor man, living in the ultimate get-away-to world we yearn for in our concrete canyons. His is not the Africa of new nations struggling with politics and trade balances, but rather the jungle of his creator, who never saw the 'dark continent'. His is the Africa of our imagination, eternally mysterious, with the limitless horizons teeming with heroic lions and elephants and vast areas forever unexplored, where undiscovered cities of gold lie ruled by semi-clad barbarian women. Tarzan is a folk-hero, perhaps the first folk-hero accepted the world over; a simple, universal idea expressed in a human form that everyone can understand and identify with—the man we'd rather be.[3]

Tarzan never falls prey to the lure of other women, for Jane's image is firmly anchored in his heart. His Jane, whom he took into his strong arms at their very first meeting, pressing her to his glistening, naked body and sealing her half-open lips with a long and passionate kiss! Tarzan, the monogamous hero loves his wife with faithful ardour and is devoted to his family. The most beautiful queens and wild, half-naked priestesses of jungle deities may be burning with love and longing for Tarzan—all in vain.

Wherever Tarzan turns he will find undiscovered, secret lands or remnants of old civilizations hidden away in deep, secluded valleys. Whether it is Opar, last city of Atlantis (H. Rider Haggard's 'She' motif), or Cathne, the city of the golden treasure, or Nimmr in the 'Valley of the Sepulcher' (the undying Prester John motif), or the primeval land of Pal-Ul-Don, surrounded by impenetrable swamp, Tarzan is always roaming through the forgotten worlds of our subconscious mind. And in his enormous territories somewhere in or around former German East Africa, Tarzan, the 'great Bwana', reigns benignly over his faithful Waziri.

The adventures of this hero of our subconscious dreams are all designed according to the same basic formula; for a series of this kind to be successful, it must repeat the formulas which the public has come to expect. The pattern is always the same: the effective solution of the problem posed, which will give Tarzan reasons for ever new activities.

The formula only became really rigid in the Tarzan stories produced in Mexico, which are usually thirty-two pages long. Each booklet contains at least one battle with some wild animal—lion, gorilla, leopard or crocodile. The stories begin almost invariably with Tarzan being asked for his assistance which he readily gives of course. And they end with him leaving the rescued parties—either after a prolonged feast, or after having led them safely out of the jungle.

But Burroughs himself always knew how to vary the formula so that it never became tedious. His secret lay in his simple but almost magical method of story telling: at the height of suspense a chapter will close with a 'cliff hanger' and the next chapter will take up one of the other numerous strands of action which are only drawn together at the end. Only rarely did this method misfire, and then it was because of lack of time and attention to detail.

In contrast to the stereotyped Mexican comic books mentioned—which only exploit the commercial value of the 'Tarzan' title—the Gold Key collectors' editions revive Burroughs' gripping story-telling techniques. In Tarzan's adventures as drawn by Foster, Hogarth and Manning, the primitive Tarzan

This Tarzan strip (John Celardo) shows the typical end of a villain. The evil one brings about his own death—the hero does not have to sully his hands with the blood of his antagonist.

The Phantom by Lee Falk, drawn by Sy Barry. This 'lone ranger' of the jungle is an ancestor of the super-hero. The Phantom, the 'immortal' wandering spirit of the jungle, protects his realm (somewhere off the coast of Africa) with the help of his jungle patrol.

lives again, reminding us that there is a beast within the human breast, covered only by a thin layer of 'civilization'. However the scar on Tarzan's forehead, which turns blood-red whenever he is seized with overpowering rage, is reserved almost exclusively for the Tarzan of the novels. Some of the comic strips are certainly as rich in adventure and entertainment value as the original novels.

The jungle background is also used in several other comic strips because it is eminently suited to the production methods of a series. Exotic countries and endless narrow jungle paths where adventure lurks behind every tree and camp-fires burn on every clearing, heroic men and women facing devilishly clever adversaries: all help to open escape routes for the imagination. A few minutes each day are enough: the reader is drawn out of the boredom and frustration of his workaday life and his existence is made a little brighter.

Among the strips that lead their readers to faraway places is *The Phantom* by Lee Falk, a series of adventures around a masked rider who is a lord of the jungle. This strip was destined to become famous. It started in 1936 and was drawn by Ray Moore, Wilson McCoy and Sy Barry in succession. However *The Phantom* is one of the forerunners of the super-heroes, and so it is discussed in the next chapter.

Lyman Young's *Tim Tyler's Luck* is also set in the jungle but it does not have a costume and mask as *The Phantom* does. *Jungle Jim,* drawn by Alex Raymond, brings the reader the adventures of a big game hunter and guide in the jungles of Asia. This strip always appeared on the same page as *Flash Gordon*, and it was drawn—exquisitely—by the same artist. For a long time it was a generally accepted practice to give a whole page to the same designer, who could add a second, additional strip to his main offering. *Jungle Jim* was the 'top strip' to *Flash Gordon*; *Colonel Potterby and the Duchess* was the 'top strip' for *Blondie* while *Sappo* was the 'top strip' for *Thimble Theatre*.

The adventures of jungle heroes were featured in comic books as well as in comic strips.

The Foster reprints which Dell published as comic books, enlarged by one new picture for each daily instalment, evolved into the series of *Tarzan* comic books which Gold Key published until 1971, when *Tarzan* moved over to DC. United Features brought out its own comic books and produced Hogarth's *Tarzan* reprints in a series called *Sparkler Comics*. *Jungle Jim* and *The Phantom* also tried their luck in comic books and in the process changed their publishers as often as the designers changed their shirts. The characters in the comics go on wearing the same shorts—presumably for easy identification—so that we feel like asking if they are ever washed!

Other comic books also reached eagerly for the jungle world. Innumerable male and female imitations of Tarzan swung from tree to tree in vain attempts to appear as fascinating as their model. Loincloths and the snapping of lions' vertebrae became the indispensable requisites of jungle sagas drawn in the Hogarth or Foster style. The only thing that distinguished Kaänga from Tarzan was his name and the slightly puzzled expression on his face—though of course his adventures were more banal. One of the better uses of the Tarzan concept was Frank Frazetta's *Thuda, King of the Congo* (1952). *Nyoka, Sheena* and *Rulah* all described exploits in the jungle. Indeed these modern amazons glide into trouble or fall into the most dangerous traps faster even than their male counterparts—but luckily there is always a 'totem animal', a 'helper' or a brilliantly saving 'idea' waiting in the wings to rescue them in the nick of time. *Ka-Zar* (does the linguistic resemblance to 'Zar' or the German word 'Kaiser' (emperor) denote a true potentate of the jungle?) rules over a vast underground primeval jungle empire. He, too, like Tarzan, has climbed out of the pages of 'trivial literature'. In *Ka-Zar* Burroughs has fused two separate localities from his own imaginary world, Tarzan's jungle and 'Pellucidar', the primeval world deep within the bowels of the earth. Of all the many successors to Tarzan that vanished into the comics' limbo during the recession after 1955, only *Ka-Zar* has a chance of a new life in the seventies. As Tarzan's fame became world-wide, it was inevitable that he should be imitated in countries outside the United States. There were European series like the French *Artagon, fils des Dieux*, for instance, which emerged a year after Tarzan's first appearance in France; others include *Targa, Yorga, Akim, Tarou* and *Djeki la jungle*. They 'swiped' not only the style of drawing used in *Tarzan* but also the form of story telling, making minimal modifications.

This widespread copying seems to indicate that the Tarzan theme satisfies some deep-seated, latent longing within the reader's psyche. The European imitations had a much longer life span than their American counterparts, and this was mainly due to the fact that the original Tarzan drawings appeared in French newspapers only in censored—that is mutilated—versions. The French reacted with incredible prudery and covered every inch of nudity with rampant foliage; graphically effective shading was lightened. The magazine *Tarzan* was denounced for its 'Americanism' and its 'immorality' as far back as 1941 and had to be discontinued after only nine months of existence. The field was free for a thousand and one successors.

Closely related to jungle comics are comics about primeval worlds. Not many of them exist in pure form, because the theme can be easily integrated into other genres with the help of a few simple tricks of the trade; of the few that do exist, the comic book series *Turok Son of Stone* is worth mentioning. It is the tale of two Red Indians who live in a primeval valley completely cut off from the outside world. They go through adventures with dinosaurs, pterodactyls and cavemen. This adventure series obviously takes place in the eighteenth or nineteenth century, which means that the valley need not be exactly located and the fact that this 'lost valley' is nowhere to be found today can be put down to some natural catastrophe that may have happened since.

Tim Tyler's Luck by Lyman Young and Tom Massey. This series proves that men on jungle patrol can—in contrast to Tarzan—stay young for decades without using an 'elixir of youth'.
© 1970 King Features Syndicate

What makes this series particularly interesting is the mixture of epochs and the motif of a lost world (beloved also of Burroughs and many other writers of adventure stories). There is a discrepancy between the primeval world and modern man and the two heroes of the tale know two secrets which give them the upper hand over the cave-dwellers: they can produce fire and they know how to prepare a poison for their arrow tips which will kill the dangerous animals they encounter. The most important element, however, is the theme of the quest, in this case for a way out of the valley into which Turok and Andar have strayed. Sometimes the incompatibility of reality and a world of fantasy is hinted at when a path leading to the outside world suddenly opens up and the monsters try to flee out of their primeval valley; then the two heroes must save the 'real' world from a dreadful invasion and so they always find themselves back in their strange imprisonment. For more than fifteen years *Turok Son of Stone* has expressed man's search for his own individuality and his constant battle against a hostile environment. Strips set entirely in primeval times, without connection with modern man, like the Belgian *Tounga*, cannot portray this eternal theme of the search symbolically; but in their return to the very beginnings of *homo sapiens* they nearly always show how our ancestors lived, how the events they experienced could have turned out this way, or perhaps another way, and how they were never just adventures to early man but signified the same stark battle for existence that today, in our modern world, is fought out in terms of ideologies, politics and the day to day struggle for economic survival.

Science fiction

Science fiction, a mixture of present-day ideology and futuristic technical development, shows man in his relationship to a world ruled by technology; and according to the author's 'message' super-technology is presented either as a blessing or a curse. Jules Verne and H. G. Wells had been picked over by the pulps, America's cheaply produced trivial literature, and authors like Edgar Rice Burroughs[4] and a host of others writing under their own names or under pseudonyms had mixed ideas taken from Jules Verne or H. G. Wells with elements of other fantastic genres. Comics continued this trend.

The first science fiction strip appeared, as already mentioned, together with the first *Tarzan* strip on 7 January 1929. *Buck Rogers*,[5] set in the twenty-fifth century, was translated into eighteen languages and was published in forty countries. A Buck Rogers craze gripped the world: Buck Rogers dolls, moon-pistols and rockets became popular toys. All that is left of this money-spinning saga today are copies locked in archives and a book published in 1969 entitled *The Collected Works of Buck Rogers in the 25th Century*, reproducing twelve adventures dating from 1929 to 1946 in one colossal volume of 370 pages. Ray Bradbury, who considers himself a true child of the twentieth century, writes in the foreword that when he was a boy 'Buck Rogers burst upon our vision like some grander July Fourth, full of rockets celebrating tomorrow'. Describing the significance the series had for its readers, Bradbury said:

Alley Oop by V. T. Hamlin. *Alley Oop* used to be a rather amusing strip set in a primeval world. Later on a time machine made it possible to experience adventures in any epoch.
© 1970 Newspaper Enterprise Association Inc./UPI

Beaten down by dull reality, dying for romance, we waded out into a sea of space and happily drowned.

The enemy of every boy is gravity, and here in the first few days of Buck Rogers that incredible stuff 'inerton' plucks us off our feet and hurls us through the sky, free at last. And free not only to jump over dogs, rivers, and skyscrapers, but to challenge the stars.

As adventure strips (of any genre) were not easily accepted at the start, characters had to be found with whom the reader could identify. With Tarzan, this had not been difficult, but in the case of Buck Rogers a bridge had to be built across centuries to a far distant future. Obviously, the best thing to do was to take a man of our own era, transport him by some means to the twenty-fifth century and let the reader explore together with him the marvels of a future world.

Buck Rogers was based on Philip Nowlan's novel *Armageddon 2419 A.D.* and it starts with the hero telling his readers (in first person narrative) how he had landed himself in a future era. He had been a pilot, he relates, in the First World War, and after his demobilization he had been given the job of measuring the deepest tunnel of a mine near Pittsburgh. The air down there had had 'a peculiar pungent tang and the crumbling rock glowed strangely'. When he had started to take measurements the ceiling of the tunnel had come down behind him. He had only been able to gasp out a few disjointed sentences: 'Trapped!! Gas knocking me out, too . . . getting sleepy . . . guess I'm done for . . . goodbye all . . . Mother!' The unknown gas had, of course, not killed him, but had held him in 'suspended animation' for 500 years, and when eventually the rock shifted and fresh air blew into the tunnel, he awoke. He stumbled out of the mine, his memory still linked to the accident that had trapped him, and his first thought was to notify his parents and his friends that he was alive and well. But then he discovered that it was now the year 2430. Wilma, a girl he met straight away and who shared his adventures for the next 39 years, at first did not believe his tale. He managed to convince her, however, by showing her his wartime (1914–18) service medals. 'I believe you now', whispered Wilma, overwhelmed, confronted by such irrefutable evidence, and for the next few decades *Buck Rogers* readers too believed his every word.

In contrast to social utopia (of the Thomas More type), the world of science fiction is not normally blessed with peace. As for the 'science' in this fiction—it has to be taken with a large grain of salt as far as all the apparatus is concerned—the sight of rockets as drawn in *Buck Rogers* would make an expert rock with laughter.

But even if the technical details of future ironmongery are less than accurate, they are not altogether figments of an author's fertile imagination. John Flint Dille, the innovator of the *Buck Rogers* series, was in constant contact with scientists at Chicago University who used to discuss with him some of the problems they were investigating at the time and bits of scientifically correct information certainly found their way into the strip. Much thought was given, for instance, to the construction of space suits and to ways and means of preventing the moon being infected by germs carried by astronauts. It is also interesting to note that the idea of an atomic bomb appeared in *Buck Rogers* as early as 1938; but this was mere speculation by the authors, and not based on information received from scientists.

Buck Rogers' world is highly rationalized and ruled by technological data; still, it has its romantic side: Wilma, the young woman who introduces him to the world of 2430, is also his fiancée throughout the stormy years, and *Buck Rogers* would not be a first-class science fiction story if his romance with Wilma did not lead to ever new adventures. 'Killer' Kane, one of Buck's arch enemies, wants to enslave the world and tries time and again to use Wilma as a pawn in his evil plans. Needless to say he never succeeds. Buck Rogers sees to it that even in those far remote times the United States will remain democratic.

Despite all the futurity expounded in *Buck Rogers*, it remains firmly anchored in our own epoch. This is shown less in the sometimes sadly antiquated machinery, than in its flow of action. Science fiction strips do not prepare us for a better way of life to come, but help us to escape into a (usually) far-off archaic future world in which the hero finds his own form of self-identification or idealistic satisfaction.

The idea of futuristic-archaic worlds needs to be explained in a little more detail and the best example of such an idea as expressed in a comic strip is *Flash Gordon*. Drawn by Alex Raymond it appeared first in 1934 as a Sunday series; in 1948 Mac Raboy took over and today Dan Barry draws the Sunday and the weekday instalments.

In *Flash Gordon* the technical details, so important in *Buck Rogers,* take second place. The series starts with a planet coming near the earth. Flash Gordon, his fiancée Dale Arden and Dr Zarkov, a brilliant scientist, fly to the planet in order to avert the danger threatening the earth. The planet is inhabited and its people call it Mongo. All the kingdoms of this planet are technically far advanced, but there are blank spaces on the maps of Mongo indicating unexplored territories: dense jungles and arid deserts where strange animals live. Here too we find conspirators and also men whose aim is world domination. Ming the Merciless wants to dominate the planet and, if possible, also the earth. But thanks to Flash Gordon his plans never succeed. Seemingly killed a thousand times, Ming always pops up again with new dastardly plans to lure Flash to his doom.

Cities suspended in the air, heat-shields for expeditions to the ice-bound regions of the planet, countless flying objects, strange means of transport and the inevitable bizarre death-ray pistols (ZZZAP!) give the series its element of futurity; but monarchic governments, and the environmental conditions of the planet with their jungles, their deserts of ice or sand, their impenetrable swamps and landscapes pitted with craters, the daggers and swords drawn by inhabitants, their clothes trimmed with ermine and many more anachronistic details give the strip a comfortably archaic and familiar look. Such science fiction is probably also an attempt to present the old idea of romantic knightly deeds in new forms; to cloak it with the mantle of modern technology and so to make identification with the heroic archetype easier.

Flash Gordon is the incarnation of good and is therefore

Flash Gordon drawn by Alex Raymond. In 1938 Alex Raymond dispensed with speech balloons and inserted narrative text at the bottom or in corners of the picture; but designers who followed him later re-introduced the speech balloons.

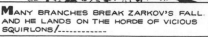

Brick Bradford by Paul Norris. A 'time top' and other fantastic
inventions allow the reader to take part in adventures set in any
century—past, present, future.
© 1970 King Features Syndicate

engaged in continuous battle against evil in the shape of Ming
the Merciless. During the Second World War Flash Gordon's
struggle became a great, united campaign of all the allied states on
Mongo against the 'evil one' who threatened them all. Such
symbolic significance was attained by most comic strip heroes
of that time and added, no doubt, to the war effort.

When Raymond finally dropped *Jungle Jim* and *Flash Gordon*
in order to devote himself entirely to his new character *Rip Kirby*,
Mongo had once more drawn away from the earth. *Flash Gordon*
was now free for new adventures and turned his attention to the
exploration of space. This gave the series a more definite science-
fiction touch; archaic details became less obvious but were not
entirely dropped. To this category of science fiction belongs
Drift Marlo, a series with present-day action, concerned with the
problems of space travel today or in the very near future.

Brick Bradford, a series drawn by Clarence Gray and written
by William Ritt, started in 1933 and combined, just as *Flash
Gordon* did later, elements of several different styles. The invention of a 'time gyroscope' not only added to the futuristic appeal
of the series, but also made it possible to treat any theme from
crime to Wild West adventures to the investigation of the

microcosm.

Comic books too profited from excursions into mankind's
future. On the one hand through reprints of popular comic strips
like *Flash Gordon, Buck Rogers* and *Drift Marlo*, on the other
through original comic book series. The latter include *Planet
Comics,* which appeared from 1940 to 1954 and whose heroes,
Futura, Red Comet, Mysta of the Moon, Star Pirate, etc., had
erotic as well as science fiction stories appeared in the E.C.
booklets *Weird Fantasy* and *Werid Science* and were later
published as series under the titles *Weird Science-Fantasy* and
Incredible Science-Fiction. Among such stories are, for instance,
the comics versions of Ray Bradbury's *I, the Rocket, King of the
Grey Spaces* and *Mars is Heaven*. In a pocket book edition of
these tales Ray Bradbury writes:

> One of the reasons we go into Space is to lose ourselves
> again, know magic, plumb mystery, ride high, be glorious,
> and have the heck frightened out of us. And we will be
> frightened not only by other worlds and creatures on those
> worlds, but by ourselves. We are still the greatest mystery
> and we shall spend several million more years trying to figure
> ourselves out.[6]

Twin Earths by Oscar Lebeck, drawn by Alden McWilliams, shows the earth in competition with a planet with very advanced technology, called Terra; Terra is almost an exact replica of the earth. A. McWilliams now draws *Dateline: Danger!*
© 1962 United Features Syndicate Inc./UPI

Other firms placed less ambitious reading matter in the hands of newspaper vendors. *Space Adventures, Space-War* and *Tommy Tomorrow* all whisked their readers—more or less successfully—away from earth, into the future, or both. Contrary to McLuhan's maxim, the present is personalized and rationalized in terms of the future in such science fiction comics, not in terms of the past.

Newcomers to this genre in recent times were, among others, the Gold Key series *Magnus Robotfighter 4000 A.D., Space Family Robinson, Mighty Samson* and *M.A.R.S. Patrol*. The two

Magnus by Russ Manning. German version. Magnus and Leeja are trapped in another dimension, which is ruled over by Mogul Badur, an evil potentate. Magnus is a kind of futuristic super-hero and he fights against the robots which are trying to enslave the human race.
© 1968, 1966 Western Publishing Co. Inc./Bildschriftenverlag

last mentioned series mirrored the fear of an all-destructive world war. *Samson* shows the aftermath of such a war in which a new world emerges; traces of the old civilization which perished are found near N'yark (New York). *M.A.R.S. Patrol* tells the story of an integrated group fighting against a hostile invader. After three really good issues the level of quality dropped and the invader turned out to be fiend from outer space; the story began to resemble a series called *The Invaders*, which had been adapted from a popular television programme. *Space Family Robinson* told the Odyssey of an ordinary American family trapped in space in the year 1999. This series was taken up by television and presented to viewers under the title 'Lost in Space'. *Star Trek* had a similar theme and was also shown on television. The most intelligent of all these science fiction series was probably *Magnus,* which started in February 1963: in the year 4000 mankind is technically so far advanced that all work is being done by robots. Man is about to be enslaved by the robots he created. At this point a man with a fighting spirit, called Magnus, appears on the scene. He had been brought up by a wise robot, kindly disposed towards mankind. Magnus takes up the fight against robots and against tyranny of any kind. Russ Manning's graphic art lent this series a particular charm. The twenty to twenty-seven pages allotted to each story allowed comparatively complex tales, but the series did not survive Manning's change-over to newspapers. Together with the titles in the Gold Key range already mentioned, *Magnus* disappeared into the half-limbo of reprints.

DC brought out two booklet series of the science fiction genre worth mentioning: *Mystery in Space* and *Strange Adventures*. A group of graphic artists and authors co-operated in these series and produced stories of special interest to science fiction enthusiasts. Their approach was broad to start with, aiming to interest a large readership; but it soon became clear that the stories attracted a rather specialized public. Many of the stories were conceived by John Broome and Gardner F. Fox, both of them prodigious writers of novels.[7] None can accuse Fox, who for many years also wrote the stories for *Justice League of America,* of catering for mediocrity. His tales are quite full of intriguing sub-plots; they are logical, complex in construction, demand the reader's intelligent attention.

The most complicated adventures are experienced by the hero of the series *Adam Strange*: on earth he is an archaeologist, but on the planet Rann he is a saviour from dangers in a world of the future. Fox and Broome let their hero span the distance between the earth and Rann (25 trillion miles) with the help of a zeta-ray sent out from Rann—which reminds us of *Buck Rogers* and Burroughs' *John Carter of Mars*, where unusual aids are also used to reach certain far-flung places in space. On Rann, a planet revolving round Alpha Centauri, Adam finds his mate Alanna, but maddeningly the zeta-ray weakens after each adventure and the frustrated lover finds himself back on earth. Adam Strange, originally appearing in *Mystery in Space,* is reprinted today in *Strange Adventures*, and a series called *From Beyond the Unknown* has replaced the vanished *Mystery in Space.*

Apart from pure science fiction comics, adventure series exist which combine elements taken from various types of 'fantastic' literature. *Nick Fury* or *Agent of S.H.I.E.L.D.,* for instance, or European stories like *Blake et Mortimer, Tintin, Dan Cooper, Bob Morane,* and super-hero tales like *Superman* or *Fantastic Four.*

The struggle against the super-technology of mad scientists often carries an element of science fiction into super-hero stories. Particularly in *Fantastic Four* (Marvel) where the evil technology of a brilliant scientist is challenged and fought; this involves all manner of strange apparatus making possible adventures on far-flung planets, in the macrocosm, the microcosm, or inside the earth.

If you enjoy being scared out of your wits . . .
Science fiction is closely allied to literature of the supernatural and their elements often mix. The legends of vampires, werewolves and the host of monsters that haunt the human mind; terrors that rise from open graves, spooks and spirits and things that go bump in the night—they all belong to the vast treasure of tales of all nations, told to make our flesh creep and our hair stand on end. For comics, however, they seemed to be out of bounds, because it was almost impossible to find a main character who could tumble from one spine-thrilling adventure into the next without causing undue alarm.

Comic books seized an opportunity of publishing several different (complete) stories in one booklet. E.C. Comics introduced special story-tellers for this purpose: the crypt keeper, the vault keeper and the old witch, who give their ironic comments on the outcome of each tale in the comic books *The Haunt of Fear, Tales from the Crypt* and *The Vault of Horror.* These series,

The genre of horror and of the mysterious was continued in comic books after the introduction of the Comics Code; but in contrast to earlier publications these booklets were in good taste and published no gory trash. The stories were all very moral and their conclusion was usually the victory over some dreadful danger threatening the earth.
© 1958 Charlton Comics Group

together with some other E.C. publications, precipitated the introduction of a comics code and the cleansing operation that swept through the whole of the comics market.[8]

The stories collected in these comic books continued the tradition of the gothic novel—the work of such geniuses of the genre as Horace Walpole, Ann Radcliffe, Matthew Gregory ('Monk'), Lewis and Mary Shelley; in America Charles Brockden Brown, Edgar Allan Poe, Nathaniel Hawthorne; and in our century H. P. Lovecraft and Ray Bradbury have developed the theme and added new dimensions to old ideas.

Comic books which tried to follow the tradition of making fantastic themes plausible made use of the stories of some of these authors; E.C. Comics, for instance, published versions of Ray Bradbury's *The Small Assassin, The Handler* and *Let's Play Poison.* Unfortunately, together with versions of Edgar Allan Poe stories of the Dracula or Frankenstein variety, an increasing volume of crude and ghastly blood-dripping horror tales appeared, which brought the whole genre into disrepute. It is, of course, quite possible that many young readers' nerves were strained beyond endurance by the offerings of these particular comics; but the greatest horror was felt by educational experts who preferred to frighten children with the good old-fashioned fairy-tales.

Tales of mystery and of horror satisfy a natural desire for irrational explanations of a complex environment. Technological societies have need of a little superstition, of an escape into transposed forms of ideas and beliefs held in childhood.

The tradition of the uncanny or horrific novel continued despite the fact that horror comics had ceased to exist, and one day the idea of publishing comics versions of creepy stories was reborn. In 1965 Warren Publishing Company produced two magazines, *Eerie* and *Creepy*, which once more drew inspiration from the realm of the uncanny; both are far removed from the cheap rubbish that had brought comics into disrepute. They are not comic books, but journals telling their stories in the form of comic strips, and first class graphic artists are employed on both. (Some of them also worked for E.C. Comics.) The stories, though they do not bear the Comics Code's stamp of approval. are in good taste and can in no way be compared with the sensationally presented comics which deserved nobody's admiration. The Warren magazines are good additions to the magazines which reproduce the stories of horror films, like *Famous Monsters of Filmland*, *Monster World*, *Screen Thrills Illustrated* and *Castle of Frankenstein*.

But fantastic themes and strange ghostly worlds have also reappeared in comic books. Gold Key published two series, *The Twilight Zone* (inspired by Rod Serling's television series) and *Thriller*, continued under the title *Boris Karloff's Tales of Mystery*; DC brought out *House of Mystery, House of Secrets, The Unexpected, The Witching Hour* and *Beware . . . the Monsters are coming!*; and Marvel's *Tower of Shadows, Chamber of Darkness, Where Monsters Dwell, Where Creatures Roam, Fear, Monsters on the Prowl* and *Creatures on the Loose.*

Nearly all these comic books have their storytellers: the dramatist and novelist Rod Serling, Boris Karloff of Frankenstein fame, Cain, the housemaster, the three witches, the house of mysteries which tells its own tale, the authors or designers of the stories. Some of these strips are really thrilling, some are a little antiquated and others are once more adapting novels or short stories by H. P. Lovecraft, but none of them offend against the principles of the Comics Code. Since 1971 it is also possible (within certain limitations imposed by the Comics Code Authority) to present once again stories handled in the literary tradition of Edgar Allan Poe, Mary Shelley and Sir Arthur Conan Doyle whose works are read in schools all over the world.

Another not-to-be-forgotten category of that type of literature is the 'sword and sorcery' saga. The best examples of this genre are to be found in the works of Abraham Merritt, Robert E. Howard, J. R. Tolkien, Edgar Rice Burroughs, L. Sprague De Camp and Otis Kline, and quite a few themes from their novels have found entry into comic books in series such as *Conan the Barbarian, Nightmaster, The Viking Prince* and into the *Dr Strange* stories. The last mentioned character, acting in the modern world, deals mainly with magic—in contrast to Nightmaster and Conan—but even Dr Strange's psychedelic adventures take him sometimes to worlds where swords are not unknown.

The way in which Steve Ditko introduced the occult into comic books gave the Marvel series of *Doctor Strange* its special flavour. It began—as any decent occult strip should—in a Tibetan monastery in the style of Shangri La, where Dr Stephan Strange, under the tuition of the Ancient One, gradually changes from a down-at-heel, morally not very laudable surgeon into a paragon of virtue who nobly desires nothing but the good of all mankind, and becomes a Master of the Mystic Arts. It is only thanks to Dr Strange that the Dread Dormammu and the sinister Baron Mordo have not yet turned the lot of us into zombies without a will of our own and enslaved the whole of mankind. The magicians wage their wars with terrible curses, calling on the might of the Crimson Bands of Cyttorak or the Hoary Hosts of Hoggoth. Personifications of eternity, of Kismet (fate) and of nightmares appear, and over all these goings-on watches the eye of Agamotto.

Creepy. Title page by Frank Frazetta. Since 1965 it has been possible to enjoy exquisite horror in comics. *Eerie* and *Creepy* also cater for fans of horror film.
© 1967 Warren Publishing Company, New York City, USA

Dr Strange by Steve Ditko. The deciding battle between the great magicians, the evil Baron Mordo and the noble Dr Strange. As always the earth is the prize for which the contestants battle. Never have curses and magic formulas appeared in such impressive portrayal as in Steve Ditko's drawings of Dr Strange's adventures. From Strange Tales, No. 132.

The old tales of chivalry

The very first example of a tale of chivalry that presents itself in comics is at the same time also the best: *Prince Valiant* by Harold R. Foster (started in 1937), presents the figure of a knight whose adventures in the fifth century A.D. take us to the court of King Arthur. The young prince who comes from a legendary country far north (somewhere near Norway) wants to become a knight at King Arthur's court. He makes himself useful to the King in many ways and finally after long and arduous endeavours he is made a knight.

Hal Foster, who always maintained that Val was all he himself would like to be, led the prince through adventures that had the glory and fascination of the great old legendary epics. *Prince Valiant* is also known as the legend of *The Singing Sword* and joins the many tales woven round Excalibur, King Arthur's magic sword, and around the Balmung and the Nagelring. The young prince has to battle with dragons and giants and all manner of beasts of fable before he attains his knighthood. Sir Gawain, the Don Juan of King Arthur's court, instructs him in all the arts a knight has to master and Merlin, the wise old magician, never refuses to give him advice.

Prince Valiant, the great epic of a young prince and his 'Singing Sword', lets all the old characters of the King Arthur legend (and many others) spring to life: Lancelot, Gawain, Modred, Merlin and Queen Guinevere people Camelot, King Arthur's splendid castle, and act out their stories to our entertainment and delight. Foster's genius lets the era of the knight-errant, of valour, love and honour rise before our eyes in glowing colours.

The news that the Huns had invaded Europe gives Prince Valiant, who pines for adventure, cause to rejoice. He plunges into action, demoralizes Attila's barbaric hordes through guerilla tactics and weakens them so seriously in a great battle that it later becomes easy for Aetius to defeat Attila on the fields of Catalonia. Thus Prince Valiant becomes the decisive figure of the whole era, and indeed of world history! Much has been written about Prince Valiant's struggle against the Huns. It is usually taken as another example of how heroes of comics were used for propaganda purposes in the war against Nazi Germany. The fact that 'Hun' is a derogatory term for 'German', like 'Kraut' or 'Fritz' seems to support this theory, and in 1939 it must have looked pretty obvious. France's free zone published *Prince Valiant*, but changed the Huns to some imaginary barbarians called Patagos. With hindsight, however, it becomes questionable whether Foster really intended Prince Valiant's one year long campaign against the Huns to be a morale boosting propaganda effort. Foster spent two years in research on the subject before he actually started work, which disproves the idea that his work was influenced by the outbreak of war. However, when the strip began to appear and war broke out in Europe it was easy to connect the Huns of Prince Val's day with the 'Hun' threatening Europe in 1939.

Extensive historical research allowed Foster to give an accurate

Mediaeval Castle by Hal Foster. At times used as bottom strip to *Prince Valiant*, it depicted mediaeval customs and tradition. A rather passionless account in which Foster could use the results of his extensive research. Beneath the strip a panel showing the well-known characters from *Prince Valiant*.

Our Story: EACH MORNING ALETA, QUEEN OF THE MISTY ISLES, MARCHES HER FAMILY DOWN TO THE SEASHORE FOR THEIR SWIMMING LESSON. AND THEY LEARN QUICKLY, FOR THEIR MOTHER IS EQUALLY QUICK WITH THE PALM OF HER HAND OR AN ENCOURAGING SMILE. IT IS ALSO RECORDED THAT MANY YOUNG GALLANTS BECAME INTERESTED IN SWIMMING INSTRUCTION AND CAME TO OBSERVE THEIR LOVELY QUEEN (IN A WET BATHING SUIT) GIVE LESSONS TO HER BROOD.

IT HAS BEEN CLAIMED, AND WITH SOME LOGIC TOO, THAT ALETA'S MOTHER HAD BEEN A MERMAID, FOR BOTH WERE AS MUCH AT HOME IN THE WATER AS IN THE PALACE. NOW, THE LESSON OVER, ALETA GLIDES FAR OUT TO SEA.

PRINCE VALIANT COMES SAILING HOME FROM THE PILGRIMAGE TO THE HOLY LAND. AS THE SHIP NEARS THE MISTY ISLES HE SEES A SPOT OF GOLD GLEAMING AMONG THE SPARKLING WAVES.

WITH A SHOUT OF JOY HE FLINGS ASIDE HIS CLOTHES, HIS CARES AND HIS COMMON SENSE AND LEAPS INTO THE SEA.

COPR. 1954, KING FEATURES SYNDICATE, Inc., WORLD RIGHTS RESERVED. 923 10-17-54

IT IS A WET AND SALTY KISS, BUT QUITE SATISFACTORY.

NOW THAT HE CAN TAKE HER IN HIS ARMS, WHAT DOES THE POOR FOOL DO? HE KNEELS BEFORE HER, TONGUE-TIED, DUMB, HIS HEART POUNDING. BUT THEN HE NEED NOT SPEAK. HIS EYES ARE SAYING QUITE PLAINLY: *"I LOVE YOU!"*

NEXT WEEK:- *Cupid Strikes Again.*

Prince Valiant by Harold R. Foster. In the saga of the Singing Sword, adventure has had to take second place to love.
© 1954 King Features Syndicate

picture not only of the British Isles and the feuds between the Angles, the Saxons and the Picts in the fifth century A.D., but also of the world of antiquity and the Mediterranean in the fading glory of a decadent and rapidly declining Roman empire. Returning from a pilgrimage to the Holy Land, Prince Valiant finds his great love Aleta, the legendary queen of the Misty Isles; but before he can win such a prize the gods make him face certain obstacles, and before Prince Val can marry his queen he has to undergo numerous adventures. He is sold as a slave, endures many hardships, faces many dangers until, at last, the lovers are re-united. At first marriage does not slow down the pace of the prince's adventurous life; on the contrary, the pace quickens, for together with a trusted friend, the Viking Boltar, he follows the kidnappers of his wife westwards to a new world only a few seafarers have ever seen. (When, years later, Arn, Valiant's son, also travels to this new world he establishes there the Algonquin Society for the welfare of Red Indians!)

Much later only, after the first children have been born, does the valiant prince curb his lust for adventure. Gradually his son Arn moves to the middle of the stage and Valiant himself appears in the more domestic aspects of the strip.

A few years ago two historians who were said to have dis-covered the legend of the Singing Sword suddenly appeared in one of the instalments and declared that at this point there was a gap in the text of the legend and that the prince is only mentioned again after a considerable lapse of time, when he reappears in a different part of Europe. This clever ruse kills two birds with one stone: a gap in time is painlessly bridged and the reader is once more made aware of the excellence of the research that goes into every detail of the saga. Foster's great epic ascribes historic events to Prince Valiant, or at least credits him with great influence on chronicled happenings; he lets him, for instance, play an important part in the spreading of Christianity throughout the British Isles—but all legends try to fit their heroes or heroines into the framework of history.

Although *Prince Valiant* has become in the course of time a kind of adventurous family strip, it still provides that rare

mixture of historical fact and fiction which distinguishes it from any other strip. In January 1971 Foster slowly withdrew from his strip which was then taken over—anonymously—by John Cullen Murphy.

Knights as heroes are relatively more numerous in comic books than in comic strips. *Black Knight* and the European *Thierry la Fronde, Sigurd* and *Robin Hood*, to give a few examples. The knights of American comic books usually turn out to be prema-ture super-heroes leading a double life and possessing all the necessary equipment. A very similar phenomenon also appears in 'Western' comic books.

High melodrama

Comic strips which take a slice of daily life and appeal to the emotions are called 'human interest' strips in the jargon of the comics business. 'Human interest' encompasses certain profes-sions: doctors, photographers, journalists, fashion designers and people of the film and theatre world, because they offer splendid backgrounds for romantic entanglements.

Emotion-laden radio and television series with advertisement spots for soap or detergents inspired the expression 'soap opera'. The equivalent of such offerings in comics can be found in the human interest strip, especially if the main character is a woman. One of the first series of this type was *Winnie Winkle*, started by Martin Branner in 1920 as a gag strip; gradually, however, the characters aged and become more than just caricatures. Winnie's brother Perry, who had spread his pranks across the Sunday paper strip, gave way to a continuous series, appearing weekdays and Sundays, about the apparently widowed Winnie Winkle, a fashion designer, and her family. Her husband is missing, after having been involved in an accident. There are hints, from time to time, that he may still be alive, but no evidence is given that this could be true. Instead, the heroine lives through the trials and tribulations of a middle class family.

The best example of a pure soap opera comic strip is *Mary Worth*, a series which arose in 1938 out of Martha Orr's instal-

Winnie Winkle by Martin Branner. A melodramatic moment in the life of Winnie Winkle, fashion designer.
© 1960 Chicago Tribune — New York News Syndicate

ments of *Apple Mary*; it relates (after radical modifications of the whole concept) the experiences of a middle-aged woman with grown-up children. Since her own family no longer need her, she throws herself with boundless energy into the task of helping and advising friends, relatives and acquaintances alike.

The ludicrous adventures of journalist *Brenda Starr* (invented by Dale Messick), a child of the early 1940s, have one aim only: to catch and marry the man who in her eyes is the only male worthy of her love. Brenda is faithful to her ideal man, though time and again she is separated from him. (Since Richardson all heroines suffer according to this recipe.) At each parting floods of tears pour over her copy—oh, romantic heart, could you wish for more?

Perhaps for *The Heart of Juliet Jones*, a series invented by graphic artist Stan Drake in co-operation with Elliott Caplin in 1953. It depicts the experiences of career girl Juliet Jones and her sister Eve. This strip satisfied the longing of lovelorn readers to such an extent that it soon spread across most of the known

Looie, an amusing little strip, also by Martin Branner. The drawing technique is unique among comic strips.
© 1960 Chicago Tribune—New York News Syndicate

Brenda Starr by Dale Messick. One of the rare moments Brenda is allowed to share with her mysterious lover. No wonder there is a starry sky.
© 1965 Chicago Tribune—New York News Syndicate

Abbie an' Slats by Raeburn Van Buren. Main character in this melodrama is the good-looking Slats, who can always count on his Aunt Abbie, an old maid, whenever he is in trouble.
© 1962 United Features Syndicate/UPI

world. (France calls it *Juliette de mon cœur*, in Germany it appears under the title *Das Herz der Julia Köster* or *Die beiden Schwestern*.)

The Jones sisters enjoyed their spinsterdom for seventeen years. Sometimes they broke their own or somebody else's heart, and in hours of sadness always found solace in the love of their dear old father. But in 1970 the unbelievable happened: Juliet Jones married . . . and a wealthy man at that! This has in no way interrupted the series' march of triumph, for it is quite possible to take a tear-laden interest in the vagaries of a married woman's life, and besides, there is always sister Eve who can still fall unhappily in love and experience many a new turmoil. Stan Drake was probably much relieved to turn—after seventeen years—to new facets of the Juliet theme.

The theatre forms a splendid background to Leonard Starr's *Mary Perkins on Stage*, a melodrama which began in 1957 (under the title *On Stage*) with Mary leaving her small home town for the bright lights of Broadway and the glamour of New York. The fairy tale of success came true for Mary Perkins and she found her man—an equally successful journalist—into the bargain. Of course Mary Perkins, the successful actress and famous film and television star, lives a life of melodrama; but to call it soap opera would be unjust, for this series is no tear-jerker. Its success rests on the glimpses the reader is given of upper class life. The glamour of Broadway, beautiful clothes, people, gestures and emotions are all depicted in an exquisite drawing technique.

There are many more women in comic strips: in *Apartment 3-G* we meet three girls all at once, who share this New York apartment for economic reasons; the rent is exorbitant. The love of life and gaiety of the three flat dwellers is well expressed in Alex Koteky's racy drawing style. The romantic interludes sometimes seem to be inspired by Jacqueline Susann's *Valley of the Dolls*, but without a hunt of any immoral 'goings on'. In 1970 a new-comer appeared to woo the readers' sympathy and interest: the dark-eyed photographer *Friday Foster*, brought to life by Jim Lawrence and Jorge Longaron.[9]

Not only in comic strips, in comic books too love is a favoured theme; but with one proviso: the stories must be 'clean' and project to teenagers the right kind of attitude towards sex. Comic books like *Young Love, True Love* and others of the same kind relate normally irreproachable 'young girl romances' and in many cases are much more popular among youngsters than sexy novels about love and passion. The great success of such comic books as *Sweetheart, Teenage Romance, Romantic Secret* and *Life Story* showed this trend clearly as far back as 1949. Top of the popularity poll were the Fawcett booklets *Sweethearts* with a circulation of one million and *Life Story* with a circulation of 700,000.

Today romance is returning to comic books in a big way. The Charlton Comics Group alone published in 1971 *I Love You, Sweethearts, Love Diary, Time for Love, Just Married, Secret Romance, Romantic Story, Hollywood Romances, Teenage Love, Teen Confessions* and *Career Girl Romances*.

It is always true love, or first love, that causes endless pain until at last wedding bells ring in the beginning of bliss, or the parties concerned realize that it was not yet the real thing.

Not only girls, men too can be the centre of a whirlwind of romantic passion. Physicians are much favoured in this role *(Dr. Bobbs, Rex Morgan M.D., Dr. Kildare, Ben Casey)*, so are judges *(Judge Parker)* and up to a point also parsons *(David Crane)*. Hospital theatres, where life or death decisions are taken, have an aura of melodrama, of complications arising from competition from other specialists challenging the famous surgeon, or from the fact that nurses or patients fall passionately in love with him. Sick people, and this includes the socially sick who are brought before a judge, are ideal vehicles for emotional themes and never fail to make their impact on the reader. The idealism which motivates doctors, judges, parsons, etc., is, of course, stressed and doctors and judges are always drawn a little larger than life in order to instil in the reader the desired confidence in the nation's great healing and corrective institutions, or to familiarize him with some of the problems that can arise in such professions. An investigation of readers' reactions to *Rex Morgan, M.D.* showed that such series are certainly able to influence their public's attitude, particularly if they dispense free medical advice.

The Heart of JULIET JONES by Stan Drake

opposite
Mary Perkins on Stage by Leonard Starr. This strip takes the reader into the glamorous world of stage, film and television. It shows a carefully executed cinematographic style of drawing.
© 1968 Chicago Tribune—New York News Syndicate

Little Orphan Annie by Harold Gray. This example from one of the Sunday strips epitomizes the whole philosophy expressed by this series: Daddy Warbucks possesses the secret weapons and the know-how necessary to defend his country from its enemies. Providence has appointed him to the task.
© 1967 Chicago Tribune—New York News Syndicate

A melodrama with a completely different slant is *Little Orphan Annie* by Harold Gray, which has a political (right wing) background. It started in 1924 as a continuous gag strip and showed Mrs Warbucks taking Annie into her house. Her motive is to show high society how generous and idealistic a *nouveau riche* family can be; but the exercise proves bothersome and after a few weeks Mrs Warbucks decides to take the orphan back to where she belongs—the orphanage. On the way, however, Mrs Warbucks' car is stopped by Miss Fair (!), member of an old established family which, though not rich, belongs to the aristocracy of the town. Much embarrassed, Mrs Warbucks explains that it is 'a lovely day for a drive'. Annie would have much preferred adoption by Miss Fair to adoption by the snobbish Mrs Warbucks. However, back Annie goes to the Warbucks household. What had started as a veiled criticism of snobbish behaviour soon turned into blatant admiration and promotion of capitalist ideas.

Mr Warbuck, his oriental servant Punjab and the Asp are never far away when little Annie, accompanied by her faithful dog Sandy, stumbles into adventure after adventure, dastardly plot after plot. Annie irons out all that does not fit in with her strictly conservative notions. Anything that does not comply with Daddy Warbucks' ideas of free enterprise and *laissez faire* economy has to be changed. He who is against Warbucks, engages in espionage, or commits a crime, has to reckon with Warbucks' and Punjab's revenge. *Little Orphan Annie*'s symbolism reached its pinnacle when Warbucks, the great exponent of capitalism, fell desperately sick at a time when Roosevelt's New Deal put the brakes on some of the excesses of free enterprise. The poor fellow nearly passed away, but with Roosevelt's death he took a sudden and miraculous turn for the better and under Eisenhower he returned to full health and vitality. In *Little Orphan Annie* capitalism is allied to strict puritanical faith, providence and pious hope, but it takes the law firmly into its own hands if there is any danger of its being undermined. The Sunday strip uses meaningful quotations in its first picture to bolster Annie's message.

Detectives and policemen

On Sunday, 4 October 1931, *Dick Tracy* was born. He was the child of Chester Gould's imagination and arrived on the scene after Joseph M. ('Captain') Patterson, founder of the *New York News* and director of the Chicago Tribune–New York News Syndicate, had accepted the idea. Gould had bombarded Patterson in vain for six long years with suggestions for comic strip themes. *Dick Tracy* finally made it.

Enraged at the growth of gangsterism in the United States, Gould wanted to unmask and combat the doings of criminals by means of a comic strip. Captain Patterson, who had an instinct for titles that put the message over, changed the original *Plainclothes Tracy* to *Dick Tracy*. ('Dick' is American slang for 'policeman'.) Gould attacked the lax attitude of local police forces and tried to illustrate how easy it was for gangsters to have

it all their own way. His crusade was directed against government bodies which had either become helpless against organized crime or were actually aiding and abetting it. The recipe was simple: Tracy was for hard, effective methods and the mere fact that an ordinary policeman could get at criminals and land them in jail delighted readers. Red tape was of no interest to Tracy. He excelled in action, in direct confrontation with evil.

Dick Tracy's first appearances were on two succeeding Sundays in the *Detroit Mirror*. He unmasked a hotel thief and arrested the big boss of a criminal gang. On 12 October 1931 a weekday series started in the *New York News* and on 13 December the Sunday strip too was taken over by that paper. The first weekday instalments showed Dick Tracy visiting the Trueheart family, where he asks father Trueheart for the hand of his daughter, Tess; but as he is pressing his suit bandits storm into the house and kill Dad Trueheart when he refuses to hand over his hard-earned dollars (on 16 December). On 19 December the robbers kidnap Tess and hold her as a hostage; Tracy is twice knocked down, and on 22 December he becomes a member of the police plain clothes squad. He immediately starts on the task of undermining the criminal gang from within. Gould and Patterson knew what they were about when they made Tracy a policeman: when gangsters break the law Tracy must not be seen to take private vengeance. He is the law and as such entitled to take action.

Dick Tracy depicted violence right from the start; up to that point brute force, blood and the techniques of criminals had been taboo in comic strips and in the beginning the public reacted against this aspect of the strip. But Gould was not to be drawn away from his chosen style of narrative, for he maintained that reality was much more violent than anything shown in his series; and so *Dick Tracy* was sometimes banned from the comic pages of some papers during the first few years of his stormy career. Never for longer than a week, though:[10] as soon as the blood was mopped up Dick Tracy turned up again.

Chester Gould uses a very flat style of drawing, designed to give an impression of reality though the characters involved are unreal. A legion of heavily caricatured criminal types with names indicative of their appearance entered the scene: Pruneface, Flattop, Miss Egghead, Mole. Some criminals betray their particular nastiness if one reads their names backwards: John Naem, Junky Doolb, Professor M. Emirc, Frank Rellik, Frankie Redrum. Once, in 1936, Chester Gould wanted to break through the illusion of reality he himself had created. He had brought his hero into an impossible situation, a trap out of which he could not escape. He therefore turned to the reader in one of the instalment's pictures with the words: 'Gould, you have gone too far', whereupon the hand of the artist appeared in the (next) picture and erased the rock that had blocked the entrance to the mine. But Patterson refused to accept this solution and a 'natural' one had to be found. Since then Gould has been careful to keep within the framework of illusion.

In the first twenty-four years of his existence Dick Tracy has been shot at and wounded twenty-seven times and a collection of

Dick Tracy by Chester Gould. Plenty of action—and force if needed—in the service of the law. Gould's bluntly effective style of drawing emphasizes the 'cops and robbers' flavour.

roughly fifty bullet-holed hats shows the extent of near misses; but not only with bullets do his enemies try to eliminate him: he has been beaten up, chloroformed, blown up by explosives, dragged along behind a car and once nearly frozen to death; when his house was set on fire he went blind for a while. His injuries all heal very quickly, even his gun hand, though squashed almost to pulp by some antagonist, returned to its usual 'quick draw' in double quick time. His sharply etched profile and famous hooked nose, however, have never been touched.

Will Gould's *Red Barry*, a detective who stormed through the *New York Journal* from 1935 to 1938 was less long-lived. A violence which betrayed the strip's relationship to 'black' series of films *(série noire)* made for its early demise.

Dick Tracy's adventures rank with some of the longest ever depicted in comic strips and sometimes take over six months to unfold, and as Gould never determines the end of a sequence in advance, he can spin it out until he tires of it and wants to create something new. He reckons that his readers tire of a story around the same time he does and then usually lets the criminal die a violent death.

The series takes the work of the police as its main theme and Tracy's private life has remained very much in the background. This is probably also the reason why he did not marry Tess Trueheart, who had been his sweetheart from the start, until 24 November 1949. The union was blessed in 1951 by the arrival of daughter Bonny Braids.

Besides Dick Tracy and his rogues' gallery a collection of minor characters assembled over the years, such as Junior, Dick Tracy's assistant Sam Catchem, policewoman Lizz, Dick's boss Chief Patton, and many others, including the whole population of the moon—yes, *Dick Tracy* even shows elements of science fiction. Flights through space are commonplace and on earth it is easy to move about silently in flight buckets and to be in constant communication with colleagues through two-way wrist TV.

Rip Kirby by Alex Raymond. German version. The adventures of an intellectual type of detective who loves books, classical music, good living; they became a great success with readers, though the syndicate had been sceptical when the series started. In this sequence Rip Kirby rescues a beautiful girl and later takes her out to dinner.
© Kings Features Syndicate/Bulls Pressedienst

86

Chester Gould comments cleverly on the world of comics in two strips within the strip. He introduced the first in 1964, as a subplot in a specific criminal case. It was called *Sawdust* and told of sawdust gifted not only with human speech, but also with a talent for outrageous puns. The inventor of the series has four assistants who work together and all four sign the sequences. The other one is drawn by one of the regular minor characters, Vera Alldid, that is, she only writes the text, for the strip is about the *Invisible Tribe* which is, as its title states, invisible. In both strips, but particularly in *Sawdust*, Gould seems to make fun of himself.

Other policemen strips, coming after *Dick Tracy*, portray more of the human side of a policeman's life. *Mickey Finn*, for instance, a strip begun in 1936 by Lank Leonard, which contains an ethnic element, and Jay Irving's humorous strip of patrol policeman *Pottsy*.

Private detectives also enliven the comics scene, but although they act on their own volition and at their own peril, they must be sanctioned by the law. The best one is surely Rip Kirby, the intellectual who wears glasses and enjoys the good things in life. He is well read, loves classical music, but can nevertheless hit hard when necessary. He also plays golf, drinks moderately, and is an adept at chess and at handling women. This strip runs contrary to all the well-tried recipes of comics successes, and yet it paid King Features handsome dividends. After the Second World War Alex Raymond had returned to drawing *Jungle Jim* and *Flash Gordon* before inventing *Rip Kirby* in 1946. After 1948 he drew only the latter, until he was killed in a car accident and John Prentice— a worthy successor—took over the strip. Before the war Raymond had also drawn *Secret Agent X-9*, written by Dashiell Hammet, but neither of the two stayed long with this particular series. It was continued first by Mel Graff and then by Bob Lewis. In 1967 Al Williamson took over and, with the intention of making the strip's hero a little more human, changed its title to *Secret Agent Corrigan*.

Ian Fleming's *James Bond,* popular though he had become through the novels and films, found no American syndicate to distribute it, because the licence fees were too high and so *James Bond* stayed at home in England, in the pages of the *Daily Express*. In the USA he remained tied to two comic books which appeared in conjunction with the film *Dr. No*.

Secret Agent Corrigan by Al Williamson. Originally invented by Dashiel Hammett and Alex Raymond under the title *Secret Agent X-9*, taken over by Mel Graff and Bob Lewis and finally by Al Williamson, who recaptured the excellence of Raymond's drawings.
© 1968 King Features Syndicate

Al Williamson not only continues Raymond's high quality of drawing, but is also a worthy successor to Raymond's art of storytelling. In the spy strip *Secret Agent Corrigan* he often introduces fights with swords and daggers.
© 1968 King Features Syndicate

Mandrake by Lee Falk. Drawn by Fred Fredericks. Part of a Sunday strip sequence which shows Mandrake's old tricks: he gestures hypnotically.
© 1967 King Features Syndicate

Alfred Andriola had drawn the detective series *Charlie Chan* for seven years, the first comics series to have an Asian as its chief character (modelled on the novels of Earl Derr Biggers), before he offered his readers *Kerry Drake* in 1943. A strip with both a private and a police detective as its main protagonists, it made clever use of the detective story technique which gives private detectives either a friend at court, or a special antagonist at police headquarters, like Mike Hammer and Pat Chambers, or Michael Shayne and Inspector Lefevre. Batman and Police Commissioner Gordon follow the same precept. (Batman, the super detective, will be discussed in the next chapter.)

A very special species are detectives who use magic or supernatural powers. There is, for instance, *Mandrake,* a magician and hypnotist who has been active since 1934 (invented by Lee Falk). He solves the most intricate problems by means of hypnotic manipulation; whether they are earthly or inter-galaxy problems matters little. At the height of the James Bond craze Mandrake joined the general spy-fever and helped an international organization, reminiscent of Interpol (called Inter-tel), fight a dangerous espionage ring. Mandrake's factotum Lothar, an African prince, assisted his master from the very beginning in all his battles against evil and gradually progressed from servant to equal partner.

Will Eisner created *The Spirit* in 1940. The singularly enterprising special detective of this series suffered a very special initiation before he attained his status: his first attacker knocked him unconscious and his colleagues thought he was dead; then when he had come round he underwent a mock burial so that afterwards, disguised as The Spirit and always wearing a mask, he could outwit the gangsters. From 2 June 1940 to 28 September 1952 *The Spirit* appeared in complete stories which were added to Sunday newspapers, as sixteen-page comic book sections. From 1941 the adventures of *The Spirit* (whose headquarters was a cemetery) were also published in a regular comic book.

The Shadow, who possessed the faculty of confusing men's minds to such an extent that he became invisible to them, also spooked through comic books after he had first conquered the pulps and made successful broadcasts—always asking and answering the pertinent question: 'Who knows what evil lurks in the hearts of men? The Shadow knows!' He also used to say: 'The weed of crime bears bitter fruit! Crime does not pay!' and this was always followed by satanic laughter.

Other detectives and agents appearing in comic books include Ellery Queen, Sherlock Holmes, Perry Mason and Mike Shayne; sometimes, however, they only survived for a few issues.

The adventurers

In 1934 a series by Milton Caniff, *Terry and the Pirates*, began to fill a wide, exotic landscape with thrilling adventure. Once again the title had been Captain Patterson's choice. Caniff made thorough researches into all aspects of China, scanning all the material he could find, becoming quite a China expert in the process. In 1937 Terry fought on the Chinese side against the Japanese invaders, but on advice from the syndicate 'Japanese' was dropped and they were just called 'invaders'. During the Second World War they reverted to being 'Japanese' invaders.

Captain Patterson had seen Milton Arthur Paul Caniff's strip *Dickie Dare* and had been impressed by it. He decided to give Caniff a chance with *Terry and the Pirates*. *Dickie Dare* had been the story of a boy who had wanted to join Robin Hood's Merry Men. Terry was, to begin with, a pale-faced boy looking for treasure (a disused, forgotten mine) in China. He never found the mine, but he found adventures galore among pirates—including beautiful female ones—and all kinds of Asiatic characters, good and bad. Patterson's wish that this series should become as habit-forming as a soap opera was fulfilled. The strip achieved such popularity and its characters were so real that millions of

opposite

Steve Canyon by Milton Caniff. Among the many women in the life of the gallant pilot Steve Canyon, Summer Smith Olsen is the only one he really loves. He had to wait for many years before he could marry her—when she became a widow. The example here shows that the square pictures, intended for a whole page, could be adjusted to fit a third of a page. The montage of the panels was originally two rows, but it has been altered here.
© 1953 Field Enterprises/King Features Syndicate

Smilin' Jack by Zack Moseley. Flying, loving, romancing, these things go together: particularly when the main character is an adventurous Erroll Flynn or Douglas Fairbanks type.
© 1960 Chicago Tribune—New York News Syndicate

Americans mourned when heiress Raven Sherman was pushed out of a truck by villains and plunged to her death at the foot of a Chinese mountain. Students all over the USA turned their faces eastwards in respectful silence, and Caniff received flowers and condolences from scores of readers.

Caniff's young hero grew up and as he was already engaged in fighting for the Chinese and against the Japanese, he started to take an active part in the Second World War from 1942 onwards. On 17 October 1943 the series shifted its direction: the hero joined the category of gallant flyer-adventurers. This move brought Terry into the tradition-laden genre of flyer-strips and soon *Terry and the Pirates* outflew *Skyroads* (Dick Calkins), *Tailspin Tommy* (Hal Forrest), *Ace Drummond* (a series by C. Knight modelled on Eddie Rickenbacker, the American air ace

of the First World War), *Barney Baxter* (Frank Miller), *Smilin' Jack* (Zack Mosley) and *Scorchy Smith* (John Terry, 1930, Noel Sickles from 1934) in popularity.

Milton Caniff also drew *Male Call* free of charge for 300 army newspapers (from 1942), designed civilian defence posters and countless insignia for air force squadrons, and illustrated confidential military instruction manuals. Because of the highly secret nature of some of the material in his possession, Caniff's house was classified a 'war plant' and anybody visiting him had to check in and out on a special visitors' list.

When the Second World War was over Caniff earned $70,000 a year, but he did not possess the rights over his strip. In 1944 Marshal Field offered him a five-year contract with a guaranteed weekly salary of $2,000 if he would draw a new strip for the Chicago Sun Syndicate. Caniff accepted with the proviso that he should retain all rights over the new strip, that the Sun would in fact only hire his strip. Field's syndicate and King Features were to distribute the series. Caniff waited patiently until his contract for *Terry* ran out two years later. In the meantime Field and Hearst could do no more than hawk around Caniff's name and reputation. This they did with resounding success.

As soon as it became known that Caniff would start drawing a new strip in 1947 more than 200 daily papers contracted the series without knowing its name or its theme, long before Caniff drew the first tentative line. Tension grew until at last, two weeks before *Steve Canyon* was to be published for the first time on 19 January 1947, Caniff showed his work to the syndicate. Everybody breathed a sigh of delighted relief: *Steve Canyon* was Caniff at his best.

Steve was an adult, mature man-of-the-world version of Terry; a courageous, devil-may-care, ex-airforce pilot (the airforce actually gave both Terry and Steve identification numbers), who had entered into the flying taxi business after the war. Caniff stuck to his cinematographic technique of drawing which had become a style to be copied by the young aspiring comics artists of the day.

In 1970 it happened: Steve Canyon and Summer married. They were both madly in love, but soon Mrs Canyon started to take matters into her own hands.
© 1970 Field Enterprises/King Features Syndicate

Working to his own particular method, Caniff drew material for his stories from newspaper articles, radio programmes, books, films, and many other sources. (*Newsweek* commented that his work technique and manner of storytelling could best be compared with that of the Dumas family.[11]) He was always well informed and his instinct for coming events was almost uncanny. Two days before a *real* paratroop invasion into Burma took place, a Burma invasion appeared in *Terry and the Pirates*. It had been drawn weeks previously. (British newspapers even suspected Caniff of espionage!) In 1949 Steve Canyon suggested that Russia might be building submarines in her southern ports. A few months later this proved to be actually true. Steve Canyon later returned to China (1949) to fight against an invader from the north.

Stevenson Burton Canyon is always on the ball. Many minor characters take part in his various exploits and are usually modelled on living people—names, of course, are altered. Since 26 April 1970 Steve has shared his adventures and his bank account with Summer Smith Olsen, a widow with a son, whom he had met many years ago when the strip was young.

But he is not the only flying hero; he shares the air with others. Roy Crane's *Buz Sawyer* started his career in 1943, when Crane left *Captain Easy*. *Buz Sawyer*'s territory of action was the war in the Pacific. In order to escape from time to time from drawing the essential but tedious details of planes and military hardware, Crane let Buz be shot down every now and then, to crash land on one of the beautiful South Sea islands. Ample opportunities here to let lovely dusky maidens take over! After the war Buz Sawyer helped in various capacities in the developing countries and also acted as detective in criminal cases. His pal Rosco Sweeney became the hero of a humorous Sunday strip. Just as Terry Lee and Steve Canyon, Buz Sawyer too moved to Vietnam. But only Steve Canyon was mentioned in *Pravda* as a fighter for imperialism—an incident later mentioned in Caniff's strip.

During the Second World War Frank Robbins started to draw *Johnny Hazard*, after discontinuing his temporary work on *Scorchy Smith*; perhaps Johnny experienced the adventures which had been invented for Scorchy Smith. Stylistically Frank Robbins' work is akin to that of Caniff. For some years now Johnny Hazard has been busy in a secret service world with a distinctively futuristic flavour; but Robbins' designs do not include such elaborate technical details as those depicted in U.N.C.L.E.'s television and comic book series. Inevitably, beautiful women weave in and out of the strip and supply the necessary element of romance. Heroes of such stories are always chivalrous towards

Buz Sawyer by Roy Crane. During World War Two Buz fought in the Pacific for the USA. Today he lends a helping hand anywhere—even in developing South American countries. The effective grey shading in Crane's drawings is achieved through the famous 'Craftint' method which Crane, among others, pioneered.
© 1965 King Features Syndicate

ladies—even ladies who try to murder them. Emancipated women do exist in comic strips, but they are usually minor characters or particularly wicked antagonists, like the Dragon Lady, one of Terry Lee's female enemies.

At the beginning of the adventure era in comics sportsmen appeared in the pages of newspapers and comic books, together with the many sky-storming flyers. One of the first was Ham Fisher's *Joe Palooka*, a boxer. Ham Fisher had tried for many

Captain Easy by Crooks and Lawrence. Started originally by Roy Crane, this series is even today almost indistinguishable in style from *Buz Sawyer*.
© 1970 Newspaper Enterprise Association Inc./UPI

Johnny Hazard by Frank Robbins. Planes, women, politics and hidden treasure are the ingredients: Rapidly moving, casual style of drawing.
© 1970 King Features Syndicate

years to sell his series to one of the syndicates, but it was only after he had joined the McNaught Syndicate as a representative and had proved his worth as a knowledgeable salesman of series, that he could promote his own strip. In 1930, when his boss was away, he took *Joe Palooka* along on his round to the various papers and offered it for sale together with other series. Three weeks later twenty newspapers had bought his strip which proved an instant success. *Joe Palooka* has always been one of the most sentimental series of the United States, and after the hero had married it turned into a family strip with emphasis on emotional matters.

The problem with boxers is that it is impossible to show them as world champions for any length of time without losing credibility. John Cullen Murphy, whose boxing genius *Big Ben Bolt* had remained world champion since 1950, realized this predicament and withdrew his hero (unbeaten) from the ring to let him loose on the world of adventure.

The war: G.I. Joe's heroic deeds

The name G.I. Joe for American soldiers stems from the comic strip *Private Breger* by Dave Breger which since 1942 has shown the humorous side of a soldier's life. During the Second World War many comic strips and books had started to take part in world events. The paper heroes too went to the front and fought for their country and did their bit for the reader's morale.

The flyers already mentioned had taken to fighting for home, family and apple pie as a matter of course—and even Tarzan confronted the Nazis who invaded his jungle. Mickey Mouse and Donald Duck were staunch in their support of the propaganda for the war and they were magnificent morale boosters. Today some heroes still turn up in Vietnam, and for some years *Tales of the Green Beret*, a series based on a novel by Robin Moore, led its readers to Vietnam and Latin America. But the involvement in today's war is much more tentative.

The Vietnam War is much too controversial for an all-out engagement. This came to be understood by the producers of comic books when Vietnam stories received many more refusals than acceptances. As far as comic books are concerned, the First World War and the Second World War are still raging. Heroes like Sgt. Fury or Sgt. Rock and their combat troops are almost super-heroes. The nucleus of the group survives, the minor, additional characters die. Moral conflicts arise and the deeds of G.I. Joe are held up as great epics of heroism.

Opinions on war comics differ sharply. Jules Feiffer states that they 'are harmful, distorted, Pentagon manipulated and, more often than not, boring'. On the other hand the representatives of a firm which does not handle any war comics feel 'that the readers of war comics realize that most of the stories are fantasy and consider them as entertainment'.

Certainly, war comics conjure up war heroes like puppets and distort their characteristics to such an extent that at times they become mere caricatures; but it should be remembered that they are primarily meant to entertain. Joe Kubert, editor of the war comic books of National Periodical Publications, stresses on his

readers' letters pages that it is not his intention to glorify war in comic books, but rather to show what a human being has to endure, or can achieve in times of extreme peril. In the last analysis there are never any victors in war, only losers.

Heroes like Sgt. Fury in *Sgt. Fury and the Howling Commandos* or Sgt. Rock of Easy Company in *Our Army at War*, are always completely invulnerable. They always appear at the centre of any engagement where the fighting is fiercest (hence the tattered and torn uniforms), bullets whirr past them, bombs explode, but they are never wounded—at least never mortally wounded. They are leaders of men who take their groups of warriors behind enemy lines to go into action against newly invented super-weapons, or stride in and out of headquarters on important missions. The enemy is often reduced to just a handful of men, as in the case of Baron Strucker and his Blitz squad, for instance. War comics experts make a harmless game out of war: the side armed with the better ideology must win. Even in battle against an enemy vastly superior in numbers the brave warriors will be proved better, more courageous, more tenacious and much

Sgt. Fury and His Howling Commandos drawn by Jack Kirby and Geo Bell. This elite squad wins wars in the twinkling of an eye thanks to its daredevil missions. From *Sgt. Fury*, No. 6.
© 1963 Marvel Comics Group

Enemy Ace by Joe Kubert. Eddie Rickenbacker and Baron von Richthofen are the models for this World War One epic in which both sides are shown.

© 1968 National Periodical Publications Inc.

more intelligent fighters and will win—if all else fails—by using their fists in close combat. In *Sgt. Fury and His Howling Commandos* a German, Eric Koenig, fights with Fury against the Nazis. Remarkable is the fact that in the last few years, perhaps inspired by the film *The Blue Max* and encouraged by Snoopy's preoccupation with the Red Baron, National Periodical Publications have published a comics series under the title *Enemy Ace* in which a German pilot of World War One plays the main part. Baron von Hammer, the enemy ace, is presented in such a way that the American reader can identify with him; and as the ace is an 'enemy', the series is well able to work out an underlying anti-war attitude. *Enemy Ace* often reflects on the madness of war and it also ridicules absurd concepts of honour. The latter theme can be well illustrated with examples from World War One. Is the Enemy Ace therefore an anti-hero and the comic book that relates his story an anti-war tract? Almost; but an honest critic

has to admit that most of the pictures are so fascinatingly beautiful that they would tend to prevent the message from reaching the reader's consciousness.

If Coulton Waugh's experimental anti-war strip *Hank* (1945) had had a similarly entertaining wrapping it might have become a success and lasted longer than just three-quarters of a year.

The Western: The frontier—an American Garden of Eden?

As long as the frontier still existed Americans could expand, could move ever farther west. 'Go West, Young Man! was the advice endlessly repeated. The will of the individual was law. Man was master of his environment and could shape it to his liking. But the freedom to move into this promised land was the very reason for its gradual decline, for it was inevitable that as more and more settlers 'went West', they imported, in time, all the problems of civilization into their paradise. Written law advanced much more slowly into the West than man and the violence that accompanied him. Though the West was anything but a Garden of Eden, it was painted as such in the memory of men and glorified by all the mass media.

The period between 1870 and 1890 in particular has been given an aura of glory. This was due to the fact that a particular section of white Westerners had sent the whole population of the USA into a paroxysm of admiration: the cowboys. At a time when urbanization of the West was beginning to darken the horizon of the future, cowboys were still free and unfettered. They still fought against the perils of nature rather than man-made perils; and so, apart from American pioneer folklore (with characters like Johnny Appleseed and Paul Bunyan) the cowboy legends were born. 'Tall tales'; shameless self-glorification and absurd exaggeration; myths around individuals and their heroic deeds.

The stories around Pecos Bill, in particular, belong to the 'tall tale' category. They tell of a cowboy who grew up with wolves and understands the language of nature. He can do practically anything: one day he accepts a bet that he can ride a cyclone. He gallops off to Kansas, lassoes himself a tornado, jumps on its back and rides it all the way through Oklahoma down to the Panhandle. When the tornado realizes that Bill cannot be shaken off, it simply dissolves itself into rain and patters down to earth; as Pecos Bill now has nothing left to ride, this must be the only recorded case of his being unseated from his mount. It would have been reasonable to presume that such tales of Pecos Bill would be portrayed in comics; but, apart from a Walt Disney version, no. The Westerner was glorified because through him it was possible to gloss over the systematic murder of the Red Indian, or even to legitimize it. Owen Wister writes in *The Virginian* (1902): 'He (the cowboy) will be here among us always, invisible, waiting his chance to live and play as he would like. His wild kind has been among us always, since the beginning: a young man with his temptations, a hero without wings.' To Wister the cowboy is the last romantic figure on American soil.

The cowboy hero is chivalrous and morally as clean as driven snow. Women to him are creatures to protect. He comes from nowhere and rides off into nowhere. He does not talk much, but when he does it is to the point. He has his own particular brand of humour, expressed in such sentences as: 'When you call me that, SMILE.' The Westerner is surrounded by an aura of purity far removed from the complexities of love, of family ties, work or vacation time. The cowboy is the personification of an ideal capable of fulfilling all dreams—and not only those of adolescents. His ruling principle is honour, coupled with the law that 'might is right'.

This glorified image of a brief historical period was painted by cheap novelettes, films, books and finally by radio, comics and television.[12]

But the Western draws its attraction not only from its heroes, it nourishes itself on its landscapes, the vastness of its prairies and on the freedom of movement it conveys to people trapped in cities, people who can only dream of wide open spaces. For all these reasons the Wild West has remained for decades one of the most successful money spinning themes of Hollywood films. Other media have also profited, among them comics.

There have not been as many Wild West comic newspaper strips as comic books, but the strips that made it all told their stories with considerable gusto. Fred Harman's *Bronc Peeler* and *Red Ryder* belong to early Westerners who rode through comic strips. Successes in films and radio series helped some heroes to additional fame in comics. Tom Mix, Hopalong Cassidy, Roy Rogers, Gene Autry and Cisco Kid conquered all media, and though the golden voice of Gene Autry remained inaudible to comics readers, singing cowboys rode to world fame in many of the comic books published by Dell.

One of the most long-lived cowboy sagas is that of *The Lone Ranger* (invented for radio by George W. Trendle), who from 1933 to 1954 rode the ether waves to the tune of the William Tell overture three times a week and delighted radio listeners with his cry, 'Hi-ho, Silver, away!' In 1938 *The Lone Ranger* made his debut in comic strips and soon afterwards also in Big Little Books and other comic books.

The legend of the Lone Ranger has long since become a generally accepted American myth. This is proved by the assertion that anyone who is not instantly reminded of the Lone Ranger every time he hears the William Tell overture can be classed as a snob. But why a 'lone' ranger? Well, the story goes that six rangers were trapped in Bryant Gap by Butch Cavendish's gang. Among the six rangers were two brothers. One survived the massacre through the help of Tonto, a Red Indian. When Tonto was a little boy, this man had saved his life and since then Tonto called his saviour 'Kemo Sabay'—'faithful friend'. Whilst the white man still lies unconscious, Tonto buries the five dead rangers and digs a sixth grave to give the bandits the impression that all have been killed. The man Tonto had saved became the Lone Ranger. He resolved to bury his name and to hide his face from the world so that, with his identity unknown, he might track down the murderers of his brother. Since then he roams the Wild West in a constant battle against all law-breakers. Bullets made of silver from a hidden mine, which the Lone Ranger and his brother once discovered, are his trade-mark. The silver bullets have a deeper meaning: vampires and werewolves can be killed with silver—and so the silver bullets symbolically kill all evil.

A white horse called Silver carries the Lone Ranger in all his battles against bandits. The horse could be white simply to make it even clearer that his rider is a good guy, a kind of knight in shining armour. But symbolism goes deeper here: herds of beautiful horses roamed on the prairies and the most beautiful horse, the most coveted one was the white stallion, a splendid animal said to be stronger, faster and of greater endurance than any other. According to Washington Irving's *A Tour on the Prairies,* stories of this type, which were told around the campfires, were first mentioned in 1832. In the light of these tales we see that the Lone Ranger is not just the good guy: riding a mythical animal, having subdued the strongest, noblest and most beautiful of all horses, he rules over the prairies as a symbol of omnipotent good and becomes himself a myth. He sees to it that law and justice always win but he never kills for 'When the Lone Ranger shot, he shot to disarm or to wound, but he never shot to kill.'[13]

The Lone Ranger drawn by Charles Flanders and written by Paul S. Newman. Since he was first heard over the radio in 1933, the Lone Ranger has fought untiringly for law and order in the Wild West. When he gallops across the prairie everybody begins to hum the opening bars of the 'William Tell' overture.

Billy the Kid by John Severin. Up to 1971 the real-life Billy the Kid could not be presented as a comic strip hero. A cousin was invented who was a goody and used his gun against the baddies. Comics Code bullets always hit their target without shedding blood. From *Billy the Kid* No. 22.
© 1960 Charlton Comics Group

The adventures of *Cisco Kid*, drawn by the Argentinian artist José Luis Salinas, are remarkably effective. *Cisco Kid*, like the *Lone Ranger*, was not invented by comics; he was the brainchild of author O. Henry; but later he too was taken up by all the mass media.

Rick O'Shay (first appearance 1958) is the latest addition to true Western comic strips in American newspapers. Other Western series, like *Tumbleweeds* and *Redeye*, are humorous strips which make fun of the Wild West genre. In some ways *Rick O'Shay* is an in-between. On Sundays the series offers a single, complete gag story, on weekdays it runs a continuous story in instalments. The strip is drawn by Stan Lynde in an intentionally simplified, realistic style. Though there is humour, it seems more logical to class this strip as a true Western rather than a humorous strip; particularly if one considers the resemblance of this series to the morality plays of the Middle Ages.

The names of the actors, Rick O'Shay, Hipshot Percussion, Ouyat Burp, Sudden De Mise, are not just a play on words; they denote the character of each person (just as names in mystery plays do) and give the reader some idea of what to expect. Film and television have behaviour patterns for their Westerns, which telescope social events and reduce them to a manageable scale. The purest method of fitting adventure to the pattern of a morality play can be found in this particular strip, which underlines the virtues and the paradisiac aspects of the Old West.

For a long time Wild West adventures could be enjoyed in comic books much more often than in newspaper strips. Famous names of film and television crowded the pages of many comic books: *Hopalong Cassidy, Tom Mix, Rocky Lane, Lash La Rue, Gene Autry, Roy Rogers*, and later *Cheyenne, Maverick, Wanted: Dead or Alive, Gunsmoke, Shotgun Slade, The Rifleman, Wagon Train, Rawhide, The Lone Ranger, The Cisco Kid, Bonanza, Laramie, Wild Wild West* and many more. Like other feature films, Wild West films had their comics versions: *Rio Bravo, Last Train from Gun Hill, McLintock* and *How the West was Won*, to name but a few; and apart from all those, hundreds of newly invented Wild West heroes, or heroes modelled on some character of history or folklore sprang to life in the pages of comic books. Some to make the West safe, some, like Jesse James, to make it unsafe. Old heroes like *Buffalo Bill, Kit Carson, Wild Bill Hickock* and *Davy Crockett* rubbed shoulders with such newcomers as *The Trigger Twins, Johnny Thunder, Nighthawk, The Masked Raider, Maverick Marshal, Tim Holt, Tony Barrett, The Black Rider, The Ghost Rider*, and the long row of famous 'kids': *Cheyenne Kid, Durango Kid, Kid Colt Outlaw, Kid Montana, Kid Sloane, Outlaw Kid*, two different *Rawhide Kids, Two-Gun Kids, Ringo Kid, Wyoming Kid* and finally *Billy the Kid*. Under the Comics Code it would have been impossible to classify Billy the Kid as a hero and therefore the comics Billy is only a cousin of the real Billy. His career started after Pat Garrett had already shot the true, historically verified Billy the Kid. Billy the Kid number two is as noble as most other heroes of the Wild West. The accumulation of 'kids' is perhaps a sign that this type of Western comic caters for youthful tastes in particular and tries to give its young readers characters with whom they can readily identify.

One of the two Rawhide Kids deserves a special mention, because he is always fleeing from something or someone, though he is a helpful youngster and yearns for peace and quiet; but perhaps you automatically become an anti-hero if you insist on dressing in black in a Western strip, despite the fact that you are a good guy. Under the guidance of some artists, Jack Davis for instance, this particular *Rawhide Kid* came very near to being a parody of a Western strip. All stories however comply with the strict rules of a morality play: the culmination point, the confrontation between good and evil, comes with the showdown.

What seemed impossible in films was easily achieved in comic books: in some series Red Indians, like *Strong Bow, Straight Arrow, Lone Eagle* and *Indian Chief* are the heroes. Lone

Gun Law by Harry Bishop. Wild shooting in the streets of Dodge City. Marshal Matt Dillon must take punishment too at times—just as he does in the radio and TV series. The series *Gunsmoke* exists as a comic strip only in Britain.
© 1968 CBS/Daily Express

Ranger's Red Indian friend Tonto had a comic book series all of his own; but then Silver, the Lone Ranger's horse, was also allowed his solo adventures.

Similar in aim to Western comics are series which tell the adventures of the Royal Canadian Mounted Police: *King of the Royal Mounted* (modelled on Zane Grey) and *Sergeant Preston of the Yukon* among others; both, of course, always get their man. Attempts at a modern Western have also been made, notably in *Vigilante* and some of the *Pow-Wow Smith* stories.

In recent years the Italian Western has been in sharp competition with the Hollywood Western, and in the wake of the new Western film boom the European comics industry has followed suit. Some series, like *Gun Law* (taken from the American television series *Gunsmoke*), have been popular in Britain for more than a decade and there have been European comic books with Western themes; but some of the best series, like *Fort Navajo* (France), *Jerry Spring, Ray Ringo* and *Comanche* (Belgium) appeared only in the last few years. They are serials, first published in comics magazines and later also in book form. As continued sequences they have more epic breadth than the conclusive stories of American comic books; but they cling almost fanatically to realism and therefore tend to be burdened with too much detail.

Masks are in high demand among Western heroes. The Lone Ranger was only the first—he set the trend. Outlaw Kid, Durango Kid, Tim Holt (Redmask of the Rio Grande), Calico Kid, the

Western comics glorify not only historically verified heroes. Many Lone Ranger copies ride across the prairie; but most numerous are the sharp-shooting Kids.
© 1954 Charlton Comics Group (left)
© 1958 Charlton Comics Group (middle)
© 1960 Marvel Comics Group (right)

Ghost Rider, the Black Rider, the Masked Raider, Nighthawk and one of the Two Gun Kids all wear masks or some sort of disguise. Some have double identities. Durango Kid, explaining why he wears a mask, says that the guardians of the law are usually not masked and therefore at a disadvantage; but no bandit has an advantage over him because he too is masked. Nobody knows him and therefore he can do things which no ordinary guardian of the law could dare to do.[14]

This explanation puts the Western hero who leads a double life on a par with the super-hero. Uncanny accuracy and lightning speed are the indispensable prerequisites of these quick-firing sharp shooters. And just like super heroes they must forget about sweet love and wedding bells as long as danger threatens; but if we may believe some of our modern authors, the Western hero gets all the satisfaction he needs from his ersatz penis—his gun.[15] Nobody, however, knows for certain. From one issue to the next is a whole month or more. What does our hero do in the meantime? It is a long time to wait, and even the most strong-willed ascetic may weaken. Who knows?

Rawhide Kid. German version. One of the best and most long-lived Kids. During the 1960s particularly, this series came near to a delightful parody of the Western style under the Stan Lee, Jack Kirby, Dick Ayers team.
© 1962, 1968 Marvel Comics Group/Bildschriftenverlag GmbH

4 Super-heroes

Clark decided he must turn his titanic strength into channels that would benefit mankind. And so was created . . . SUPERMAN, champion of the oppressed, the physical marvel who had sworn to devote his existence to helping those in need!

Superman Comics

But we must have [enemies]—our patriotic fervour is so intense that we must use it against someone.

Gustave Doré, *L'Histoire de La Sainte Russie*

Modern myths

Superman—the man of steel, helper of all those in distress, defender of the weak and oppressed, strongest of all men, invincible, handsome as a god, noble and gentle—in short, a man far superior to any other human being. He is the ultimate hero, the epitome of his young readers' dreams.

There are so many heroes with superhuman qualities. Jules Feiffer once said that if they joined together with the even more numerous super-villains they would darken the skies like locusts. And all of them experience adventures without a break—mostly adventures of dimensions, Countless times the earth, no, whole galaxies are rescued from destruction or enslavement and, on a smaller scale, America is made safe for democracy. Cosmic super-policemen, they patrol the universe, but they do not seek adventure in the same way as the old legendary heroes of mythology and legend did. They do not have to search for evil to combat: evil positively leaps at them and never lets them rest. Without pause they have to prove their super-faculties and powers, for their *raison d'être* is constant battle. They go to battle as the ordinary man goes daily to his office.

The concept of the super-hero was new to comics. It arrived in 1938 in the shape of Superman. Tarzan, The Phantom, Flash Gordon and Buck Rogers, already established in comics at that time, were of course also superior beings; just like The Shadow, Nick Carter, Doc Savage or Sherlock Holmes, who had hunted down villains for decades in millions of cheap pulps.

But Superman and Co. presented a new species of hero to the comic book world—godlike, invincible creatures. Even the way they dressed was quite different. They wore colourful tights, with or without mask or cape, and this intriguing garb was a kind of trade-mark, like Hercules' lion skin.

Superman is as old as the ages. Achilles and Siegfried stood at his cradle—and they are all three invulnerable, except for Achilles' heel, the spot on Siegfried's back and Superman's susceptibility to kryptonite.

Super-heroes, these new 'characters' as they were at first referred to in the comics industry, all bore traces of old myths and legends. Joe Siegel described his 'Man of Steel' as 'the world's greatest adventure strip character', a 'character like Samson, Hercules and all the strong men I ever heard tell of rolled into one'.[1] (In the beginning Superman did not have the exaggerated powers he later assumed.)

But not only Superman, other characters of comics also had mythical ancestors: the first *Flash* is a reincarnation of Mercury (note his costume!); the modern Icarus, *Hawkman*, of the Egyptian prince Knufu (a later version of Hawkman hails from the planet Thanagar); *The Green Arrow*, based on an Edgar Wallace tale, is a descendant of Robin Hood; *Hawkeye* is a modern Philoctet. Bill Finger must have had Aladdin in mind when he created *The Green Lantern* (he wanted to give Green Lantern the name of Alan Ladd to indicate his secret identity!) and Bill Everett, creator of Namor (Roman read backwards) was inspired by some lines in Coleridge's *The Ancient Mariner*.

Most super-heroes draw their special faculties from very ancient sources, but their characters are modified and changed to such an extent that today, with their modern images, they may be regarded as original. They express in today's idiom the ancient longing of mankind for a mighty protector, a helper, guide, or guardian angel who offers miraculous deliverance to mortals.

Marvel Comics have chosen the Nordic gods as their speciality. Olympians, such as Hercules, drop in on occasional visits. The noble Sif now prefers black hair, Thor is blonde, clean-shaven and no longer as uncouth as he used to be. He is super-hero and god rolled into one; with the help of lesser gods, goddesses and heroes he protects 'Midgard' (the Earth) and the whole of the universe. Stan Lee and Jack Kirby, creators of this commercialized heroes' paradise, have dressed up Thor, God of Thunder, and the *Tales of Asgard* so expertly, in such thrilling modern versions, that American readers of Marvel Comics know more about Ragnarök, Yggdrasil or Bifröst than the direct descendants of the Old Teutons.

Is it surprising that the adventures of super-heroes are called modern myths and that Marvel's Stan Lee, the great bard of these modern epics, is hailed as the Aesop and Homer of pop culture?

Thor by Stan Lee. German version. A saga
woven around the Norse god Thor. Jack Kirby
drew the pictures for this cosmic epic. From *Hit
Comics* No. 34.
© 1966 Marvel Comics Group/Bildschriften-
verlag, GmbH

History of the super-heroes

The first super-heroes of modern comic epics were unleashed upon mankind at the end of the 1930s, after thousands of years of preparation through myth and legend. A foretaste of things to come was given in 1936, when Lee Falk's *The Phantom*, a mixture of mythological figure and super-hero, appeared on 17 February.

Although he was not endowed with supernatural powers the Phantom seemed immortal, for behind the mask he wore his personality remained forever hidden. True to the first Phantom's oath, his successors kept up the tradition throughout four centuries and created the impression of immortality. The absence of reality is expressed not only in the behaviour and the legendary deeds of the main character, but also in the localities chosen: the Phantom's realm is a large island called Bengali, off the East African coast. He rules in the deep forests, where his skull throne stands in the depths of the skull cave. This cave of memories is a forerunner of the super-heroes' haunts and hiding places where they keep their trophies and souvenirs, like Superman's fortress of solitude, or Batman's bat-cave.

The double identity aspect of super-heroes is also outlined in *The Phantom*, though in reverse and in a particularly complicated way: The Phantom divests itself of its individual personality in order to become a hero and the hero in turn takes on the additional aspect of Mr Walker (the Ghost Who Walks). Superman, in contrast, is first and foremost hero, and he dons his second identity (Clark Kent, the reporter) to hide his true 'super' nature from the ordinary mortals amongst whom he works.

The dream of a Superman is about to be realised: Lee Falk invented *The Phantom*, the forerunner of the super-heroes, in 1936. From *The Phantom* No. 33.
© 1969 King Features Syndicate Inc./Charlton Comics Group

Superman (German version). The tragedy of the planet Krypton had great significance for the planet Earth, for little Kal-El was fired off into space by his parents. He landed on Earth and became Superman, the man of steel, most powerful of all the super-heroes. Here we see his parents firing the rocket which they have aimed at the planet Earth. From *Superman* No. 1.
© 1966 National Periodical Publications Inc./Ehapa Verlag Stuttgart

Jerry Siegel and Joe Shuster, spiritual fathers of *Superman*, hawked their brainchild around for five years before they persuaded Action Comics to start publishing *Superman* in June 1938. The verdict of publishers had always been that it was too fantastic or not commercial, but time was ripe for the superman idea and Action Comics reaped a tremendous commercial success. Their editions doubled and in 1939 *Superman* conquered the newspaper strip columns as well. During the Second World War Superman belonged to the American soldier's equipment.

He gave them hope and became their symbol of courage and determination, almost a substitute for conventional religion—to the horror of the army chaplains. The Second World War really established the super-heroes, for the Axis Powers provided an enemy against whom they could launch themselves with no holds barred. The fight started in earnest in 1941 and chauvinistic appeal was buttressed by encouragement to buy war bonds.

The enemies were now 'Nazi beasts' and 'Banzai'-yelling 'Nips'. Super-heroes found real adversaries against whom they

Red kryptonite had strange effects on Superman; here he describes how it once made him so fat that he couldn't get through the window, how another time he became as small as Tom Thumb and was able to block up the barrel of a gangster's revolver, while another time he became as big as Gulliver and pushed ocean liners out of his way. From *Superman and Batman* No. 15. German version.
© 1967 National Periodical Publications Inc./Ehapa Verlag Stuttgart

could pit their strength, for the concept of the super-*villain* had not yet been fully developed. So far, super-heroes had mainly gone into action to combat natural catastrophes; now they found U-boats, battleships and all manner of enemy war potential to fight: 'twisting submarines into pretzels'. Superman really overshadows all other super-heroes for he possesses all the qualities imaginable for a super-hero: he is invulnerable, super-strong, superfast (he is faster than the speed of light and can therefore travel through time); he has X-ray eyes that can penetrate anything and microscopic view to detect the smallest atomic particle. His only weakness is connected with 'kryptonite', a radioactive, rock-like substance that was created through the explosion of Superman's home-planet Krypton. Kryptonite exists in a variety of colours: green kryptonite can weaken, even kill (!) Superman; it has no effect on ordinary human beings. Red kryptonite, invented in the fifties to create a new story potential, has qualities that affect Superman and other creatures of the planet Krypton in the most astounding way: it changes Superman's faculties and alters him physically or mentally; it

can give him the ability to read minds, can change his head into that of a lion, can make him invisible or even transfer his faculties to others.

The magic potential of the red rock as well as other magic, can vanquish the noble hero—at least temporarily, but usually he perceives in good time what is afoot. He realizes, for instance, when Mr Mxyzptlk[2] has played a magic trick on him, and induced by a ruse to pronounce his name backwards, the Superman-scorner disappears into the fifth dimension for another ninety instalments.

In *Captain Marvel*, one of the most successful super-heroes in competition with *Superman*, magic also played an important role. The Captain transformed himself with the help of the magic formula Shazam,[3] compounded out of the first letters of the names of ancient gods and demigods, to an accompaniment of thunder and lightning provided by a youthful radio-reporter called Billy Batson, into the superstrong hero Captain Marvel. Superman could only ask contemptuously: 'Shazam? What is Shazam?' and out of this contretemps arose one of the few disputes about plagiarism in the history of comics (launched by *Superman*'s publishers, DC National Comics).

Superman's claim to the sole rights in a whole array of super-powers forced Captain Marvel to abandon the super-world. The argument that he was a Superman imitation won and permission to continue drawing his adventures was withdrawn. It was of no avail that Captain Marvel differed from Superman in important details and that he—though inspired by Superman—was more of a take-off of the real thing, drawn in an original and refreshingly new style; nor that a band of anthropomorphic animals were regular members of his crew. Jules Feiffer maintained that he did not even look like Superman, but resembled Fred MacMurray.

Superman's publishers also brought out *Detective Comics* (March 1937), a series which has in the meantime produced over 400 issues. Into this series *Batman* was born in issue No. 27 in May 1939. Batman stands at the other end of the super-hero spectrum. In contrast to the seemingly almighty Superman, he is an ordinary human being, like the Phantom, who trains (under the guidance of his creators Bob Kane and Bill Finger) until he is so well equipped in every way that he can tackle even the most dangerous criminals. Like many of his successors he is of independent means and can attend posh social functions— which always seem to attract crime—in the guise of playboy Bruce Wayne.

Around 1960 *Batman* was slowly dying, but a television series infused new life and vigour into him. True Batman fans were horrified at this pop version of Batman. At the end of the series, however, the enraged fans were mollified by the fact that on his thirtieth birthday Batman returned to his detective role with an added touch of the mysterious. His appearance on television had, needless to say, a most invigorating effect on the sales of *Batman* comic books. Finally, in December 1969, Batman closed his bat-cave temporarily and sent his young assistant Dick Grayson—who had aged only about four years since his first appearance in 1940—to college.

opposite
The origin of Batman. This extract describes how Bruce Wayne became 'the ordinary, run-of-the-mill millionaire who fights against crime under another identity'. Batman chose the bat as his symbol and disguise, and in the last panel it is explained to German readers that this is why he was given the name Batman. From *Superman und Batman* No. 18.
© 1968 National Periodical Publications Inc./Ehapa Verlag Stuttgart

After their successful debut Superman and Batman had their own magazines, bearing their respective names as title; but they still remained faithful to the comic books that had sealed their fame. Superman was so successful that even the adventures of his boyhood were related in special series for *Adventure Comics* and *Superboy*. Some casual critics thought they were the adventures of his kid brother!

In 1950 comic books about Superman's girl friend Lois Lane[4] and his friend Jimmy Olsen started to appear. The latter had been invented specially for a radio series. To top it all Superman and Batman appeared together and shared adventures in *World's Finest Comics*, and here the two heroes took the opportunity of revealing to each other their otherwise strictly secret identities. (This instance apart, nobody, except perhaps President Kennedy, has ever been told!) The two super-heroes also appeared together in *Justice League of America*, a collection of National Comics' most popular heroes.

The success of the super-heroes encouraged many imitations; but they had to have their special gimmicks, choose their own names, apparel, town of origin, etc. Generally speaking National Comics heroes live in imaginary towns, which all belong to the same type of city: Superman lives in Metropolis (a name inspired by Fritz Lang's famous film); Batman in Gotham City; Flash, the super-sprinter, in Central City. Marvel Comics are more realistic in their approach: most of their heroes live and work in New York City.

Many heroes who followed in Superman's wake experienced a short blossoming between 1940 and 1949 before the market became saturated and the readers lost interest. The patriotic flames that had inspired the heroes and had spurred them on to action during wartime had died down. But during the years between 1958 and 1962—and this was still before the comics renaissance—some super-heroes were dug up again and reinstated in a modernized version, or were created anew. The new creations appeared together with some of the old heroes, and the super-heroes' long absence was explained by National Comics, for instance, by the existence of parallel worlds situated in the same space in the universe, but in different dimensions. So as to distinguish them these parallel worlds are called Earth One, Earth Two, etc., up to any number, and their invention opened up many possibilities for new themes and variations of themes.

It is almost impossible to prove that a comics firm has copied super-hero-ideas from another; anyhow, nowadays competition is no longer quite so keen on the hero market. It is practically divided into two groups only: Marvel and DC, and if heroes like sprinters Flash (DC National), Lightning (Tower) and Quicksilver (Marvel) all seem to have the same quality of speed, each one attained it in a different way. Flash received it through a chemical reaction induced by lightning; Lightning through a machine invented by two scientists, and Quicksilver had been born with it through some happy mutation of genes.

Other newly awakened heroes proved to be particularly tough and indestructible as, for instance, *Captain America* who lay frozen in the Arctic ice for twenty years—as this series had in fact been 'on ice' the idea had a nice, ironic touch. But Captain America had been seen to throw his shield about him in heroic fervour during the days of the Cold War around 1955! A clever reader found an explanation: the interim Captain had not been the real Captain, but only his brother. As a brother had been mentioned in earlier *Captain America* stories, it seemed a reasonable suggestion.

Publishers leave it to their readers to explain apparent incongruities arising out of the difference between real time and comics time. In comics, as in Shakespeare's dramas, a dual time system is used; but whilst in drama years are telescoped into a manageable period of action, in comics the life span of a hero is extended like elastic in order to press as many episodes into it as possible.

Flash, Green Lantern and some of the others were given a new lease of life even before the second comics boom started in the sixties; however, no new ground was broken until 1962, when Marvel Comics' Stan Lee invented *The Fantastic Four* and *Spider-Man* and a fresh wind began to blow through the wilting super-hero epics. The new, modern, more reality-orientated super-heroes were joined in the years that followed by *Thor, Daredevil, Iron Man, Hulk, Silver Surfer*, the resurrected *Captain America, Submariner* and others. The new 'Marvel Age of Comics' had broken upon mankind—at least for the next decade. For Shakespeare lover Stan Lee (in private life Stanley Lieber) the super-hero stories have the same function that fairy-tales, myths, legends and romances had for earlier generations.

When comic strips were brought up to date and re-issued, old heroes were often given doubles. This picture is taken from *Flash* and the German text reads: 'The old and the new Flash run off together, to catch the three super-criminals . . .' From *Blitzmann* No. 104.
© 1970, 1961 National Periodical Publications Inc./Bildschriften-verlag, GmbH

Zusammen laufen jetzt der alte und der neue Blitzmann los, um die drei Superverbrecher zu fangen.....

The Silver Surfer drawn by John Buscema and Joe Sinnott. A super-hero, with Messianic traits, in Asgard. From *Silver Surfer* No. 4. © 1968 Marvel Comics Group

Marvel Comics, whose heroes have very human failings, produce stories of a humorous, slightly ironic vein, and the same recipe helped many an ailing hero of the great competitive firm National Periodical Publications to new life and vigour.

The enthusiasm for new experiments, which triggered off the boom of the sixties, led also to more socially orientated themes. Some of the heroes such as Green Lantern and Green Arrow even cast off their uniforms—at least for a while—and in their search for truth found themselves face to face at last with reality and the social problems that beset the land.

Marvel—a new era

1962 the new 'Marvel Age of Comics'—as Marvel themselves modestly called it—started triumphantly. Nostalgic memories of days when Stan Lee and Jack Kirby produced all that was best in comics almost single-handed!

Marvel continued the work of the Timely Comics Group which had started this 'squinky division of the comics business'— the super-heroes—in November 1939. When, at the end of the forties, the super-heroes lost their hold on the public, romances and modified horror took their place. At this point Timely changed their name to Atlas Comics. In 1962 they decided to start again where thirteen years earlier—as Timely—they had stopped. Stan Lee was at the head of the undertaking and they now changed their name to Marvel, because of the tremendous success of *Marvel Comics* during the Golden Age.

Marvel called itself the 'House of Ideas' right from the start, and many of the themes taken up really were new. Not only were the heroes themselves fresh products of their creators' imagination, the ways in which they were presented had an entirely new and original approach. Serials, in many instalments, made it possible to give the characters a much greater complexity than they had ever had before.

The first of the new super-heroes were *The Fantastic Four*. On the title page of their booklets the words 'The World's Greatest Comics' were printed in all modesty, starting with the very first issue. Through cosmic radiation the scientist Reed Richards changes into a rubber-like man (reminiscent of Plastic Man and Elongated Man) called Mr Fantastic; the same cosmic incident turns Benjamin Grimm into an orange-coloured colossus, 'The Thing', with only four fingers on each hand (like Mickey Mouse); Sue Storm becomes the Invisible Girl and her brother Johnny the Human Torch. Thus endowed by fate with superhuman qualities, these chosen ones decide to stay together as a group and they call themselves The Fantastic Four.

In his own way each Marvel hero is also an anti-hero. *The Hulk*, for instance, described by a reader as the 'true existential man', is the comic's Dr Jekyll (Dr Bruce Banner) and Mr Hyde (Hulk). The Hulk's green-coloured body and square-cut face call Frankenstein to mind. He is a truly tragic character.

Dr Strange, master of the mystic arts, explorer of every dimension of every fantastic realm, whose psychedelic adventures were superbly drawn by Steve Ditko and Gene Colan, attained his powers only after he had experienced and overcome a depression so deep brought him to the very edge of crime.

The Hulk, a super-hero resembling Dr Jekyll and Mr Hyde. From *The Hulk* No. 6. © 1962 Marvel Comics Group

Daredevil is a blind lawyer who finds new dimensions in his blindness; his 'radar sense', brought about through radioactivity, allows him to 'see' with his ears.

One of the heroes, Marvel's *Spider-Man*, has to tend his torn spider's costume again and again and experiences in business and in private life one mishap after another. He goes through traumatic crises of identity and suffers from almost paranoiac attacks of self-doubt; but he never gives up, despite all his near misses, disappointments and outrageous accidents. He is the most tenacious and absurdly heroic character of them all.

Spider-Man, in his secret identity of Peter Parker, is handicapped by constant fear for his Aunt May, for whom the slightest excitement could mean death. He is always short of money and earns a precarious living by photographing himself in battle with an automatic camera, and selling the pictures to the *Daily Bugle* for a pittance. J. Jonah Jameson, editor of the paper, has out of envy of the hero denounced him to the press and television as a public menace, so that the police as well as the public are in doubt as to whether Spider-Man is a friend or a foe of society.

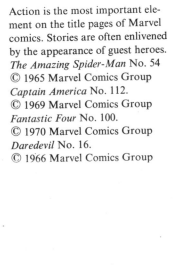

Action is the most important element on the title pages of Marvel comics. Stories are often enlivened by the appearance of guest heroes.
The Amazing Spider-Man No. 54
© 1965 Marvel Comics Group
Captain America No. 112.
© 1969 Marvel Comics Group
Fantastic Four No. 100.
© 1970 Marvel Comics Group
Daredevil No. 16.
© 1966 Marvel Comics Group

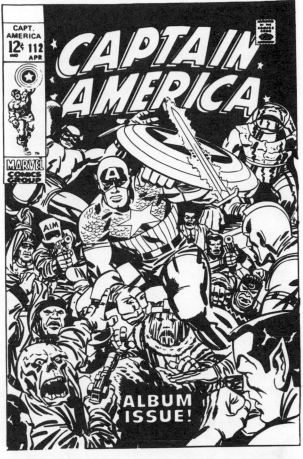

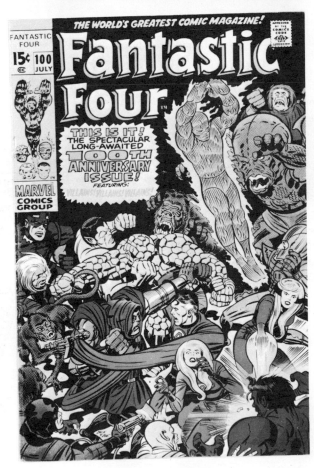

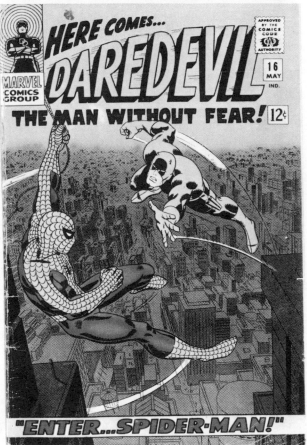

Spider-Man, absurd hero of the comics. Here he tries to repair his torn spider's costume. From *Hit Comics* No. 88. (German version.) © 1969, 1968 Marvel Comics Group/Bildschriftenverlag GmbH

Peter Parker could become a brilliant scientist if he were not so preoccupied with his super-hero existence. He is an outsider at college, just as he had been at high school, and as he keeps on missing his lectures his marks are not as good as they should be. His Spider-Man *alter ego* constantly comes between him and the normal joys of a healthy young American; his love life too is just one long misery.

His intense suffering and frustration make of Spider-Man the most human of all the super-heroes, and because the reader himself suffers with his hero, Spider-Man is above all other Marvel heroes the most popular on the university campus. Readers' letters from his fans, the 'spidophiles', beg that their 'Spidey' may at last be given just a little bit of good luck; but whatever happens one thing is certain: any good luck coming the way of the 'friendly neighbourhood wallcrawler' will be of short duration only!

The most controversial Marvel hero is *Captain America*, super patriot and spirit incarnate of the USA. Dressed in the Stars and Stripes he incorporates American ideology and the establishment-perpetuating principle expressed by all the super-heroes. Captain America's first action on the title page of his first issue (March 1941) was to crash his fist into Hitler's face. He went on fighting in this vein, his little battle companion Bucky at his side, against Nazis and Japs until 1949. It strikes one as odd that this fervent defender of American democracy, of all people, should personify an idea preached by Nazi ideology: the concept of breeding supermen. Captain America starts as plain Steve Rogers, a weakling who is not accepted by the army despite all his patriotic enthusiasm. Steve, however, is taken in hand by Professor Reinstein (!) who turns him, through a scientific experiment, into a superman. He is the first of a planned series of super-agents. But Professor Reinstein is killed by Nazi agents and takes the secret superman formula with him to the grave, and so Captain America (alias Steve Rogers) remains the only Super-American.

It all started with the bite of a radioactive spider—and hey presto, a new super-hero was born. From *Hit Comics* No. 96. © 1969, 1968 Marvel Comics Group/Bildschriftenverlag GmbH (German version)

A hero's frustration. For Spider-Man, unlike Superman, victory is not always easy and effortless. On this extract we can see the proof corrections: a speech balloon has been changed to a thought balloon. From *The Amazing Spider-Man* No. 82.

The good old days, when the world still was as Captain America and his sidekick Bucky knew and understood it: clear cut fights—the goodies (Americans) and the baddies (Nazis or Commies). From *Captain America* No. 104, artists Jacky Kirby and Syd Shores.
© 1968 Marvel Comics Group

Times have changed for Captain America. Now Cap is torn by self-doubts: the Hamlet of comics. This picture series imitates the technique of the moving camera. From *Captain America* No. 122. Artists: Gene Colan and Joe Sinnott.

In the McCarthy era 'Cap', as he was affectionately called, awoke to brief life again as a 'Commie-Smasher'; but he only came back permanently in 1964, as a 'Living Legend of World War Two'. Towards the end of the sixties, when America's image began to alter, Captain America became something of an anachronism. His creators are aware of this. Torn by self-doubt, Captain America even searched for a new image as a sort of Easy Rider (1970)—whilst controversy still rages on around him.

The one hero through whom Stan Lee openly moralizes—if we forget about the many short Marvel Westerns through which a strong moral wind blows—is the *Silver Surfer*, a quasi-messianic figure. 'We try to portray this without satire,' says Stan Lee. The Silver Surfer's former name was Norrin Radd and he used to live on the planet Zenn-La (!). He becomes the messenger of Galactus, a super-super creature who feeds on the energy of whole worlds; but one day, when Galactus' appetite turns earthwards, Norrin refuses to obey his master. In punishment, he loses some of his powers and is banished to earth. Norrin has to accept the cruel exile from his home planet, and gliding through the air on his surfboard, he tries to better mankind. Sometimes he despairs of his self-imposed task and feels like destroying the whole, graceless globe. What puzzles him most of all about human beings is the fact that they are the only inhabitants in the universe who kill in the name of justice.

Marvel also produced the first black super-hero. *The Black Panther* appeared for the first time in July 1966 on the pages of the *Fantastic Four* comic book. The name, however, was chosen in ignorance of later developments.

The ingredient which above all others contributed to the success of Marvel Comics was a new special type of communication with the readership. Readers' letters pages were nothing new and 'Brand X', or 'Ecch' (Marvel's name for their competitors) ran them as well; but the long, witty replies to readers' comments, written in a personal and friendly tone, extended the 'letter corner' to two pages and it became the most popular feature of the comic book. Marvel invented the 'No-prize', which is not given for the best readers' letter, and the non-existent Irving Forbush. The reader was made one of the Marvel family, a 'keeper of the flame'. Marvel started a comics club, just as the defunct E.C. Comics had done, and called it 'MMMS'.[5] But unfortunately after having fallen into other, purely commercial hands, and lost its connection with the publishers, the club had to be disbanded in 1971. Since 1962 the author's and the artist's credits appear in Marvel publications on the first page of each story. This means that the reader can always see straightaway who wrote and drew the comics; other comics publishers have never done this. In 1965 the 'Bullpen News' page was introduced, which revealed editorial secrets and made of readers true insiders. This personal approach was later successfully copied by other publishers.

The high standard of Marvel publications made them interesting also to older readers, and the average age of the Marvel Comics readership is far higher than that of any other comics publishing concern. In the mid-sixties Marvel was favourite reading matter on the campus for both students and professors.

The super-hero boom

Anything that is successful is imitated or produced in series. This principle is valid in America for all popular arts. No wonder, then, that Superman and Batman started the first super-hero boom in the forties. But it took twenty years before something similar happened again.

The contents of *Superman* and *Batman* stories were direct continuations of the type of adventure-novel themes around Doc Savage, Black Bat and other characters published by the pulps. The firm Timely (now Marvel) also picked up threads of pulp stories in their comics when the penny dreadfuls themselves were suffering heavy readership losses. Pictured in comics, those stories became even more exciting.

In this highly praised incident Marvel Comics turn to more profound ideas. From *Fantastic Four* No. 72. Artists: Jack Kirby and Joe Sinnott. © 1968 Marvel Comics Group

Marvel rose to great heights in the sixties. Adventures assumed galactic proportions and the characters became more and more titanic. Here Galactus utters the often quoted words: 'Emotion is for lesser beings.' From *The Fantastic Four* No. 50. Artists: Jack Kirby and Joe Sinnott.

Silver Surfer loses his powers (cont. from p. 115). From *The Fantastic Four* No. 50. Artists: Jack Kirby and Joe Sinnott. © 1966 Marvel Comics Group

The greatest prize a super-hero can win: the gratitude of the nation, expressed by the President of the USA. From *Strange Suspense Stories* No. 75. Artist: Steve Ditko.
© 1961 Charlton Comics Group

During the first, wild founder years, plagiarism was considered at the worst as ungentlemanly; 'swiping', that is copying other artists, or pinching ideas and producing them slightly modified, was common practice and accepted as a legitimate means of improving output. A firm inventing an original character, a first-born among super-heroes, had to expect a series of imitations tions to spring up in all the other comics. Great artist like Alex Raymond, Hal Foster or Burne Hogarth would find imitations of their work an everyday occurrence. Timely's *Human Torch* soon had his descendants—such as Firehair, Firefly, Fiery Mask, Firebrand and Pyroman, to name but a few. 'Swiping' was simply part of the business. Bill Everett, creator of Timely's *Submariner*, designed two copies of his own character for other firms and drew for them Hydroman and The Fin.

The number of super-heroes grew and became legion. To name only a few of the most important: The Angel, Atom, Blue Bolt, Comet, Crimson Avenger, Destroyer, Dr Fate, Dr Mid-Nite (!), Guardian, Hangman, Hour-Man, Hurricane, Johnny Quick and his magic formula $[3 \times 2(9y)4A]$, Ka-Zar, Manhunter, Marvel Boy, Plastic Man, Robotman, Sandman, Skyman, Starman, Thunderer, Web and Wildcat.

Captain America began in March 1941 by practically deciding the outcome of the war singlehanded; and on the crest of a tremendous patriotic wave were born no less than forty (!) *Captain America* imitations, among them *The American Avenger, The Super American, The Flag, The Patriot*, and *Major Liberty*. Chauvinism was mirrored in such titles as *The American Comic Book, All Star Comics, Star-Spangled Comics, All-American Comics*, etc. Timely even produced a comic book called *U.S.A.* and a hero of the same name.

The pulps had been only a kind of foundation stone for the super-heroes; what really triggered them off were tensions within the social structure of the country—just as happened again later, in the sixties. Superman and Batman were born just before a great world conflict. They mirrored the spirit of the era and America's attitude towards political problems; they expressed the idea that America was the saviour and preserver of all true social values, guardian of democracy, deliverer of the oppressed from the bondage of Fascism and National Socialism.

After the Korean War interest in super-heroes began to dwindle. Cheap patriotic morale boosters and bloodthirsty horror comics were no longer in demand.

Patriotic enthusiasm could not always find the outlet against someone which Gustave Doré had pointed out but in comics such emotions could be kept alive, compensated, and guided into suitable channels. Publishers of comics kept a finger on the public's pulse and had an instinct for trends among their readership. Comics written and designed on Government contracts for the army were, of course, a different matter. They mirrored the government's political line.

Then came the renewed American comics boom of the early sixties. This boom too was initiated by super-heroes. But the new type had their own particular neuroses and foibles: a reaction to the public's growing boredom with stereotyped black and white presentation of good and evil by all the mass media. To this were added the explosions of social conflict and the Vietnam War. Once again the success of comics was promoted by war; but this was not the only reason for their resurrection. The first boom still glowed across two decades. The old comics awakened nostalgia for lost childhood and the new generation of grown-ups did not forbid their kids to read comics—as their parents had done.

Other comics publishers too profited from the super-hero boom
Marvel had initiated. Plagiarism was rife: here Charlton's resurrected
Blue Beetle fights in true Spider-Man style. From *Blue Beetle* No. 1.
Artist: Steve Ditko.
© 1967 Charlton Comics Group

Publishers of comics took note of the trend. The reappraisal
of the American consciousness was taken into account. That is
why the 'message' of comics is no longer as crystal clear as it
used to be. It is still oriented towards law and moral principles,
but it has at least become thoughtful and probing. The innocent
naïvety of the Golden Age of comics has been lost and the
concept of the super-hero is being questioned; comics are drawing ever closer to reality and the great problems of our day.

For these reasons the second boom is also drawing to its end,
but the near future has certainly some surprises in store for us.
Marvel will have to kindle fresh enthusiasm and will surely come
up with ideas of how to modernize the family of super-heroes.

Extended powers
Only one hero is mightier even than Superman: *The Spectre*, a
spirit who walks the earth and has practically unlimited powers.
He can alter his appearance at will, can make himself invisible,
can transform matter, etc., etc. Compared with Superman and
Spectre, all other super-heroes have very limited powers. They

possess only one, or at best a few specially developed faculties.
Their particular 'speciality' or sometimes their origin, is ex-
pressed in their name: *Spider*-Man, *Aqua*-Man, or the *Elongated*
Man, and often alliteral second names are lovingly added, like
The Winged Wonder for Hawkman, The Sultan of Speed, The
Viscount of Velocity or The Scarlet Speedster for Flash; Batman
is The Caped Crusader.

Any one of us can become a super-hero by mere accident! It
is so easy: usually no more is needed than a scientific experiment
that slightly misfires; the inhaling of vapours released, the
accidental touching of a substance, chemicals combined with
the striking of lightning (shades of Frankenstein?) and hey
presto! a new super-hero is born!

Batman, however, shows us that we can attain to super-hero-
ship through sheer industry, tenacious endeavour, and a large
enough private fortune—running into millions—to acquire all
the necessary super-hero equipment. There is no bodily function
except sexual prowess (strictly taboo) that could not be suitably
extended or adjusted to serve super-hero purposes.

Flash, for instance, can run at such speed that even the surface

Daredevil's 'radar sense' explained. From *Marvel Super-heroes* No. No. 25. Artist: Wallace Wood.
© 1969 Marvel Comics Group

Green Lantern, a type of super-Aladdin. Here Green Lantern swears to use the magic power of his ring only secretly and only against evil. He calls himself Green Lantern, after the lantern which is the source of energy supplies. From *Top Comics* (German version) No. 3. Artists: Gil Kane and Murphy Anderson.
© 1970, 1969 National Periodical Publications Inc./Bildschriftenverlag GmbH

of water seems to be solid; he can deflect bullets with air compressed by a wave of his hand, or he can agitate his atoms into such high vibrations that bullets pass straight through him without causing any damage. He can also 'vibrate' himself through locked doors and solid walls by the same method. Speed has, in his case, also a most detrimental effect: in his private life he seems to be the slowest, most unpunctual of human beings. No wonder, when he has to tear off on some tricky mission just as he is supposed to keep some ordinary humdrum appointment as plain Mr Barry Allen.

Green Lantern has, at first glance, no special faculties. He achieves his incredible feats with the help of a ring; but the ring functions at the will of its master. Hal Jordan, in his Green Lantern identity, finishes off any adversary with his unlimited fund of clever ideas and his unbreakable willpower; but he must also do the bidding of the guardians on planet Oa, for they supply the energy (which always lasts for 24 hours) from a lantern-shaped source of power. The ring, however, has one weakness: it is powerless against anything of yellow colour. A man who sees (nearly) all his endeavours crowned by success thanks to such a device is always in danger of gradually losing faith in his own personal abilities and so Green Lantern started to hit out with his own fist from time to time, instead of conjuring a giant plasma fist from out of the ring. To restore his self-confidence the guardians of Oa cut down the supply of energy, so that he could no longer rely on a last power reserve to get him out of mortal danger. Now that Green Lantern knows he has to apply his own strength and mind and can no longer rely on completely automatic salvation, he has become much more human and understanding and willing to tackle ordinary problems of everyday life instead of battling endlessly against a host of imaginary enemies.

To augment their various super-powers and use them collectively, super-heroes often band together in super-hero organizations or groups. Among such bands of super-heroes are DC's *Justice League of America* (a new group modelled on *Justice Society of America* of Golden Age days), the *Legion of Super-heroes* and the *Teen Titans*. Marvel drew several of its heroes together in *The Avengers*, so that they could unite in battle against super-foes who had formed themselves into super-villain organizations. For the reader the main attraction probably lies in the opportunity of seeing several super-darlings in action at the same time.

Super-sex

Due to the strictly enforced rules of the Code Authority (1954), it is only in caricatures like those in *MAD* that Superman gives rein to his exhibitionist tendencies whilst changing his clothes in a telephone box (in reality he prefers broom closets or dark alleys), or used his X-ray eyes to glance furtively into the ladies' toilet.

For one super-power is denied all super-heroes: super-sexual powers; and the widespread longing among ordinary mortal men for a penis of super dimensions can never be compensated through the figure of a favourite super-hero. Super-heroes as well as super-villains seem to have absolutely nothing to show underneath their tight-fitting tights; they all appear to be poor androgynous beings—hermaphrodites who lack the primary sexual organs. Jack Kirby's figures, who always stand with their feet at least four feet apart, make this lack pretty obvious.

In DC's Imaginary Tales the stiff schema of the *Superman* stories could be relaxed. For example Lois Lane was not even married to Superman but (as we can see from this cover) to Lex Luthor, Superman's greatest enemy. Drawn by Kurt Schaffenberger. From *Lois Lane* No. 34.
© 1962 National Periodical Publications Inc.

Sexless super-heroes? Jack Kirby's figures, who are always drawn with their legs at least four feet apart, make this lack particularly plain. From *Mighty Thor* No. 160 © 1968 Marvel Comics Group

By simply omitting to mention sex, comics authors achieve the same effect as the loincloth or the fig-leaf does in some paintings or sculptures, and the youthful reader is denied compensation for his most secret and private inferiority complexes.

A sterile, 'clean' world is created in which all the heroes are—at least to look at—androgynes.

The sexual self-denial of the super-heroes may be based on masochism connected with their high battle morale. Their chaste, at best monogamous behaviour stands in glaring contrast to their potential virility. What a paradox, that super-heroes should have to act towards women like ordinary, shy, merely human men! And so the super-hero remains, in one of the most important and vital aspects, a highly unsatisfactory figure of identification for ordinary, frustrated men.

Just imagine Superman's sexual possibilities! He could offer wish fulfilment to every male; he could possess the most beautiful women of the universe, either by subduing them with charm like some super-Casanova, or by taking them by force—and enjoying super-orgasms at any time and for any length of time. But as it is the question must remain: Portnoy Superman still going strong after thirty-two years?[6]

Super-heroines have to behave in an even more absurdly Victorian manner. What possibilities have been missed here! What about supergirl, Superman's female counterpart? The professionally trained female Circassian slaves of Suleman the Second's harem would appear as naïve beginners compared with Supergirl's super-powers of vaginal muscle contraction.

It is idle to try to imagine the sexual practices of super-heroes. As far as we know, Iris Allen, Flash's wife, has never yet complained; and what would Captain America's girl friends say if they saw that their hero's underpants also bore the Stars and Stripes?

Possibly, but not very likely, further liberalization may loosen the Code in the course of the seventies and allow heroes with hypertrophied sexual powers to appear not only in the pages of underground comics.

The 'side-kick'

When comics were accused of having a bad effect on youth, critics pounced on seemingly homosexual traits in super-heroes. Dr Wertham saw (1954) a direct link with homosexual fancies in Batman and the Boywonder Robin. His attitude triggered off a controversy, if not to say a libellous propaganda campaign, that is still raging today.

The youthful 'side-kick' is really based on an old tradition of American minor fiction and serialized pulp literature. Tough, resilient, self-reliant, unafraid and honest: this was the image of the typical, one-hundred-per-cent American boy. He was also expected to be clever, humorous and clean. More often than not he was an orphan boy who had had to stand on his own feet from a tender age. Horatio Alger Jr's books had a great part in creating this archetype of the All-American boy. In his many cheap novelettes such boys blossomed in the asphalt jungle of New York—they usually hailed from Brooklyn—and on their way from rags to riches they caught many a grown-up gangster. Such boys, salt of the (American) earth, were of course immediately snapped up by comics and made into boy heroes. Much better identification-figures for young readers than the grown-up heroes! There were also boys who clubbed together in teams and the leader was always the toughest and most American of them all. They fought in countless booklets of the Golden Age during the forties and naturally helped win the war. The *Boy Commandos* under the leadership of Captain Rip Carter, *The Young Allies, The Tough Kids Squad* fought behind or in front of the enemy lines. The *Newsboy Legion* fought at home against crime and the infiltration of enemy agents. When Jack Kirby changed over again from Marvel to DC in 1970 he could take his *Newsboy Legion* into battle again; but now a little Negro boy had joined their ranks.

It was natural that publishers should try to enhance the success of grown-up heroes by letting boy heroes fight at their side, or by giving the boys a grown-up helper. The Newsboy Legion fought together with the Guardian! Kids were so popular as comics heroes that they quite often pushed a super-hero out of his own comic book; many heroes went into battle with smaller editions of themselves at their side: The Human Torch and Toro, The Sandman and Sandy, The Shield and Rusty, The Green Arrow and Speedy, Captain America and Bucky, and many other teams. All of them, just as Superman and Jimmy Olsen, or as Achilles and Patrocles, Dietrich of Bern and Hildebrand, King Arthur and the Knights of the Round Table, for that matter, may be suspected for their friendships.

In *Love and Death in the American Novel* Leslie Fiedler explains that there is more between men than just the sacred element of friendship and cites Ishmael and Queequeg, Natty Bumppo and Chingachgook, Huck and Nigger Jim as examples. And so, if we follow the Freudian interpretation, the super-heroes and their young battle companions are but an extension of a truly American tradition. This is neither the time nor the place to contradict Leslie Fiedler, one of the few quotable apologists of the comics culture.[7]

Feiffer adds his comment when he says that American society as a whole takes a misogynist's view of women: 'not only homosexuals, nobody likes them'. This is expressed in all American forms of entertainment from the party joke to comics to films and literature.

Stereotyped clichés of the early comics era naturally fostered the idea of repressed sexual undertones; but for a long time now the tendency has been towards emphasis of the heterosexual, and modern super-heroes have proved their virility by the many marriages that have taken place in their ranks. The Fantastic Four couple has already produced—after the appropriate time lag—splendid progeny. Batman has sent teenage-wonder Robin to college where he seems to show a normal and lively interest in the opposite sex. Young battle companions, however, since they have aroused such unhealthy suspicions, are no longer popular with publishers.

Motivation

Super-heroes have little or nothing in common with Nietzsche's Superman. They live by comparatively conventional morals; they are for good against evil, whereby they adhere strictly to the law's definition of good and evil.

They are always ready to avert catastrophes, help damsels in distress, prevent crimes being committed or injustice being done and to save the earth, or even other, faraway planets from destruction; under the Code Authority rules they undertake never to kill intentionally in their battles against villainy.

Super-heroes mete out their punishment in such well-measured doses that the enemy is either knocked out, can be captured without difficulty, or is able to flee—suitably humiliated, of course—only to return to a revenge attack. This saves the authors from having to invent ever new antagonists, and if they cannot think of anything new they can fall back on a series of hard-boiled, tough villains who, either out of greed or lust for revenge, are always willing to risk another round. The noble super-heroes enjoy their role of helper in distress which allows them to jump into the arena when some worthwhile heroic deed beckons—without being saddled with the responsibility of solving social problems. The criminals they fight are super-criminals and the big gang rings are just super-criminal syndicates; that crime is a symptom of sickness in a society is never stated, because the super-heroes are interested primarily in the *battle* against crime, not in the removal of its causes. They are rarely concerned with the rehabilitation of a criminal, even less with circumstances that led him into crime. Sometimes (as once in an adventure of Spider-Man) a hero can persuade a criminal to change his ways, but on the whole super-heroes accept that a power of evil exists which not even they can break. All they can do is to fight against it. A Sisyphean task that has kept them young for decades.

For a long time super-heroes believed that they were faultless knights in shining armour. They had so many gallant deeds to perform that they never found time to think; or the thought of revenge that had prompted them to take up super-heroism as a career (Batman) closed their minds against the realities that ruled society. They thought, spoke and acted in clichés, were fitted with spiritual blinkers and saw everything in harsh contours of black and white; in-between shades did not exist: democracy was good, Fascism, Nazism, Communism bad. In Senator McCarthy's days they were his allies and staunchly toed the government line and the line of Hoover's FBI; their spiritual heritage was middle-class and petty bourgeois; they were liberal-conservative like their inventors, belonged to the silent majority and believed that tough measures resolved conflicts.

In the course of time and with the birth of a new species of the genre, however, super-heroes have changed. They have undergone (and are still undergoing) a process of reappraisal. Suddenly heroes like Green Lantern are becoming aware of the existence of racial problems, and of the fact that villains sometimes sit behind desks. Nothing is resolved as yet; but this is only natural. Today's problems are too complicated to be treated to rash quick-fire action solutions—and to prove entertaining into the bargain. But it is to be expected that progressive publishers, editors, authors and artists will continue to humanize their heroes; which means, among other things, that they will have to accept a defeat from time to time.

The secret identity

What is not going to change in the forseeable future is the rigid convention of giving super-heroes a secret identity. It is part of their psychological defence mechanism. Each super-hero chooses in the beginning of his career a disguise and a battle name. Usually he decides to frighten his adversaries, so as to defeat them psychologically as well as physically. He dons a mask and in doing so reaches back to the age-old custom of exorcising demons and evil spirits by frightening them with a terrifying disguise. Today the villains stand in the place of evil spirits. The super-hero's disguise has therefore a mythical element.

Apart from any deeper meaning, costume and mask satisfy a natural urge to have fun, to dress up. The super-hero divides himself into two component parts, each playing its role: the *alter ego* and the secret identity. The dream half (*alter ego*) expresses all that the author or designer—and with him the reader—would like to be; the other half, rooted in reality, is a symbol of the ordinary everyday man following the behaviour pattern ordained by society. It is a division of life into dream and reality typical for the average citizen and serves to strengthen the individual's self-confidence and to justify his personal way of thinking.

There is a serious drawback, though, to the super-hero's dual life: he cannot (and usually does not want to) marry. A family would lay him open to blackmail and all kinds of pressures. 'Darling, I can't marry you, you wouldn't be safe,' are the words the marriage-bent Lois Lane, Superman's girlfriend, has to hear again and again. Celibacy does, of course, aid the popularity of super-heroes; just as it enhances the success of pop stars. To compensate for marriage DC comics have hit upon the idea of imaginary stories; that is, stories are told within the story, in which Superman marries and goes through imaginary experiences. This leads to the paradox that Superman remains single but can, nevertheless, enjoy married bliss in his own personal dreamworld; the reader, of course, gets the best of both worlds.

Lately, however, weddings have not been as taboo in the super-hero world as they used to be. Reed Richards (Mr Fantastic) and Sue Storm (Invisible Girl) of the *Fantastic Four* have become Mr and Mrs; so have Yellowjacket (alias Goliath, alias Ant-Man, alias Henry Pym) and the Wasp of the Avengers. Barry (Flash) Allen took an ordinary mortal as wife: his girlfriend of long years standing Iris West, the journalist. On the first day of their marriage he confesses that he is Flash—only to be told that she has known this long since, because he talks in his sleep.

Could not each one of us be a disguised super-hero? Our visible appearance only the façade of our much more exciting *alter ego*? The super-hero's secret identity is made in our own image, and it is not a particularly flattering one, as the example of Clark Kent shows. Super-careers force super-heroes to lead particularly drab private lives. They cannot make use of their special faculties in the course of normal, everyday life without betraying their secret; their tragedy is that they have to live one half of their lives as normal, humdrum mortals without being able to find fulfilment in that sphere. (Feiffer calls it the super-heroes' masochism.)

The 'little man' likes to project his wishful thinking into the shape of a big, strong man. Super-heroes are no more than the expression and fixation of narcissistic self-aggrandisement; they show how the adolescent reader, or the infantile grown-up sees himself in his dreams. Super-heroes fulfil the youngster's longing to be like the heroes of legend, fairy-tale and myth, and offer him a perfect identification figure.

It is interesting to note that characters like Superman, Captain America and Batman were invented by their creators when they were still of school age.

As identification figures the super-heroes also express the current ideals of masculine beauty; and it is not always packed muscle, but more often the movement of the figure in action that primarily interests the designer. Jack Kirby supplies his heroes with muscles no anatomy chart would ever show, and yet they appear organically quite sound; not because they enhance the quality of strength portrayed in the figure of Captain America or Thor, but because they introduce an impression of explosive action into a static picture. Bull-necked Superman and Captain America were fashioned according to the taste of their time: modelled on the Charles Atlas body-building-school ideal with Herculean muscles as a narcissistic aim for which to strive. Modern super-heroes mirror a different ideal of male shapeliness and the Silver Surfer, for instance, reminds us of statues by Praxiteles or Lysippos.

Super-heroines

The relatively small number of beautiful females in comic books of the sixties seems to reflect America's misogyny, but is, in fact, mainly the result of the strict censorship introduced in 1954; also most comics writers and artists are male and they quite naturally express their own dreams and repressed wishes first.

In the glorious days of the forties, the heyday of the comics hero, a great many shapely heroines firmly stood their ground in comics pages and competed with the men. Captain America had a whole range of female imitations: Miss America, Liberty Bell, Miss Victory, Pat Patriot and Yankee Girl, all of them even more patriotic than their male model. Captain Marvel had his female counterpart in Marvel Girl, Hawkman in Hawkgirl, and today, as then, a Batgirl sometimes crosses Batman's path.

In the world of legends and fairy-tales it is always the prince who rescues the maiden, never the other way round. Girls who act like men could only be found among Amazons, and so the first and most famous of all super-heroines was a descendant of the Amazons. *Wonder Woman*,[8] created in 1941 by William Moulton Marston, inventor of the lie-detector, under the pseudonym of Charles Moulton and drawn by H. G. Peters in a strangely flat, two-dimensional style, was the daughter of the Queen of Paradise Island, an Amazon realm no male was allowed to enter. These Amazons were under the protection

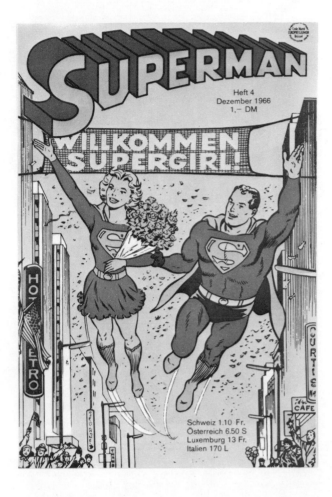

of Aphrodite; like her companions Wonder Woman was created by breathing life into a statue—the problem of the Amazons' procreation was solved.

Wonder Woman was sent to America to help defend democracy against Fascism. She wore, as befitted her mission, Stars and Stripes on her shorts and her breasts were supported by the wings of the American Eagle. For two and a half decades she fought with her magic lasso, her invisible aeroplane and her bracelets of Amazonium (which deflects all missiles) against all sorts of crimes, which often took the shape of an evil female adversary.

Wonder Woman was no creature of harsh masculinity.[9] In her secret identity of Diana Prince, the bespectacled[10] W.A.C. nurse, she could be of almost helpless femininity. She also had strict moral principles. Helpless girls, gagged and bound, struggled through many a Wonder Woman story and a fat little friend called Etta Candy was for a long time battle companion in most of her adventures. No wonder that the critics not only cried sado-masochism, but also suspected the same goings on between Wonder Woman and Etta which they suspected between Batman and Robin.

Up to 1968 Wonder Woman remained an Amazon. She held Steve Trevor, the pilot who had fallen in love with her, at arm's length, though she had fallen for him at first sight. In October 1968 she took off her uniform—at least for the time being. Her role had become anachronistic. She opened a fashion boutique and plunged headlong into the sorrows of love, because she now fell for the wrong guy.

Feminine softness in the midst of the hard, cruel battle against evil—girls who could put men on the rack—it needed a very delicate touch to make such things acceptable to the mainly male readership. Lee Elias was superbly successful with his black-haired *Black Cat* (appeared 1942 in *Speed Comics*) and so was Syd Shores when he launched *The Blonde Phantom* in 1944.

After 1948 sex was beginning to be strongly emphasized in comics and Gregory Page created *The Phantom Lady*, a very feminine super-heroine indeed, as her generous décolleté proclaimed. But after 1954, when the Code Authority had come into being, all the girls except Wonder Woman, whether they had super-powers or lived in the jungle, disappeared into the comics limbo, and only a few made a comeback in the sixties, notably the Black Canary and The Black Widow. For a while comics denied American matriarchy and sexual behaviour and showed a world ruled exclusively by men. Even the slightest suggestion of sex stimulus was avoided; censorship would have clamped down immediately on any accentuation of the female form. What, girls in tight-fitting tights? Impossible!

Some years after Superman's cousin had landed on earth—

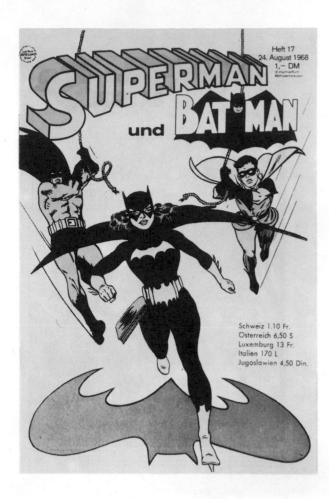

When Marvel introduced the new 'Marvel Age of Comics' in 1962 and censorship was beginning to loosen its iron grip, the firm poured more and more heroines onto its pages: Invisible Girl (now a mother), The Wasp, The Scarlet Witch, Medusa, Crystal and Marvel Girl.

Super-villains

Super-heroes and super-heroines upset the balance between good and evil by their mere existence and to redress this balance super-villains were invented. Normally, each super-hero has his counterpart in the world of villainy. This is a method well tried by many authors of serial novels. We only have to think of Sherlock Holmes and his adversary Dr Moriarty. Comics copied the theme and produced Captain America and the Red Skull, Superman and Lex Luthor, Batman and The Joker, Reed Richards and Dr Doom, and many others.

Each super-hero has an enemy tailored to challenge and match his own particular faculties. The perfect examples are Human Torch and his adversary, The Asbestos Lady; but to match, for instance, The Spider-Man against Galactus would mean the hero's certain death, and to avoid such outrageous catastrophes each hero fights only within his own heroic class.

But in the long run one enemy alone is no challenge for a full-blooded super-hero. The enemy has to disappear behind bars from time to time or even to be presumed dead. If the same villain arrested at the end of one story should reappear at the beginning of the next, the reader might be tempted to conclude that the punishment did not fit the crime. Criminals must always get their just deserts in the end and are often seemingly killed stone dead; a few stories later, however, the reader learns to his surprise that once again, as many times before, a miracle has saved the evil-doer's worthless life. Once more, he can go into action and challenge our hero with his deeds of villainy and deceit.

If the popularity of a hero drops to such a low level that his

'She's been among us for years, and we never suspected! Imagine that!!'—she became *Supergirl*, the world's greatest heroine. Superman introduced her to the astonished world in February 1966 (*Action Comics* 285). 'She's terrific! Cute, too!' and 'What a Superdoll!!' were some of the delirious comments. In the same story Kruschev remarked laconically: 'It must be a capitalist hoax!'

A new readership draw had been found. Supergirl's second identity is that of Linda Lee Danvers, model of the perfect American college girl; and that is probably the reason why the Code Authority did not object to Supergirl's well-shaped legs being set off to their best advantage by the shortest of mini-skirts.

particular comic book has to be discontinued, it still does not mean that he has to die. In a few years' time readers may like to hear of him again—and up he pops in a modernized version. Hence the saying goes in comics: 'Old super-heroes (like soldiers) never die, they only fade away. . . .' They fade into the comics limbo, that uncertain region where jobless heroes and villains go until recalled.

Since the censorship of 1954 came into force death is only shown as fiction in comics: a kind of unreal state of non-existence which can never figure as a satisfactory solution to any problem. There are only a few exceptions and these made history: Tower Comics let Menthor, hero of *Thunder Agents*, die a true hero's death in issue No. 7 and Marvel allowed Zemo, an old Nazi villain, to be well and truly killed. The latter event did not deter another Nazi fiend from appearing in Zemo disguise and threatening Captain America. No fan would seriously believe that Dr Xavier of *X-Men* was really dead, and sure enough, three years later he re-emerged.

Each super-hero has 'pro bono contra malum' invisibly stamped on his forehead and can, therefore, never be defeated. No wonder that under such a scheme the super-villains are often drawn much more interestingly and hold more fascination for the reader than the hero himself. Just as super-heroes, super-villains too usually acquire their super-gifts through some accident; but when they realize their new potentialities, their warped brains think only of the advantages they can gain for themselves, the power they will be able to wield over their fellow beings, the damage they can inflict on society in revenge for some injustice they suffered in the past.

Lex Luthor, Superman's arch enemy, enjoyed experimenting with chemicals in his youth. Carelessly released vapours robbed him of every hair on his head. It had been Lex's own fault, but he blamed Superboy who had wanted to rescue him—taking the vapour clouds for the smoke of a fire—for the accident and his ensuing baldness. Luthor convinced himself that Superboy was envious of his scientific genius, broke off their friendship and decided henceforth to use his powers in the furtherance of crime.

An important part in the Superman saga is also played by Brainiac, a green-faced computer in human shape, largely immune against Superman's attacks. Brainiac's particular hobby was to scale down whole towns, including inhabitants, to minute size and add them to his growing collection; but when he started on terrestrial towns Superman managed at last to stop this fiendish pastime. He successfully returned towns and inhabitants to their normal size, only one town he could not help: Kandor, a town which his green adversary had popped into one of his bottles, just before the final destruction of the planet Krypton. Brainiac's bottle was filled with an atmosphere which permitted the inhabitants to survive. Since then Kandor—in its bottle—stands in Superman's fortress. Sometimes a group of mini-super-heroes issues from the bottle, to aid Superman in particularly tricky cases. This town is, by the way, the town of Supergirl's parents and they still live there—in reduced circumstances.

Another super-villain who was given a fiend's appearance by a chemical reaction is Batman's adversary, The Joker. His hair turned green, his face white and his lips blood red. At first he was one of those particularly sinister fiends who torture their victims just for the fun of it; but gradually he became the real 'joker' of the world of crime, who commits his villainies for the sole reason of annoying Batman.

The best and most effective villains personify the greatness in evil; they are lonely, tragic figures, demanding our pity. Their crimes are committed out of a desire for revenge, a feeling of bitterness, for they are denied the ordinary human emotions—soulless, despairing creatures. Frankenstein was made of such stuff, and also Marvel's Dr Doom, a super-villain so popular with readers that he became the first evil character to be title-hero of his own series of stories.

Dr Doom, dictator of Latveria, has the greatness as well as the loneliness of Shakespeare's Richard III, and resembles him in more than just an unprepossessing appearance. He is absolute master over his realm. Human beings are no more to him than figures on a chessboard, and he pushes them around as he pleases. He is also a scientific genius—just like his adversary, Mr Fantastic (Richard Reed).

Another highly successful Marvel villain is *The Red Skull*, the man with the red death's-head mask. He was originally created by Hitler to do his bidding, but gradually became the power behind Hitler's throne, and is now the personification of dictator-ship, world-domination and enslavement of mankind. His driving motive is blind hatred against Captain America who for over thirty long years has thwarted his wishes, humiliated him, beaten him in countless battles and repeatedly seemingly killed him; but Red Skull always rises like a phoenix out of the ashes to make another attempt at bringing Hitler's heritage to the USA.

Apart from the great ones there are the smaller evil-doers who have attained some sort of super-faculty through long, pains-taking efforts. They are no less inventive in brewing trouble and confront lesser heroes, like Flash; but their super-villainies never succeed in amassing the fortunes for which they pine and the tailors who fashion their costumes never receive payment for their bills.

Brain versus brawn
Some critics see in the super-heroes' fights a simple brain versus brawn theme which labels the intellectual as negative and inferior.

Super-hero wars are always fought for the highest possible stake: 'Shall earth survive?' It is only logical to give the super-heroes enemies with the most advanced technical know-how and the scientific means to blow earth right out of the universe. Only mad scientists have this particular know-how in comics, and so a simple, straightforward analogy with reality exists. (The comics' atom bomb appeared long before the real one.) The American archetype of the 'tinkerer' of the Edison brand became the Mad Scientist who dabbles in world destruction as a scientific experiment.

In the cruder stories of the Golden Age, when mad scientists and thinkers most often worked for the Nazis (rumours of

Red Skull, like most other super-villains, seems immortal. Beaten innumerable times, he always turns up again. Cap will have many more occasions to beat him. Both are shown here one year after Red Skull's first appearance. From *Fantasy Masterpieces* No. 6. Drawn by Jack Kirby.
© 1966, 1941 Marvel Comics Group

German 'wonder weapons' abounded), they were usually portrayed as small, misshapen men with large 'egg' heads. Later designs were subtler and much more inventive. Brainiac, Lex Luthor and Marvel's aptly-named Mad Thinker are not displeasing to look at and are rather tragic characters. Super-heroes, however, need enemies they can tackle physically and so mad scientists generally work via robots or other artificially created beings. The Frankenstein theme is endlessly varied and modified.

A repeated show of primitive physical strength and superiority on the part of super-heroes would be boring in the long run, and

Superman therefore functions in many a story as super-sleuth. In such cases he becomes a veritable Sherlock Holmes, and Batman too has to make good use of his grey matter when he tries to unravel the mysteries left behind by the Riddler. Batman's super-detective adventures in *Detective Comics* are well worth reading. On the whole it is intelligence rather than crude strength that wins the final super-hero victory.

Except for Benjamin Grimm, The Thing of the Fantastic Four. He just likes to 'smash 'em', and when he goes into action his battle cry can be heard loud and clear:

From *Fantastic Four* No. 48.
© 1965 Marvel Comics Group

opposite
Confrontation between good and evil assumes gigantic proportions: Dr Richard Doom, Marvel's Richard III, has one of his great triumphs. From *Fantastic Four* No. 57. Drawn by Jack Kirby and Joe Sinnott.
© 1966 Marvel Comics Group

5 Criticism and censorship

Senator Kefauver: Here is your May 22 issue. This seems to be a man with a bloody axe holding a woman's head up which has been severed from its body. Do you think that is in good taste?

Mr Gaines: Yes, Sir; I do, for the cover of a horror comic. A cover in bad taste, for example, might be defined as holding the head a little higher so that the neck could be seen dripping blood from it and moving the body over a little further so that the neck of the body could be seen to be bloody.

Senator Kefauver: You have blood coming out of her mouth.

Mr Gaines: A little.

Congressional Interrogation of the Creator of Horror Comics,
W. M. Gaines[1]

Dr Wertham on horror

Even today, after three decades of uninterrupted controversy, it is still not possible to prove conclusively whether comics, films and television have a damaging effect on youth or not. Do comics stimulate, canalize or reduce aggression? Are they catalyst or outlet-valve? Do they lead to a catharsis or do they encourage violence and crime? All these contradictory effects of the mass media have been scientifically analysed and the conclusion is that the effect of comics (as of the other mass media) varies tremendously and is dependent on so many different factors, that it is impossible to give a definite verdict.

Reaction to comics depends largely on the widely differing psychological states of readers, and indeed an individual reader's reaction may vary considerably at different times. The state of mind of any given reader is influenced by his (or her) age, social status, education, upbringing and many other factors. Weak, unstable characters will show a greater tendency towards heightened feelings of aggression than strong, stable minds. However, what is really being debated is not whether portrayal of sex and violence stimulates or reduces feelings of aggression, but rather the question of what kind of social values and standards of behaviour the comics are offering their readership. It seems that the so-called good, harmless comics are the ones that have so far been neglected in any such investigation.[2]

As it is impossible to bring positive proof of the comics' guilt, their opponents in the USA will have to continue watching them corrupt the fibre of the nation. They have made up their minds: universities in revolt, family life endangered, school dropouts, illegitimate children, mental disease, venereal disease, drug addiction are being fostered by the mass media—and the government does nothing beyond appointing one investigations committee after another.

In 1968, after the assassination of Robert Kennedy, President Johnson appointed the National Commission on the Causes and Prevention of Violence. Its brief extended to the mass media, inclusive of comics. The Commission's findings were that the causes of the problem were deeply rooted in American society itself; but despite this verdict the comics' enemies are once more

This particular E.C. comic book was used as evidence of the corrupting influence of crime and horror comic books on youth, and was defended by William M. Gaines from E.C. (See the quotation at the beginning of this chapter.) From *Crime SuspenStories* No. 22. © 1954 E.C. Publications

A good example of the way criticism of the medium was incorporated into comic books. Donald Duck is raging against comic books. He says: '"Superman"! A fantasy picture of a detective who can jump over skyscrapers and bend iron bridges with his bare hands.' He goes on: 'Have you nothing better to do than read rubbish like that?' An accurate caricature of the emotional, prejudiced attitude of many of the early opponents of comics. From *Die tollsten Geschichten von Donald Duck (The craziest stories about Donald Duck)*, drawn by Carl Barks.
© 1965 Walt Disney Productions/Ehapa Verlag Stuttgart

on the warpath. An increasingly liberal application of the rules of the Code, which, so they say, did not curb violence anyway, the growing number of pre-Code comics being reprinted and the large number of publishers who do not adhere to the Code, have prompted critics to revive all the old worn-out anti-comics arguments fashionable in Dr Wertham's heyday in the forties and fifties.[3]

Many of the new anti-mass media crusaders have chosen television as their main target, but comics get their share of abuse, for the formulas are more or less the same in all the mass media. The average American spends 3,000 whole days, that is nine years of his life, looking into the 'boob-tube'. Television has altered ways of life as well as political attitudes much more radically than comics. Violence has come to be accepted as something perfectly normal. To grown-ups, films like Sam Peckinpah's apotheosis of violence, *The Wild Bunch* and also his film *Straw Dogs* are already old hat. But the innocent little ones, already endangered by sex instruction in schools, must be protected from the effects of visually demonstrated violence!

Content of comics is dictated by the type of society in which they appear. Taboos, censorship or control do not change the aspirations, wishes and longings for which comics offer compensation; that is the reason why the controversy raging around comics has never bothered the readership—comics continue to be avidly read by young and old alike.

True, most comics serve to introduce the young to the conditions prevailing in society and must therefore be kept under scrutiny. The hysterical shouts of guardians of our morals, however, attacked only the surface symptoms of sex and violence, never getting near the root of the evil and detracting attention from the fact that reality was much worse than anything ever shown by the mass media. No form of censorship whether of film, television or comics, has been proved to have influenced crime statistics in any way.

Two of the most famous and most influential critics of comic books were Gershom Legman and Frederick Wertham. Legman's theory, expounded in his book *Love and Death* (1949), is that the violence in pulp literature and in comics is transformation of and compensation for sexuality repressed and restricted by society. Legman's exposition was brilliant and came much nearer to answering basic questions than Wertham's or any of his followers' theories; though Legman too overshot his goal at times: 'That the publishers, editors, artists and writers of comics books are degenerates and belong in jail, goes without saying . . .' (page 45), or: '. . . the two comic book companies staffed entirely by homosexuals and operating out of our most phalliform sky-scraper' (page 43).

He does not interpret the transformation of sexuality into violence as a general result of repressive civilization, but as a commercialized perversion—sanctioned by a hypocritical society—of normal sexual desires. As far back as 1949 Legman hinted at the fact that the primary cause of damage done to the youthful psyche lay not in the mass media but in the society that produced them.

The reader is not allowed to aim his aggression against the real cause of his frustrations, the system itself, and so the mass media give him figures of identification, scapegoats. Legman believes that the world of fantasy into which children flee is also caused by frustration—the restrictions imposed by parents and school:

> Children are not allowed to fantasy themselves as actually revolting against authority—as actually killing their fathers —nor a wife as actually killing her husband. A literature frankly offering images for such fantasies would be out-lawed overnight. But, in the identifications available in comic-strips—in the character of the Katzenjammer Kids, in the kewpie-doll character of Blondie—both father and husband can be thoroughly beaten up, harassed, humiliated, and degraded daily. Lulled by these halfway aggressions— that is to say, halfway to murder—the censorship demands only that in the final sequence Hans & Fritz must submit to flagellation for their 'naughtiness', Blondie to the inferior position of being, after all, merely a wife. In other words, the *status quo* must be restored in some perfunctory genuflection as the reader leaves. This is the contract under which direct-attack fantasy is allowed: the attack must be incomplete; even so, being against authority, it must be punished; and, in the last analysis, it must change nothing. (Page 48.)[4]

The greatest responsibility for the introduction of a comics code and the cleansing operation which followed undoubtedly falls on Dr Wertham. His crusade against comics started in 1940 and in 1954 he published his accusation in a book called *Seduction of the Innocent*.[5] Frequent appearances on television and many articles in the press gave him publicity and he became a well-known national figure. He has not changed his ideas to this day, and has restated them recently, in his book *Sign of Cain* (1964). He has, however, turned his main attention to the evils of television as the primary cause of the country's moral decline.

Wertham saw in producers and publishers of comic books veritable vampires who sucked the blood of the innocent. Comic books, in his opinion, systematically poisoned the wellspring of children's spontaneity and prepared the ground for later aggressive behaviour (*Seduction of the Innocent*, page 296).

After he had been incorporated into some comic books as 'Dr Frederick Muttontop' or 'Dr Frederick Froyd' and thoroughly ridiculed, this Savonarola of comics soon saw to it that his opponents stopped laughing. The young delinquents Dr Wertham questioned had all read comics. A young, parentless murderer had read comics. In the room of a youngster who had committed suicide, comic books were found. Seen from his point of view, Dr Wertham's demand for legal censorship did not seem unreasonable; but his clinical findings as well as later laboratory tests on the effects of comics do not necessarily give an undistorted picture of the true effects, and even if they did, they would only apply to a small group of delinquents whose social environment and family background had already done them such irreparable harm that it did not need the added influence of comics to bring them into conflict with the law.

The examples of picture material Dr Wertham gives in his book are indeed horrific. There is, for instance, an illustration from the famous E.C. story drawn by Jack Davis in which a very special type of baseball is played: the ball is a human head, the torso is used as defence guard and the intestines are laid out as markings on the field. Another picture in the booklet has in the meantime become famous for its jolly text: two corpses are being dragged along the road behind a car. Text: 'These *****!! GRAVEL ROADS are tough on tires!' 'But ya gotta admit, there's nothing like 'em for ERASING FACES!' No child could remain untouched by such horrors.

'I want to be a sex maniac', reads the heading of one chapter in Wertham's book. It is just one answer given by one of the children he questioned; for in Dr Wertham's view comics do not only seduce the reader into crime, but also into sexual perversions. At the end of the forties bosoms came into fashion, not only in films: comics too went in for them in a big way. Female protagonists of comic book stories could be proud of ample proportions and certainly did not hesitate to grant the reader generous insight into blouses, or to show off the contours of their tight-fitting pullovers. Hence the name 'headlight-comics' given to booklets of this genre by their attentive young readers. Phantom Lady, and particularly the jungle heroines, went about their adventures in the scantiest of clothes.

In 1948 Kinsey enlightened Americans to the fact that masturbation is not harmful *(Sexual Behaviour in the Human Male)*. Instead of worrying about sexual stimulation we should be concerned about the channelling of children's sexual impulses into masochism, sadism and fetishism. Apart from the obvious flaunting of the female form, scandalized critics imaged phallic emblems and other sex symbols to lurk everywhere. Someone rejoicing in a particularly vivid imagination might, perhaps, find in the detail of a muscular shoulder (enlarged by Dr Wertham) the image of a *mons veneris*. Wertham saw even in *Wonder Woman*'s magical lasso a vaginal symbol; but he missed the subtlety of her name Diana (the huntress) *Prince* (not Princess).

He also maintained that the comic heroes were clearly homosexual—differing sharply from those critics who saw them as completely sexless creatures. Of Robin, Batman's side-kick, Wertham writes: 'He often stands with his legs spread, the genital region discreetly evident.' (Page 191.) How else could he stand? Fans, moreover, know that Robin, in contrast to other super-heroes, prefers trunks of thick, green corduroy-like material, which explains the effect of fullness the drawing gives.

Here is a famous passage from Wertham's book:

> Sometimes Batman ends up in bed injured and young Robin is shown sitting next to him. At home they lead an idyllic life. They are Bruce Wayne and 'Dick' Grayson. Bruce Wayne is described as a 'socialite' and the official relationship is that Dick is Bruce's ward. They live in sumptuous quarters, with beautiful flowers in large vases, and have a butler, Alfred. Batman is sometimes shown in a dressing gown. As they sit by the fireplace the young boy sometimes worries about his partner: 'Something's wrong with Bruce. He hasn't been himself these past few days.' It is like a wish dream of two homosexuals living together. Sometimes they are shown on a couch, Bruce reclining and Dick sitting next to him, jacket off, collar open, and his hand on his friend's arm. (Page 190.)

A television adaptation of *Batman* tried to forestall such criticism by introducing an aunt into the misogynists' homo-erotic household.

Wertham's book ends with a passage in which he assures the mother of a juvenile delinquent that the way she brought him up could not possibly have been the reason for his delinquency. It was so easy to blame the comics for everything!

The McCarthy era, that heyday of the blindly hysterical, was also Dr Wertham's great time. It is easy, though, to judge with hindsight; today we know the importance of the elementary stage for a child's whole future development. Our primary concern is no longer whether comics have a harmful or a beneficent effect, but what social values and standards comics offer youngsters.

A child's fundamental character traits are moulded by the parents. 'Parents should set the standards, keep track and stick to their guns' is the sensible advice Dr Spock[6] gives parents who worry about the influence of film, television and comics.

The most violent and cruel portrayals take place in cartoon films and comics where anthropomorphic animals like Bugs Bunny and his friends or Tom and Jerry blow each other up, flatten each other with steam rollers and invent all manner of loving treatment for their enemies. Grown-ups as well as children love them, and they show most clearly that such violence serves the purpose of giving an outlet to aggressive feelings through illusory aggression. In this way anybody can identify himself (or herself) in an approved manner with the aggressive character and enjoy the enactment of violence second-hand. But the illusion alleviates the frustrations which caused aggressive feelings in the first place only very temporarily, and imaginary outlets for aggressive tension, as a substitute for solving conflicts, only condition man from childhood to an alienated, unreal life.

History of crime comics

The history of comic books can be told in the history of attacks made against them. In 1940, for instance, just as they were beginning to establish themselves, the *Chicago Daily News* called them a poisonous mushroom growth; in the same year the comic book industry began to prepare its defence. DC National formulated its own comics code to which all its authors and designers had to adhere.

Comic strips remained comparatively immune to attack—after initial difficulties, like an attack on *Jeff and Mutt* in 1911—because stringent self-censorship had already been imposed. The comic strip syndicates objected most strongly to being mentioned in the same breath as comic books, because the latters' reputation was so bad that they had become synonymous with crime, horror and corruption of youth—a stigma that still attaches to them.

After the war, crime began to be featured in comic books with increasing emphasis. The definition of crime comics, however, can be a debatable point. To Legman and Wertham the act of violence alone counted; whether it happened in a Donald Duck(!) or a Western comic was immaterial, they classed the offending issue as a crime comic book. According to Wertham's definition, only a tenth of the entire production could be classed as crime comics in 1946; in 1949 roughly one half, and in 1954, shortly before the official Comics Code was introduced, the majority of all booklets on the market were crime comic books. Approximately 80 million comic books were sold per month and free competition resulted in publishers outbidding each other to offer ever larger quantities of trash to the public. In the end some critics feared that a kind of Gresham's law was operating under which bad comics were gradually pushing out the good ones.

Real crime comics were a genre which portrayed American society with realistic brutality. As a species they ceased to exist abruptly with the introduction of the Comics Code. Critics accused these booklets of glorifying crime, of presenting crime for crime's sake. Defenders argued that the portrayal of violence was simply a necessity; Shakespeare, they pointed out, also showed violence and so did legends, myths and fairy tales. But in classic literature, violence (and anything else comics have in common with classic literature) stands in a definite relationship to certain norms of behaviour so that individual acts of violence break through the confines of such norms; whereas in pure crime comics the crime or violence is the driving force and the *raison d'être*: it demands no reflection on the part of the reader.

CRIME was written in enormous letters across the cover of the most successful booklets of this genre, accompanied by an appropriate picture. Beneath the large heading those who looked very carefully could read the legend 'does not pay' in minute lettering; a statement which certainly did not hold true for the publishers! When they were placed on shelves for display, the beholder's eye would instantly be caught by *one* word: *GANGSTERS—can't win; CRIMINALS—on the run; Justice traps the GUILTY; GUNS against gangsters; There is no escape for PUBLIC ENEMIES; LAWBREAKERS—always lose; MURDER Incorporated; CRIME and punishment*, etc., etc. At very close scrutiny the words 'Dedicated to the eradication of crime' could be seen—but this was considered very hypocritical.

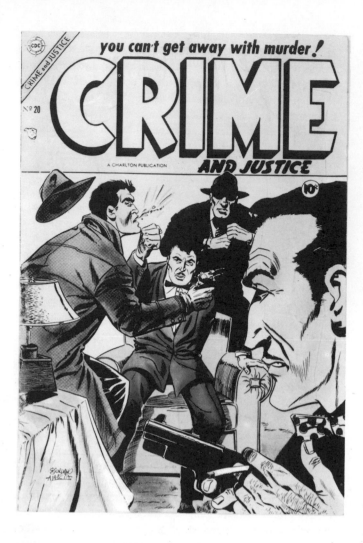

The word CRIME was always displayed prominently on comic book covers; 'justice' or 'law' appeared in small print.
© 1954 Charlton Comics Group

Many stories were advertised as 'true', but only the general public, not the critics, were suitably impressed by such legends as: 'True facts from the files of the FBI', or 'Adapted from true Police and FBI cases'. Titles such as *All-True Crime, Official True Crime, Authentic Police Cases, Famous Crimes* or *True Crimes* tried to cloak the content with a mantle of 'authenticity'; they were, however, no different from any of the other crime booklets.

One of the strongest objections voiced by critics was that crime comics taught youngsters the technique of crime. They only needed to be just a little more intelligent or quicker than the protagonists of a given comic, to escape the police in the end. The crimes committed in crime stories positively asked to be copied (so said the critics) and the bank raid of the comic book could become the real life raid on the candy store round the corner.

The greed of youngsters for more and more violence and sadism was diagnosed as a pathological social trait, induced by the brutalizing effect of the Second World War. One aspect which aroused particularly heavy criticism was the occasional hoodwinking of the police. This found great approval among readers, who liked to see the police beaten, but was later expressly forbidden by the Comics Code. Hatred of the police as an instrument of repression finds its outlet in today's underground comics. The fascination of the crime comics lay in the fact that crime or vice always seemed to be so much more exciting than virtue; and quite apart from that, the gangsters portrayed had all the characteristics of the ideal American male: they were tough, hard, went all out for success and as American ideology rates success the highest goal, crime came to be seen as no more than a means to an end and was only bad if it did not succeed.

The gangster, stalking through the city with his gun, is the modern version of the archaic hunter; besides, he has heroic traits, for does he not confront overwhelmingly powerful enemies? Society's taboos demand that he be caught and punished. The reader, however, always sympathizes with the underdog and a Robin Hood touch will make the gangster even more acceptable as an identification figure.

But the most attractive feature is probably the courage the criminal shows in doing what the reader would like to do if he dared, in carrying out the actions which are buried in his subconscious mind. Crime comics re-awaken the reader's aversion to the repressions and restrictions of society, to the laws and taboos; they appeal to a fundamental ambivalence in his mind. On the one hand the reader is on the side of the gangster—even if he does not admit this—because he finds it dull to identify with a normal, virtuous protagonist, but at the same time he is relieved when the criminal gets his just deserts, as this strengthens his sense of security.[7]

Comic books were spared one danger: Mickey Spillane had originally invented his private detective Mike Hammer for the comics under the name of Mike Danger, but Timely was not interested, because at that time the market was already saturated with crime comic books. Spillane worked out his idea and later published it under the title *I, the Jury*. It became a sensational bestseller, but as a comic book it would most certainly have speeded the introduction of the Comics Code.

Crime comics showed not only gangsters and other professional criminals, they offered quite a variety of identification figures to their public; very popular were, for instance, frustrated husbands or wives who committed murder, but were prevented from executing the perfect, undetected crime by some unfortunate and unforeseen circumstance, and here the transition from crime to horror comic took place. The horror comic book did not aim at compensation for feelings of aggression, but at delightful shivers of horror down readers' spines. For this reason more attention was paid to the text, because terror induced by the reader's own imagination is much more potent than prefabricated, pictured terror. Limits had to be imposed because of the demands of good taste, but they were pretty generous. Here are two examples of techniques used:

Case 1: A man is shown lifting an axe preparatory to striking his wife on the floor. In the next frame he lowers the axe; the wife is not shown, but the caption reads: 'Bertha squealed as Norman brought the axe down. The swinging of steel and the thud of the razor-sharp metal against flesh cut the squeal short.' In the next frame he holds the axe poised again, the body still not exposed, and the caption reads: 'He brought the axe down again and again, hacking, severing, dismembering.'

Case 2: 'His victim's shrieks died to a bubbling moan . . . then a final death rattle. . . . You did not stop swinging the chair until the thing on the floor was nothing but a mass of oozing scarlet pulp.' No body is shown but the entire frame is *coloured red*.[8]

The murder takes place 'off', but the explicit text makes it all the more effective.

No wonder that long before 1950 crusades against comic books took place all over the USA. In 1948 The Greater Cincinnati Committee on Evaluation of Comic Books was formed; a sermon by the Methodist preacher Dr Jesse L. Murrel had sparked off its formation and Dr Murrel became chairman of the Committee. This was not the only case of objections against comics being raised from the pulpit. Usually local parent-teacher associations initiated the campaigns, but the National Congress of Parents and Teachers was also involved.

There were even public burnings of comics, and warned by all these unpleasant happenings the Association of Comics Magazine Publishers tried, as early as July 1948, to formulate a code for the industry which would oblige the members of the Association to keep their products free of sex, obscenities and sadism; but the member firms represented only thirty per cent of the industry. National Publications, Fawcett and Dell would not join because they judged their comic books to be blameless and were anxious to prevent their names being used as a cover for other producers connected with this control body. In 1950 the Association was dissolved.

Crime comic book producers tried in 1949 to change from crime to melodramatic romance for teenagers, but sales sank so alarmingly that by 1950 they were forced to return to the old crime formula. At the same time William Gaines introduced horror as a new genre into his E.C. Comics. The letters E.C. stood for *Entertaining Comics* and were certainly in no danger of being confused with the E.C. Comics of William Gaines' father, the Educational Comics.

Bill Gaines and Al Feldstein changed *Crime Patrol* into *Crypt of Horror* (April 1950) which was later renamed *Crypt of Terror*. At the same time *Vault of Horror* and *Haunt of Fear* were substituted for E.C.'s war comics which had been edited by Harvey Kurtzman, whose genius later produced *MAD*. In May 1950 *Weird Science* and *Weird Fantasy* were started. Later on these two comic books merged to form *Weird Science-Fantasy* which was soon renamed *Incredible Science Fiction*. In October 1950 *Crime Suspense Stories* were added to the lineup; *Shock Suspense Stories* and *Two Fisted Tales* followed suit. These comics were the best products on the market—and not only because of their aesthetically pleasing drawings. Wallace Wood, Jack Davis, Johnny Craig, Frank Frazetta, Reed Crandall, Bill Elder, George Evans, John Severin, Joe Orlando and Al Williamson (who joined later) belonged to the E.C. élite. They tried to work in the tradition of Edgar Allen Poe and within that tradition they were quite justified in using all manner of necrophilous paraphernalia in their tales of terror. Their attempts at achieving subtle horror and the high artistic standard of the work produced by E.C. Comics is perhaps featured most clearly in their adaptations of Ray Bradbury's stories.

The critics, however, screamed new abuse. No matter how excellent the standard—horror and violence were condemned. Publishers had meanwhile engaged psychiatrists and psychologists to give scientific advice on the content of comics and to defend them from a professional point of view. Dr Wertham suddenly found himself confronted by colleagues' statements

This 'Pledge to Parents' appeared in all Dell comic books, until the partnership between Dell and Western Publishing Co. ended in 1962.

The Comics Code seal, which guarantees that a booklet is wholesome, entertaining and educational; in use since 1954.

which appeared in abbreviated form on the cover of comic books as a kind of legitimizing pass.

But by now government bodies had also been alerted and the Kefauver Crime Committee held an inquiry into the effect of comics. (See quotation at beginning of chapter.) Walt Kelly, Joe Musial and Milton Caniff, members of the National Cartoonist Society, had been invited to give evidence on comic newspaper strips. After they had answered questions, they drew their comics characters for the members of the committee to take home. No wonder the committee found no definite connection between juvenile delinquency and comics. One interesting point came to light, however: the fact that under the prevailing *en bloc* distribution system retailers were forced to carry horror comics along with the others if they wanted to sell comics at all.

Other, smaller commissions pronounced comics guilty and a law against youth-endangering comic books was expected at any moment. Five years earlier the governor of the State of New York had prevented a law against crime and horror comics being passed on the grounds that it would contravene the Constitution and could also be used against authors like Poe or Conan Doyle. Such arguments would no longer work and it was high time for the publishers themselves to take some kind of action.

On 26 October 1945 the Comics Code of the C.M.A.A. (Comics Magazine Association of America) came into force. This Association had been joined by all the principal comics publishers except Dell Publications and Gilberton Company. As in 1948, Dell refused to join, because the Code only regulated the production of horror and crime comics instead of eliminating them; but Dell was quite prepared to co-operate with the C.M.A.A. and under its own code, formulated after 1954, undertook to publish only 'clean' comics. Proudly each Dell booklet displayed the 'Dell-Pledge to Parents':

The introduction of the Code was a heavy blow for the comics industry. The publishers of crime comics who had not joined

disappeared altogether; of the twenty-nine firms that had according to Dr Wertham's definition produced crime comics, twenty-four ceased publishing; a success of which the good doctor frequently boasted. The Code alone did not, however, achieve these results. In May 1955 it became illegal in the State of New York to sell obscene, objectionable comics to minors, or to carry words like 'crime', 'sex', 'horror' or 'terror' in any title; and a dozen more states also introduced laws against such types of comic books. A radical 'shrinking process' took place in which crime and horror comics disappeared completely. In the case of E.C.'s comics this was a real loss to the grown-up readership—in the meantime partially made good by the appearance of *Creepy* and *Eerie*, the two horror magazines, and *MAD*, which had started before the introduction of the Code. E.C. stopped publishing its comic books one month before the Code came into force: 'In answer to the pleas of America's parents,' as was sarcastically explained. Apart from all this it must be pointed out that at that time the whole comics industry suffered from overproduction and the Code had a healthy effect in cutting it down to size; before the Code came to the rescue retailers could hardly cope with the three hundred and fifty odd titles per month.

Crime lingered on for a while in very subdued versions with guardians of law as the main protagonists, as, for instance, in DC's *District Attorney*. Comic books had been purged of all objectionable material and the committees dissolved in the proud knowledge of total victory.

Code and censorship

'The seal on the cover means this Code-approved comic magazine is wholesome, entertaining, educational.' This visible sign of the Code Authority's approval meant, at least up to 1962, that the comic book thus honoured contained nothing remarkable and was usually plain boring.

136

The Code is divided into three main parts (see Appendix) and forbids the portrayal of crime and violence; it demands 'clean' dialogue (slang and colloquialisms are allowed), decently dressed characters and good taste in the treatment of all matters relating to sex and marriage. There are also rules regulating advertisements in comic books, which had been another bone of contention with critics.

How strong the influence of the Code Authority still is, even today, can be measured by the fact that drugs, though one of the most topical subjects, had been completely taboo until 1971. The opinion prevailed that narcotics addiction, no matter how carefully approached, was not a fit theme for treatment in a medium catering mainly for children.[9]

The Code was, and still is, strictly applied. In 1969, 309 books out of 1,000 failed to satisfy the Authority; but on the whole offences against the Code are but minor lapses. Sometimes they are just grammatical errors, or perhaps the dress of one character in one picture of a booklet does not meet with approval. Publishers try their best to comply with the rules of the C.M.A.A. before submitting material. Between the autumn of 1954 and end of 1969 the C.M.A.A. tested exactly 18,125 comic books.

If no objections have been raised, a comic book may go straight into print; if it has come back with some criticism, matters have to be put right. Objections could read as follows: Page 18—Panel 1—Position of girl in relation to man is very suggestive. Change her position to indicate that both her legs are on the other side of the man. We suggest that her leg, shown in the foreground, be removed and man's body be extended downward. Page 28—Panel 1—'Mush' should be 'Must'.
These examples are taken from the files of the C.M.A.A.

The most potent argument used by the comics industry against the indictment of 'endangering youth' was the First Amendment to the American Constitution: 'Congress shall make no law . . . abridging the freedom of speech.' To avert the danger threatening the industry and appease public opinion, comics publishers created their own moral code. In the USA self-censorship and control are always brought in when pressure from organized bodies, like the Parents–Teachers Association, becomes too strong. In such cases self-censorship becomes self-defence in order to allow the affected medium to continue as a commercially viable part of the entertainments industry.

The comics magazines *Eerie* and *Creepy* have catered, since 1965, for horror fans. They use themes which were portrayed in horror comics before the introduction of the Code, but the artistic level of the stories and the drawings is higher than ever before. From *Eerie* No. 14, drawn by Angelo Torres.
© 1967 Warren Publishing Company, New York City, USA

When attitudes alter and trends have become more liberal, even in organizations formerly opposed to progressive ideas, self-censorship is once more abandoned; we have seen this happen in the film industry. At one time the Film Production Code had become absolutely necessary for the continuance of Hollywood's industry—this self-censorship held back development in films for decades. In the television media of the USA free artistic development is curbed by the self-interest of commercial sponsors who wish to reach the broadest possible range of viewers and therefore oppose anything that may offend any one section. The larger the viewer public to be contacted, the more harmless and bland the programmes offered.

Self-censorship is a kind of barrier society erects to protect the *status quo*. In the case of crime comics the intention was to prevent a distortion of children's imagination and to keep it within the norms decreed by society.

The Comics Code also had its positive effects. More attention was given to dialogue and the standard of drawings rose, because after the shrinkage of the overall production incompetent graphic artists no longer found employment. Stories did not become less fanciful, but they tended to suffer from academic, stereotyped boredom—especially in the realm of science fiction—because violence in action was forbidden.

Self-censorship of comics had in one respect the same result self-censorship had on films: heroes of the Wild West shot much more accurately than ever before. Instead of just hitting a body, they now planted their bullets with breathtaking precision into a man's upper arm, or shot their opponents' guns clean out of their hands.

In the early sixties Stan Lee of Marvel showed the way out of the creative (and commercial) stagnation that had gripped the comics industry—without breaking the Code. His magic formula was to humanize the hero.

Comics in the classroom

Because of the combination of picture and text, comics can be a very useful aid in learning to read. Things and actions are made visual and names of objects are repeated many times in the course of a story so that new words are easily learnt and remembered.

Comics have been used in education for a long time. Their expressive way of imparting knowledge rivets the reader's attention and helps him to absorb the content. After the Second World War—in which they had so gallantly served as propaganda

material—comics began to be used for advertising government services. Pamphlets in comics form praised the army, the navy, the Department of Health, Education and Welfare (HEW) and many other government departments.

Results achieved in the educational process through comics are most gratifying. In the late forties more than 2,500 classes of primary schoolchildren learnt to read with the aid of a *Superman Work Book*, and today kids are still enjoying their lessons, because such well-loved comics-characters as *Steve Canyon* make it all so interesting and easy. Those of a scholarly bent can learn Latin or other languages together with *Peanuts*, though it sounds a bit odd to hear Charlie Brown declare in the middle of a baseball game: 'Garrulitas magna in campo interno magnopere

The Bible as comic book was a bestseller. Apart from the original *Picture Stories from the Bible*, various other editions were published. Shown here is the *Classics Illustrated* version, used in Sunday schools.
© 1947 Gilberton Company Inc.

jaculatorem cohortatur!' ('Lots of chatter in the infield is very inspiring to a pitcher!')

In 1941 The Parents' Institute, publishers of the *Parents Magazine,* brought out George Heckt's *True Comics* to prove to crticis that comics had their positive side. *True Comics* featured factual matter and true adventure stories concerning great (American) personalities of the past. *True Comics* were much praised—but not by the children. Commercial success was not overwhelming and after a few years they were discontinued.

M. C. Gaines, on the other hand (father of Bill Gaines of *MAD* fame), scored a phenomenal success with his *Picture Stories from The Bible.* During the forties this great innovator of comic books —he had, for instance, promoted *Superman* and *Wonder Woman* —experienced the joy of seeing his 'biblia pauperum' read in more than 2,000 Sunday schools. Up to date over five million copies have been sold. The crown of thorns, the crucifixion, the blood and the death produced the same awe-inspired thrills in readers of comics as they had in the readers of scores of American religious bestsellers. (*Life of the Martyrs* was later also available as a comic book.)

In 1945 M. C. Gaines started a publishing firm called Educational Comics and produced his famous *Picture Stories*; written under the guidance of educational experts, they became valuable teaching material in schools: *Picture Stories from Shakespeare. Picture Stories from Science, Picture Stories from Mythology, Picture Stories from Natural History, Picture Stories from American History.* Later, *Classics Illustrated* continued this type of comic book with their series, *The World Around Us.* E.C. also published comic books for adults, such as *Desert Dawn* (for the American Museum of Natural History) and *The Bible and the Working Man* (for the C.I.O. union).

The idea behind educational comic books is to give the child reading matter that entertains as well as teaches and to present informative matter in an interesting and enjoyable way.

Treasure Chest of Fun and Fact, still read in Sunday schools in the USA and Canada, is a perfect example of such comics. When *Treasure Chest* first appeared it dealt mainly with religious subjects. The publishers specialized in religious and educational publications, but had no direct connections with the established church. Later this policy was changed when it was realized that,

SIMPLY A Saint
The Story of Saint Gabriel

IN 1856, A YOUNG MAN FROM ASSISI, ITALY, SHOCKED HIS FAMILY WITH HIS DECISION TO GIVE UP A CAREFREE LIFE AND ENTER THE SEMINARY. HIS NAME WAS FRANCIS POSSENTI. ONE DAY HIS CHURCH WOULD NAME HIM SAINT GABRIEL OF OUR LADY OF SORROWS!

BUT YOU'RE NOT FIT TO ENTER THE SEMINARY, FRANCIS! IT WILL RUIN YOUR HEALTH. BESIDES, YOU HAVE A BRILLIANT FUTURE AHEAD OF YOU.

I WILL NEVER HAVE ANY PEACE, FATHER, UNTIL I GIVE MY LIFE COMPLETELY TO GOD. AND AFTER ALL, THAT IS THE MOST BRILLIANT CAREER ANY MAN CAN HAVE.

AS A YOUNG BOY, FRANCIS WAS KNOWN FOR HIS GENEROSITY.

THAT YOUNG BOY IS ALWAYS GIVING SOMETHING TO THE POOR.

IT SEEMS HE CAN'T STAND TO SEE ANYONE SUFFER.

...BUT FRANCIS HAD HIS FAULTS, TOO...

FRANCIS! WHAT HAPPENED TO YOU?

OH, NOTHING! I JUST HAD A LITTLE DIFFERENCE OF OPINION WITH ONE OF MY FRIENDS!

People very soon began to realize that comics could be used as educational aids. The *Treasure Chest* series of comic books started with mainly religious subjects for use in Sunday schools. From *Treasure Chest* Vol. 19, No. 5, drawn by John Tartaglione.
© 1963 T. S. Denison Co./Treasure Chest

in contrast to Gaines' *Picture Stories from the Bible, Treasure Chest* was not much used as educational material.

Nowadays harmless Disney-style dialogue, the achievements of great men, together with facts and jokes make up the contents of *Treasure Chest*.

On the whole comic books do not pretend to offer more than entertainment and the reader knows what he is buying; but as comics are read most avidly at an age when they could influence the development of literary taste, there is great anxiety that such reading matter may prevent literary taste from ever forming. Dr Spock allays such fears by commenting, quite rightly, that a child's taste in literature is not determined by what it reads at the age of (let's say) ten, but by the atmosphere in which it grows up.

Flaubert describes how the young Madame Bovary had been intoxicated by the contents of novels of the Walter Scott kind. Similar effects from comics are basically harmless. Critics fear that the ready-made images of comics, with their visual impact, might inhibit childish imagination; comics, they say, are no more than a waste of time, filling the mind with matter that does not enrich it.

But in comics, just as in fairy tales, the unreal quality of scenery and action stimulates imagination. In contrast to film and television which make an entirely passive reception possible, comics demand the co-operation of the reader in piecing together the pictures. The text alone does not furnish the story. The books for children which are always held up in preference to comics, but which have the same linguistic level, are in no way superior. The after-effect on a child's imagination is probably stronger with comics.

The *Classics Illustrated* aim at a symbiosis of comics appeal and 'good book'. The world's classics, so appetizingly arranged in comics form, are not meant as a substitute for the real thing, but try to awaken the reader's interest in great literature. They also offer an alternative to bad, violent or trashy comic books.

At the end of each booklet it says: 'Now that you have read the *Classics Illustrated* edition, don't miss the added enjoyment of reading the original, obtainable at your school or public library.'

Purists find this emasculation of the world's great literature unpardonable; but such objections are petty. *Classics Illustrated* take infinite pains in producing as near as possible a copy as the comics format will allow. That Goethe's *Faust*, part II, seems a bit short compared with the original version is a forgivable lapse, bearing in mind the readers' ages!

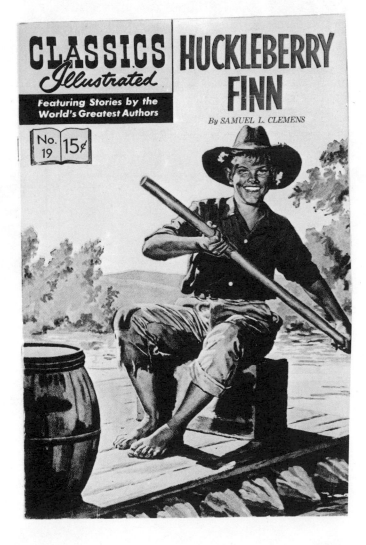

Classics Illustrated, a successful comics book version of classical literature. This series was not meant to replace the classics: it was meant to act as an introduction to them.
© 1967 Gilberton Company Inc.

JULIET, NOT KNOWING THAT ROMEO WAS IN THE ORCHARD, CAME OUT UPON HER BALCONY AND SPOKE ALOUD.

O ROMEO, ROMEO! WHEREFORE ART THOU
    ROMEO?
DENY THY FATHER AND REFUSE THY NAME;
OR, IF YOU WILT NOT, BE BUT SWORN
    MY LOVE,
AND I'LL NO LONGER BE A CAPULET.

SHALL I HEAR MORE, OR SHALL I SPEAK AT THIS?

'T IS BUT THY NAME THAT IS MY ENEMY;
WHAT'S MONTAGUE? IT IS NOR HAND,
    NOR FOOT,
NOR ARM, NOR FACE, NOR ANY OTHER
    PART
BELONGING TO A MAN.

O, BE SOME OTHER NAME!
WHAT'S IN A NAME? THAT WHICH WE
    CALL A ROSE
BY ANY OTHER WORD WOULD SMELL AS
    SWEET;
SO ROMEO WOULD, WERE HE NOT ROMEO
    CALL'D,
RETAIN THAT DEAR PERFECTION WHICH
    HE OWES*
WITHOUT THAT TITLE.

*possesses

Classics Illustrated are well able to awaken a child's or a young person's interest in the complexities of good literature.

Shakespeare, Dumas, Scott, Dickens, Cooper, etc., form the basic stock. In the first thirty years of publishing *Classics Illustrated* over one billion copies have been sold, including translations into over thirty foreign languages. There is also a *Classics Illustrated Junior Edition* which caters for children under ten years of age and tells fairy tales and legends.

C.I., too, has a sort of code which forbids the portrayal of cruelty, torture, etc., and asks writers and artists to observe the rules of good taste. The great majority of their issues are very well drawn by such excellent artists as George R. Evans, A. McWilliams, Jack Kirby and the naïvely-original Alexander Blum.

Thanks to *Classics Illustrated* out of the mouths of children may be heard:

From *Hamlet. Classics Illustrated* No. 99. Artist: Alexander Blum. © 1965 Gilberton Company Inc.

opposite

The *Classics Illustrated* adaptations of Shakespeare were particularly well prepared and faithful to the original; the artists were instructed to make sure that the costumes and decor were accurate. This extract is from *Romeo and Juliet, Classics Illustrated* No. 134. Artist: George R. Evans. © 1963 Gilberton Company Inc.

6 Society as portrayed in comics

The image of society imposed by censorship

At a meeting of the National Cartoonist Society in April 1962 Hal Foster told delegates of the many furious letters of protest he had received, because he had included Nubian Negro slaves, a Jewish merchant and an Irishman in his *Prince Valiant*. 'The only people you can draw are white, rich Protestants,' Foster commented.[1] This readership reaction only confirmed the syndicates in their policy to distribute only comics which did not give offence to any section of the public. Not only *Prince Valiant* (where it amounts to distortion of historical fact), but all strips, and particularly those with modern themes, were therefore cleaned of any controversial matter.

When Dale Messick included a Negro girl in a group of teenagers in *Brenda Starr*, the syndicate had her removed in order not to 'offend' readers in the Southern States.[2] Alfred Andriola told at the Comics Congress in Bordighera how he had to alter his strip *Kerry Drake* more than once before the syndicate would accept it. At one point he wanted to give a mysterious woman writer the name Jet Black, though she was not a black girl. The syndicate's censor objected, because he thought it might annoy black people among the readership. Andriola changed the name to Sable Black, because, like all compromises it did not shock anyone or mean anything.[3]

Asked whether he had ever had to alter a strip because of some real-life incident, Creig Flessel related how once, after the assassination of President Kennedy, he retouched a sequence from *David Crane*. In the first version a bank robber had been shot dead by a policeman whilst trying to escape. The syndicate feared that at that point in time the portrayal of an act of violence would not be a good thing;[4] so Flessel removed the policeman's revolver and the robber died of a heart attack.

Not even *Peanuts'* creator Charles Schulz was allowed to work entirely without restriction. He too had some of his *Peanuts* instalments returned. One sequence, in which Linus' blanket had come to life and jumped at Lucy, was turned down. The syndicate was of the opinion that such violence was unacceptable to the readership![5]

These particularly well-known examples of censorship all

In 1970 *Beetle Bailey* was suspended from papers of the southern states and the Pacific Edition of the *Stars and Stripes* for a while, because a Negro soldier called Lt Flap had been introduced into the strip.
© 1971 King Features/Bulls

The figure of Captain America, clad in the Stars and Stripes: the unconquerable spirit of the USA. An incarnation of the all-American ideal, he is indisputably an American institution. From *Captain America* No. 113. Artist: Jim Steranko.
© 1969 Marvel Comics Group

occurred some years ago; but newspapers also influence what 'goes' and what does not. They often alter series or ban 'offending' strips from their comics pages temporarily or permanently. Mort Walker's *Beetle Bailey*, for instance, was banned from the pages of *Stars and Stripes* from 1954 to 1955 because, so the pundits decreed, *Beetle Bailey* was bad for the soldiers' morale. After twenty years of exclusively white faces in the ranks of the *Beetle Bailey* army, Mort Walker thought it about time to include a black face and so he introduced Lt Flap, a black soldier with an Afro hairstyle and a goatee beard; whereupon the Atlantic Edition of *Stars and Stripes* appeared in October 1970(!) without *Beetle Bailey* and some papers in the deep South also banned this mildly satirical strip from their pages.[6]

These examples show only too clearly how strongly the image of society portrayed in comics is influenced by self-censorship. So as not to offend or annoy any citizen, sex, violence, social problems—in short all controversial matter—are brushed under the carpet.[7] The King Features Syndicate, for instance, states:

> . . . we have a 'Code of the Comics'. No blood, no torture, no horror, no controversial subjects such as religion, politics and race. Above all, is the important matter of good taste. The comics must be clean. No suggestive posturing and no indecent costumes. The figures must be natural and lifelike. In other words, 'Blondie', for example, is the daily doings in humorous form of a normal American family.[8]

Through many decades comics portrayed an idealized image of the 'America of the good old days'; an America which never existed outside the mass media. It was Norman Rockwell's America, as he used to paint it for the cover pictures of the *Saturday Evening Post*. It is of symbolic significance that the original *Saturday Evening Post* has ceased to exist.

Society's image in comics, expressed in statistics

Statistics arrived at through empirical investigations prove that comics do not give a 'true' picture of society. Publications dealing with comics rely heavily on the few investigations that have been undertaken.[9] They are almost invariably analyses of newspaper strips, offering a definite and circumscribed area for studies 'in depth'. Comic books, however, have been sadly neglected, because of the great difficulties involved in obtaining samples of discontinued editions.

The percentage of adventure, crime and family themes in comic strips is particularly interesting when we consider the picture painted by comics in the past. Rarely, though, have any researchers looked behind the scenes and evaluated these figures in the light of the comics' self-censorship.

It has been proved repeatedly that newspaper pages containing comics are the most widely read pages of any newspaper; also, that comics are read equally by all classes of society.

Francis E. Barcus' research into the world of the Sunday strip, in which he used a representative selection of strips that had appeared between 1943 and 1958, gave a clear picture of the distribution of various genres at that period. 64·2 per cent were humorous strips, 35·8 per cent adventure or melodrama-strips (of all kinds). 73·8 per cent of all strips with stories taking place in America were concerned with city life, whilst 80·9 per cent of foreign countries portrayed were shown as rural.

Characters in the strips of Barcus' survey seemed to be mainly either lower or middle class (10 and 68 per cent respectively). Gerhart Saenger, in a differently arranged breakdown, found 53 per cent belonging to the lower middle class. In Saenger's analyses two thirds of all male characters were white collar workers and only 12 per cent manual workers; despite this fact,

Frank King's *Gasoline Alley*, one of the institutions that accompany the average American from the cradle to the grave. In this sequence Skeezix, who arrived on the scene on 14 February 1921, is five years old (1925). In the background is the usual stereotyped black Mammie. © 1926 The Chicago Tribune/New York News Syndicate

Pottsy by Jay Irving. This strip about the good-natured policeman Pottsy gently sings the praises of the police force. Harry Hershfield's Abie the Agent reappears in this strip: he had previously introduced a little ethnic humour into the funnies.
© 1970 Chicago Tribune—New York News Syndicate

comic strips are often referred to as the proletarian novel, light entertainment for the Bumsteads of America.

72 per cent of the comics population is male; but whilst the bachelor adventurer is master of any situation, the married man tends to be ruled by his wife. Often the wife is drawn taller than the husband, as she definitely rules the roost. Aggressiveness shown by the male and female protagonists often changes at marriage: the formerly aggressive bachelor becomes meek and mild whilst the formerly defenceless little woman turns into a household dragon. Example: Blondie.

Ethnic minorities
Barcus found only one solitary Negro in 1958; 1950 strips, investigated by Spiegelmann, revealed none at all. Like all the other media, comics offered a world of social myths to the recipient and contributed among other things to the fact that the 'Black Man' became to many Americans an 'invisible man' (Ralph Ellison).

A strip not included in any of the surveys, because it was not a particularly successful series, was Tom Little's *Sunflower Street*; it did, however, run from 1934 until right into the fifties. In this strip Negroes were the main protagonists, but they were exclusively of the naïve, always jolly, Sambo type. Servants, who abounded in strips before the Second World War, were also more often than not of the black Sambo variety. Walt Wallet in *Gasoline Alley* was not the only character looked after by a black Mammie.

Early strips did show a certain amount of ethnic humour as, for instance in Harry Hershfield's Abie the Agent; but Schlemihl Abie Kabibble's humour was gentle and did not flow from the particular features of a Jewish minority, nor from its confrontation with the Goyim.

The humour in *Bringing Up Father* and *Mickey Finn* was at least in part drawn from the Irish origin of its main characters, though the only thing left to link Jiggs with the Emerald Isle seems to have been corned beef and cabbage. Policeman Mickey Finn, drawn by Lank Leonard, is also of Irish descent. He first went on patrol and later became Sheriff of a small town; but gradually his domineering Uncle Bill became the strip's main character. That Mickey's roots had been in Ireland can be guessed from his profession. (Most New York policemen were of Irish origin thanks to a wave of Irish immigration; hence the stereotype of the Irish policeman.) Only the knowledgeable reader will recognize the name Finn as that of a legendary Irish figure.

Not only blacks, but also poor whites, Puerto Ricans and the most neglected of all minorities, the Red Indians, were shamefully under-represented in comic strips; all those who did not fit into the ideal conception of an All-American USA never became protagonists in American comics. Only the concept of the Anglo-Saxon White, in short the WASP (White Anglo Saxon Protestant) was acceptable. Religion, however, was also taboo and at weddings the denomination of the couple was never made clear; as it was equally impossible to ignore religion, weddings

were limited to the words 'I do!' which are used by all denominations. Tarzan's wedding was apparently not quite neutral, for a New York newspaper of the Russian Orthodox Church eliminated the wedding scene and mentioned only the registry formalities in the text. If the religious affiliation of some character is, by chance, mentioned in a strip, they usually turn out to be Roman Catholic—a religion popular also with Hollywood.

If blacks or Red Indians were ever mentioned in comics, then it was always in such a way that the ethnic minorities among readers would identify themselves with the white protagonists, thereby denying their own origin and cultural background. In comics, just as in all other media, the chance to create a 'cultural and racial pluralism' was missed. By simply ignoring the members of ethnic minorities the great myth of the 'equal chance' for all Americans regardless of race, colour, origin or social class, could be preserved.

This split panel symbolizes the equality of all men and it prepares us for the end of the story, when the white racist (on the left) will be reformed thanks to the noble deeds of the Negro. From *Our Army at War* No. 179. Artist: Joe Kubert.
© 1967 National Periodical Publications Inc.

War: the great leveller

Worse almost than ignoring the very existence of the black man was the way he was so often portrayed when he did manage to appear in a strip. From about 1960 onwards the occasional token Negro appeared in comics to show how progressive the firm in question was. It was a kind of hypocritical, sham integration whereby in a quite unnecessary and dramatically inconsequential way 'white' roles were taken over by blacks.

In the mid-sixties the two most important battalions active in comics wars seemed to be thoroughly integrated: Easy Company in *Our Army at War* (DC) and the Howling Commandos in *Sergeant Fury* (Marvel) include all possible ethnic minorities in their ranks. The Howling Commandos sport Gabriel Jones, the Negro who can blow the trumpet so well(!): Dino Manelli, the Hollywood star of Italian origin; Izzy Cohen the Jewish mechanic from Brooklyn; Dum-Dum Dugan, the red-haired Irishman and Rebel Ralston, the guy from the deep South. Pinky the Englishman and Eric Koenig, the German, joined later.

Easy Company is similarly equipped; only here the token Negro, Jackie Johnson, is a former boxer and world champion. One better than the Howling Commandos, they even have a Red Indian: Little Sure Shot! (Marvel makes up for this lack in *Lieutenant Savage and His Rebel Raiders*.) Like many war films of the same kind, these comic strips include a white racist, who at the end of the story emerges as a reformed character. Usually the despised ethnic underdog (in the cases of *Our Army at War* and *Sergeant Fury* it is either Gabriel Jones or Jackie Johnson or Little Sure Shot), comes up trumps at a moment of grave peril, whereupon the benighted white racist sees the light and admits the equality of all races.

In the DC story 'What's the Color of Your Blood?' (November 1965), introduced with: 'Only Sgt. Rock dares to bring you the battle tale that's too hot to handle!', a member of the German master race is converted. Storm Trooper Uhlan (=Max Schmehling) is given the blood of Jackie Johnson (=Joe Louis) in a blood transfusion and has to admit that black men too have red blood.

An ethnically integrated fighting group had already been shown in *Blackhawk*, a comic book created by Will Eisner. Here the American leader of the group was joined by André, Chuck, Olaf, Stanislaus, Hendricksen and the Chinese factotum Chop-Chop. But all fighting troops are led by a real, all-American guy. Sergeant Rock of Easy Company comes from a mining district in the mid-west, and Sergeant Fury of the Howling Commandos from the slums of the Bronx. They demonstrate, by the fact that they are 'natural leaders', the true superiority of the real, one hundred per cent American.

In 1965 a German was made the
hero of an American comic book,
for the first time. Erich von
Hammer, 'The Hammer of Hell',
is the bravest of the fighter pilots
who appear in this story about
World War One. Both sides observe a very strict code of honour.
From *Star Spangled War Stories*
No. 138. Artist: Joe Kubert.
© 1968 National Periodical
Publications Inc.

The same distribution of roles goes for other genres too. In *Lone Ranger* it is always the white man who is the leader, the hero, the identification figure. Tonto, his Red Indian pal, invariably has to play second fiddle; as he still speaks in broken English after so many years it is perhaps no coincidence that *tonto* is Spanish for 'clot'[10]—and that is the reason why he is called Toro in the Mexican version of *The Lone Ranger (El Llanero Solitario)*.

Mandrake's right hand, Lothar, served for many years as the dumb, faithful factotum of the intelligent white man. But this black man, dressed in a lion skin and wearing a fez, could be trusted at first to perform only the simplest of tasks for the intellectual Mandrake.

Law and order

Ideological conflicts are tackled in comics—as in all the entertainment media—on the individual level. The main protagonists are the identification figures and what the identification figure does is always right, but in all presentations that serve to entertain, problems can only be shown in shortened, telescoped versions.

Jules Feiffer tells of a comic book of the forties which is a perfect example of society's image in comics: the story *Muss 'em Up Donovan* (*Centaur Funny Pages*) concerned the policeman Donovan, who was dismissed from the police because of his brutality (hence his name 'Muss 'em Up'!) but he is eventually asked to rejoin, because the legal methods of combating crime are too soft. The law cannot hold the gangsters in check: Muss 'em Up's methods are better![11]

Methods of eradicating crime by taking the law into one's own hands in order to hasten the return of law and order, without waiting for judicial procedure were given high praises. In Wild West stories these methods were elevated to the level of heroic myths. (John Ford's film *The Man Who Shot Liberty Valance* is the perfect example.) They also form the basic theme of the detective pulps. Mickey Spillane's Mike Hammer and Richard S. Prather's Shell Scott act exactly like 'Muss 'em Up' Donovan. Comic books use this theme (of taking the law into one's own hands) with particular gusto in super-hero stories; though Superman and Batman were relatively quickly promoted to honorary policemen, so that they would no longer act outside the law in their private wars against crime. In practice, however, nothing in their behaviour changed: action, violence and fighting for fighting's sake remains the main motive for all Superman and Batman stories.

Critics like Wertham claimed to detect fascist tendencies in super-heroes. In Wertham's view Superman glories in the right of the individual to take the law into his own hands.[12] In the super-heroes' overpowering might Wertham saw a relationship to the 'Nazi-Nietzschean "Übermensch" in his provincial apotheosis as Superman'. In Wertham's opinion the main task of these heroes was the elimination of foreign-looking villains. He maintained that super-hero comics 'showed us the world against a kind of fascist backcloth of violence, hatred and annihilation'.[13] This world is a 'crime-ridden Megalopolis'; it

has been given an almost mythological significance, for it has become the stage for adventure in the twentieth century, over which Superman watches from above.

Wertham was grateful for the fact that the S on Superman's breast was not an SS. Other critics saw in the jagged lightning portrayed on Captain Marvel's tunic one half of the SS troopers' emblem; and the get-up of Blackhawk and his troop reminded some of them fatally of the Storm Troopers' black uniforms.

Leslie Fiedler commented very perceptively on this controversy:

This is not quite the 'fascism' it is sometimes called. There is, for instance, no European anti-Semitism involved, despite the conventional hooked nose of the scientist-villain. (The inventors and chief producers of comic books have been, as it happens, Jews.) There is also no adulation of a dictator-figure on the model of Hitler or Stalin; though one of the archetypes of the Deliverer in the comics is called Superman, he is quite unlike the Nietzschean figure—it is the image of Cincinnatus which persists in him, an archetype that has possessed the American imagination since the time of Washington: the leader who enlists for the duration and retires unrewarded to obscurity.[14]

The super-heroes re-establish the rule of order: at the end of each story the *status quo* is once again the same as it was before the threatened danger had appeared. Whatever these heroic leader figures do is right, and so the wish-dreams of readers are fulfilled in both directions: the longing for law and order and the longing to break out of the tight circle of authority.

Comics producers and public taste

In the early fifties Charlton produced a booklet in which the main protagonists were Negroes; but it did not sell and the attempt at publishing a Negro romance comic book was discontinued. Time and time again it was proved that there had to be a definite demand for any special type of comic book unless, of course, profits were not important. Negro comic books? 'If we could sell them, we would make them. As simple as that.'[15]

A representative section of readers is questioned before a new comic strip even starts and further enquiries are made to ascertain whether it is a success and should be continued. Popularity of comic books is assessed month by month. To give just two examples: Marvel's *Silver Surfer* and DC's *Deadman* sank below a certain sales level and both of these excellent series ceased to be published. In order to be commercially viable as a mass medium comics must be addressed to the general public. Publishers of comics cover this up by calling themselves the servants of public taste. Success, they say, indicates what the majority likes, and besides, there are a great variety of comics to choose from; no reader is forced to buy what he or she does not like.

Both changes in public taste and ideological conflicts can be mirrored in any of the mass media, including comics, and the growing presentation of all such subjects in all the media shows how the rising generation is increasingly concerned with such matters.

However the conditions of production overrule most other considerations, for the contents of popular escapist mass media reflect the economic background of the nation. If a mass medium initiates new trends, as Marvel did by humanizing comics heroes, such moves are dictated by the opportunities the market offers, not by any deeper sociological reasons.

Producers of comics must have their ear to the ground and take note of the public consensus. Nothing goes out of demand more quickly than yesterday's formula. All the mass media profit from each other and from the current waves of fashion. They seize the new trends and make them popular in order to exploit them.

This type of topical reaction can be seen most clearly in the comics for teenagers, the *Archie* comics, for instance. In the seventy years of their existence comics have grown into a chronicle of changing public tastes. The image of society mirrored in comics has been conditioned by the mass media; the authors and artists themselves are influenced by the mass media and so is the work they produce.

The motto: 'If you've got a message, send it by Western Union' was appropriate for comics and films at a time when pseudo-engagement in ideological problems and explicit moral stories were not profitable, but they have now outgrown this phase. However the idea still prevails that comics (and particularly war comics) are pure entertainment, mindless distraction which conveys no message.[16]

Those who adhere to this concept believe that comics—as a mindless distraction—cannot do any harm. Humorous strips offer relaxation and imagined adventures satisfy the desire to flee from humdrum everyday existence. Comics, like film and television, are a substitute for unobtainable real life ambitions and desires, and each strip, each comics figure, has its relevance and its social function. The movies, the theatre, the books and magazines and newspapers—the whole system of mass culture as creator and purveyor of ideas, sentiments, attitudes and styles of behaviour—all this is what gives our life its form and its meaning. Mass culture is the screen through which we see reality and the mirror in which we see ourselves. Its ultimate tendency is even to supersede reality.[17]

Many a publisher of comics is only too aware of the social relevance of his products. Stan Lee of Marvel, for instance, who does try to be didactic to influence society through his publications.[18] Marvel is the perfect example of what Marshall McLuhan described as 'talking back to the media', for their contact with readers is expressed through a gigantic volume of readers' letters (and their replies).

Firms who maintain close contact with their readers receive a particularly heaving mailbag. (*MAD* received in 1960 over 2,000 letters per week.) The same applies to the big comic books publishers and only the 'best' readers' letters can be printed in the correspondence columns of comics. Each Marvel comic (over 20 titles) and each DC comic (over 50 titles) has one or two pages reserved for letters; they are sometimes the most entertaining part of the whole book! Through their letters readers give their verdict on any newly produced comic book—and the publishers take heed.

Marvel began very soon to answer readers' comments at length and often gave replies peppered with irony. A regular letter writing competition developed. Fans—all of them know the names of each author and artist by heart—used to make only brief comments as to mistakes or inaccuracies they thought to have discovered and, of course, changes among writers or graphic artists working for Marvel were always noticed with interest. But this was in the good old days, before the letters pages began to branch out.

In those blessed days design, text and content of comics formed the main topics of discussion, but today readers' letters pages are a forum for ideas on subjects like the value of American ideals, or the rejection of such ideals. (See the controversy raging around *Captain America*.)

Marvel's position on all questions raised is maintained not only in the strips presented and in the answers to readers' letters, but also in the soapbox, Stan Lee's regular column, where Marvel's moving spirit holds forth on any problem; he has developed a kind of Marvel philosophy. Stan's soapbox of March 1969 may serve as an example:

> One of the things we try to demonstrate in our yarns is that nobody is all good, or all bad. Even a shoddy-villain can have a redeeming trait, just as any howlin' hero might have his nutty hangups. One of the greatest barriers to real peace and justice in this troubled world is the feeling that everyone on the other side of the ideological fence is a 'bad guy'. We don't know if you're far-out radical, or Mr. Establishment himself —if you're black militant or a white liberal—if you're a pantin' protest marcher or a jolly John Bircher—but, whatever you are, don't get bogged down by kindergarten labels! It's time we learned how fruitless it is to think in terms of us and them—of black and white. Maybe, just maybe, the other side isn't all bad. Maybe your own point of view isn't the only one that's divinely inspired. Maybe we'll never find true understanding until we listen to the other guy; and until we realize that we can never march across the Rainbow Bridge to true Nirvana—unless we do it side-by-side!
>
> Excelsior!
> Smiley

Comics and advertising

Comics get their revenue not only from sales, but also to a large extent from advertisements. Large editions attract the advertiser, small editions are uninteresting from his point of view. Comics have an important voice in the ever-growing chorus of advertising.

Advertising agencies very soon realized the potentialities of comics in this respect, and just as in the case of radio (and later television), agencies sprang up to cater for comics advertising as early as the forties.

Analyses of readers' reactions showed that advertising was most effective when it was tailored to the style of the medium, and so advertisements in comics are styled like the comics themselves and are often drawn by well known comics artists. The advertising

Because of their great popularity, comics characters were very good material for advertisements. Al Capp's use here of his Fearless Fosdick in an advertisement for hair oil is as tasteless as most of his comic strip material.
© 1954 United Features Syndicate Inc./UPI

world recognized the expressiveness of comic strips as an excellent medium for advertising long before pop artists discovered the potentialities.

Popular comics figures can advertise directly, as the Peanuts do for Ford, Little Lulu for Kleenex, Blondie for Kodak or Al Capp's Fearless Fosdick for a hair oil, or comics figures specially designed for an advertisement experience adventures in short comic strips. 'Fresh Up' Charlie praised a make of lemonade, Captain Tootsie a brand of candies. Some, like the toy figures of Major Matt Mason or Captain Action, even had their own little comic books, or Big Little Books. How close the links are between the toy industry and comics becomes evident in the figure of Barbie the doll with its own very special comic book. Firms that advertise through comics benefit also from secondary exploitation of comics characters, that is they sell plastic figures, pictures and all manner of comics paraphernalia, or give such 'presents' away with the sale of their products. Breakfast cereal firms are particularly active in this field. Collectors now pay high prices for these paraphernalia.

Much more useful is Smokey, the bear who warns of the dangers of forest fires. He pleads his case in comic strips and also has a comic book devoted to his efforts.

In 1944 an advertisement of a third of a page in *Puck the Comic Weekly*—supplement to papers of the Hearst newspaper chain, with a circulation of roughly 7 million—already cost $9,500.

Comic books charged up to $3,000. In 1971 a four-colour whole page advertisement on one of the title pages cost, with DC for instance, $10,600; on one of the inside pages $7,475. The price charged gives the advertiser one published advert in all the DC comics, with an edition of 6·5 million copies per month. Terms vary, of course, according to how often an advertisement is placed; but it is possible to get an idea of how much up to fifteen pages of adverts (in a thirty-six page booklet) can bring in in a month! Funds raised by advertising serve, as they do in newspapers, to cover high costs of production and to keep retail prices low, so that, together with licence fees from abroad and direct sales, enough comes in to guarantee a profit. Only a large range of series can maintain a comics firm at a profitable level.

Even Western Publishing Company's comic books (Gold Key, published by Dell up to 1962), have carried advertising since 1969; they had not found this necessary at first, as Dell's publisher George T. Delacorte Jr. had taken over from the pulps the practice of enormously large editions which kept the dollars rolling in —despite the fact that around one third of the print run was not sold. But in the fifties the first adverts began to appear in Dell publications.

Advertisements in comic books aim at the age-group for which the book is designed: comics with lots of anthropomorphic animals for tiny tots carry adverts for candies and toys, Wild West comics will advertise air-guns.

153

An example of the behaviour accepted—
and expected—in Love Romances.
Stories like this are still very popular with
adolescent readers. The Code demands
that Love Romances stress the values of
home life and the sanctity of marriage.
From *Young Love* No. 80. Drawn by
Gray Morrow.
© 1970 National Periodical Publications
Inc.

Super-hero comic books go in for bodybuilding in a big way and used to advertise exclusively Charles Atlas gimmicks. Today, bodybuilding adverts still abound; and in the romance comic books girls are encouraged to buy bust-enlarging products.

One comic strip told the story of a poor weak man who had sand kicked into his eyes by some great big muscle-laden character on the beach. As he was a weakling, the little man not only had to pocket the insult, but he lost his girl friend as well, who now despised him for his lack of muscle power. Back home, eyeing his pitiable reflection in the mirror, he realizes that a course of Charles Atlas' bodybuilding is the only means of changing his lamentable fate. He enrols in a Charles Atlas home course and after a few short weeks emerges packed with muscles in all the right places. ('I was a 34 lb. weakling and gained 374 lbs. in a week. Send for free catalogue . . .' as *MAD* put it in a hilarious caricature.) Our friend now reappears at the beach where he socks muscle man number one a mighty blow in the face, whereupon errant girl friend returns to her former lover with glowing eyes: 'Why, you are a REAL He-man now!'

Direct advertising (Charles Atlas) and indirect publicity (Superman) work hand in hand. Comics offer in their characters the ideals which the consumer industries need. Straightforward advertising and indirect pressures which influence the subconscious mind of the reader complement each other; with muscles and busts it is the illusory expectation of perfect partners that is fostered in the readers' minds.

Publicity has long since forced the reader to accept the myth: 'blondes have more fun'! It is true that some raven-haired characters like Tarzan, Mandrake, Prince Valiant and Superman are distinguished by the bluish-black shimmer of their locks or sleek heads; but it is perhaps no coincidence that none of these heroic figures are 'true Americans' by birth, whilst Sgt Rock, Steve Canyon, Terry Lee and Captain America, in short all the typically American boys, have blond shocks of hair. (Whether they are also blue-eyed cannot be ascertained; printing methods make this a debatable point.)

Profits can rise to undreamed-of heights in a real boom, like the 'shmoo' wave (*Li'l Abner*) or the latest *Peanuts* enthusiasm. In 1955 it was the Davy Crockett wave which rose from the Disney Studios to swamp the entire nation. Everybody and everything wore Davy Crockett headgear—even Charlie Brown. Batman caused an even greater boom which was exploited by the production of one thousand and one Batman accessories.

Comics help, as part of the 'culture industry' (to borrow Adorno's expression) to condition readers, like Pavlov's dogs, to life in a consumer society, demanding that ever new needs be created which the consumer-industry can then exploit. Mass media, advertising and publicity combined see to it that public demand is currently created and expanded and the wheels that drive the economy of capitalist systems are kept running smoothly.

Comics: an American institution

300 million comic books sold in a year[19] and an estimated 100 million people reading comic strips every day; these figures give an idea of the gigantic spread of the comics mass media throughout the USA alone. Day after day comics entice readers into their world of fantasy. An endless stream of pictures, eternally churned out for all who were born after the turn of the century, with fixed patterns of behaviour and story contents to be exploited until doomsday: comics—the American institution.

How strong an influence the American institution has on comics readers can be gleaned from the intimate relationship between the public and its favourite comics characters. The flood of letters received at Raven's death in *Terry and the Pirates*, at Cookie's birth in *Blondie*, at the appearance of Lena the Hyena in *Li'l Abner*, or when Sandy in *Little Orphan Annie* had got lost—to mention only four All-American strips—is always held up as an example of the great popularity comics enjoy.

When in the thirties, for economic reasons, plans were made to cut down the space given to comics in newspapers, or to eliminate some strips altogether, Gallup Polls came up with the fact that comics were in many cases the main reason why people bought newspapers. (It was war-time austerity that forced comics formats to become smaller before and during the war years.) After having quickly scanned the headlines, the majority of newspaper readers pounce on the comics section. The frantic desire for relaxation and escapism could not be better illustrated; and the reader enjoys the escapism he gets from comics all the more because, thanks to censorship, comic strip contents mirror the tastes of the great majority. As the longing for this type of escapism is as strong today or stronger than it was seventy years ago, comics have continued in existence, have become a habit and a tradition with ritual overtones, and will go on flourishing as an important institution.

7 Inter-media dependencies

Faster than a speeding bullet! PWYONNG!—More powerful than a locomotive! . . . WHOOO-OOOT!—Able to leap tall buildings at a single bound! . . . WHOOOOOSH!—Look! Up in the sky! It's a bird! It's a plane! It's . . . SUPERMAN!

Title of the radio 'Superman' series

I must admit that 90% of comics are garbage, but I believe that to be the average for other fields as well—and nearer 100% for television.

Wallace Wood

History of the mass media

When in 1830 a steam-driven printing machine was invented, it meant not only the beginning of a mass-produced press, but also of mass-produced literature. Together with the need to produce a readership arose the now economically vital necessity to abolish illiteracy. Machines would be able to offer more than just the Bible as reading matter and so gradually, in the course of the nineteenth century, it became fashionable to learn to read—that is reading began to spread from a small elite to the masses. Newly won readers were attracted by cheap entertainment as much as by the offer of speedy information. Cheap entertainment began to be churned out in the form of serial stories which appeared in 'story papers'. In the States they were made to look like newspapers, so that they could qualify for cheaper postal rates; in England everything was done not to publish in newspaper format in order to avoid stamp duty.

New publishing firms, like Beadle & Adams, had small financial resources and as international copyright laws did not yet exist, the cheapest way to fill pages was to copy stories from abroad. American publishers pinched English and French stories; English publishers American and French stories; and only the French possessed their own regular story-tellers, such as Sue, Dumas and Féval, who wrote daily instalments of 'feuilletons'.[1] (In America and England stories appeared weekly.)

But soon America and England too began to produce home-grown authors bent on quick earnings. One of the first to become known as a writer of romances was Professor (Joseph Holt) Ingraham. Longfellow mentioned him in 1838:

A new American novelist has arisen; his name is Professor (Joseph Holt) Ingraham. . . . I think we may say that he writes the worst novels ever written by anybody. But they sell.[2]

Ingraham informed Longfellow in 1846 that he had by now written eighty romances, twenty of them in the preceding year.

Apart from their prolific output such authors were characterized by a passionate and sweeping style of writing; among them were Reynold and Lippard who were highly successful. American readers became used to the new style of literature and digested products much worse than those of Ingraham. Periodicals like *Uncle Sam* (1841), *Yankee* (1843), *Omnibus* (1844), *Flag of the Free* (1848) and *News of the World* (1848) did well on the new literary market. Two story papers which started in 1850, *New York Ledger* and *New York Weekly* were particularly clever in forcing sales. After 21 May 1859 the *Weekly*, having been taken over by Francis S. Smith and Francis S. Street, appeared as *Street & Smiths New York Weekly* with the sub-title 'A journal of Useful Knowledge, Romance, Amusement, &c.'. This journal and the *Ledger* employed their own authors and only occasionally

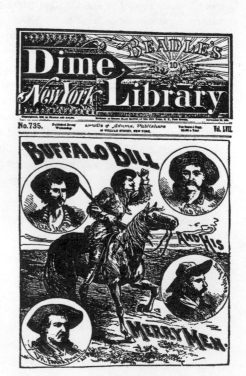

Dime novel of the nineteenth century. *Buffalo Bill* 1892 by Beadle & Adams is reminiscent of *Robin Hood and His Merry Men*. Beadle & Adams created the dime novel with Beadle's Dime Library which first appeared in 1860.

pinched foreign stories to fill gaps. The *Weekly* published series by Francis S. Smith and romances by Mary J. Holmes, the 'Queen of the Human Heart'. The Queen moved away from the general run of stories filled with ruffians, villains, mixers of poison and kidnappers and wrote exclusively of love's joys and pains. Her heroines were usually school-mistresses or poor seamstresses who pursued more or less tearful paths through life.

The first 'authentic' Wild West stories began to make their appearance side by side with love and adventure tales. Ned Buntline (Edward Zane Carroll Judson), famous in his day, told the Buffalo Bill stories; but Buntline's hero never spoke a rough or indecent word and never, never swore. The series about Nick Whiffles was a little more life-like. Nick did not figure simply as a kind of clothes horse on which to hang a story. The tall tales about him were written with a light hand; but Buffalo Bill, Kit Carson and Texas Jack became the heroes of the first Dime Novels, which glorified the killers of Red Indians and slaughterers of buffalo herds. This genre soon swamped the mass-literature market and produced trigger-happy heroes out of characters such as Wyatt Earp and Jesse James.

Ledger and *Weekly* were stiff competitors who used to entice each others' authors away by offering them higher fees—a mild forerunner of the sort of warfare that later raged between Pulitzer and Hearst. Well-known authors of the day were also approached, and some with success. In 1864 Horatio Alger wrote *Marie Bertrand, or the Felon's Daughter* for the *Weekly* and then turned to story writing for Boston newspapers; and in 1868 his *Ragged Dick; or, Street Life in New York* turned out to be a sensational success. Then in 1871 he returned to *Weekly* with *Abner Holden's Bound Boy or the Poor Relation*, and stayed on as permanently employed author. His innumerable stories— which up to 1907 also appeared in Dime Novels—successfully exploited the rags to riches theme and reached editions of one million.

But the end of the story papers was in sight. The newspapers' Sunday supplements and the cheaply produced reprints of English novelettes gradually edged them out of the market. After 1880 story papers tried to economize by publishing more and more reprints of old stories or taking over stories from other papers. A few publishers managed to change over to the production of cheap booklets, forerunners of the pulps which gained tremendous popularity a few decades later.

In the meantime the readers' interest had shifted to newspapers, the first comic strips and, most glowingly, to an entirely new medium: film. Films soon began to concentrate on themes similar to those the story papers had treated and on humour of the crazy type shown in early comic strips. The idea of filming endless series which left the viewer each week in new agonies of suspense, stemmed from the early serial stories, whilst the gag had been borrowed from comics.

J. Stuart Blackton drew the first cartoon film for Vitagraph, *Humorous Phases of Funny Faces* in 1905. It had a successful première in 1906 and marked the beginning of a most fruitful relationship between comic strip and film. The first cartoon film with a proper little story to it was *Gertie the Dinosaur* (1909),

drawn by Winsor McCay, the inventor of the *Little Nemo in Slumberland* series. In the same year the *Newlyweds*, George McManus' comic strip, appeared in a theatre version in the musical comedy *The Newlyweds and Their Baby (Snookums)*. The screens of that era showed *The Great Train Robbery* (1903), the first feature film, which at the same time was the first Western; after Edison's attempts in 1894 to present Annie Oakley and Buffalo Bill on film, and after the first coloured cartoon film, Paramount's *The Debut of Thomas Kat* (1913), came the first full-blown film series: *The Adventures of Kathlyn* (1913). It had thirteen instalments and was based on Harold MacGrath's novel, first published in 1913 as a serial in Hearst's newspapers and later, in 1914, also in book form.

To keep the public interested beyond the first wave of enthusiasm, the new medium relied mainly on series shown in instalments. Full-length feature films appeared only by and by; but right up and into the fifties, a full-length feature film would usually be accompanied in the USA by film serials continued in weekly instalments. In the end television wiped the film series off the cinema screens.

Exchange of ideas between the various entertainment media resulted in comic strips like *Mutt and Jeff*, *Happy Hooligan* and *Snookums* appearing as cartoon films; and in films like the Charlie Chaplin comedies, the exploits of the Keystone Cops or of Laurel and Hardy, supplying comics with many an excellent gag. In those days, when films were still silent, the relationship between comics and film was even closer. Film versions of Mutt and Jeff, for instance, used no title cards to explain the action, but worked the speech balloons into the cartoon film drawings; when the spectators had read their messages, the balloons would float away and explode.

All mass media, however, have one great disadvantage: they cost money; in most cases a lot of money—progress demands its price. Newly invented aids to the smooth working of the media were therefore closely inspected as to their probable capacity for aiding not only the technical processes, but also the promoting of greater profits. Nobody was willing to introduce expensive novelties unless they made the cash registers ring more impressively. Whether the outcome was artistically valuable or simply a load of trash was of minor importance, but once the financial potentialities of the mass media had been recognized, business went ahead and flourished. To make profits worthwhile, as large as possible a public had to be attracted and given the opportunity to partake in the enjoyment of mass media at the lowest possible price: only thus could films, newspapers, periodicals, or any other mass media, turn into viable and profitable undertakings.

Pulps—forerunners of comic books

The mass media which developed in the twentieth century, radio, television, pulps and comic books grew out of previously existing media, and the close interrelationship of all the media created a network that encompassed the old and the new.

If we proceed from the premise that film and comic strip influenced each other, it seems odd that thirty-two years passed—

Tarzan by Russ Manning.

between the *Katzenjammer Kids* and the first *Tarzan* strip—before adventure found its way into comics. The reason was that comic strips began simply as a continuation of the tradition of caricature and satire, and films, whilst making use of this tradition, drew also on the romantic novelettes and adventure stories of nineteenth-century story papers for inspiration. Demand for adventure in printed form, however, did not slacken and in the beginning of the twentieth century the pulps were the medium that satisfied it; only the gradual transition of comics from the grotesque, via the humorous everyday-life, to the adventure-story strip, prompted the pulp publishers to consider a changeover to comic books.

Pulps were mostly uncut periodicals and were printed—as their name suggests—on wood pulp. They had a handy format of 19 × 24 cm. Two thirds of their 128 pages (average number) covered the title story, the rest were given over to short stories. There were always roughly 250 different titles on display in newspaper shops and kiosks. The whole range of themes treated by the pulps appeared later also in radio, television, comic books and strips and even in films.

One of the most successful themes in pulps and later on the screen, and in radio and comics adaptations, was Edgar Rice Burroughs' *Tarzan of the Apes*. It was first published in 1912, in the *All Story Magazine* (later re-named *Argosy*). Eventually Burroughs published all his novels in book form, but most of his Tarzan, John Carter of Mars, Venus and Pellucidar tales appeared first in pulps like *All Story Magazine*, *Blue Book*, *Red Book* or *Amazing Stories*; and in 1918 Burroughs' most popular hero, Tarzan, began to conquer the film screens. In all, thirty-eight Tarzan feature films and film series were made.

Most films, starting with *Tarzan of the Apes* and *The Romance of Tarzan* (both 1918 and with Elmo Lincoln as Tarzan) borrowed only the motives and broad outlines of Burroughs' novels; only two much later films, *The New Adventures of Tarzan* (1935) and *Tarzan and the Green Goddess* (1936) show something of Burroughs' original concept of his hero; this was probably due to the fact that the production of these films was in the hands of Burroughs' Tarzan Enterprises, and that Herman Brix who played Tarzan was ideal for the part.

As Richard Lupoff[3] points out, Burroughs' tales were influenced by Rudyard Kipling's Mowgli stories, H. Rider Haggard's *Nada the Lily* (1892), the legend of Romulus and Remus and also by Harry Prentice's *Captured by Apes; or How Philip Garland Became King of Apeland* (1886). H. Rider Haggard's *She: A History of Adventure* (1886) may—perhaps together with Mabel Fuller Blodgett's *At the Queen's Mercy* (1897)—have stood at the cradle of some of Burroughs' Tarzan motives.

Tarzan's success went beyond the twenty-four published novels and a string of successful films and film serials. He proceeded to conquer the other media as well, after having initiated the adventure genre in comic strips[4] (1929). He swung through Big Little Books[5] and comic books, and first entered radio in a series of programmes called *Tarzan of the Apes*, written by Burroughs in successive instalments; starting in 1932, beginning with episode no. 287 (from 1934), it presented the many episodes of the adventure *Tarzan and the Diamond of Ashair*. This, in turn, was then published as a novel under the title *Tarzan and the Forbidden City* (1938). *Tarzan and the Fires of Thor* was presented in thirty-nine episodes in 1936, and in 1940 was illustrated by Rex Maxon for use in the daily *Tarzan* strips. In 1952 CBS

158

introduced the first of sixty-five half-hour shows dedicated to the adventures of *Tarzan, Lord of the Jungle*.

In 1921 Tarzan had lept on to the stage in a London theatre production of *Tarzan of the Apes. Li'l Abner, Superman* and *Peanuts* had to wait until 1956, 1966 and 1967 respectively, for their admittance through the stage door. Tarzan, always one jump ahead, graduated to television in 1966 in an American series that stretched across two years and which enriched Gold Key's comic book Tarzan instalments by four extra adventures taken from the television version. In 1972 the *Tarzan* comic book was taken over by DC Comics and Joe Kubert is now the artist. The new *Tarzan* comic book has an additional feature *John Carter of Mars*. Two other Burroughs series were featured in the same magazine as *Korak, Son of Tarzan*; they were *Pellucidar* and *Carson of Venus*.

Burroughs died on 19 March 1950, as he lay in bed reading the comics supplement of a Sunday paper. People say that he died just as he turned his attention to the *Tarzan* strip.

Another and most important American contribution to the literature of adventure was the Western, which appeared around the middle of the nineteenth century and rapidly gained popularity. During the peak years of pulp culture (1920–45) Westerns were in high demand. A ceaseless flood poured from the pens of authors with suitable pseudonyms like Ernest Haycox, Luke Short, Jonas Ward or Harry Sinclair Drago, and series included such titles as: *Western Rangers, Star Western, Bullseye Western, Ace High Western, Pioneer Western, .44 Western, Pecos Kid Western, Western Raider, Quick-Trigger Western, Western Trails, Pete Rice Western, Buck Jones Western, Range Riders Western, Rio Kid Western, Western Rodeo Romances, Masked Rider Western, Mavericks, Rangeland-Lore, Outlaws of the West, Texas Rangers, Golden West*, or simply *West*. Frederick Schiller Faust, the 'King of the pulps' whom most readers only knew under the name Max Brand or one of his other nineteen(!) pseudonyms, lived and wrote his novels (mainly Westerns) for a long time in Florence, where Aldous Huxley and D. H. Lawrence were his neighbours. At the height of his career he received a fee of 10 cents *per word*, a colossal sum compared with the customary rate of 1 cent per word for authors of pulp novels.

Faust, who hailed from California, was a man of perseverance and steady slogging. Every day he rattled off fourteen pages on his typewriter and his oeuvre grew to twenty-two million words distributed over 196 novels, 226 novelettes, 162 short stories, 44 poems and 56 films. Films included the *Dr Kildare* and *Destry* series; but he did not write the film scripts, only the novels on which the scenarios were then based. Decades later *Dr Kildare* was adapted for television, which in turn produced a comic book series and a comic strip; and Faust's Western series which had a hero called Silvertip was taken up by Western Publishing Company in 1958 and brought out as a comic book.

One of the best of the Western authors was possibly Zane Grey who was no pulp writer. His first book, *Betty Zane*, was published in 1904 and his novels headed the bestsellers' lists for years. Many of his themes were used in films, they inspired a television series (*Zane Grey Theatre*) and many comic books. Zane Grey was also the creator of the comic strip *King of the Royal Mounted*, which ran simultaneously as a radio series. He wrote some of the strip's episodes, but very often he only gave a story outline which was then turned into a strip by his son Romer Gray.

Apart from the Western the pulps offered a colossal range of subjects and comic books drew inspiration from all genres; only the comics' humorous series sprang from different sources. There seemed to be no theme that had not been tackled by pulps. Hersey Publications alone presented the bewildered reader with series like: *Flying Aces, Fire Fighters, Sky Birds, Loving Hearts, Underworld, Spy Stories, Mobs, Prison Stories, Speakeasy Stories, Strange Suicides, Quick-Trigger-Western, Thrills of the Jungle, Ghost Stories, Miracle Stories and Fantasy Stories, Speed Stories, Danger Trail* and *Dragnet*.[6]

Then there were already the so-called 'true' stories: *True Story, True Romances, True Experiences, True Ghost Stories, True Proposals, True Strange Stories, True Lovers*; all published in periodicals of the McFadden Group. How true they were has never been established; still, the magical word 'true' seemed irresistible to the addict and all such series (except *True Comics*[7]) had tremendous success in pulps as well as in comic books.

But the most lucrative idea the comics ever drew out of pulps was that of the masked super-hero. One of the most popular models was *The Shadow*. He appeared first in *The Shadow of Wall Street*, published in 1929 in Street & Smith's periodical *Fame and Fortune*.

At that time publishers sought and made connection with radio.[8] Broadcasters too were constantly searching for new material. The Street & Smith mystery series went on the air on Thursday night. The commentator was a hollow-voiced mystery man known to listeners only as The Shadow, who never neglected to draw attention to a new magazine, the *Detective Story Magazine*, soon to be published. Listeners liked the idea of a ghostly voice and to prevent other radio stations from imitating The Shadow, Street & Smith protected their idea with the copyright for a magazine called *The Shadow*. Nobody expected the magazine as such to be a great success and it was to be published as a quarterly, but the first number, *The Living Shadow*, sold like hot cakes, and so number two, *Eyes of the Shadow*, was published the following month. Walter Brown Gibson, who had written the first novel in the series, now took the pseudonym of Maxwell Grant and proceeded to write 282 of the 325(!) *Shadow* novels. They appeared regularly until the summer of 1949. Bruce Elliott, author of the Flash Gordon television series, wrote some of the forty-three remaining tales. An author writing for pulps had to write fast; in this Maxwell Grant (alias Walter Brown Gibson) excelled and some of his novels were written within a week.

The success of *The Shadow* in pulps influenced the radio series and the firm of Blue Coal offered to sponsor broadcasts in which The Shadow would be the star, but with some modifications. In the novel the Shadow had a threefold identity; in real life he was Kent Allard, who roamed the world as Lamont Cranston, who in turn, with the help of friends, played the role of The Shadow in order to fight crime. Radio cut out Kent Allard but kept the

The romances in the pulps were echoed in the comic books of the forties, and even today a large number of comic strips are love stories.
© 1954 Charlton Comics Group (top left)
© 1967 Charlton Comics Group (top right)
© 1970 National Periodical Productions (bottom left)

double identity Lamont Cranston/The Shadow; a girlfriend called Margo Lane was introduced; and whereas the pulp version of The Shadow could make himself invisible by some mysterious means, the radio Shadow's hypnotic personality had the gift 'to cloud men's minds so that they could not see him'.

The radio series was given the introduction, spoken by The Shadow in the hollowest of voices: 'Who knows what evil lurks in the hearts of men? THE SHADOW KNOWS!' and was already highly popular when Orson Welles took The Shadow's part (1937–9).[9] The series, now broadcast on Sunday afternoon, survived until 1954. It unleashed a flood of Shadow paraphernalia: book editions, games, torches, writing pads, masks, suits; Big Little Books, films, comic books and a comic strip by Vernon Greene followed. An attempt was made to revive the Shadow comic book in 1965, but it failed; pocket book editions of the novels, however, published since 1969, are still going strong.

Another Street & Smith success was *Doc Savage*, a pulp series starting in 1933 with *The Man of Bronze*. 165 of the 181 novels in the series were written by Lester Dent under the pseudonym of Kenneth Robson. *The Shadow* fought against cruel and cunning foes like The Black Master, Green Eyes, The Blue Sphinx, The Creeper, Quetzal, Silver Skull, The Voice, or against whole groups like The Crime Cult, Six Men of Evil, Brothers of Doom or the Hydra. Doc Savage, 'The Mental Marvel', had to do battle with The Red Skull, The Czar of Fear, Mad Eyes, The Black Black Witch, The Thing That Pursued and The Pure Evil (names foreshadowing the later super-villains of comic books). Doc's war against crime always took place in broad daylight—in contrast to The Shadow's nocturnal exploits—and Doc confronted enemies the world over, whilst The Shadow limited his crusades against villainy mostly to his own City (as Batman and Spider-Man did later).

Doc Savage lasted till 1949 and was in the end pushed off the stage—like so many of the other pulp heroes—by the rising popularity of comics. He may have been a direct forerunner of *Superman*; he was always called Superman in advertisements.[10] The Shadow, with his bat-like cloak and another series called *The Black Bat*, may have inspired such early comic book characters as Batman, or Mandrake the Magician, or any of the other magic manipulators. Doc Savage has in the meantime found a new lease of life in paperbacks and he appeared—briefly—in one comic book in 1966.

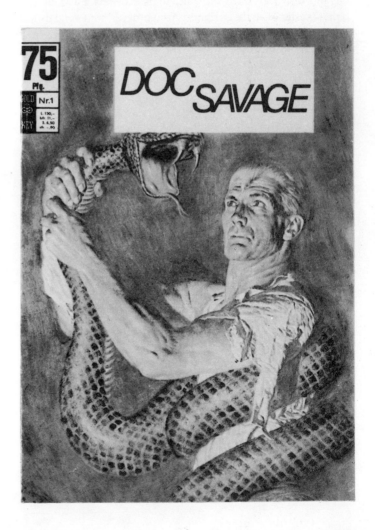

Doc Savage, a rival of *The Shadow*, figured in the pulps and was a forerunner of *Superman*.

The Phantom Detective (1933–53) and *The Spider* (1933–43), two modern avengers leading double lives, belong to the playboy-detective type (like *Batman* and *The Green Hornet*). This species also appears in other genres: in cloak and sword romances like *The Scarlet Pimpernel* or in early Westerns, like the figure of Don Diego de la Vegas in *Zorro*. (The latter graduated from pulps to film, television and comics.) *The Spider* was different in that he took the law very firmly into his own hands and eliminated criminals without a qualm; he represented the extreme Right in the pulps and was heartily hated by underworld and police alike. Seen from this point of view *The Spider* series is a forerunner of the Italian *fumetti neri*. Columbia produced a film series based on the Spider novels in 1938; it was called *The Spider's Web*.

The concept of the masked avenger had already become known in 1913 through the French film series *Fantomas* (Louis Feuillade) and it had spread to America, where a similarly negative hero, Fu Manchu, appeared. He was created by Sax Rohmer. The first novel in the series, *The Mystery of Dr Fu Manchu*, was published as a serial in *Collier's Weekly* in 1913; in 1923 a film series appeared under the same title (in fifteen parts!) and at least eleven further films and film series followed. In 1931 a *Fu Manchu* comic strip was produced in the USA and in 1962 a strip based on the novels appeared in France; finally a television series around this anti-hero held Americans glued to their TV sets. Fu Manchu is the ancestor of all the intriguing Asiatic 'devils' who wend their sinister way through the mass media. In comic books Fang, Archfiend of the Orient, and The Mandarin (both Marvel villains) were the two most prominent examples of the species.

Two further types of pulp novels greedily absorbed by film, radio, television and comic books were horror and fantasy. Robert E. Howard's *King Kull* and *Conan the Cimmerian* belonged to the 'sword and sorcery' variety, developed from Burroughs' themes. Most of Howard's stories appeared in *Weird Tales*, a magazine that also published most of Howard Phillips Lovecraft's 52 stories. The latter's 'sorcery sagas' dispensed with the sword and concentrated entirely on the supernatural; on the Cthulhu myth and the dream land of Kadath. Lovecraft, today considered by many the legitimate heir of Edgar Allan Poe's kingdom of horror, was indeed the best of a bunch of authors dabbling in the supernatural. The others, whose work was published in *Dime Mystery Magazine*, *Horror Stories* or *Terror Tales*, were responsible for the name 'Bloody pulps' which people began to give to any periodical of that type. Horror pulps were good business, were bought at a rate of 150,000 copies per month and created the same kind of furore that later raged around horror comics.

When the first comic books appeared, publishers of pulps were delighted. They realized that this new medium could tell tales more quickly and more interestingly than even the pulps had done. In *Timely Comics* (today's Marvel) Martin Goodman used the same formulas that had served him so well in his pulps; and Fiction House turned its dime novel booklets *Planet*, *Jungle* and *Wings* into comic books. Standard, Fawcett and Donenfeld did the same with their pulps. Pulp heroes fell left, right and centre—to be reborn in comic books.

A few pulps survived as superior entertaining magazines printed on better paper, among them *Argosy*, *True*, *Analog*, *If*, *Red Book* and *Ellery Queen's Mystery Magazine*;[11] today the old type seems to be reappearing sporadically under titles like *Gothic Romances* or *Horror Stories*, trying to open up once again the money-spinning possibilities of cheap pulps.

Radio series—comics without pictures

America's broadcasting networks started to get going at roughly the same time as the pulps. On 2 November 1920 the results of the Harding/Cox Presidential elections were broadcast on station KDKA—the radio era had arrived. In 1922 the first melodrama went on the air and soon all kinds of entertaining series were carried into American homes. Apart from themes lifted straight out of pulps, broadcasting studios offered quite a variety of home-grown productions.

One of the most long-lived adventure series of American broadcasting was no doubt George W. Trendle's *The Lone Ranger*. Three times a week, starting Monday 20 January 1933, to Friday 3 September 1954, episode after episode poured out of radio sets all over the USA. The success was phenomenal and soon all the paraphernalia dreamt up by astute business interests for such occasions cascaded onto the market: Big Little Books, hard-back books, sundry textile and stationery articles, toys, etc. etc. Then came two feature films, several television films and, as the latest contribution, a coloured television cartoon-film series; apart from all that *The Lone Ranger* triumphed not only in his immensely popular comic strip, but also in roughly 160 comic books.

The radio series had no picture—the comics no sound, and just as the comics tried to substitute the missing sound by all manner of onomatopoeic text, speech balloons and the like, so the broadcasting studios tried to create the illusion of a picture by clever sound effects. Comic books have titles that almost leap out at you —and each radio series has its own distinctive introduction: in *The Lone Ranger*'s case it was the 'William Tell' overture. Detroit's broadcasting station, which broadcast *The Lone Ranger* produced two other, equally successful series: *Sergeant Preston of the Yukon* and *The Green Hornet*; both were later enthusiastically received as comic books and on television. These series, too, had well-known musical leitmotifs.

Quite apart from the many radio series, broadcasting also tried to make use of the sound film. Feature films became 'radio novels', or were broadcast, in Hollywood Radio Theatre for instance, as radio plays acted in front of a studio audience. Many popular actors and actresses liked broadcasting and Al Jolson, known as The Singing Fool, had his own radio show; so did Gene Autry and Roy Rogers, the singing (film) cowboys. Gene Autry, discovered by Will Rogers, was for many years the star of his own radio programme and became equally popular in his television Westerns. His peak years were 1935 to 1950. Both these cowboy types also featured in comic strips and books. The Roy Rogers comic books were drawn by such fine artists as Albert Micale, John Buscema and Alex Toth. The Wild West adventures of Dale

The Lone Ranger. (German version.) Since 1938 the Lone Ranger has been featured in Big Little Books, comic strips and comic books. From 1948–61 Clayton Moore acted the part of the Lone Ranger on television and also in two feature films. From 1933–54 there was a radio series devoted to the Lone Ranger.
© 1971, 1960 The Lone Ranger Inc./Bildschriftenverlag GmbH

Evans, Roy Rogers' wife, were mostly drawn by Russ Manning.

Comic strips and books also became material for radio series. Strips like *Blondie, Flash Gordon, Buck Rogers, Dick Tracy, Red Ryder, Prince Valiant, Little Orphan Annie, Mandrake, Terry and the Pirates* and comic books like *Batman, Superman* and *Green Lantern* did very well on radio, and the popularity of the programmes reflected back on the strips and comic books and in turn heightened their popularity.

Superman broadcasts started on 12 February 1940 and quickly developed into a great success, particularly with children. In the comic books, thought balloons explain Superman's motives, but radio cannot produce thought balloons and so Jimmy Olsen was invented to give Superman someone to whom he could open his mind and heart whenever the listener needed explanation or comment. Radio also added green kryptonite which, together with Jimmy Olsen, then found its way into the comic book *Superman*; roughly a decade later Jimmy Olsen had become so popular that he was actually given his own comic book. The radio adventures of Batman and Robin were part of the *Superman* series.

Interaction between film, radio, television and comics

Superman and Batman became film stars as well as radio stars. In 1941 eighteen Superman cartoon films were produced by Paramount under the direction of Dave Fleischer. Mort Weisinger, who had taken over the editorship of the *Superman* comic books (also 1941) had come from the comics' science fiction sector and it was therefore natural that he should underline science fiction appeal in *Superman*. He wrote two film series for Columbia: *Superman* (1948) and *Superman versus the Atom Man* (1950); *Superman and the Mole Men* (1951) was followed by a television series in which the same actors took part, and in 1967 Superman reappeared on the TV screen in cartoon film series.

Batman and his pal Robin appeared in 1943 in *Batman and Robin*, a Columbia film series in which the two heroes fought against the Japanese villain Dr Daka and his zombies; one of the few instances in which Batman took an active part in the war. (A background of music by Wagner added to the film's attraction.) In 1948 *The New Adventures of Batman and Robin* was filmed, and finally, in 1966, there followed a television series and a Cinemascope film of the two buddies' exploits.

Batman became a highly successful TV series which in turn resulted in a Cinemascope film. Drawings by Carmino Infantino.
© 1966 National Periodical Publications Inc./Centfox Film

Films breathed new life into the stereotyped pictures of comics. *Mandrake, Buck Rogers, Phantom* and *Flash Gordon* were admired on the screen and afterwards fans returned to reading their comics. *Prince Valiant*, filmed in 1953 under the direction of Henry Hathaway and with Robert Wagner in the title role, spanned only one episode of this vast epic; but it proved to be the most successful film version of any comic strip. In the meantime the comic's Prince Valiant continued to enthral his admirers year after year. Prince Valiant's film and the television series featuring Steve Canyon, were also responsible for the fact that these two comic strips appeared in comic books. Reprints of strips became scarce, once comic books had appeared on the market, and even the most popular strips reached the comic books only via different media (*Tales of the Green Beret*) and in new adaptations (*Brenda Starr* and *On Stage*).

But film companies also swapped, pinched or enlarged each others' ideas. Sometimes a particularly successful film would be copied—in a slightly modified version—by some other firm, or the same firm would expand it into a series; whereby the quality of the 'follow-up' usually sank far below that of the original film. Examples of series developed from an original film include *Dr. Kildare* (based on Max Brand's novel), *Going My Way* (Oscar winner of 1944), *The Thin Man* and *Lassie* and all these film series were later also turned into television series. As well as these fifteen-part instalment films, many B-films were also developed into series; each instalment would be shown together with the main feature film of the current programme. They include the Western series about Hopalong Cassidy, Wild Bill Elliott, Roy Rogers, Gene Autry, Cisco Kid, Gabby Hayes, Lash La Rue, Rocky Lane and Tom Mix. (It goes without saying that these film series all had their own comic books.) The advent of television has made this type of film series obsolete, but film companies still try to exploit certain trends (the Western wave or the sex wave, for instance) and every now and then series based on particular characters are filmed: James Bond, Flint, Django.

opposite
Flash Gordon by Al Williamson. Created by Alex Raymond in 1934. There was also a radio series and eventually a television series and a series of films starring Buster Crabbe. From *Flash Gordon* No. 5.
© 1967 King Features Syndicate

Maverick. Left: scene from the TV series with James Garner as Bret Maverick. *Right:* the same scene in the comic book. Note how the action from various film takes is condensed into one single scene. From *Maverick* O.S. 962; drawn by Dan Spiegle.
© 1958 Warner Brothers Pictures Inc./Licensing Corporation of America/Western Publishing Company Inc.

Gradually, thanks to ever increasing production, constant demand for novelties and the parallelism of the media, there developed a catastrophic dearth of ideas. New themes had to be found, new trends invented. Each medium hoped to get some benefit out of another medium's success and so the interrelationship between the different media became ever tighter. Radio, film, television, comic strips and books, magazines, story magazines, hard-back books, paperbacks and newspapers are dependent on each other. The pulps had made their contributions to film, radio, television and comics. Comics strips and books gave ideas to film producers, broadcasters and authors; films, in turn, produced the book, or the comic 'book of the film'. The theatre and the fine arts are part of this gigantic network, and neither 'folk art' nor inter-personal communication should be excluded.

After an initial struggle the mass media have developed into industries. These industries in turn created secondary industries to supply the incredible paraphernalia that backs up the success of a film, a radio series, a comic strip or a comic book: images of heroes, dolls, parts of a hero's uniform (Green Lantern's ring, Buck Roger's helmet, Tom Mix's guns, Matt Dillon's Sheriff's star), calendars (Peanuts), Disney wallpaper, children's mugs

formed like the head of Fred Flintstone, Superman and Batman costumes. Countless fan clubs aid and abet these industries by creating ever new demands for such gimmicks.

Film and television tie-ins readily exploit the popularity of any given character; hence the comic book versions of films. There has to be a certain similarity between the beloved hero on the screen and his counterpart in a comic book, but usually the resemblance is confined to a more or less successful portrait of the character in question. *Movie Classics* (comic book versions of films) must be produced well in advance of the publishing date, because they are supposed to reach the public at the same time as the film they complement. They are therefore designed with the original film script—and not the finished film-version—as model, and consequently there are differences; necessary cuts add to the divergencies. Scenery can be very different, as the designer works from his own research material and not from the film setting (except, perhaps, for an important scene where scenery or decor influence the action); though comics have great potentialities for expressing film-ideas, specific scenes or sequences of a film are only shown if they happen to fit into the general pattern of the comics version. The same applies, of course, to television series turned into comic books.

Among the many films that have inspired comic books—in the hope of reciprocal publicity—were practically all the famous screen spectacles, such as *Mutiny on the Bounty*, *Ben Hur*, *Last Train from Gun Hill*, *Rio Bravo*, *How the West Was Won*, *Lord Jim* and *The Fall of the Roman Empire*; and all the Disney films (comic books by Western Publishing Co.) and after 1962 John Ford's *Cheyenne Autumn*, Howard Hawk's *El Dorado*, Henry Hathaway's *The Sons of Kathie Elder* (published by Dell); and horror films like *The Mummy* or *Frankenstein* appeared in shortened versions in the appropriate magazines *Eerie* and *Creepy*, and in the other specialized booklets of the Warren Publishing Company.

Over 150 comic book series and one-shot issues were based on television series. Particularly successful ones became regularly published comic books. The tremendously successful 'adult Western' radio series *Gunsmoke* by John Meston and Norman Macdonnell (broadcast from 1950 to 1961) was taken over by television with equal success and became one of the longest running Wild West series. The first number of the *Gunsmoke* comic book appeared in February 1956 and after it had reached number six it established itself as a regularly published comic book series. Numbers 15 to 26 were designed by Alberto Giolitti, a particularly gifted artist, and since then *Gunsmoke* illustrations have often been swiped (or quoted) by European Western series; but some American graphic artists also take *Gunsmoke* as their model. The London *Daily Express* has carried *Gunsmoke* as a comic strip under the title *Gun Law* for over a decade, and Gold Key has even published a booklet showing stills from the television film with appropriate text underneath each photo.

From *Eerie*. Comics version of the horror film *The Mummy* (1932). The illustrations keep close to the character of the film, down to the lighting and Boris Karloff's make-up (by Jack Pierce). Drawn by Wallace Wood. © 1967 Warren Publishing Co., New York City, USA

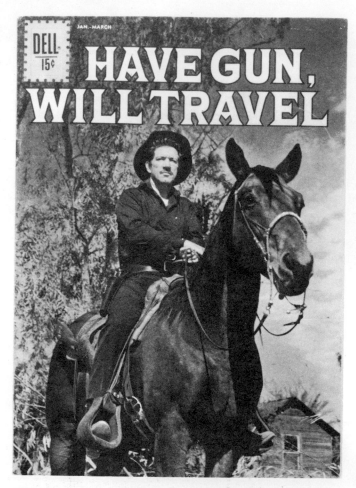

Have Gun, Will Travel. Paladin, the hero of this strip, was always dressed in black. He was a skilled marksman and he also had a surprising love of Shakespeare.
© 1962 Columbia Broadcasting System Inc./Western Publishing Co. Inc.

Gunsmoke. The most popular television series became popular comic books; those drawn by Alberto Giolitti were especially successful.
© 1960 Columbia Broadcasting System Inc./Western Publishing Co. Inc.

Have Gun, Will Travel by Sam Rolfe and Herb Meadows, a series which reached television via radio on 14 September 1957 also blossomed into a comic book; as did *Tales of Wells Fargo* by Frank Gruber (television series started 18 March 1957), *Sergeant Preston of the Yukon* (television via radio) and *The Cisco Kid*. Many booklets in these series were drawn by Alberto Giolitti, the *Gunsmoke* artist, who also designed *Turok Son of Stone*, some of the Tarzan books and sundry other television or film-based comic books. The series turned into comic books are legion: *Bonanza, Cheyenne, Rawhide, Lawman, Sugarfoot, Tales of the Texas Rangers, Wagon Train, Casey Jones, Rin Tin Tin, The Rifleman, Laramie, Maverick, Wyatt Earp* are just a few of the Western lines; *77 Sunset Strip, The Untouchables, The Man from U.N.C.L.E., Peter Gunn, The Detectives, I Spy, John Drake,* in the detective and spy-fever genre; *Star Trek, Voyage to the Bottom of the Sea, Land of Giants, Time Tunnel, The Invaders,* in the science fiction stakes; *Sea Hunt, Lassie, Circus Bay, Fury* and sundry other adventure series, including *Walt Disney's World of*

Adventure; and light entertainment like *I Love Lucy, The Three Stooges, Leave it to Beaver, Father Knows Best, The Munsters, Mister Ed, My Favourite Martian, The Real McCoys,* and *Oh! Susanna Gale Storm.*

In some cases only a few numbers or just a single booklet (called a one-shot issue) was published, as with *The Texan, The Gray Ghost, Shotgun Slade, The High Chapparal, The Virginian, Tombstone Territory, Men into Space, Ripcord, Wanted: Dead or Alive, The Troubleshooters, Whirlybirds, Flipper* and *The Aquanauts.*

Books based on television series, produced by Western Publishing Company, proved so successful that Dell (with 6 million booklets per month) was at times the biggest comic books publisher. But lately the demand for comic books based on films or TV series has slackened; partly because of high licence fees and profit-sharing demands, partly because television has lost its novelty appeal and fans no longer wish to re-live series in comic books.

Exchange of themes between the media tend to take place at definite and crucial periods, when the necessity to progress with the times, to adjust entertainment to social and political developments becomes pressing. The mass media received new impulses in the restless era around the turn of the century, during the First World War, the great economic depression, during the New Deal era, the Second World War, the Korean War and the Vietnam War with its attendant reassessment of values.

This parallelism in the media also affected the artists who worked in them. Techniques of film photography and cutting influenced the designers of comics, the storytelling techniques of novels and comic strips had influence on film and television. Orson Welles' film *Citizen Kane* was 'comics-oriented', some critics said; but much more important than a possible effect of comics on *Citizen Kane* was the stimulus comics *received* from this revolutionary experimental film. Steranko said that *Citizen Kane* had influenced comic books in particular. Bill Finger, Bob Kane and Jerry Robinson, author, designer and assistant designer

of *Batman*, went to see *Citizen Kane* a dozen times to learn from its dynamic style of narrative.[12] Other films too had significance for producers of comics and influenced their work.

Naturally, influence exchanged between media can be good or bad, but the effects flow from changes in storytelling techniques rather than from the quality of material exchanged. Silent film and comic strip techniques, for instance, resemble each other in the way they tell a story. Text is blended into the picture in a similar way in both media; film-cutting techniques and sequences of pictures in comic strips follow the same principles. The idea of a commentator is shared by all the media. In radio series such as *Lights Out* and *Inner Sanctum Mystery*, and in television programmes like *Thriller, Alfred Hitchcock Presents* and *Twilight Zone*, a storyteller gives the necessary outline and comment; the same applies to comic books: *Boris Karloff's Tales of Mystery, The Twilight Zone, Tower of Shadows, House of Mystery*, for instance; and the pulps have editors who write comments to stories and act as compère to their readers.

Lawman. Both a television series and a comic strip.
© 1960 Warner Brothers Pictures Inc./Licensing Corporation of America/Western Publishing Co. Inc.

77 Sunset Strip. Both a television series and a comic strip.
© 1962 Warner Brothers Pictures Inc./Licensing Corporation of America/Western Publishing Co. Inc.

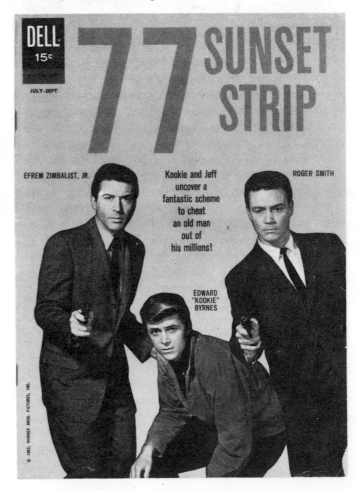

The Cisco Kid by José Luis Salinas; long before O. Henry's Cisco Kid arrived in comic books he had appeared on radio, television and in film. Salinas sent his drawings for the strip from the Argentine.
© 1968 King Features/Bulls

Films have given a new impetus to comics and comics, in turn, have reflected their image into films. European film directors were the first to admit they were using ideas taken from comics. Alain Resnais's *Last Year in Marienbad* is said to have a comics style of story telling, and in *8½* Fellini made use of the comics technique, emphasizing particular characters or scenes by contrasts of light and shade. In France it is above all Alain Resnais, Louis de Broca, François Truffaut and Jean-Luc Godard who have been inspired by the comics style or, as in the films *Pierrot le fou* and *Fahrenheit 451*, have used comics as a feature of the action. In 1971 Marvel's Stan Lee even wrote the scenario for a film which Alain Resnais was to produce.

Konga by Steve Ditko. The film *King Kong* was responsible for the King Kong Comics and also for a number of imitations, such as *Konga*. For a long time Steve Ditko produced fantastic stories for Marvel and Charlton. From *Fantastic Giants* No. 24.
© 1966 Charlton Comics Group

Snow White and the Seven Dwarfs (1937). This was Disney's first full-length cartoon film. The comic book of the film was so successful that it was reprinted four times in the USA alone.
© Walt Disney Productions

The cartoon film

The most obvious direct relationship exists between comics and cartoon films. The idea of the animated cartoon is almost as old as comics and the artist who drew the first successful cartoon film was a comic designer. *Mutt and Jeff*, *Felix the Cat* and many other series were turned into cartoon films between 1916 and 1925; but the breakthrough came with Mickey Mouse, invented 1925, who triumphed in the first cartoon film with sound: *Steamboat Willie*. Walt Disney's cartoon films ushered in a whole new era: The *Silly Symphonies* popularized the colour film and with *Snow White and the Seven Dwarfs* the first full-length cartoon film enraptured children and adults alike. The seven dwarfs were drawn and 'animated' by Vladimir (Bill) Tytla and Fred Moore; but although Disney could obviously not do all the work by himself alone, he planned each film and supervised each detail. Disney was, for instance, not only the inventor of Mickey Mouse, but also Mickey's voice!

Disney soon recognized the fact that the public was not only delighted by cartoon films, but also by comic strips that brought the little trick-film heroes into their homes; and so *Mickey Mouse* began his career in comics in 1930 and Donald Duck in 1938. Cartoon feature films appeared in comic books and relieved fans of the task of collecting the stories strip by strip. With the publication of *Walt Disney's Comics and Stories* the cartoon film heroes started to lead a double life: apart from their film exploits they now experienced additional comic strip and book adventures. In the meantime the big Disney feature films and documentaries have also found their way into comics.[13]

Other cartoon film ideas have established themselves equally in two media: Paul Terry's *Mighty Mouse* films, Walter Lantz's *Woody Woodpecker* cartoons, Loew's *Tom and Jerry* and the Warner Brothers' series *Bugs Bunny*, *Daffy Duck*, *Beep Beep the Roadrunner* and *Tweety and Sylvester*.

Walt Disney's Mickey Mouse initiated a new trend of cartoon films. There followed films about Donald Duck, Goofy and the rest of the Disney gang.
© Walt Disney Productions

Pinnacle of success for *Peanuts*: the feature film *A Boy Named Charlie Brown*.
© 1969 United Features Syndicate/UPI/Centfox Films

William Hanna and Joseph Barbera, designers of animated cartoons, scored a fantastic success on TV with their *Huckleberry Hound* and *Flintstones* produced by much faster, improved techniques. *Huckleberry Hound* and *Flintstones* appeared promptly also as comic books and strips. *Yogi Bear*, *Pixie and Dixie*, *Magilla Gorilla* and *Space Ghost*—also by Hanna and Barbera—fared equally well. Some of these series form the basis of Saturday morning 'all-cartoon' television programmes. In 1963 *Krazy Kat* became a cartoon film series and in the wake of the new Marvel era of adventure such strips as *Spider-Man*, *Hulk*, *Captain America*, *Thor* and many others speedily turned into money-spinning cartoon films.

Superman, *Aquaman* and some of the other DC heroes also leapt onto the small screen. *The Archies*, which cleverly combined the beat craze with the teenage appeal of the comic strip *Archie*, were received with particular enthusiasm. From animated cartoons originally produced for the big screen, new television series were made, because some of the old films had been shown so often that like Fleischer's *Popeye*, for example, they could no longer be used.

Some of the new successful comic series like *Beetle Bailey* and *Snuffy Smith* were also made into TV series, and the *Peanuts* triumphed first on the small screen and then, in 1966, also on the cinema screen in their very own feature film *A Boy Named Charlie Brown*.

In Europe too themes were exchanged between film, television, novels, comic strips and books. *Michel Vaillant*, *Tanguy et Laverdure*, *Perry Rhodan*, *Diabolik*, *Barbarella*, *Astérix* and *Tintin* are just a few examples to be discussed in the following chapter.

Marvel comic heroes appeared on television, in animated cartoons, in 1966.
© 1966 Marvel Comics Group

Nick Fury—Agent of S.H.I.E.L.D. was one of the best examples of the super-spy strips in comic books, which were a direct result of the super-spy craze on film and television. Jim Steranko, who drew this strip, had a great talent for visual effects and some of the apparatus and wonder-weapons he invented surpassed even the outfits of James Bond or The Man from U.N.C.L.E. From *Strange Tales* No. 167.
© 1967 Marvel Comics Group

8 The European comics scene

They're crazy, those Romans
Astérix

Schnorch, Sack, Räbäh
Mickey Mouse

The European comics tradition

The form which the Genevese author, painter and university professor Rodolphe Töpffer (1799–1846) gave to his imaginative picture stories about Cryptogame or Jabot influenced the development of early European comics for about half a century. European picture stories were drawings with a text of varying length underneath. This applied as much to W. F. Thomas's ne'er-do-well *Ally Sloper*, which appeared (with interruptions) from 1884 to 1920, as to Tom Brown's *Weary Willie and Tired Tim*, which was published from 1896 in the children's magazine *Illustrated Chips*, to the picture pages of the Germans F. Steub and Wilhelm Busch or those of the French artist Georges Colomb.

Georges Colomb, a professor of natural science who signed his drawings Christophe, exercised a particularly strong influence on the content and structure of other picture stories through the success he had in 1889 with his *La Famille Fenouillard (The Fenouillard Family)*. His stories in which, as in the case of his predecessors, picture and text were strictly separated, appealed almost exclusively to children. In the USA a greater readiness to experiment resulted in a relatively quick development away from the trend of European picture stories, towards comic strips which appealed to a broader and above all adult public in the newspapers. But European picture stories were tied to an accompanying text and appeared only in children's magazines or as supplements for children in magazines or newspapers.

The French painter Jean-Pierre Pinchon followed this tradition in 1905 when he improvised a short story for *La Semaine de Suzette*. This story so pleased the readers that it was turned into a series on the adventures of the small, naïve girl from Brittany, called Bécassine.

Even the scurrilous series *Les Pieds Nickelés (The Nickel Feet)* by the Frenchman Louis Forton was published in 1908 in a children's magazine, *L'Epatant*, though the political allusions of this series had been aimed more at adults. In addition to captions for pictures, onomatopoeia and speech bubbles also appeared in the series occasionally.

Similarly in Italy we find picture stories in the *Corriere dei Piccoli*, the children's magazine founded in 1908. From 1909 onwards it published Antonio Rubino's imaginative and poetic picture series and Attilio Mussini's *Bilobul*, the adventures of a versatile Negro boy in an imaginary Africa where everything was taken literally and turned into pictures. Sergio Toffano's *Bonaventura* which appeared in 1917, is part of these early series. Just as in *Krazy Kat* the same gag is continually being used: at the end of each sequel the title figure is given a million as reward for help he has accidentally rendered.

The same style was also followed in England. Magazines like *Comic Cuts* (from 17 May 1890), *Illustrated Chips*, *Dan Leno's Comic Journal*, *Puck*, *Chuckles*, *The Rainbow*, *Comic Life*, *The Funny Wonder*, *The Firefly* and finally *Film Fun* or *The Play Box* used amusing short picture stories to appeal to their public, the children. Germany did not lag behind either. After the occasional publication of politico-satirical picture stories, mostly a juxtaposition of caricatures prepared by Olaf Gulbrannson, E. Thöny or K. Arnold for *Simplicissimus*, *Jugend*, *Kladderadatsch* and *Fliegende Blätter*, in 1921 the children's magazine *Der heitere Fridolin (Cheerful Fridolin)* appeared on the scene. Every fortnight children could read stories from Barlog's *Laatsch und Bommel* or Schäfer-Ast's *Benjamin Pampe*. Barlog, who also drew the adventures of *Professor Pechmann* for *Der heitere Fridolin*, succeeded in getting the *Berliner Illustrierte* to publish his series *Die fünf Schreckensteiner (The Five Schreckensteins)*. This series is about the ghostly ancestors of the Schreckenstein family, who always play their tricks during the witching hour. It is closely related to pantomime strips like the *Vater und Sohn (Father and Son)* series started in 1934 by Erich Ohser under the pseudonym: e. o. plauen.

While Europe still persisted with this form, America had long since changed to another, more racy comic form. The new combination of picture and text eventually made itself felt in Europe, at first because of the acceptance of translated comic strips. As early as October 1906 the Danish weekly magazine *Hjemmet* published the strip cartoon *Lile Svends Gavtyvestreger (Little Svend's Pranks)* which was *Buster Brown* translated by a schoolmaster(!) Then two years later, on 27 September 1908, the

Katzenjammer Kids appeared in number 39 of the illustrated magazine *Hjemmet* under the title *Knold og Tot*. These early imports laid the foundation for Bulls Presstjänst, one of the largest comics and features syndicates in Europe, which takes a large proportion of its material from King Features Syndicate.

In England picture stories came out in daily newspapers relatively early with *Pip, Squeak and Wilfred* appearing in the *Daily Mirror* in 1919 and the small bear *Rupert* in the *Daily Express* in 1920. *Rupert*, which was only drawn by his creator Mary Tourtel until 1935, still appears in the *Daily Express* today. Two pictures appear in the paper every day with captions below—lovable relics of the early form taken by comics. In 1921 the first European daily strip cartoon was published in the *Daily Sketch*: *Pop* by J. Millar Watt, an amusing cartoon strip for adults which from 1929 also appeared in the *New York Sun*.

Although European strip cartoons enjoyed considerable success, attempts at indigenous production were rather submerged when the American comic strip was renewed during the world slump. An aggravation of this tendency was the fact home-made cartoon series cost seven times more than imported ones. Also an initial mistake was made in regarding comics as reading material only for children, because until then only children had been given picture stories. In the USA, on the other hand, comic strips were also aimed at adults. So in Europe comics were put in children's or young people's papers and the stories were bowdlerized, often without motive. At the same time the first European comic books with reprints of American comic strips were published.

In France one of the first figures to be shown speaking was Martin Branner's *Winnie Winkle*, who appeared as *Bicot* in *Dimanche Illustré*. Because of the many americanisms these imported series were edited and adapted to the French environment.

Alain Saint-Ogan produced the first genuine French comic strip in 1925 with his *Zig et Puce*, a childish Laurel and Hardy couple who were joined in 1926 by the little mascot penguin Alfred. Although it was still linked to the archaism of the early comic forms, *Zig et Puce* breaks with the tradition of having captions below the pictures and bases the story exclusively on speech balloons. Saint-Ogan's series was published in *Le Dimanche Illustré*. It differed from all earlier European series in that it did not consist of self-contained gags, but of amusing adventures which ran from one week to the next. Originally any adventure had only twelve sequences, but soon they extended to thirty and forty. It was only in 1929 that *Zig et Puce* was faced by a competitor—Hergé's *Tintin*.

One day Alain Saint-Ogan was visited by the young Belgian artist Georges Remi in Paris. Remi presented *Totor, Chef de la Patrouille des Hannetons (Totor, Chief of the Cockchafer Patrol)*, a boy-scout picture story, which had already been published in 1923 in *Le Boy-Scout Belge*. Saint-Ogan advised him to adapt himself to modern times and to take up the American idea of using speech balloons in comic strips. Remi, whose pseudonym Hergé is merely a phonetic transcript of his initials R.G., followed Saint-Ogan's advice. The result was *Tintin au pays des Soviets (Tintin in the land of the Soviets)* a comic strip which was published by instalments in *Petit XXème*, the children's supplement of the daily newspaper *Le Vingtième Siècle*, from 10 January 1929. At the same time Hergé had a go at gag strips with *Quick et Flupke, Gamins de Bruxelles (Quick and Flupke: kids in Brussels)*.

Apart from the first French daily strip, *Les aventures du Professeur Nimbus (The Adventures of Professor Nimbus)*, by A. Daix (1934) and English series like Stephen Dowling's *Buck Ryan* (1937), a detective comic strip for the *Daily Mirror*, or Dowling's *Garth* (1943), not many new comic strips were produced in Europe. This was because the Second World War produced a shortage of newsprint, resulting in less space being available for comic strips. Children's pages were also thinner, or even stopped publication altogether. In Germany national isolationism resulted in no American comics being imported. And all satire ended in 1933. The introduction of American comic strips and comic books which occurred after the war with the entry of the allies came therefore as a real surprise and overwhelmed the guardians of culture and virtue.

Comics in Germany

Comic strips in German translation were published in daily newspapers from 1948 onwards. The strips and their publication in paperbacks from 1950 opened the way for comic books in Germany. *Superman*, who had eagerly fought the Nazis during the war, was one of the first to try and break into the German comic book market. But he only appeared in three issues. The heroines *Blonder Panther (Blonde Panther)*—called the *Panthera Bionda* in Italy—and *Nyoka (Nyoka, the Jungle Girl)* did not obtain any permanent success either.

The first, greatest and most lasting success was gained by Walt Disney's *Micky Maus*. The first issue of this series, which was the only comic book series admitted for postal distribution, was published in September 1951. Monthly publication was soon insufficient to meet the steadily rising demand. So from April 1953 *Micky Maus Sonderhefte (Mickey Mouse Special Editions)* appeared regularly in the middle of the month, reproducing mainly comic versions of Disney's films. Finally in 1955 *Micky Maus* was published fortnightly and in December 1957 it began appearing weekly. The circulation of *Micky Maus* had already reached some 400,000 per book by 1954. Even after the switch to more frequent publication, sales did not decline. They have now stabilized at 437,000 copies.

In October 1962 *Micky Maus* was joined by *Walt Disneys Mickyvision*, a comic book which provided scope for Disney's films and television series. In order to increase its readership, *Mickyvision* started running the adventures of racing driver Michael Voss from 8 March 1965. This series was nothing more than the Belgian series *Michel Vaillant* under another name. Only after the comic strip *Michel Vaillant* was also screened on German

television was it decided to drop the German version of the title, which had been designed to make it easier for the reader to identify with the main character in the series.

As more and more Belgian series were included in *Mickyvision*, in August 1966 the book was renamed *MV 66* and in 1969, some time after the introduction of *Astérix, MV-Comix*. Apart from the occasional publication of *Mickyvision* in comic books every three weeks *Die tollsten Geschichten von Donald Duck (The craziest stories about Donald Duck)* appeared. This book devoted its sixty-four pages mainly to the inimitable stories of Carl Barks. *Walt Disneys Lustige Taschenbücher (Walt Disney's Comical Pocket Books)*, imported from Italy, completed the publisher's catalogue.

[1] Lat.: Was? [2] Lat.: Soll geschehen! [3] Lat.: So ist es! [4] Lat.: Wehe den Besiegten!

In September 1966 Ehapa Verlag issued *Superman*, thereby giving him a third chance, after his second entry on the German market in 1953–4 had only lasted for 21 issues. A little later the series was renamed *Superman und Batman*. As the adventures of these super-heroes also appeared in *MV-Comix* and both series were issued fortnightly, they appeared alternately on the market so as to appear to be available on a weekly basis.

Only Kauka-Verlag, one of the few German publishers to produce comic books of its own, has been able to achieve results comparable to those of Ehapa Verlag. Rolf Kauka started at the

beginning of the 1950s with *Till Eulenspiegel* and *Münchausen*. Fix and Foxi, originally subsidiary figures in *Till Eulenspiegel*, very quickly became the main feature and in 1953 the title of the comic book was changed to *Fix und Foxi*. As years went by Fix and Foxi and their antagonist Lupo became increasingly stylized, and *Fix und Foxi* was also gradually switched to weekly publication. By 1970 the circulation had settled down to an average of 300,000 copies sold. As in the case of *Micky Maus*, children aged from seven to fourteen coming from every level of society, made up the bulk of the readership. The only differences

It was only at the third attempt that *Superman* and *Batman* managed to establish themselves in Germany.
© 1968 National Periodical Publications Inc./Ehapa Verlag Stuttgart

The last animated cartoon film produced under the direction of Walt Disney was *The Jungle Book*. The comic book was published throughout the world at the same time as the film was released.
© 1969 Walt Disney Productions/Ehapa Verlag Stuttgart

Fix und Foxi and their delightful opponent Lupo were the most successful comics characters produced in Germany. They also enjoy considerable popularity in other countries.
© 1970 Rolf Kauka Verlag

which can be discovered are regional preferences. While *Micky Maus* sells somewhat better in northern Germany than in southern Germany, the south is a bigger market for *Fix und Foxi*. It is assumed that the reason for this is the slightly more Anglophile attitude of the inhabitants of northern Germany.

Kauka-Verlag was also successful when it tried its hand at publishing further comics. *Lucky Luke* was brought to Germany for the second time when he appeared in *Lupo modern* and Astérix and Obélix emerged as *Siggi und Babarras*. In order to make it easier for German readers to identify with the characters, the whole series was adapted to German conditions. But the attempt to turn a French satire into a German one misfired, as the critics immediately sensed political conservative rubbish. The licence was withdrawn and passed to Ehapa Verlag in Stuttgart, whose translation was closely watched by the French producers. Kauka, however, continued to publish stories about Siggi and Babarras, as long-term supply contracts had been signed. In every country the purchase of a foreign series in principle gives the right to change the title and permits the publisher concerned to produce his own stories under the new title. Since Kauka-Verlag was convinced that its Astérix versions had failed and because the *Siggi*

und Babarras series could not change its image, it was gradually withdrawn from circulation. *Super Tip Top* followed *Lupo modern* (and in 1969–70 was finally absorbed by the Kauka comic book series, which could equal the circulation of *Fix und Foxi* paperbacks and were produced in order to persuade grown ups to read comics). In the pocket book comics German readers are getting to know Lucky Luke, the Schtroumpfs (*Les Schtroumpfs*) and Prinz Edelhart (*Johan*), all Belgian products.

In addition to the humorous comics of Disney and Kauka, an attempt was made to introduce adventure comics into Germany at the beginning of the 1950s. Thus in June 1952 the series of *Phantom* comic books was started, in which each issue was given a separate title: that of the hero of the series. Towards the end of the series in 1955 however only *Prinz Eisenherz* (*Prince Valiant*) and *Phantom* were left as titles. In the *Phantom* paperbacks translated reprints of comic strips also appeared—*Phantom*, *Mandra* (from *Mandrake*), *Prinz Eisenherz* (from *Prince Valiant*), *Rip Korby* (from *Rip Kirby*), *Blondie*, *King der Grenzreiter* (from *King of the Royal Mounted*), *Bob und Frank* (from *Tim Tyler's Luck*), *Steve Canyon*, *Der Oberst und die Herzogin* (from *Colonel Potterby and the Duchess*), *Gorden* (from *Flash Gordon*), *Lilo* (from *Teeny*), *Felix der Kater* (from *Felix the Cat*), and several sequences of the comic book series Hopalong Cassidy. While the *Phantom* paperbacks always consisted of complete stories, from January 1953 Aller-GmbH published *Buntes Allerlei* with instalment stories, which meant that this series was a collection of the Sunday sequences of American comic strips. *Phantom*, *Rip Korby*, *Gorden*, *Blondie* and *King* were again included, but other series also appeared, like the *Katzenjammer Kids*, *Schmerbauch* (from *Bringing Up Father*), *Kasper und Liesel* (from *Toots and Casper*), *Ein lustiger Vagabund* (from *Pete the Tramp*), *Oma* (from *Grandma*), *Die liebe Familie* (from *Polly and Her Pals*), *Präriewolf* (from *The Lone Ranger*), *Ricki* (from *Rusty Riley*), *Hannelore* (from *Etta Kett*), *Zirkusvolk* (from *Tommy of the Big Top*), *Theobald* (from *Henry*), *Meisterdetektiv X-9* (from *Secret Agent X-9*) and *Schifferkal* (from *Popeye*). In 1954 *Buntes Allerlei* switched to *Superman* and, in addition to *Superman* adventures, published filler series such as *Tom von Morgen* (from *Tommy Tomorrow*), *Rote Maske* (from *Vigilante*), *Johnny Quick* and *Tomahawk*.

In 1953 a Swedish publishing house in Germany published *Tom Mix* with the adventures of the title hero and the series *Lash La Rue*, *Adlerauge (Eagle Eye)*, *Buffalo Bill* and *Roland der Riese (Roland the Giant)*. But this series of paperbacks did not last very long. It came to an end because of the campaign against comics started up by German guardians of culture who were following the American example, and the resulting movement called Books for Young People in Exchange for Rubbish. But as there were never any real horror, sex or crime comics of American origin, the comics inquisitors contented themselves with adventure comics. In the case of *Tom Mix* the end of the series was mainly due to the American firm Fawcett giving up its comics series, with the result that supplies to Germany dried up.

Buntes Allerlei and *Phantom-Hefte* with their strip series had too little comic book character to retain the loyalty of their 100,000 readers for any length of time. Pure comic books such as *Yabu*, *Wild West* and *Der fidele Cowboy (The Faithful Cowboy)*, however, had relatively long runs before they were stopped.

At the beginning of the 1950s Mondial Verlag started *Tarzan*, *Pecos Bill* and *Der kleine Sheriff (The Little Sheriff)* imports from America and Italy. Although they were cut down and rewritten to make them more like Italian and French comic books, the *Tarzan* paperbacks reveal up to a point the genius of Burne Hogarth's draughtsmanship, which is supported by clever colouring, though this colouring is sometimes too dense. It is frustrating for comics researchers and purists that even the peak performances of comics should be curtailed and forced into the Procrustean bed of small and absurd formats. Cinema experts have been fighting in vain against similar abuses in film editing.

Pecos Bill and *Der kleine Sheriff* were, like *Tarzan*, notable in that speech balloons were not used. But it was particularly in the case of the two Western series that the censor frequently interfered. Knives, clubs and pistols were almost always left out of the picture due to a curious retouching job. They emerged always at the last moment in the hand of the marksman, who in the previous picture was still aiming with an empty hand.

In some cases violent actions were replaced by text passages if those responsible for publishing felt that the educators and youth officers were breathing angrily down their necks. In view of the concern of the guardians of culture, it should be remarked that in these paperbacks more and more text passages were inserted in order to invalidate the reproach of picture illiteracy. In the end, two comics pages were always followed by two pages of text—and the magazines were passed over to other people: a glorious success for voluntary self-control.

Andy Capp (Willy Wacker) by Reg Smythe. Andy Capp's lifestyle has a universal appeal and this strip was one of the quick starters in the international comics business.
© 1970 Syndication International/Publishers—Hall Syndicate

But it was impossible to kill *Tarzan*. Already in the 1920s this story had found numerous friends in Germany through the excellently translated novels of Edgar Rice Burroughs. Lehning Verlag, following Pabel Verlag, continued the editing of the *Tarzan* strip until 1964, and in 1965 Bildschriftenverlag started the German version of Gold Key's comic book *Tarzan of the Apes*.

When Lehning Verlag published *Tarzan*, only four years remained before it was forced to close down. In this space of time the publishers imported titles like *Kit Carson* and *Spider* from England, *Kalar* and *Marco Polo* from France and Italy. But it was particularly Lehning Verlag which, at the beginning of the 1950s, started German adventure comics, like *Sigurd, Nick der Weltraumfahrer (Mick the Space Traveller)*, *Tibor* and *Falk*, and then from 1 July 1953 published the series *Akim, Carnera* and *El Bravo* —which were imported from Italy as weekly mini-books. These paperbacks enjoyed a certain popularity for some time—enough to get them on the official publishers' index—but they did not compare favourably with other series because the stories were short and their quality was inferior. Only the comics versions of the Karl May novels, published under the titles *Kara Ben Nemsi* and *Winnetou*, were above average. Drawn by the German Helmut Nickel, they were of a surprisingly good quality, compared to other German comics, a fact which was recognized by exports to other European countries.

As is common in almost all countries, the early adventure stories were provided with a horizontal handwritten text. But in the case of *Micky Maus* and very soon in the case of *Fix und Foxi* letterpress text was preferred and eventually this became accepted as the usual style for captions in German comic books. This was possibly because in this way the impression of a product which had been completely drawn was avoided and because this was closer to the typeface of books and newspapers.

Illustrierte Klassiker were respectable enough to enable Bildschriftenverlag, a subsidiary of National Periodical Publications, to build up its comics series. In 1962–3 *Bildschirmklassiker (Television Classics)*, *Detektivklassiker (Detective Classics)* and *Filmklassiker (Film Classics)* were issued for a year only; while permanent series were added with *Sheriff Klassiker* in 1964, *Tarzan* in 1965, with *Gold Key* and *Hit-Comics* in 1966 and *Top Comics* in 1969. With the exception of *Tarzan* most of these titles are so-called 'head series', series which provide a framework for comics series of varying length or which make it possible to bring several series under one roof.

Thus *Sheriff Klassiker* published and still publish alternately *Kid Colt, Rauhfell Kid (Rawhide Kid)* and *Texas Kid (Rawhide Kid* No. 1*)*. In *Hit-Comics* we find the Marvel Comic books *Die Spinne (Spider-Man)*, *Die Fantastischen Vier (Fantastic Four)*, *Halk (Hulk)*, *Die Räscher (The Avengers)*, *Captain Marvel*, *Devil-Man (Daredevil)*, *Der mächtige Thor (Mighty Thor)*, *Der unsbesiegbare Eiserne (The Invincible Iron Man)*, *X-Männer (X-Men)* and *Prinz Namor, der Sub-Mariner (Prince Namor, the Submariner)*. *Top-Comics* are in the DC series *Wassermann (Aquaman)*, *Die Schwarzen Falken (Blackhawk)*, *Blitzmann (The Flash)* and *Die Grüne Laterne (Green Lantern)*. The Gold Key

series generally took over its own series, such as *Magnus*, *Astronautenfamilie Robinson (Space Family Robinson)*, *Korak Tarzans Sohn (Korak Son of Tarzan)*, *Dr. Solar, Bonanza, Lancer, Der einsame Reiter (The Lone Ranger)*, *Mündundgsfeuer (Gunsmoke)*, *Samson (Mighty Samson)*, *Turok Sohn der Steinzeit (Turok Son of Stone)* and a few one-shot issues.

Bildschriftenverlag with its adventure series holds a special or perhaps even an outsider position, as it does not use the normal channels of distribution but has built up its own distribution network which however only reaches about a quarter of newspaper dealers. Therefore the circulation of the comic books averages some 30,000 and in some cases, such as with *Tarzan*, 80,000 (about 160,000 per month). As the magazines are undated, returns can be offered to other dealers for sale, a method which the American publisher Delacorte applied to his pulps in the 1940s. In addition, all series are published in co-operation with other branch companies of National Periodicals all over Europe. The printer only alters the captions on the strip depending on the country. As in this way the individual titles achieve high total circulations, the low circulations within individual countries still remain profitable.

Just as Bildschriften and Ehapa Verlag imported television comics, so in 1962–3 Neue Tessloff Verlag tried television exploitation on a larger scale. With *Wyatt Earp, Mike Nelson, Lassie*, etc. the series lasted for 190 comic books of 24 pages each; 39 comic books in pocket form were also published, featuring American television adventure series even if they had not yet been shown in Germany. *Detektive (The Detectives)* was for instance screened on the second German television channel under the title *Kein Fall für FBI*, several years after the series had been published in comic books.

In the 1960s the publishers of paperback novels tried to enter the comic book business. In addition to publishing Westerns and detective stories, Bastei Verlag brought out *Felix* and eventually *Lasso, Buffalo Bill, Wastl, Silberpfeil (Silver Arrow)*, *Bessy, Der rote Korsar (The Red Corsair)* and for some time its own *Roy Tiger* as a comic book. (So far 50 million copies of *Bessy* have been sold, almost as many as the total world sales of *Peanuts* books.) Part of the series is taken from abroad or in connection with Bulls Pressedienst, part is ordered by Bastei Verlag itself. The artists, with a few exceptions, work in Italy or Spain.

Since 1968 Moewig and Pabel have also tried their hand at comic books once more. Moewig's *FBI—G-Man Bruce Cabot* and *Perry* (following the novel series *Perry Rhodan*, which was highly successful, but was attacked by critics because of its marked Fascist features) were able to hold their own in contrast to the children's periodical *Plop* and the Barbarella imitation *Uranella* (from Italy) which was published as a pocket book. Pabel's *Tom Berry* was also sold successfully.

It should incidentally be noted that in the German Democratic Republic (GDR) comic strips were banned as vehicles of imperialistic propaganda. Children's magazines like *Mosaik* therefore stopped at the level of development reached by picture stories in 1920. Perhaps their only counterpart are the children's magazines put out by department stores in the West. *Mosaik*, however, does not sell Salamander shoes as *Lurchi* does (to give one of the best examples), but expresses an ideology. Compared with this type of ideological brainwashing Captain America's adventures in the early 1950s as 'Kommunistenzerschmetterer' (Commie Smasher) are almost nice and harmless. But at the end of 1969 the East German cultural-political magazine *Sonntag* called for 'popular counter-images' against the bourgeois comic figures.[1] We arc still waiting for the result of the appeal.

In West Germany however it is certain that every month some 12 million comic books are sold. Of these Ehapa Verlag publishes about 3·5 million, followed by Kauka-Verlag with 2·8 million. The next largest market share is held by Bastei Verlag with 2·6 million and by Bildschriftenverlag with barely 1 million.

Apart from a few exceptions, one type of comic book has never existed in Germany—the war comic. For one thing, the war featured in the penny novels, the so-called foot-soldiers' paperbacks; for another it was hardly likely that German readers would identify themselves with the American protagonists in existing war comics. There were also fears that there would be furious reactions from critics both at home and abroad. But in other European countries American and English war comics found a market. The scenes in these paperbacks are limited to Germany, North Africa and the Pacific. The Germans—referred to as 'Nazis' (Hans and Fritz)—and the Japanese are the enemies.

Even in other types of comics the image of foreigners is almost always determined by national stereotypes. Frenchmen have little Menjou moustaches, Englishmen drop their 'h's, the Germans belong to the blond master race. Very often Germany is equated with Bavaria. All these cliché notions are also to be found in the translations. Producers have differing views about the image of America presented by American comics to countries abroad. Bildschriftenverlag believes that comics can hardly influence the image of America held by young readers, but they could possibly deepen the picture of the pioneering period in Wild West comics which is conveyed to them in films and literature. Bulls Pressedienst believes 'that comic strips could influence the picture of America which their readers visualize. In our opinion this picture is created in its essential aspects by other media like newspapers, films and television and mainly by news and social reporting.' Jules Feiffer, cynically restricting the issue, felt that one could get a pretty accurate picture of America from *Steve Canyon* and *Buz Sawyer* (both are conservative strips with typical idealized Americans as their heroes). Stan Lee says there is a precondition before one can recognize the picture of America inherent in comics—a picture which he considers less accurate than that given by other media. 'It is necessary first to have a good understanding of comics before one can glean a "true image" of America.' This advice is mainly directed to sociologists and adult interpreters of comics.[2] In addition, the picture of America conveyed by comics is filtered by translation, since through this process the original can be censored. Thus Ehapa Verlag: 'We have no special instructions for our translators. The content can be radically changed for the sake of humour, topicality or modernity.'[3]

There are also certain rules for the processing of comic strips.

It is obvious that the language has to be adapted to the country in which the strip is to be published. In general, however, a correct type of language is used. But if it appears expedient, a modern, local slang is used. In the case of translations of funny strips, what is involved is 'above all to bring out the funny points. If this cannot be achieved by fairly direct translation, the strip must be rewritten and must be given a new point or it must be dropped.' Adventure strips 'can usually be translated fairly accurately'. However, if in the view of the Pressedienst 'unsuitable events with violence, vulgarity and similar happenings occur' the text and drawings of the scenes involved are re-edited.[4] Similar ideas to those of Bulls Pressedienst also govern United Press International, which amongst other things has a comic strip with rigid instructions concerning translation—*Peanuts*. Charles Schulz watches closely to make sure that no bad language infiltrates his series. If in a German translation the word 'damn!' should ever appear instead of 'rats!', you can be sure that it does not originate from UPI.

Just as German illustrated papers in Austria and Switzerland are mainly imported from Germany, comic books and comic strips are brought in from Germany. The circulation of comic strips in German-speaking areas is almost entirely left to Bulls Pressedienst and United Press International. UPI mainly supplies *Peanuts* (to ten daily newspapers with a total collective circulation of around one million) as well as other contributions by United Features Syndicate such as *Tarzan* or *The Captain and the Kids*, by Newspaper Enterprise Association such as *Captain Easy* or *Bugs Bunny* or by Register and Tribune Syndicate such as *Tumbleweeds* and *Wee Pals*.

Bulls Pressedienst represents, amongst others King Features, the largest newspaper syndicate in the world; they also represent English, Scandinavian and German syndicates. The distribution and circulation figures show clearly that in German-speaking areas not only comic books but also comic strips are widely circulated. It is true that not every newspaper devotes a whole page to comics as the *Hamburger Morgenpost* does, but in view of the increasing popularity of comics even as conservative a newspaper as the *Frankfurter Neue Presse* included *Peanuts* (as its first strip). It is not surprising that in September 1970 Bulls Pressedienst was already supplying 79 papers in Germany (not including their regional editions), 15 in Austria and 6 in German-speaking Switzerland, with a varying number of comic strips. For comics attract a great deal of attention in these countries. Today newspapers are using comic strips more frequently as it has been recognized that—in Germany at least—they offer a new way of following the trend towards the visual.

The reaction to comic strips in German papers is generally positive. As the readers are accustomed to the fact that they cannot go against the will of the editorial staff, they also accept it when the editorial staff ban comic strips from their papers. Thus *Bild-Zeitung* stopped their strips because their editorial staff did not want them. The *Abendzeitung* of Munich interrupted the publication of *Blondie* and *Phantom* because allegedly nobody paid any attention to the strips. It was not without a certain irony that when *Phantom* made his last appearance in *AZ* on 21

Taró by Fritz Raab, drawn by F. W. Richter-Johnsen. This excellent series appeared in *Sternchen*, the children's supplement of *Stern*, until the middle of the 1960s. This exotic strip about the Indian Taró, who wants to act as a peacemaker between Indians and Whites, has so far been unsurpassed in Germany as far as quality is concerned.
© F. W. Richter-Johnsen and Fritz Raab

October 1969 his longstanding girlfriend Diana thought: 'Away as if he had never been here! Come back soon darling!', and there was a notice on the lower margin of the picture about the next instalment (which never occurred): 'Tomorrow. The Missing One.' The readers accept the dictates of the editorial staff. Direct questioning would probably have produced different reactions from the readers.[5]

In addition to the newspapers illustrated magazines have been increasingly taking up comic strips. *Stern*, for example, has been publishing *Peanuts* for some time. *Stern* is one of the few magazines to publish its own comic strips. Thus for some time it has published Roland Kohlsaat's *Jimmy das Gummipferd (Jimmy the Rubber Horse)*, now appearing under the title *Julios abenteuerliche Reisen (Julio's Adventurous Journeys)*, a mixture of comic strip and picture story. In the youth supplement *Sternchen* a picture sequence with rhymed text has been appearing for some time. It is called *Reinhold das Nashorn (Reinhold the Rhinoceros)* and is by Loriot (=Pirol=Victor von Bülow), one of the most important cartoonists and promoters of cartoon humour in Germany. Until the beginning of the 1960s *Stern* also published *Taró*, one of the few excellently drawn German adventure series. *Taró*, by Fritz Raab and the cartoonist F. W. Richter-Johnsen, describes the adventures of an Indian in the Mato Grosso area in a sustained style which does not aim at spectacular effects.

Bulls Pressedienst—probably rightly—holds the view 'that the interest in comic strips in Germany is increasing visibly and that the attitude of reserve towards comics which was noticeable earlier in several quarters is now giving way to an objective judgement and appraisal. And the newspapers which have understood the idea of comic strips and made strips a natural part of their contents have been successful as a result.'[6]

Bulls Pressedienst has also exported this success to several East block countries. Thus *Rip Korby* appears in the Czech newspaper *Smena* in Bratislava *v nemeckon originali a slovenskom preklade* (in German original with a Slovak translation). The German text of this American series is published with speech balloons as in Germany, with the translation below the pictures. The Czechoslovak newspaper *Svet* published *Káčer Donald (Donald Duck)* and now *Micky Maus*. In addition to mediocre productions of their own, the Prague youth magazine *Ohníček* publish the series *Rex Star* (from *Flash Gordon*) and *Kida a Pida* (from *The Katzenjammer Kids*).

Independent Yugoslavia can show a multitude of comic book series including imports from England (Westerns, adventure and war comics), from Italy (Westerns), from France (*Lucky Luke*) and from America (*Tarzan*, for example). Moreover comic books from Germany are available in kiosks for visitors from West Germany, and naturally for Yugoslavs as well.

Flash Gordon (Rex Star) by Mac Raboy (Czechoslovakian version). *Flash Gordon* appears in Czechoslovakia under one of the two titles used in Germany. Here Flash and Dale (Rex and Veronika) are visiting the Czechoslovakian pavilion at the World Fair—in the original version they visited the Swiss pavilion, because Switzerland is a neutral country and nobody could take offence.
© 1965, 1970 King Features/Bulls

Tobias Seicherl by Ludwig Kmoch. Already in the 1930s Austria had a local dialect strip in inimitable Viennese style. With his dog Struppi and his practical common sense, Seicherl, the prototype of the 'little man', masters the most complicated situations. The strip deeply influenced the life and work of the Viennese graphic artist and sculptor Alfred Hrdlicka.

Comics in France and Belgium

France and Belgium had their own comics tradition which they were able to resume when there was enough paper available for comics at the end of the Second World War. On 26 September 1946 the Belgian Raymond Leblanc published the youth magazine *Tintin* in his publishing house, Editions du Lombard, set up in 1945. The title was taken from Hergé's comics figure. And thus from the first issue onwards the Tintin adventure *Le Temple du Soleil (The Temple of the Sun)* appeared in the magazine. In 1969 the same adventure was filmed by Belvision, the film division of Editions du Lombard. *Tintin* magazine reached a weekly circulation of 650,000(!) copies sold in various editions throughout the world. The popularity of the magazine is not only based on its comics series, but also on the fact that good editorial texts accompany the comics pages.

Tintin is one of the most successful, if not the most successful European comics series. Tintin, the boy from next door with the round face and the indomitable bush of hair, has no family ties and therefore can always go out after adventures. On his adventure trips, which take him all over the world, even as far as the moon, Tintin is accompanied by his crafty fox terrier Milou. In the course of over forty years Hergé invented for *Tintin* thousands of figures which all have their special characteristics, as well as thousands more subsidiary figures which remain without influence on the story. The main character, Tintin, has gradually been joined by a core of people who appear regularly: the absent-minded, deaf professor who is always ready with new, slightly eccentric inventions and whose pendulum always proves its usefulness, the officers of the Crime Squad, Dupont and Dupond, who are convinced of their ability although they are generally

183

Tintin by Hergé. With *Tintin* Hergé created one of the longest surviving European comics series, in which realism in detail is coupled with stereotyped caricatures of people.
© 1967 Editions Casterman, Tournai

the last to find a solution to their cases, and since 1940 Captain Haddock. This affluent, irate seaman, who is always ready to hand out abuse appropriate to the situation, creates additional complications through his ill-temper and foolhardiness, which Tintin with a cool, reasoning brain is able to solve as easily as the most complex course of action.

The stories first appeared in instalments in *Tintin* magazine and then two years later they were published as an annual, in the form of a hardback book. By 1971 some 22 of these annuals had been published. Some of the adventures which were issued between 1930 and 1968 were entirely redrawn over the years. *Tintin*'s creator Hergé was also the author and artist of the stories about *Jo et Zette* which appeared in five annuals, and the stories about *Quick et Flupke* which appeared in eleven annuals. Like *Tintin* they were translated into a dozen foreign languages. Hergé's 38 annuals reached a total world circulation of 22·5 million. But Hergé also had other projects and successes for Tintin apart from comics. Together with J. van Melkebeke he had by 1940 completed two plays about Tintin: *Tintin in India, or the mystery of the blue diamond*, and *Monsieur Boullock has disappeared*. After the war other uses were made of the stories. There were Tintin records, a puppet film, a semi-animated television series, an animated cartoon series for television by Belvision

which was also shown in the USA, two Tintin feature films with actors and a full-length animated cartoon film.

Tintin stories mainly appeal to a young public and therefore the features of the characters are simplified in cartoon fashion. Their only concession to Tintin's adventure world is an almost excessive naturalism and realism in the details of the environment shown. For this reason, as well as to obtain a precise harmonization of colours, to look for locations and construct accurate scale models, Hergé set up the Hergé Studios.

In issue number one of *Tintin* Edgar-Pierre Jacobs's series about the English detectives *Blake and Mortimer* appeared. The first adventure was still strongly influenced by the doomsday mood of the war and was strongly permeated with science fiction elements. This is less surprising if we take into account the fact that in 1942 Jacobs had provided the final instalments for the American series *Flash Gordon* in the French magazine *Bravo*, because the supply from America had been interrupted. In 1945 he had drawn the science fiction series *Le Rayon U (The U-Ray)* for *Bravo* in the same style. His characters are less caricatured than Hergé's. In the detail, however, Jacobs applied the same meticulous realism which is also found in Jacques Martin's historical comic *Alix l'Intrépide (Intrepid Alix)* and his adventures while looking for the reporter Lefranc.

Lucky Luke by Morris, author René Goscinny. American habits and customs in a series which exposes every cliché and lovingly makes fun of the skinny hero Lucky Luke. It is not just a matter of the usual sunset. The Daltons, Calamity Jane, Billy the Kid and even bulb-nosed W. C. Fields contribute to the gags.
© 1970 Journal Pilote, Dargaud S.A. Paris

The style of *Tintin* magazine and of its staff influenced the Belgian periodical *Spirou*, set up in 1938, as well as the children's periodicals *Coq Hardi* and *Vaillant* which were set up in France in 1946. In 1947 the Belgian Morris (Maurice de Bevere) invented for *Spirou* his Western lampoon *Lucky Luke*, for which he personally provided the captions and drawings until he met René Goscinny who then wrote humorous parodies of Western adventures. In 1968 Morris moved with his series to the French magazine *Pilote* which he set up together with René Goscinny. René Goscinny soon became its editor-in-chief.

A strong opposition to the spread of American strips in France built up in 1949. The Communists attacked comics because they were American and because they stressed an individualism which was incompatible with Marxist teaching. The right wing wanted to ban them because they were American and because they threatened the national spirit. Theologians turned especially against the 'excesses' of comics books and, as is common in such cases, applied the same judgements to them as they did to comic strips. Finally comics met opposition from French comic artists and editors who were really not particularly pleased at the return of competition. The Communist party's bill banning all foreign comics was rejected, but the proposal submitted by their Catholic opponents, which was morally better camouflaged, became law on 16 July 1949: a control board set up under this law has strictly supervised French comics production since then. On 23 December 1958 sanctions were strengthened by an additional decree, penalizing breaches of the 1949 law. The self-censorship imposed by the legislators also affected Belgium, as newspapers were exported from there to France or were published in France in special periodicals. Finally in 1960 a European federation for youth periodicals was set up, which laid down directives similar to those of the American Code Authority. The Moral Code issued by Europress Junior places even greater emphasis on protecting the young than the American code.

Apart from comic papers with the same format as *Tintin* and *Spirou* (20 × 31 cm.) innumerable comic books were published in France and Belgium in every possible form and in various sizes. Paperbacks in pocket size, which were often produced in co-operation with Italy or taken over from Italy, were very popular. Thus among the various titles published by Editions Aventures et Voyages there were *Les aventures du Chevalier Bavard (The Adventures of the Garrulous Knight)*, *Tipi* (with *Pecos Bill*), *Lancelot, Ivanhoe, Marco Polo, Shirley, Rouletabille, Brik, Kris le*

Pecos Bill. This character from America's 'tall tales' enjoyed a long life especially in Europe.
© 1970 Editions Aventures et Voyages

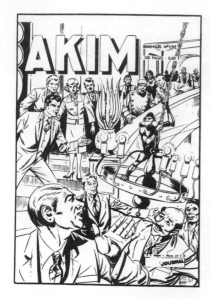

Series like *Akim*, *Kris le shérif (Kit the Sheriff)*, *Lancelot* or *Marco Polo*, which were produced in France and Italy, were soon distributed throughout Europe.
© 1965 Editions Aventures et Voyages

Shérif (Kit the Sheriff), the Italian Tarzan imitation *Akim* or *Captain Swing*. Certain publications by Verlag Artima-Tourcoing such as *Hefte Ardan*, *Cosmos*, *Eclair (Lightning)*, *Tarou—Fils de la Jungle (Tarou—Son of the Jungle)*, *Dynamic*, *Sideral*, *Aventures Fiction (Fiction Adventures)*, *Vigor*, *Red Canyon*, *Audax*, *Atome Kid*, *Spoutnik*, *Olympic*, *Big Boy*, *Meteor* and *Monde Futur (Future World)* were slightly larger than the *Tintin* and *Spirou* series. They were partly translation from American comic books, partly mediocre productions by German publishers. These small format paperbacks are mainly published in black and white, while the large format ones are entirely based on colour. In the case of *Strange* and *Marvel*, the French editions of the Marvel

Comics which have been issued since 1970, small pocket book comics at least used decorative colours. The two hundred and eighty page quarterly pocket editions of *Super Pocket Pilote* (stopped after ten issues) and *Tintin Sélection* are partly in colour, partly in black and white.

While all types of comics books emerged, *Journal de Mickey* presented Disney stories adapted to periodicals, and *Tintin* and *Spirou* came along with new series which again mostly began as short stories in loose sequences and were then established as instalment stories. Individual instalments were limited to one or two pages so that with an average length of forty-four pages per story they ran for a period of between twenty-two and forty-four weeks. Thus *Tintin*'s publications included: in 1954 *Dan Cooper*, the adventures of a Canadian pilot drawn by Albert Weinberg; in 1955 *Ric Hochet*, the reporter and detective by Tibet (Gilbert Gascard); at the end of 1956 *Michel Vaillant*, the adventures of the racing driver devised by Jean Graton. In 1965 *Ray Ringo* was published, a Western in the style of *Tales of Wells Fargo* with a very realistic style by William Vance (William Van Cutsem). Vance also drew the mariner strip Howard Flynn and in Bruno Brazil a James Bond-style spy thriller, which were published in *Tintin* in 1964 and 1968 respectively. He also drew several of the adventures of Bob Morane in *Pilote*. Ever since 1966 Hermann (Hermann Huppen) has drawn for *Tintin* the adventures of the globe trotter and former Interpol inspector Bernard Prince. When the young, white-haired Bernard Prince

inherits the yacht Cormoran, he is enabled to experience adventures in localities throughout the whole world. Thus he takes up the traditions of the untrammelled playboy hero and offers wish fulfilment to his confined readers. In this case the appeal is to a considerable extent based on the illustrations, a fact which also applies to Hermann's other series, *Jugurtha* and *Comanche*. In this context it is not surprising that the French special comics periodical *Phénix* in 1970 awarded the Belgian comic artist Hermann the Phénix prize for the best foreign artist. The scenarios for Hermann's stories as well as for Eddy Paape's science fiction series *Luc Orient* and for William Vance's *Bruno Brazil* were written regularly by Greg (Michel Regnier), who resumed Alain Saint-Ogan's series *Zig et Puce* for *Tintin* in 1960, doing both the text and the drawings.

Dan Cooper by Albert Weinberg—Europe's answer to *Steve Canyon*. From *Tintin Sélection* No. 8.
© 1970 Editions Aventures et Voyages

The comic pocket book of some 280 pages, which originated in Italy, has been popular in Europe for several years. On this cover (from the pocket book *Tintin Sélection*) heroes from different series, such as Ray Ringo (by William Vance), detective Ric Hochet (by Tibet) and the Japanese Taka Takata (by Jo-El Azara) are brought together.
© 1968 Editions du Lombard

Howard Flynn by William Vance. Vance is one of the young European artists who are noted for their particular attention to detail. From *Howard Flynn à l'abordage*.
© 1968 Editions du Lombard

As in the case of *Tintin*, the title of the periodical *Spirou* is derived from its main figure. The hotel page boy Spirou, who has the most exciting and amusing adventures, was invented by Bob-Vel (Robert Velter) and from 1946 onwards was drawn by André Franquin. Spirou also had a team of fellow adventurers. As Spirou's friend, there is the reporter Fantasio, who is in fact characterized by his name. The Comte de Champignac, a scientific genius and a sworn enemy of all world conquerors, intervenes if the situation requires it. To make the series lighter and to provide additional humour there is Gaston Lagaffe, the oaf, wit

and speculator, who even has his own gag series, in which he regularly makes Fantasio see red. During the years a pale, subsidiary character was replaced by Kokomiko, the mythical Marsupilami from South America. The sly Marsupilami with his tail of indefinable length at once won the sympathy of the readers. The *Spirou* series even appeared in a German translation for a short time in 1960, under the title *Der heitere Fridolin (Cheerful Fridolin)*, until it gained a permanent place with Kauka Verlag under the title *Pit und Pikkolo* (Spirou and Pikkolo).

In 1952 Peyo (Pierre Culliford) produced for *Spirou* the

Bruno Brazil by William Vance. A mixture of *James Bond, Man from U.N.C.L.E.* and *Mission: Impossible* is presented in this outstanding Belgian series. Incidentally European comics heroes smoke much more often than their American colleagues do. From *Bruno Brazil: La cité petrifiée*.
© 1971 Editions du Lombard

Bernard Prince by Hermann. As far as form is concerned, one of the most beautiful, brilliant and interesting European series. About a globe trotter and his companions. From *Bernard Prince: Général Satan*.
© Editions du Lombard

adventures of the knight *Johan*, for whom he provided the scurrilous companion Pirlouit in 1954. The two are known in Germany as Prinz Edelhart and Kukuruz. In 1958 the fairy-tale world of the *Schtroumpfs* was included almost as an afterthought in the eighth episode of *Johan*. The minicosmos of the blue Schtroumpfs is one of the most delightful things ever to have been shown in comics. Between the Schtroumpfmountains and the Schtroumpfriver lies Schtroumpfland where dwarf-like Schtroumpfs live in their mushroom houses. One Schtroumpf looks like another, an impression which is enforced by the white Schtroumpf trousers and their caps with a pom-pom on them. Only one of them towers above the host of minuscule neuters, the Grand Schtroumpf, the wise head of the Schtroumpf community, who is recognizable by his beard and his red garments. However, even if they all look alike each Schtroumpf has his own personality.

Comanche by Hermann. If after *Fort Navajo* any further proof were needed that Europe's Westerns can beat America's contributions, *Comanche* provides it.
© 1971 Editions du Lombard

Thus there are intellectuals, misanthropists, lazybones, inventors
and mischief makers. The main characteristic of this world of
dwarfs is their language; the word 'Schtroumpf' is used to
express almost anything according to whether it is used as a verb
or a noun. The success of the Schtroumpfs surprised even Peyo,
under whose guidance they soon became the main characters in a
series of their own. The *Schtroumpf* annuals were also a success. In
addition they were turned into books for small children. Schtroumpf figures and an animated cartoon series for television added
to the commercial value of this idea.

The setting up of the French comic periodical *Pilote* marked a
further considerable success. *Pilote* appeals to a somewhat older
public than *Tintin* and is therefore correspondingly more satirical
and characterized by well-thought-out adventure strips and
humorous strips. The author-artist team René Goscinny and
Albert Uderzo, who came from *Tintin*, secured one of the surprising successes in *Pilote* with their *Astérix*. In view of the quality
of their series and the topical allusions this is easily understand-
able. (In 1947 Astérix could already be recognized as one of the
characters in the Uderzo series *Arys Buck*.)

Astérix, the gnome from Gaul, as he likes to be called, and his
fat friend Obélix, the supplier of menhirs, are the main actors in
this series which takes place around 50 BC, the period when
Vercingetorix surrenders to Julius Caesar. Only a small Gallic
village in the North has not fallen to the Roman legions as its
Druid Miraculix has brewed a magic potion which enables the
village to defend itself successfully. But it is Astérix and Obélix
(who as a boy fell into the magic potion) who send the Romans as
it were on a conveyor belt into the land of dreams. The permanent
fight between the Gauls and the Roman occupiers becomes,
through intentionally anachronistic—in fact, topical—allusions,
a delightful satire on French society and also makes use of the
experiences of the underground Resistance fighting the German
occupation forces in the Second World War.

Apart from showing satire and the myths of resistance,
Astérix reveals a blatant chauvinism. The detailed pictures over-
flow with gags, using speech balloons to express the peculiarity of
the written word: Egyptians speak in hieroglyphics, while the
Goths talk in black Gothic type, and when everything has been
accomplished, there is roast wild boar. But this is not the only
formula used by *Astérix*, which always keeps to the same
pattern.

From the beginning *Pilote* also published Victor Hubinon's
Barbe Rouge, a pirate strip, and *Tanguy*, a pilot strip by Uderzo
and Jean-Michel Charlier. In 1963 Charlier invented the Western
Fort Navajo drawn by Jean Giraud, which captures the atmosphere exceedingly well and surpasses many an American Western.
Henri Verne also started a comic strip for *Pilote* around the book
and film character *Bob Morane*, as well as a semi-humorous
science fiction series on the character *Valérian* and many other
series like *Achille Talon*, *Iznogoud*, $4 \times 8 = 32$ *l'espion—chamé-
léon* and *Rémi Herphelin*.

From 1970 the Belgian and French comics papers *Pilote*,
Tintin and *Spirou* turned away increasingly from the instalment
stories which for decades had been their main ingredient. Instead
of publishing two pages of a story a week they started publishing
four pages a week so as to conclude the series more quickly. In
addition, series with complete episodes of seven to eight pages
were introduced. In these circumstances even strips for intellectuals such as *Lone Sloane* found their way into *Pilote*.

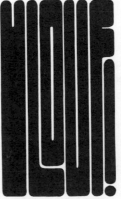

Valérian by the artist J. C. Mezières and writer P. Christin, one of the best European science fiction strips which captivates us with its easy style.
© 1970 Dargaud S.A. Paris

Comics finally established themselves in France and Belgium after 1945, because there was an indigenous production which was connected with other marketing uses. This situation was originally absent in Germany, but in France the connection with other media is closer than in Germany. Tintin's excursions into other media have already been mentioned. The Schtroumpfs found a playground in television films. The comics heroes Michel Vaillant, Ric Hochet, Tanguy and Laverdure became television heroes, the television adventures of the knight Bayard and Thierry-la-Fronde became comic books. Television and comics were based on books about the adventures of Bob Morane. And French film producers also helped to set up comics clubs with magazines, in which the phenomenon of comics was investigated. The comics club movement started in 1962, the year when the thirty-seven-year-old Parisian Jean-Claude Forest, who up to that time had drawn series for the periodical *Vaillant* such as *Jim Boum*

and *Nasdine Hodja*, launched on an unsuspecting public his *Barbarella* series in the periodical *V*. Both events were not without their impact.

Comics clubs led to comics congresses in Bordighera in 1965 and Lucca in 1966, to the setting up of the Italian periodical *Linus*, which deals with comics and offers its own comics for adults such as Guido Crepax's *Valentina*, and in 1966 to the start of the French specialist periodical dealing with comics, *Phénix*.

As a result of the clubs and *Barbarella* adult and intellectual comics established themselves either by appearing in periodicals or by coming straight onto the market in book form. *Jodelle*, *Pravda* and *Lone Sloane* entered on the scene and profited from the top trends and the increasing seriousness with which comics were being regarded.[7] The French edition of the American high-quality horror magazines *Eerie*, *Creepy* and *Vampirella*, as well as the setting up of Het Stripschap, a Dutch society for research

192

Creepy. Cover picture by Frank Frazetta. As so often happened, the French were more receptive to American specialities than other European countries were.

© 1967 Warren Publishing Company (New York, N.Y., USA)

Comics in Italy

In 1932 the American comic strip was accepted in Italy. Soon periodicals were set up in which comic strips were included until they were banned by the Fascist regime in 1938. After the Second World War American comics steamrollered Italy once again. Following the imports, home production was started, mostly rather weak imitations, but the story content compensated their readers.

When American strips were banned, enthusiasm for American comics was so great that protests against the ban were successful, at least in the case of *Popeye*. And the comic heroes gained a foothold immediately after the enforced break. When the supply of comics from America was interrupted the series had to be completed in Italy. Thus, for instance, Federico Fellini wrote the last nine to ten weeks of scenarios for *Flash Gordon*, which in addition to other strips was published in the magazine *L'Avventuroso*.[9]

After the war the shelves of Italian news-stands were again filled with home-made products like *Akim*, *El Carnera*, *Pecos Bill*, *Il Piccolo Sceriffo (The Little Sheriff)* or *Il Piccolo Ranger (The Little Ranger)*. In addition Mickey Mouse and Co. was distributed under the title *Topolino* and Superman appeared as *Nembo Kid* until 1966 when he got his original name back. As in France, comic books were sold in many different formats in Italy, the most popular being the pocket book format whether it had 32 or 128 pages. Apart from comic books with the usual format of either 16×20 cm. or 20×31 cm. the *piccolo* format invented in Italy deserves to be mentioned. It was exported to Germany by Lehning Verlag. Photonovels (photos with text bubbles mirrored into them) which are extremely popular in Italy and France, found no acceptance in Germany.

and presentation of comics, can be seen as a consequence of the European enthusiasm for comics running parallel with the enthusiasm for American films at the beginning of the 1960s. In this context Truffaut and Melville should be mentioned. Their films represented a homage to their American models. Active promoters of the scientific preoccupation with comics such as film producer Alain Resnais and his comrades-at-arms Claude Moliterni, Maurice Horn and Pierre Couperie of SOCERLID[8] made comics socially acceptable.

Just as in the case of films, it was the French who first opened the eyes of the Americans to the merits of their mass media as regards their form and content. But the wave of enthusiasm for both media also carried some along with it who in their emotional state overlooked the negative aspects of comics and simply said that comics were art in order to legitimize the reading of them and to free them from the suspicion of vulgarity and triviality.

Il Piccolo Ranger (The Little Ranger). As in the case of *Kit, the Sheriff* identification is made easier for the readers through the use of a young (small) hero.

© 1969 Editoriale CEPIM (Edizioni Araldo)

Tex by Galep. The *piccolo* (mini) format was particularly popular in Italy because of its handy size. Many *piccolo* series appeared later in a larger format.
© 1967 Edizioni Araldo

Two pages from *Tex*, which show how accurately Ticci follows the style of Giolitti. Even his use of onomatopoeia is identical to Giolitti's. From *Tex* No. 108.
© Edizioni Araldo

Italy's comics industry is mainly concentrated in Milan. This is the headquarters of Arnoldo Mondadori Editore, the Italian publisher of *Mickey Mouse*, which has many of its stories produced on the spot. The same publishing house also produces *Superman*, *Batman* and *Classici Audacia*, a series of large-format periodicals in which the complete adventures of Belgian and French comic heroes like *Michel Vaillant*, *Luc Orient*, *Bernard Prince* and *Lieutenant Blueberry* (of Fort Navajo) can be obtained.

Also based in Milan is Edizioni Araldo, which supplies the market with *piccolo* editions and with 128-page comic books in the standard 16 × 20 cm. format. Edizioni Araldo works almost only in the field of Westerns.

There are *Il Commandante Mark (Commandant Mark)* and *Zagor*, two early Westerns, and *Il Piccolo Ranger (The Little Ranger)* the adventures of a young Texas-ranger named Miki, who also found a field for his activities in German editions. The hero of *Tex*, invented by the draughtsman Galep, is spurred on through numerous adventures by his author G. L. Bonelli. These

CIRCA TRE ORE DOPO, TEX ENTRA IN GOLDEENA...

Tex by Giovanni Ticci. It is thanks to Ticci, a former assistant of Giolitti, that *Tex* can be included among the most attractively drawn Westerns. From *Tex* No. 108.
© 1969 Edizioni Araldo

Tex by Galep. The series about the Texas-ranger and the Indian agent Tex Willer, which was initiated and drawn by Galep, is one of the better Italian Westerns.
© 1970 Edizioni Araldo

adventures keep the interest of the public, although the drawings have no special distinction despite a certain inspiration from A. Giolitti. In certain cases the stories about Tex Willer, which have also been published in Germany since 1971, are given a specially visual touch by artists like Giovanni Ticci, a former colleague of A. Giolitti who is able to capture his style extremely accurately.

The adventures of Tex are given a rather more liberal description of violence than comparable American products. On this point comics vary from nation to nation. For example in the USA there is never any bloodshed when Tarzan kills a lion. In Mexico, however, a little blood drips from the knife and the knife wounds are clearly visible in the lion's body.

Apache Kid. European comics naturally thrived on the myth of the noble savage.
© 1965 SEPIM

TEX LA SFIDA
L.250

INDIETRO! DEMONI ROSSI, INDIETRO!

2-8

Some particularly good Italian Western series like *Il Sergente York* by Roy D'Amy are appearing again today in reprints. Even the story of the West is prepared with historical accuracy.
© 1969, 1968 Edizioni Araldo

Edizioni Araldo are now republishing several of their earlier successes in the series *Collana Rodeo*. In this paperback series apart from *El Kid* and *Judok* (a kind of science fiction/Western series) there is *Storia del West (History of the West)* which is the history of the West in comic format, and *Sergente York*, a cavalry Western by Roy D'Amy. His style of drawing somewhat resembles that of Hugo Pratt. Pratt's cavalry Western *Sargento Kirk* found followers as quickly as did the Western *Ralph Kendall* by the Argentinian Arturo del Castillo, which emerged relatively late in the development of Italian comic books. *Ralph Kendall* had previously appeared in England in the youth magazine *Ranger* under the title *Dan Dakota*. From the aesthetic point of view *Kendall* is one of the most successful Western comic strips. But only the Italian publication did justice to Castillo's drawings—despite a certain amount of editing and re-assembly. In England and Germany it had obviously not been appreciated that Castillo was amongst other things a master of omission, for he does not draw all the contours of an object. So his drawings were clumsily completed with obtrusive colours. Apart from certain additions on the margin of the pictures, the Italian edition is the truest to the original version, with the smallest amount of cuts. *Kendall* is published in the paperbacks *Rin Tin Tin and Rusty* and *Whisky and Gogo* as a filler as well as in *L'Uomo dell' U.N.C.L.E. (Man from U.N.C.L.E.)*. Apart from *Man from U.N.C.L.E.* this publishing house imported *Tarzan, Il Re della Prateria (The Lone Ranger)*, *Bugs Bunny* and *Tom and Jerry* and distributed its own production *Il Cavaliere Sconosciuto (The Unknown Soldier)*.

The *Kendall* comic series was produced for Europe by Eurostudio Milano; Eurostudio is one of the big studios in which Italian comics are produced and tailormade products are turned out for European comics as well as youth and childrens' magazines. All comics from the English publishing house IPC Magazines, from the Belgian publishing house Dupuis and from the Spanish publishing house Frensa y Ediciones are imported to Italy through Eurostudio.

Reprints of American comic strips are currently mainly carried out by the Rome publishers Edizioni Fratelli Spada in their series *Stanlio ed Ollio, L'Uomo Mascherato (Phantom), Mandrake* and *Gordon*. In these paperbacks of various formats other King Features series are also being processed, and processed is the right word as the stories are cut to fit the format of the paperback without showing any consideration for the composition of the page. Another disturbing factor is the colouring, which is either too pale or too strong compared with the original.

opposite
Ralph Kendall by Arturo del Castillo. Sequences like this excellently staged fight show how Castillo's *Kendall* manages to fascinate us—especially with the pictures.
© 1970 Eurostudio Milano

197

IL GIALLO A FUMETTI
DIABOLIK
di A. e L. GIUSSANI
LA DONNA SFIGURATA

NEL FRATTEMPO A VILLA TOLMAN...
LE LUCI SONO SPENTE DA CIRCA UN'ORA. ORMAI GIULIA E SUO MARITO STARANNO DORMENDO. POSSO ENTRARE.
96

52 L. 150
SUPERGIALLO SETTIMANALE
KRIMINAL
IL PREZZO DELLA GOLA

ISABELLA
l'odissea di sciusciù
FUMETTI PER ADULTI L. 150
FRANCIA 2 F.
GERMANIA DM. 1,60
SVIZZERA Fr. 1.60

But back to Milan, where, in addition to children's comics, comics for adults (*fumetti per adulti*) have found their home. One of the first *fumetti neri* (black comics) was *Diabolik*, which was invented by the school teachers Angela and Luciana Giussani and which is now as always written by them. *Diabolik* appears fortnightly in an edition of 160,000 copies. The success was not just incidental and *Diabolik* remained the best of its type. Diabolik is a negative hero, a robber and a murderer. He could perhaps be compared to Jesse James. Diabolik's opponent is the police officer Ginko, a man of extreme integrity and correctness. The two antagonists are in permanent combat 'to symbolize the battle between good and evil', the outcome of which is always in doubt as they are of equal intelligence. Diabolik is accompanied on his gangster expeditions by his faithful girlfriend Eva Kant. With the help of plastic masks the couple can assume the appearance of any person they wish. Although he is not very choosy about his methods, Diabolik is not wholly evil. One of his positive sides, which fascinates his public, is his complete loyalty to his travelling companion Eva Kant, who helps him in his enterprises.[10]

Wertham felt that an ice-pick aimed at somebody's eyeball was utterly revolting—but it seems that the Italians don't share his feelings. From *Isabella*.
© 1969 Edizioni Erregi

opposite
Diabolik by Angela and Luciana Giussani. The series of black comics started in Italy in 1962 with *Diabolik*. From then on there were picture novels for adults with *eroi neri* (black heroes).
© 1970 Casa Editrice Astorina

Kriminal by Magnus and Bunker. Kriminal, the arch villain with his skeleton costume, is one of the most popular comics heroes in Italy. A cover illustration for Freudians.
© 1966 Editoriale Corno s.r.l.

Isabella by Alessandro Angiolini. The adventures of the Duchessa de Frissac are the most frivolous and blatant strips among the *fumetti per adulti*.
© 1969 Edizioni Erregi

This 'negative hero' did not remain alone for long. He was soon joined by *Satanik, Kriminal, Sadik, Goldrake* and *Zakimort*. Kriminal, with a skeleton painted on his skintight suit, and Satanik, the young woman who is always fighting vampires and werewolves, stand out among a large number of paperbacks because of the style of their drawing for they bear the marks of the school of Kurt Schaffenberger, for many years the draughtsman of *Lois Lane*. *Satanik, Kriminal* and *Gesebel* were started by the draughtsman Magnus and the author Max Bunker, who are also responsible for *Agente SS 018*. The sadistic, sex and crime comics produced in the wake of this series are however mainly characterized by shoddy drawing and infantile sado-masochism, flagellation and fetishism. *Isabella, Jungla, La Jena, Walalla, Justine, Jessica* and *Jacula* are vulgar rather than original. And the more acceptably drawn *Uranella* is just a popular copy of *Barbarella*.

Anything that could be considered as a subject of literature is served up in the *fumetti per adulti* periodicals, in order to give these publications a veneer of originality and refinement. Preference is naturally given to all variations of De Sade, linked in the case of *Justine, Juliette* and especially *Isabella* with *genere cappa e spada* (cloak and dagger style). They have also used Roman depravity (*Messalina*), and the *Decameron* (*Belfagor*) and even Ariosto's *L'Orlando furioso* (*Angelica*, in which less interest is shown in the raving Roland than in the title heroine). Even Lucrezia (*Borgia*) herself cannot be left out. The appearance of the characters is often modelled on film stars, a technique which is also being developed in comics for intellectuals. Thus Jean-Paul Belmondo becomes Goldrake, Ursula Andress his girlfriend Ursula, and Belfagor has the features of Vittorio Gassman.

Everything which Dr Wertham saw and thought he saw in comics, before the Comics Code was introduced, is shown here. Cruelty and sadistic violence become routine occurrences. Limbs fly through the air, eyes and tongues are torn out, homosexual and heterosexual relationships, even of a torturing character, take place continually. An indication of bestiality is also popular: this is a particular speciality of *Isabella*. Bears, horses, even an armadillo must serve this purpose. In these voyeur paperbacks women play the main roles as the jungle heroines used to do in America at one time. But although jungle heroines also had to put up with a good many things, they were never involved in sexual intercourse. The Italian heroines, who were created as a reaction against America's chaste comics heroines like Dale, Nardà and Diana, are surpassed only by underground comics in their free and easy morality.

It was inevitable that the sadistic and criminal actions of many of these heroes (and particularly heroines) should run up against opposition. In October 1966 a handful of these strip figures were taken to court 'for instigating crime and violating general moral feelings'.[11] But even in Italy the strict censorship regulations had meanwhile become brittle. The judges dismissed the charges because a ban on these paperbacks would have implied a limitation on legally guaranteed press freedom.

It was certainly not primarily these comics that aroused the enthusiasm for comics in Italy—an enthusiasm which was responsible for the setting up of the periodical *Linus* in 1965, which persuaded Arnoldo Mondadori Editore to bring out American comics series in book and pocket book editions, and which inspired film producer Alain Resnais (*Hiroshima mon Armour*) and Umberto Ecco, the professor of aesthetics at Florence University, to hold the first Italian comics congress.

Comics in England and in other countries

Apart from large areas in the Eastern Block, American comic strips and books are distributed throughout the world. And practically all countries have their own indigenous comics. South and Central America with their enormous appetite for comics have produced outstanding artists like José Luis Salinas and Arturo del Castillo. Comics, which as *Revistas Infantiles* are subject to licensing not by the self-regulating economic board, but by the Ministry of Education, are to some extent exported to Spain, where a ban on *Superman* comics was issued. A poll among young people a year after the ban showed that *Superman* was just as well known as he had been when an enquiry was made at the time of the ban. In addition to imports Spain produces Westerns and crime thrillers in a small format just as Italy does. Spain is the home of many excellent comics artists whose work is not only distributed in Spain but also in France, Germany, England and even in the USA. There are such magnificent strips as Victor de la Fuente's *Haxtur*, a science-fantasy series appearing in the superb comics magazine *Trinca*. There is the periodical *Dracula*, published by Buru Lan Ediciones, a company that is also re-printing *Flash Gordon* and *The Phantom*; the quality of their reprints has as yet been unsurpassed. Besides, Spain is also a centre of comics research. Luis Gasca, an internationally re-nowned expert on comics, has written many fine books about the *tebeos*, as comics are called in Spain (the name deriving from the children's magazine *TBO*, first published in 1917). The *tebeos* are

also appraised in excellent *fanzines* such as *Bang!* and *Xanadu*.

Scandinavia can look back on a long comics tradition. In 1906, as has already been mentioned, the first American series was imported. Comic strips quickly became an integral part of family illustrated magazines. The scientific analysis of comics also started early. In 1965 for example a Swedish Academy for Comic Strips was set up. The collection of comic strips in editions for bibliophiles shows how great the interest in comics is among adults in Scandinavia.

Three of the best known and most likeable of the many Scandinavian strips are *Petzi, Pelle, Pingo* by V. Hansen, *Rickard och hans Katt* by Rune Andreasson and *Mumintrollet* by Tove Jansson. *Petzi, Pelle, Pingo*, which is available as a picture story with text and picture separate or as a comic strip, is slightly reminiscent of woodcuts in fairy-tale books. *Rickard och hans Katt (Richard and his Cat)*, known in Germany under the title *Richard und sein Kätzchen*, describes the adventures of a little boy who goes out with his cat to get to know the big city. The comics artist Rune Andreasson has also drawn picture books, painting books and children's books, as well as the paperback series *Pele-fant* which cleverly mixes picture stories, painting pages and suggestions for games which children can play.

Ever since 1949 *Mumin (Moomin)* stories have been produced by the Finnish comics artist Tove Jansson, who is widely de-scribed as the Selma Lagerlöf of comics. She works in the tradi-tion of Scandinavian fairy story tellers and with Mumintal (*Moomin Valley*) and its population she shows a world where both sensitivity and comedy exist. This series resulted in her being awarded in 1966 the Hans Christian Andersen Medal, a sort of Nobel Prize for fairy story tellers; she is the only Scandinavian ever to have received it, apart from Astrid Lindgren. Anyone who understands the world of the Moomin troll can enter a world of European fairy tales, in a way which is almost considered im-possible nowadays. This is why *Mumin* (translated as *Moomin*) was successful throughout the world and the series was adapted for radio, television and puppet films in Germany and other countries.

English comics artists based themselves less on their own fairy tales than on the tradition of youth adventure books along the lines of *Tom Brown's Schooldays* or the novels of Enid Blyton. The adventures of boarding school boys were as popular as those of football players. And as the English tradition of crime and adventure stories for adults produced its own English strips, so over the years imports were steadily pushed out of English papers.

On 5 December 1932 the *Jane's Journal* series started in the *Daily Mirror*. It went on showing Jane's amusing escapades until 1959. In the Second World War Norman Pett's *Jane* was for England what Milton Caniff's *Male Call* was for America. The *Daily Mirror* was practically the only newspaper before the war to publish several strips. Among them was *Buck Ryan*, which has already been mentioned, *Pip, Squeak and Wilfred*, as well as *Ruggles, Beelzebub Jones, Belinda Blue Eyes*, England's Little Orphan Annie, *Just Jake*, the American import *King Sweetpea* and finally *Garth*, England's Superman, the only one of the series to survive the year 1969, who was joined by Reg Smythe's *Andy*

Mumin (Moomin) by Tove Jansson. The naive and comical trolls from the Moomin Valley have achieved worldwide fame. (German version.)
© 1955 Associated Newspapers Limited

Capp in 1956. Andy Capp is, like his creator, left-handed—and comes from the north of England as well. But only Andy Capp is a lazybones, is spoilt by his plump wife Florrie or spends her money at the local pub. *Andy Capp* tells of the depressing atmosphere of terraced houses in working-class districts, of the dole, and of the constant flight from creditors. Andy Capp, whose favourite occupations are drinking and sleeping, is a lazybones with a certain style. He always finds someone to stand him a drink if he cannot deprive his wife of her hard-earned money. And he is a passionate footballer in the good old English tradition. As Reg Smythe remarked, no one has ever complained that Andy Capp sets a bad example. Perhaps this is due to the fact that 'English people seem to adore people who haven't worked yet, but have money'. Smythe adds, however, that Andy Capp does not appeal to the English middle classes 'because he is working class—he wears the hat of the working man. He appeals rather to the aristocrats and the working class.'[12]

Andy Capp has become more moderate over the years, but he still remains the sort of person husbands would like to be. This explains why he became so popular in America in so short a time, a success only rivalled by Walt Kelly's *Pogo. Andy Capp* also became quickly popular in many other countries and occasionally he even appears in the Soviet paper *Isvestia*.

It is almost pointless to look for American strips in English papers today. The only ones are *Peanuts* and *Blondie* in the *Daily Sketch* and *Rip Kirby* in the *Daily Mail*. The *Daily Mail* also has strips of its own: *Flook* by Wally Fawkes (which has been running since 1949), a children's strip, *Carol Day* by David Wright (since 1956), a romantic adventure story, and *Fred Basset*, a jolly dog strip with international appeal.

Bristow by Frank Dickens is a popular British humorous strip which also has a large international readership.
© 1970 Evening Standard, London

Modesty Blaise by Peter O'Donnell. Artist: Jim Holdaway. Modesty Blaise was the first of the female 007s, and like James Bond she soon found her way on to the cinema screen.
© 1970 Evening Standard, London

The Gambols by Dobs and Barry Appleby. England's Blondie and Dagwood share in the victories and defeats which occur in the merry routine of marriage.
© 1969 Dobs and Barry Appleby/London Express.

Ian Fleming's *James Bond*. Artist: Horak. Fleming's novels featuring super-spy James Bond had already been adapted for comic strips; this comic strip now continues faithfully along the same lines. Here James (007) Bond is, as usual, in a tight spot. He is trying to save a damsel in distress from an archfiend called (because of his appearance) Baron Sharck.
© 1972 Daily Express, London

Jeff Hawke by Sidney Jordan is England's answer to *Flash Gordon*. It is a science fiction strip and the action is placed some twenty years in the future. It is superbly drawn, with an eye for technical details, and it quickly became very popular in England and in many other countries.
© 1971 Daily Express, London

Apart from the inimitable humorous strip *Bristow*, by Frank Dickens, the London *Evening Standard* publishes *Modesty Blaise*, the spy series drawn by Jim Holdaway based on the stories by Peter O'Donnell. In addition to the family strip *The Gambols*, the *Daily Express*, which is published by the same newspaper publishers, prints the adventure series *James Bond*, *Jeff Hawke* and *Gun Law*. The *James Bond* strip was stopped in 1962 by the

owner Lord Beaverbrook because a competing paper was publishing a James Bond story. This strip, based on Fleming's novels, was however resumed after Beaverbrook's death in 1964. With *Jeff Hawke* by Sidney Jordan the *Express* introduced a science fiction series, which ably shows the progress of a technological universe; it is based on what we know today. Erich von Däniken could have been inspired by *Jeff Hawke*, for this series

Gun Law by Harry Bishop. Despite the branch, this sequence, which is by no means exceptional for English strips, is less prudish than Barbarella and company. *Gun Law* appears in the ultra-conservative *Daily Express*.
© 1969 CBS/Daily Express, London

BLACKIE TO ROY, WHO SMASHED A PILE-DRIVING SHOT
THROUGH A THRONG OF MILLING PLAYERS.

THE HANDFUL OF ROVERS' SUPPORTERS GROANED.

IT'S HIT THE POST!

ROY'S RIGHT OUT OF LUCK!

BUT ROY HAD FOLLOWED UP HIS SHOT —

GOAL

GOAL

IT'S IN! THAT'S OUR ROY, NEVER LEAVES ANYTHING TO CHANCE—NEVER EASES UP UNTIL THE BALL'S IN THE NET.

PANIAKOS 1 — MELCHESTER 1.
AGGREGATE SCORE—PANIAKOS 2—MELCHESTER 3.

Roy of the Rovers. National preferences are reflected in comics. In America it is always
boxers like Joe Palooka or Big Ben Bolt who are successful: in England it is football
teams like 'Melchester United'. From *Tiger and Hurricane*.
© 1966 Fleetway Publications Ltd

In England, as in Italy, the newspaper stands are flooded week
by week with pocket-book comics, which very often contain
excellently drawn stories.
© 1961, 1966 Fleetway Publications Ltd

Scarth by Luis Roca and Jo Addams. A fashion strip is coupled with science fiction. The effective graphic style gives a futuristic note to the strip.
© 1970 The Sun/London Express.

The FIERY FURNACE!

BECAUSE OF THEIR QUICK TEMPERS, RED AND COLE FURNACE WERE KNOWN AS, "THE FIERY FURNACES". THEY WERE LOST IN A STRANGE COUNTRY IN THE MIDDLE OF THE ANDES, AND THE PEOPLE OF THE COUNTRY BELIEVED THEM TO BE THEIR LONG LOST EMPERORS. THEY WERE FORCED TO UNDERGO A SERIES OF TESTS AND SUCCESSFULLY COMPLETED THE FOURTH...THE ORDEAL BY WATER...

WELL, HERE'S THE FOURTH KEY. WHAT'S THE NEXT ORDEAL?

THE NEXT IS THE ORDEAL OF THE TRAVELLER...

THE EYES OF LITAN, LEADER OF THE ILTEKS, BURNED WITH HATRED AS HE STEPPED FORWARD...

NO! ALLOW THEM TO PASS ALL THE ORDEALS, EXCEPT ORDEAL NUMBER TEN... LET THEM PROCEED STRAIGHT TO THE FINAL ORDEAL.

THAT CANNOT BE, LITAN...IT IS WRITTEN IN OUR LAWS. ALL THE ORDEALS MUST BE PASSED IN SEQUENCE.

THE ORDEAL OF THE TRAVELLER *MUST* COME NEXT.

OUR PEOPLE WILL NOT ALLOW YOU TO ALTER THE RITUAL...

DEFEATED, LITAN TURNED AWAY...

VERY WELL ...LET IT BE AS YOU SAY!

HE DOESN'T LOOK TOO HAPPY!

HE'S OUT TO GET US, COLE. I BET ORDEAL NUMBER TEN IS SOMETHING IMPOSSIBLE!

THE FIERY FURNACES WERE LED BACK TO THEIR PRISON PALACE...

DON'T FORGET... IF WE DO PASS ALL THESE TESTS, *WE'LL* BE THE LEADERS OF THIS COUNTRY... NOT LITAN!

AND YOU CAN BET YOUR SWEET LIFE HE'S NOT GOING TO LET THAT HAPPEN WITHOUT TRYING A LITTLE DIRTY WORK!

AT DAWN, THE FOLLOWING MORNING...

THE ORDEAL OF TRAVEL, MY FRIENDS! THE MOUNTAIN BEFORE YOU HAS EXTREMES OF HEAT IN THE FOOTHILLS —AND EXTREMES OF COLD AT ITS SUMMIT. YOU MUST CROSS IT ON FOOT... WITHIN TWO DAYS

SOME HIKE!

FIRST...THE HEAT...

...AND THEN THE FREEZING COLD ON THE PEAK:

includes in the pattern of the story elements of terrestrial myths, fairy tales and history originating from early space travel. Harry Bishop's *Gun Law* is an excellently drawn Western based on the well-known television series *Gunsmoke*. The three *Express* series (as in the case with many English strips since *Jane*) are notable for their relatively liberal presentation of sex. Sex in these strips is freer and altogether less prudish than in French and American comics strips, except in the case of intellectual comics which, however, do not show any more than the English newspaper strips do.

The old weekly periodicals have almost all closed down as time has gone by. *Chips*, *Comic Cuts*, *Film Fun* and *Radio Fun*, together with *Ranger Weekly*, *Tiger and Hurricane*, all disappeared—making way for new comics like *Beano* and *Dandy* or the Marvel Comics *Smash!*, *Wham!* and (from 1967) *Fantastic*, which were turned into comic magazines for the English market.

American comic books are imported into England in small quantities under English price imprints, as well as being published in England under titles like *Suspense*, *Sinister Tales*, *Creepy Worlds*, *Secrets of the Unknown*, *Uncanny Tales*, *Astounding Stories*, *Out of This World* and *Weird Planets*.

Comics in pocket form are produced in England in large numbers. Thus Fleetway Publications, a division of International Publishing Corporation, produces the Western series *Cowboy Picture Library*, *Lone Rider Picture Library*, *Wild West Picture Library*, the war comics *War at Sea*, *Air Ace Picture Library*, *War Picture Library*, *Battle Picture Library*, the love stories of *True Life Library* and the *Fleetway Super Library* with heroes like Maddock's Marauders, Johnny Nero, Steel Claw, Ironside—Top Sergeant, Barracuda and The Spider. These series are sold throughout most of Europe. The main exception is Germany where Fleetway publications are only occasionally published.

Batman appeared all over the world, even in Arabia. And *Superman* followed him, as Nabil Fawzi in the Near East.

opposite
English comic magazines offer a whole range of instalment series of different types. For example, there is *The Fiery Furnaces* which tells of the experiences of the adventurers Red and Cole Furnace in exotic landscapes and lost cultures. From *Tiger and Hurricane* (edition dated 31.12.1966), artist Alberto Giolitti.
© 1966 Fleetway Publications Inc.

9 Sex and satire

What does it all mean?
Phoebe Zeit-Geist

Until the introduction of the Code, a good number of comic books were fairly daring compared with the Hollywood films of the time. Very likely the young reader found the sight of buxom girls, cruelly tied up and clothed in tatters, facing a fate worse than death, stimulating in those days. Ingenious interpreters with a knowledge of psychoanalysis discovered what was generally a crude sexual symbolism in the details that filled up the rest of the panels, one that might well have a pernicious effect on the unconscious of the 'immature' reader.

Sex in comics—prior to the Code there were many girls who anticipated what Barbarella and her playmates were to offer in comparatively harmless form in new editions. Among the publishers who brought out comic books with sexual undertones and overtones until 1954, Fox and Fiction House predominated (some large firms such as Dell and DC had already been practising self-censorship since 1940). Gregory Page's *Phantom Lady* was among the frankest super-heroines. *Torchy Todd* was even more generous; a model with a predilection for showers that went on for pages, she was usually seen from below by reason of her profession. She and *Sky Girl* offered the readers of American comic books what Milton Caniff's Miss Lace in *Male Call* and Norman Pett's *Jane* (who behaved even more freely at that date in England) offered soldiers in the way of comics pin-ups during the war.

But the jungle heroines were really the only ones who managed to assert themselves properly and to establish a specific genre. Girls exposed to jungle life simply had to wear brief leopard-skin bikinis, just as Tarzan wears a G-string. Thus the female copies of Tarzan provided a pleasant feast for the eyes. They were the white goddesses before whom the superstitious black 'wild men' retreated in awe and fear, for they could dominate them at will On the model of Tarzan's faithful Waziri, every jungle heroine had her own tribe of slavish followers.

This was a return to the theme of Sir Rider Haggard's *She* (1886) that had already been taken up in the pulps by Edgar Rice Burroughs and others, except that now the Ayeshas swung Amazon fashion through the various African and Indian jungles. For there was always need to rescue white explorers (the half-witted professor of botany was a favourite), to save the elephants' graveyard that formed part of the standard equipment of every jungle from the attacks of marauding gangsters or to make witch doctors kicking over the traces see reason. And each time these goddesses of the jungle skilfully succeeded in turning their physical attributes to the best jungle advantage.

One of the first and most important of the female Tarzans in comic books was *Sheena, Queen of the Jungle*, invented by W. Morgan Thomas but usually executed by S. R. Powell, who was also responsible for drawing a number of Sheena's colleagues. Sheena's adventures lasted from 1939 to April 1953, and she was so pugnacious that Jules Feiffer, comparing her to Wonder Woman, said: '. . . why did I always feel that, whatever her

It doesn't really matter what the jungle hero's name is, so long as he is accompanied by a shapely Jane in a leopard skin bikini. © 1952 Glen Kel Pub. Co. Inc. (Fiction House)

vaunted Amazon power, she wouldn't have lasted a round with Sheena, Queen of the Jungle?'[1]

Sheena was wild and untameable and so she emerged victorious over lions, panthers and maddened elephants. She sabotaged the work of the bad whites who penetrated her domain while her friend Bob was only there to enter the fray or watch her actions in admiration. Conversely, the female companions of Tarzan imitations, like Wana, girlfriend of *Zago—Jungle Prince* and Ann, companion of *Kaänga*, did not hold them back when it was time to hurry off through the jungle.

Ann, who appeared with Kaänga in the comic of that name and in *Jungle Comics* (the comic book that also housed *Wambi, the Animal Boy* and other Tarzans and Bombas, appeared in 64-page issues at the time), was one of the few black-haired ladies of the jungle—presumably as a contrast to Kaänga who had been chosen with fair hair in order to conceal his all-too-close stylistic resemblance to Tarzan. Apart from Ann and *Rulah—Jungle Goddess*, nearly all the others were blonde goddesses: *Camilla—Queen of the Jungle Empire, Gave Girl, Jann of the Jungle, Jungle Lil, Lorna the Jungle Girl, Luana, Princess Pantha, Saäri the Jungle Goddess, Tiger Girl, Tygra* and *Zegra—Jungle Empress*, to name only some of the most important.

Only the very popular *Nyoka* by Al Jetter offered very little sex and was clad in more than a leopard-skin bikini—in fact she wore modest tropical shirt and shorts. She was a bold explorer with missionary zeal, a female *Jungle Jim*. And like Jim, *Nyoka* gave rise to several films.

In an attempt to oust all rivals by increasing the doses, the depiction of sex, 'immodest poses' and acts of violence in comics was of course soon overdone. When the Code was introduced and legal measures threatened, publishing houses such as Fox and Fiction House had no alternative but to cease production, since a *Sheena* or *Rulah* without sex and violence would have been very dull.

Besides various levels of sublimated sex, the comic book scene remained very tame for some time. But all that was to break over the head of the readers in the course of the sixties; the naked adventuresses for intellectuals, such as Barbarella, the *fumetti per adulti* of Italy and France, and even the underground comics, are a pale reflection of the sex horrors in the comic books of that era.

Before and during the Second World War even comic strips were not entirely free of sex. Most famous of these ladies was the Dragon Lady, whom Milton Caniff first presented in 1935 in *Terry and the Pirates*. The fascinating, bewitchingly beautiful Lai Choi San (=mountain of riches), as the lady was called in every-day life, was the leader of a pirate organization and the terror of the Far Eastern seas. Dragon Lady with her supercool sex appeal and ultra-sophistication, who dominated entire crews with her whip, was every masochist's dream. She was the best representative of Caniff ladies who did not tend to skimp on their charms at that time.

Caniff drew the strip *Male Call* in order to raise the morale of the troops, and lightly and only partially clad girls like Miss Lace became favourite pin-ups for the G.I.s just as *Jane* had been for the Tommies. But after the war, when the censor tightened the screws again, all this splendour faded.

Intellectual—sexy—élitist

In 1962 the title page illustrator and collaborator on *Vaillant*, Jean-Claude Forest, drew a comic strip for *V-Magazine* whose protagonist was a girl with the features and anatomical attributes of Brigitte Bardot. Two years later Eric Losfeld's *Barbarella* was published as a luxury album in a kind of bibliophile comics edition for adults. Police intervention—the French had always been the biggest puritans in the field of comics—gave Barbarella the necessary publicity. For in 1964 it was still considered scandalous if a comics girl, even in the futuristic world of science fiction, disdained the tenets of 'normal' bourgeois morality and slept with whom she pleased. Books, articles and pamphlets on comics usually quote the picture that is considered most 'shocking'. Barbarella who has just been making love with Victor, the robot says: 'Victor, you have style!' In fact this is one of the wittier passages in *Barbarella*.

The success of *Barbarella* was to determine the course of her successors. Since Barbarella was inspired by Brigitte Bardot, she has a bigger bosom than her successors in Europe—the American *Little Annie Fanny* and *Phoebe Zeit-Geist* are, however, rivals. *Jodelle, Pravda, Epoxy* and *Valentina* were content with a small bosom which is easier to draw and gives the girls the kind of aesthetic nudity that is *de rigueur* in pretentious strip cartoons and seems more artistic both to censor and reader. Since these comics for adults never offered much in the way of content, the heroines had to be naked, which for the readers meant the same as lascivious, in order to give the whole product an air of wickedness. It is only the sexual element that gives Barbarella and the others that élitist character that marks them out for the upper classes and intellectuals, whose sexual behaviour has always been less strictly regulated than that of the lower classes.

When publishers in other countries tried to cash in on the boom in comics by reprinting these intellectual comics, they were already outdated in a sense, for in the end they were merely products of fashion. This is why they must be judged from the point of view of the year of publication and country of origin; for when the underground comics appeared after 1968 all these comics for adults seemed constrained and repressive, in spite of the nudity of the heroines, since the primary sexual zones were always veiled by casually placed shrubs, stilted postures and modestly placed hands. Only in underground comics could an occasional penis hang into the picture.

Eric Losfeld also published *Les Aventures de Jodelle*, drawn by Guy Peellaert with text by Pierre Bartier, in 1966. This is a comic book in the pop style and with poster colours, full of quotations from pop art. Jodelle is modelled on Sylvie Vartan, a pop singer in fashion at the time. In *Jodelle*, and later in *Pravda* (modelled on Françoise Hardy, another pop bard for the masses) Peellaert does not use the simple trick of the *roman à clé* but takes over the method used by pop artists who first set up idols of the masses such as Elvis Presley, Elizabeth Taylor and John Wayne, and then alienated them through their use of technique.

The bike girl Pravda la Survireuse (the super-poisonous truth), 'cool' and disgusted by society, first appeared in the satirical magazine *Harakari* for which Peellaert later also drew pop-style comics.

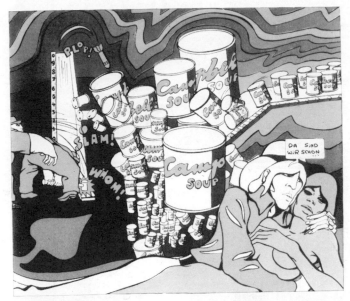

Pravda by Guy Peellaert. Peellaert uses pop art idols and the pop art style, to create a kind of pop orgy.
© 1968 Guy Peellaert. Reproduced from *Pravda* by permission of the Carl Schunemann Verlag

Epoxy by Paul Cuvelier and Jean van Hamme. (German version.) Once upon a time when I was naked in Arcadia. . . . The most fascinating thing about Epoxy is her carefree relationships with figures from Greek mythology.
© 1970 Le Terrain Vague. German edition: Verlag H.M. Hieronimi, Bonn

In *Pravda* Peellaert is quoting Warhol's Marilyn Monroe while at the same time referring to Anita Ekberg from *Boccaccio 70* and Mae West. *Jodelle* and *Pravda* integrate all the current symbols of pop art such as Campbell's soup cans and bottles of coke. For those in the know, they become a treasure house of quotations from mass culture and imply a critique of consumer society. All this is further alienated in *Jodelle* because the story is located in ancient Rome; antique SS myrmidons appear and so does François Mauriac. Peellaert skilfully exploited the craze for pop art, which was largely fed by the comics, by bringing the pop style back into comics. In *Pravda* he quotes Peter Max whose psychedelic graphic work is purely commercial in contrast to pop art; he seems to be taking an ironical view of his own work here.

Neutron by Guido Crepax appeared from 1965 on in *Linus*, the Italian magazine for comics fans. Neutron is Philipp Rembrandt, endowed with supernatural powers; but he did not have enough appeal by himself to really catch the readers' fancy for this somewhat self-willed strip. Success only came with the appearance of

the emancipated photographer Valentina who eventually became the title figure of the series. Valentina's clothes fetishism, which sends her into transports of desire, makes her nudity seem even more wicked. In *Valentina* Guido Crepax practices an unorthodox graphic aestheticism. He likes to pursue the story on several levels together on the same page, thus making it difficult to 'read'. Valentina and Philipp live in a dream, a drugged trance and in memory at the same time, but the reality around them is already fantastic enough.

Bianca Torturata by Crepax (1968–9) tells in the same style of the sexual excesses in which the boarding-school pupil Bianca indulges in her daydreams. At the end they prove to be exaggerated reality mixed with the dream world formed by the adolescent feelings of the fifteen-year-old Bianca which she notes in her diary.

Epoxy by Paul Cuvelier and Jean van Hamme (1968) is less ambiguous than her counterpart. The rather cuddly Epoxy is teleported to a mythological Greece thanks to the manipulations in time of extraterrestrial girls (naked too of course); she drifts naïvely through various Arcadias and loves, among others, Hippolyta, the Farnese Hercules, centaurs, Argus and Hermes, messenger of the gods.

One of the more important phenomena in the field of comics for intellectuals was *Seraphina*, who appeared from 1966 in the left-wing Paris journal *Jeune Afrique*. The rather poor quality of Eric Nemes's drawings had an adverse effect on its success. *Seraphina* is an Agitprop strip in which the USA and Russia have signed a pact. The SAR (Soviet American Republic) wants to

opposite
Jodelle by Guy Peellaert. The pop art style, which had to a certain extent been copied from comics, was taken up by comics. This extract from *Jodelle* shows a pop version of ancient Rome. Girls rush past Charles Aznavour to the Beatles. Sic transit. . . .
© 1966 Le Terrain Vague/Guy Peellaert. Reproduced from *Jodelle* by permission of the Carl Schunemann Verlag

Valentina by Guido Crepax. Fantasy has almost superseded reality: the narrative levels overlap to create a 'stream of consciousness'.
© 1968 Guido Crepax/Libri Edizioni/Valentina Verlag

divide the world between them. In South America, Seraphina, whose mother was sold into slavery, leads the freedom fight against enemies of the third world. Rays of energy flashing from her fingertips are the best weapon.

This still did not cover the demand for intellectual comics. Eric Losfield, that energetic publisher, continued to put his comic books for bibliophiles and his special albums on the market. One was *Saga de Xam* by Nicolas Devil from a scenario by Jean Rollin, another was *Lone Sloane* by Phillipe Druillet. Druillet also did some excellent illustrations for H. P. Lovecraft's stories. His *Lone Sloane* is now appearing semi-regularly in the French comics periodical *Pilote*. *Scarlett Dream*, drawn by Robert Gigi and written by Claude Moliterni, appeared in 1965 in V-Magazine. Scarlett Dream, like her predecessor *Barbarella*, is a science fiction strip, with less but more sophisticated sex. In 1968 Losfeld published the strip as an album.

In 1964 the American magazine *Evergreen Review* reprinted *Barbarella*. The reader's reactions encouraged them to produce an American counterpart. As a result one of the best comics for intellectuals or adults appeared in *Evergreen Review*: *The Adventures of Phoebe-Zeitgeist* from the pen of the poet laureate Michael O'Donoghue who writes for *Evergreen* and *National Lampoon* and drawn by Frank Springer, who is also active as a comic book artist. Some *Nick Fury—Agent of S.H.I.E.L.D.* issues are by him; however his style is not to everyone's taste.

Phoebe the Shining, as Artemis, sister of Phoebus Apollo was called by the Roman poets. This female ideal now appears as victim of the Zeitgeist created by the escapist mass media. With *Phoebe Zeit-Geist* O'Donoghue and Springer turn back to Samuel Richardson, whose *Pamela or Virtue Rewarded* (1740) founded the melodramatic novel in which innocent girls suffer unspeakable things; and at the same time they took over the technique of de Sade, whose *Justine* was totally opposed to the hypocritical Pamela.

Like Pamela and Justine, Phoebe is one of those naïvely innocent heroines who are constantly suffering tortures. For instance, the silent film series *The Perils of Pauline* was so successful and famous that its title became a household word synonymous with the sufferings of naïve heroines. How little this recipe has lost its effect since the days of Richardson and the *roman frisson* is proved by the success of Anne Golon's *Angélique*.

Phoebe too now went through the hell of cliché situations. Everything that can be done to a girl's body is done to Phoebe—particularly the borderline cases of sexual pathology: crucifixion, necrophilia, sodomy with a giant spider or nude object in an anti-American display in China. Certain qualifications are required of the reader, namely a knowledge of the stereotyped sequences of events in the entertainment media as inspired in particular by nineteenth-century fiction. O'Donoghue and Springer now distil and give literary form to the essence of carefully selected extreme

Phoebe Zeit-Geist by O'Donoghue and Frank Springer. (German version.) A girls' body as the object of rather unusual practices in sexual pathology. The cliché of setting together sex and Nazi bestiality (a cliché borrowed from men's magazines) gave this episode a certain notoriety.
© 1968 Michael O'Donoghue and Frank Springer/Grove Press Inc., (1970 Konkret Buchverlag)

situations. Norman Mailer also appears incidentally (he too is suitable for comics adaptation), in order to facilitate Phoebe Zeit-Geist's relations, in whatever sense, with higher regions. In the final series all those under whom Phoebe has suffered appear for the last time: a collection of mass media perversions. Phoebe's last words, 'Here Comes Everybody', in face of this apotheosis of stereotypes forge the link between this Joycean universe and the cosmos of the mass media. O'Donoghue and Springer then joined the satirical monthly *National Lampoon* and produced further satirical masterpieces.

The widest reading public ever gained by a comics series was that of *Little Annie Fanny. Playboy Magazine*, in which this product written by Harvey Kurtzman and drawn by Will Elder appears, sold an edition of some 5½ million in 1971, in addition to which we must count the number of co-readers of each issue.

Harvey Kurtzman and Will Elder have been producing *Little Annie Fanny* since 1962. Elder, who draws, or rather paints, the strip was sometimes assisted by guest artists such as Jack Davis, Al Jaffee and Russ Heath.

Little Annie Fanny is a super-playmate with regal, cantilevered bosom, doll face and—since Fanny means what the French call *derrière*—her rear proportions are equally superb. The contrast with *Little Orphan Annie*, lightly parodied here, could not be greater. Annie Fanny also has a Daddy Bigbucks (instead of Warbucks) who watches over her. Because of her naïvety Annie is constantly threatened with exploitation by a sex-obsessed world and in this way *Little Annie Fanny* mocks actual sexual fashions. But Harvey Kurtzman also shrewdly exposes more profound undercurrents in American society.

Jules Feiffer, newly popular man of letters (*Little Murders,*

'Here Comes Everybody'—everybody who ever made Phoebe suffer is gathered together here for a grandiose finale. In the general confusion Norman Mailer hardly seems out of place.
© 1968 Michael O'Donoghue and Frank Springer/Grove Press Inc. (1970 Konkret Buchverlag)

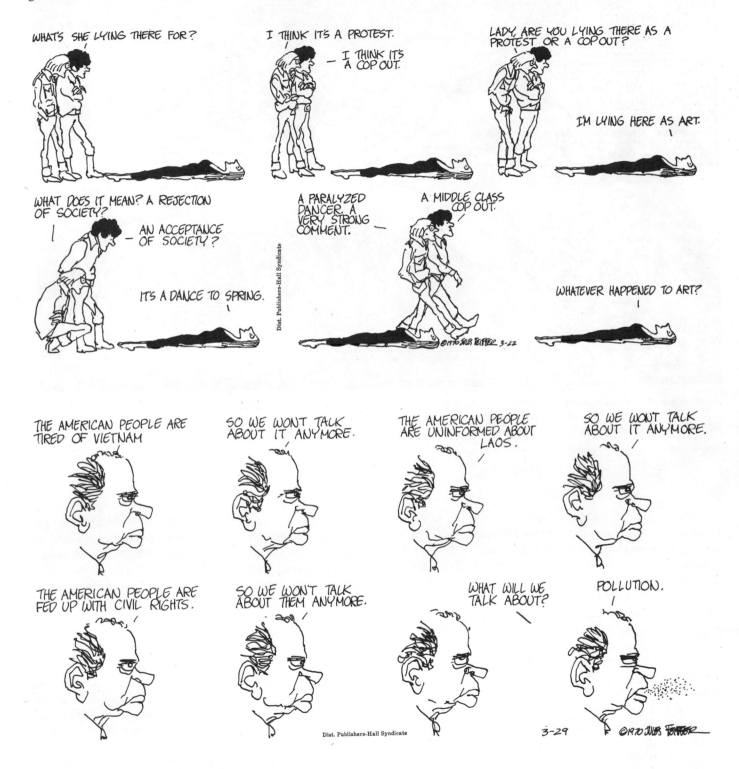

Jules Feiffer's strip *Feiffer* is an extended editorial cartoon and it is often a political caricature. It spares neither the follies of the intellectuals nor the actions of the Nixon Administration.
© 1970 Jules Feiffer

MAD began in 1952 with parodies of successful comics series. The wealth of detail, as seen in this *Superduperman* picture by Wallace Wood, was characteristic of the style in those days and especially of the style of Will Elder.
© 1954 E.C. Publications Inc.

caricature and *Feiffer* represents the transition to the 'editorial cartoon', the political caricature; Bernard Mergendeiler, Feiffer's anti-hero, is the archetypal insecure intellectual.

Feiffer also draws for *Playboy* (whose artist Shel Silverstein cultivates a similar style of humour and drawing), and it was there that, at the height of the super-hero boom from 1965 to 1969, Bernard Mergendeiler pursued his adventures as *Hostile-Man*, a witty parody of the craze for superheroes.

MAD

Harvey Kurtzman is the spiritual father of *MAD*, which was christened in April 1952. Until 1955 *MAD* appeared in the format of a normal comic book and like them cost 10 cents. The full title: *Tales calculated to drive you MAD—Humor in a Jugular Vein*, was a warning to the reader about the type of humour it cultivated. In its first years *MAD* was mainly composed of take-offs of all the most famous comics series. Will Elder, Wallace

Wood and Jack Davis drew most of the stories which exposed the weaknesses and clichés of the comics series they attacked in incisive, exact and extremely witty fashion. *MAD*, like the second satirical comic book by E.C., *Panic (This is no Comic Book, This is a 'Panic'—Humor in a Varicose Vein)*, was enthusiastically received by its youthful readers and did much to foster a critical awareness of the bad products of the medium.

Will Elder's special style was to add so many extras in his comic book take-offs, changing from picture to picture, that even the tenth reading would show up something new.

In 1955, after the introduction of the Comics Code and some months after Entertaining Comics had ceased production of their horror comics and other comic books, the format of *MAD* was enlarged and the satirical comic book turned into a satirical magazine.

Nothing is safe from the creators of *MAD* if it seems stupid, hypocritical or bad to them. By satirical exaggeration *MAD* shows what a humbug most of what the media produce is. Besides the media it also exposes and attacks the leisure and consumer

216

In *MAD*'s film and television parodies, artist Mort Drucker demonstrates his incredible mastery in the unerring caricature of the main characters. With biting irony these take-offs expose every cliché situation, as here in the TV series *Tarzan* in which even Albert from *Pogo* falls victim to Tarzan's knife.
© 1968 E.C. Publications Inc./Bildschriftenverlag

The sick humour of Don Martin fills some of *MAD*'s most popular pages.
© 1968 E.C. Publications Inc./Bildschriftenverlag

STRASSENARBEITEN

habits of the American citizen. *MAD*, whose offices are in MADison Avenue, attacks the advertising and entertainment industry which is largely based in this street. Consistently, there are no adverts in *MAD* except for final-page advertising, which attacks instead of advertising and is particularly directed against alcohol and cigarettes. Without hypocrisy *MAD* can make Hitler advertise cigarettes, since the entire editorial staff stopped smoking in the 1960s on the advice of the publisher, William M. Gaines.

The style of *MAD* in the sixties was heavily marked by the film and television satires of the superb artist and caricaturist Mort Drucker, the way-out humour of Don Martin, whose oeuvre is the best example of sick humour in comics style, and by David Berg, whose regular feature *The Lighter Side of* . . . takes the mickey out of the life styles of American suburbia. Jack Davis and Wallace Wood have repeatedly worked for *MAD* too. Will Elder followed Harvey Kurtzman when the latter left *MAD* in 1956 to start his own satirical magazines such as *Help!* and *Trump*, which had no lasting success. Yet in his own way Harvey

217

Today *MAD* is in magazine format. But the satires are still in comics style, as before. This extract is from the German version of *MAD*; a number of countries are now being infiltrated by the special *MAD* humour.

Marvel also experimented with comics parodies for a while in *Not Brand ECCH*. With take-offs of itself and its rivals, it sometimes matched the standard of the old *MAD* parodies.

Kurtzman is the man who decisively determined the style of humour and satire in the USA after 1950. In 1960 *MAD* already had a circulation of 1,400,000; in 1971 it reached 2·15 million sold issues. This is quite a phenomenon considering the high level of its contents. As before, most of the contributions are in comics style and perhaps that is why most of the readers are under twenty. The *MAD* anthologies in pocketbook format are also extremely successful, especially the first ones with their reprints of comics parodies such as *The MAD Reader*, *Mad Strikes Back*, *Inside Mad* or *Utterly Mad*, which became permanent best-sellers and sold millions.

A special feature of *MAD* is the 'self-kidding', the irony directed against itself, with which it pulls the ground from under its own critical stance in order to raise the level; this means that people grant it a certain fool's licence. This is apparent in the titles of annuals (which are anthologies of special issues): titles such as *The Worst from MAD* or *More Trash from MAD from the most sickening past issues*.

The fanatical gang of E.C. fans remained loyal to *MAD* even when the E.C. issues came to an end. Just as the members of the E.C. fan club had been, the readers of *MAD* were also imbued with an in-group feeling, the sense of belonging to an illustrious circle of elect. By means of word inventions like 'veeblefetzer', 'furshlugginer', 'ecch' and 'potrzebie' which can be applied to anything at all, *MAD* was made fully accessible only to those 'in the know'. *MAD* achieved its continuity because it had a fictitious publisher called Alfred E. Neuman who announces his motto 'What—Me Worry?' to his readers with the look of an imbecile. The importance of a fictional mascot of this kind, who personifies the publishing house for the reader, is also shown by the importance of similar figures in other successful magazines: figures like the Playboy bunny, Marvel's non-existent Irving Forbush or Sylvester P. Smythe, the little mascot figure of the only successful *MAD* imitation, *Cracked*, which was especially marked out by the style of artist John Severin.

Satires allow one to say what the ordinary critic has to omit, for it is easier to laugh at the object under attack than to examine it objectively. Like all media, *MAD* also attacks the increasingly obvious evils of American society, as well as the manner in which those evils are dealt with by the Left and the Right. But this is not the reason why the members of the *MAD* editorial staff are called 'pinkos', implying that they are 'pink' communists if not Reds. For every intellectual comes under suspicion of this in America.

Comics from the underground

'Obscene, anarchistic, sophomoric, subversive, apocalyptic, the underground cartoonists and their creations attack all that middle America holds dear.'[2] A label of this kind is a heavy burden for these products which, unlike ordinary comics, call themselves comix or even komix. After the first furore caused by their birth in 1968—a time when the police were still fairly active—they proved to be rather less progressive, subversive or radical than generally supposed. Even the designation 'underground' is more than a little dubious, for the comix do not come from an underground and neither are they produced under conditions of oppression. Their very existence contradicts their name, for Fascism is not yet so far advanced in the USA that underground activity can no longer be pursued under the protection of freedom of the press.

Nor were the comix really born in spring 1968 when Robert Crumb produced his first *Zap Comix* under a private imprint and sold them to hippies and other members of the San Francisco subculture on the street corners of Haight Ashbury. The whole thing began in the universities, in numbers of excellent college magazines where many of the future underground artists won their first spurs—and at that time they were often much fresher and more original than later in the underground where they were forced to be free. For instance one of the favourites of the underground, Gilbert Shelton's *Wonder Wart-Hog*, had already appeared in 1966 in *Texas Ranger*, the magazine of the University of Texas,[3] and in 1965 in Harvey Kurtzmann's *Help!*

The hideousness of man and his sexual complexes are the main elements in underground comix.
© 1968 Robert Crumb/Viking Press Inc. (1970 Marz Verlag)

Head Comix by Robert Crumb. (German version.) Police brutality is a fashionable feature of underground comics.
© 1968 Robert Crumb/Viking Press Inc. (1970 Marz Verlag)

Robert Crumb's *Fritz the Cat* first appeared in the men's magazine *Cavalier* and thus it is an example of the transition from underground to establishment. This extract is from the German version.
© 1968 Robert Crumb/Viking Press Inc. (1970 Marz Verlag)

Similarly the stinking super-wart-hog, which gives free rein to
his sadism in its super-hero form, was also the protagonist of a
magazine as well established as *Drag Cartoons*. Already at that
time Wonder Wart-Hog's secret identity was Philbert Desenex,
'Ace reporter of a great Megatropolitan newspaper', a paper later
identified in the comix as *Muthalode Morning Mungpie*. Even
Robert Crumb's *Fritz the Cat*, one of the successful figures of his
Head Comix, had first appeared in *Cavalier*, a successful establishment magazine of the *Playboy* type.

Underground comix appeared only when the subculture of
America had grown to such dimensions in 1968 that a ready-
made and sufficiently broad section of buyers existed who had
already been conditioned by the countless underground papers.
Moreover by this time the general climate in the media was
sufficiently liberal.

After the first issue of *Zap Comix* Robert Crumb made arrange-
ments for a firm to take over the printing and distribution.
Creative freedom and financial independence are important for
an underground artist. This is why Jack Saxon and Gilbert
Shelton founded the Rip-Off Press (*Big Ass Comix*), a kind of
authors' publishing house, to obtain a higher profit margin.
Similarly Jay Lynch and Skip Williamson (*Bijou Funnies*)
founded their Bijou Publishing Empire in Chicago. The San
Francisco Comic Book Company, a special second-hand comics
firm with a flourishing mail-order business throughout the world,
began to produce its own comix such as *Snatch* and *Jiz*. The
authors and artists are also publishers and so they derive no dis-
advantages from giving licences for publication throughout the
world.

As a sales attraction, comix are inscribed 'For Adults Only',
which promotes sales like X certificates on films.[4] They have the
same aim as the Italian and French *fumetti per adulti*, which
exploit similar subjects without the camouflage of the progressive
underground but are less free of restraint because they are
addressed to a mass public.

The American underground cinema pointed a course which
comix could not follow through because of their commercial bias.
The underground cinema broke with old visual habits in order to
create a 'new sensibility', in the sense in which Marcuse defines it,
to create new linguistic and pictorial formulae, a new aesthetic
and, finally, to broaden and change consciousness through its
content. Little of all this can be seen in the comix. They did not
make use of their freedom.

Rick Griffin and Victor Moscoso, whose work also appeared
in *Zap Comix*, offer text-free pictures of fantastic, psychedelic,
mind-shattering metamorphoses, but these are merely eccentric,
if skilful, graphic amusements. Robert Crumb's pictures of the
ugliness of the environment and man in it are still the most
honest ones, a vulgar image of reality without the usual trans-
figuring mechanisms of the media.

As though a dam had broken, all that censorship had for so
long kept out of comics flooded into the underground comix in an
orgy of sex, violence and bloodthirstiness. In an act of self-
liberation, like the graffiti artists in public lavatories, the artists

Class War Comix. The political message of underground comix usually consists in a simple bowdlerization of the Nixon Administration's policies.

depicted their own complexes and those of their fellow men, and people were extremely shocked by this.

Underground comix are polemics in comics format, emotional arguments expressing resentment of the establishment. These radical comix are addressed to a special readership, one that is more responsive to Robert Crumb's *Mr Natural* than to figures which symbolize the system like Captain America or Superman. But instead of leading to new objectives or really breaking new ground, these radical underground comix exploit the state of mind of a reactionary subculture and shock by their unconsidered portrayal of drug-addicted drop-outs.

Nard n' Pat by Jay Lynch. In their efforts to break with everything that was sacred to the comics approved by the Code, the underground comics take particular pleasure in distorting popular characters from other comics. This is one of the better examples: *Nard n' Pat* based on *Andy Gump* and *Krazy Kat* and also on Schlesinger's successful film *Midnight Cowboy*.

10 The art of comics

Comics and the High Renaissance

On 2 May 1969 the Federal Courthouse of Bridgeport, Connecticut, declared comics to be art. Mort Walker had donated 1,055 original drawings from *Beetle Bailey* to the research centre at Syracuse University, which collects both manuscripts and works of art. Since Mort Walker wanted this gift exempted from tax, he had to obtain a decision with the financial authority as to whether the drawings were trade products or precious works of art. The jury decided in favour of art and the drawings were taxed at 28,000 dollars, which was reckoned considerably lower than their value by eleven of the jury.[3] This decision established a precedent. But there are still a few narrow-minded philistines among art critics who will not acknowledge this verdict!

Comics artists themselves hardly seem bothered by this whole art dispute, and yet they are secretly proud that in 1967 their work actually hung in the Louvre (in the exhibition *Bande dessinée et figuration narrative*—arranged by SOCERLID).[4] The proximity with Leonardo surely had some effect.

The people in the business, such as Wallace Wood, do not however distinguish between museum art or fine art and trade or commercial art (popular art), saying that these different value categories are merely an invention of this century. At the time of Toulouse-Lautrec, they say, his poster art was not judged any differently from his paintings. But Wallace Wood is not alone in willingly admitting that while the major part of comics production must indubitably be graded as a trade product, some of the work in the best comics may well be considered art. The label of artist or artisan is allotted by the critic, for the creators of comics do not consider it their job to produce art but to make consumer comics.

Attempts to prove the presence of stylistic elements of fine art in comics stem from a more or less open desire on the part of those engaged in this medium to justify it by imbuing it with an aura of culture. When the same attempts were made in the early days of serious film criticism as early as 1934, Thomas Wolfe scoffed at those who tried to interpret Charlie Chaplin as a King Lear in modern dress.

Burne Hogarth, who, as he confesses himself, not only admires Michelangelo but indeed everyone from Masaccio to baroque painting, now found himself elected the Michelangelo of comics because his Tarzan had a classically ideal form—whoever drew him had to be a master of anatomy—and he offered a visual lesson in anatomy with his brief loin-cloth as a kind of model nude figure. In addition, Hogarth liked to show his Tarzan in extreme perspective foreshortening, so that every reader involuntarily cried 'Ah! Mantegna!' on sight. But there was no need to wait for realists like Hogarth and Foster to teach the comics artists anatomy. With female figures such as Nora and Maggie in

Burne Hogarth is the master of anatomical foreshortening. No wonder he was immediately likened to the Italian painters of the Renaissance.
© United Feature Syndicate/UPI

Jeden Augenblick muß er gewärtig sein, daß ihn ein Speer oder eine Kugel trifft.

224

The clear line drawing of George McManus is very strongly in-fluenced by Art Nouveau (McManus began to work for comic strips in 1903). His talent is particularly evident in the details and interiors. © 1941 King Features/Bulls

One artist whose genius cannot be praised too highly is Carl Barks who drew the *Donald Duck* and *Uncle Scrooge* strips for comic books until 1968. His effortless treatment of detail reminds us of George McManus; it is only recently that Barks has received due recognition. From *Walt Disney's Comics and Stories* No. 252. © 1961 Walt Disney Productions

Bringing up Father, George McManus is the best proof of this. His mastery of realistic expression is an essential if an impression of facility is to be achieved with the cartoon style.

But on questions of art people tend to stay with the realists, and so Milton Caniff was actually declared the Rembrandt of the comic strip.[5] Differences of style between comics artists such as Milton Caniff and Alex Raymond are even compared to the differences between Piero della Francesca and Caravaggio.[6] The game is no doubt a fascinating one.

opposite
The process of artistic creation as teamwork. Stan Lee, Larry Lieber and Johnny Romita (in the centre panel from left to right) provide greater insight into events at an editorial meeting for a *Spider-Man* issue. 'Creative freedom' is the secret of the Marvel touch. From *Spider-Man Annual* No. 5. © 1968 Marvel Comics Group

Among comics artists there is hardly one who has had an art school training purely oriented around the old masters and then descended from 'high art' to the lower depths of comics. Comics art is a vocation. Future comics artists usually begin to draw as soon as they can grip a pencil and practise on the model they have —on comics. They learn by copying their favourite artists, and so each one very soon develops a sense of belonging to a certain style. Feiffer is not the only one to have drawn comic books for himself even as a boy (one of which he proudly illustrated in his book *The Great Superheroes*).

In art schools, often in evening classes, the future comics artists train for commercial art and advertising design. One of these art schools has been run by Burne Hogarth since he gave up his *Tarzan* strip. The first commandment for all beginners is John Dewey's 'You learn it by doing it'. This basic formula of Ameri-can pragmatism is also reflected in the motto of the 'Famous Artists Course': 'You learn to draw by drawing.'[7]

Unless he is a genius the student begins his apprenticeship as assistant to a comic strip artist or executes the less important stories in comic books. In the Golden Age of comic books an old comics proverb, which still has some validity today, ran: 'Good

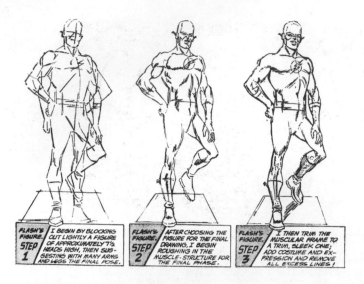

The elegant figure of the *Silver Surfer* finally ousted the muscular super-hero of the Charles Atlas school. Apollo Saurochtonos was godfather. From *Silver Surfer* No. 6. Artists: John Buscema and Sal Buscema.

swiping is an art in itself.' At that time it gave the readers special pleasure to trace back the sources of the drawings in comic books to the *Flash Gordon* or *Prince Valiant* strips.[8]

We can retrace the development of many artists very precisely. An example here is Russ Manning, who served his apprenticeship for a decade in Western Publishing (*Brothers of the Spear, Tarzan*) before taking over the *Tarzan* newspaper strip. Or there is John Buscema, who still produced *Roy Rogers* numbers without particular distinction in the fifties under ACG (American Comics Group) although there were hints of his talent in some stories; then after eight years as a commercial illustrator he reached the first peak of his creativity with Marvel (*The Avengers, Silver Surfer*).

For many artists the height of ambition is to have their own comic strip, which is also the most lucrative job in the business. There are virtually no bad artists in comic strips, while in comic books artists of lesser quality can also earn their living because of the immense demand. But not all artists can tolerate the terrible strain of fighting a deadline day in day out with a daily strip (while many others like Frank Robbins, still have enough time left to complete six weekly strips and a Sunday series of *Johnny Hazard* in two and a half days and still work as a writer for DC). But many strip artists have little or no leisure left and this is why most realistic artists have one or more assistants. As a result many artists prefer to stay with comic books.

Neal Adams is not the only one to have turned from comic strips

A brilliant example of how Alex Raymond links his masterful light-and-shade technique with a skilful use of changing camera angles. Picture and text are related, but at first glance it is only the drawing that catches our eye.

Al Williamson is a worthy pupil of Alex Raymond. He too has an outstanding talent for creating atmosphere by means of light and shade and using changing camera angles (from the total picture via the 'American' view to the close-up).

to comic books. When his *Ben Casey* came to an end he began to work with Warren Publications and DC; there he became the Batman specialist, helped *Deadman* to fame, executed title pictures for many series but never allowed himself to be pinned down to a particular series for any length of time. At the same time he also began to work for Marvel. For many comic strip artists the period with comic books was only a transitional phase of their career. Mac Raboy, who took over *Flash Gordon* in 1948, drew *Captain Marvel, Jr.* for Fawcett. He was not the only one to assist C. C. Beck, who drew Captain Marvel. David Berg, who achieved fame and honour with *MAD*, also used to draw the super-hero (in red knitted singlet) at the time. Dan Barry, who now draws *Flash Gordon*, worked on crime comics such as *Crime Does Not Pay* and *Big Town*. Before Leonard Starr began his much-praised series *Mary Perkins on Stage*, he drew stories in the style of *Terry and the Pirates* for comics such as *Air Boy*. Stan Drake, king of melodrama with *Juliet Jones*, still remembers the time in the Golden Age of Comics when he earned between five and seven dollars for a whole page (layout, pencil drawing, ink execution and colouring).

The days of the Golden Age of the forties, when there were still drawing studios delivering work to a number of different firms (incidentally the only products where one could speak of conveyer-belt work) are long past. Will Eisner tells of this era: 'I was running a shop in which we made comic book features pretty much the way Ford turned out cars.'[9]

Carmine Infantino demonstrates how *Flash* is drawn according to the conventional rules of anatomy. From *Flash* No. 169.

Frank Frazetta, the master of archaic-futuristic comics, has also been greatly praised for his illustrations of the pocket editions of Edgar Rice Burroughs' novels. From *Witzend* No. 3.
© 1967 Frank Frazetta/Witzend

It is the freelancers, who work anywhere depending on mood and orders, who have most freedom and who most often go hungry. Wallace Wood is one of the most prolific and one of the best. For instance he worked for E.C., *MAD*, Marvel, DC, Charlton, Tower, Warren, Western Publishing and King Features and also designed book covers and record sleeves. He also founded the magazine *Witzend*, the exclusive comics magazine for fastidious fans, in which the old E.C. gang also reappeared. In *Witzend* the artists retain the copyright of the individual stories.

Art in comics
Hal Foster, the first of the comics realists, was a noted illustrator and graphic designer before he worked on *Tarzan*. Indeed most of the first comic strip artists, like Dirks and Outcault, began as cartoonists and caricaturists for satirical magazines and newspapers. The stylistic tradition of the dime novel illustrations of the previous century was carried over to the illustrations in the pulps and then to the comic books to which several pulp artists switched over.

So comics have their own art history which has little in common with fine art. And yet, like fine art, they go through their various periods of experimental innovation and stylistic advances. After the magazine style of the early artists James Swinnerton was one of the first to reduce the style of illustration to simple, clear line drawing. Bud Fisher (*Mutt & Jeff*) declared in an early interview (28 December 1911): 'Art doesn't hamper my desire to express myself. . . . I use as few lines as possible . . . I never use unnecessary lines because they take the mind from the main feature, the idea. Any ability that I have is directed toward the creation of an idea with the use of as few lines as possible.'[10]

Comics have created their own criteria. As Stan Lee put it, comics should be seen as an art form in the same way as films are. Film criticism soon solved the dilemma of whether films should be measured by traditional artistic criteria or not. What is judged is the content, the values it transmits, the sociological aspect, the intention of the author and how he translates it, the manner in which the formalistic methods of the film are employed. Film is an art in its own terms and so are comics.

Comics are part of mass culture, a popular art, and should be examined as such. The art of comics lies in their perfect escapism, and in this respect they evolved their own brand of aesthetics.

Hal Foster follows in the tradition of the great illustrators. His masterly work contains all the forms of realistic portrayal. The bold architecture of the island castle in the Mediterranean reminds us of the distant lights of Camelot.
© 1955 King Features/Bulls

The crucial point is how perfectly, how absorbingly and dynamically a story is told in picture and text, how effectively the linguistic and pictorial jokes interact. It is bad—that is it lacks effect—if it is too wordy where a picture would be more striking. The interaction of picture and text are all-important. Furthermore the pictures in comics must be examined as to the various camera positions and the montage employed. Of course the artist's particular preferences can be employed as a stylistic element, for each artist has his own imagery, his own pictorial language and style. Foster, Hogarth and Raymond are comics artists because there is a close relation between picture and text in their works too. But since they wanted to achieve their primary effect through pictures they pushed the speech balloons and text to the edge of the picture and left out the line round the balloon, which they considered distracting. So they were not comics artists in the narrow sense of the word but story illustrators, whose work can be judged by the same criteria as painting or graphic art. It is

logical that Hal Foster was the first comics artist whose pictures were prized by museums, for he does not integrate the text into the picture.

So Hal Foster, Burne Hogarth and Alex Raymond are not to be praised for building a bridge between the High Renaissance and comics. Rather they are the Eisensteins and Pudowkins of comics, bringing the technique of the film—cutting, different camera angles and montage—into comics with their adventure strips. Will Eisner, the ingenious artist who drew *Spirit*, gave just as much to comic books in his own way as Foster and Hogarth gave to comic strips. Before Eisner, to paraphrase his own words, comics were only a sequence of pictures, and it was he who made them variable. Will Eisner was also very influenced by film ('film influenced me tremendously'[11]) and transmitted its techniques to comics. Many later artists like Jack Kirby and Bob Kane were equally fascinated by the film and studied its formal techniques.

230

A. Giolitti is one of the great masters of perspective and three-dimensional effects. His clear, expressive style made him into one of the most imitated comics artists in America and elsewhere. One finds Giolitti copied time and time again in Europe too, especially in Italy. From *Have Gun Will Travel* O.S. 982.
© 1959 Columbia Broadcasting System Inc./Western Publishing Co. Inc.

In comics, as in films, downward- and upward-angle shots can often be found in Westerns, for instance in the depiction of the showdown. A master of 'staging in depth' (which Orson Welles first used in *Citizen Kane*) is A. Giolitti who likes to work with 3-D effects (*Gunsmoke, Have Gun Will Travel, Tales from Welles Fargo*). Giolitti was also one of the artists who broke away from the rigid layout of six panels by placing a double picture in the most effective spot. He did this in Western Publishing comic books.

Jim Steranko, one of the new recruits to the illustrious circle of widely acknowledged comics artists, describes his work as follows:

I regard my stories as periodic and personal statements of adventure and heroic fantasy. More often than not, they embody new and occasionally quite subtle visual efforts but always toward a functional total concept. Experimentation has led to a truly fulfilling introspective of storytelling, which is what comics are all about. Of primary importance, is the

Arturo del Castillo is a great virtuoso of Western comics. The economy of his style evokes the vastness of the country and the loneliness of the cowboy.
© 1970 Eurostudio Milano

In the second half of the sixties Jim Steranko and Neal Adams introduced works of art of a very high quality into comic books. In this extract from *Deadman*, a series for which he had done some brilliant and unusual drawings, Neal Adams pays tribute to his colleague: if you look at them from below the flames read: HEY, A JIM STERANKO EFFECT. From *Strange Adventures* No. 216. © 1969 National Periodical Publications Inc.

arrangement or orchestration of elements or panels. This structure of organized long, medium and close-up shots; their space relationships and related images create a kind of visual tension. This tension is applied to the problem of story formula: conflict, crisis, climax.[12]

For the producers of comics the only essential is the effect on the public and the knowledge that this public rewards high-quality drawing very well. Marvel had to admit that it was a heavy blow to the 'house of ideas' when first Steve Ditko and then (in 1970) Jack Kirby left the firm to hire themselves elsewhere. When a good artist leaves a comic book series the comic may well perish for lack of success, even if the story writers remain the same.

Style and technique

To be accepted as a genuine connoisseur of comics art it is not nearly enough now to mention only the three stars of comics realism, Foster, Hogarth and Raymond. The true connoisseur can immediately—without cheating by a quick glance at the imprint on the first page—give the name of the penciller, inker and perhaps even the layout man in any comic put before him. The trained eye recognizes the minimal and yet so significant differences in the individual stylistic trends. It goes without saying that the shrewd reader can, of course, also recognize the author of the story by his stylistic peculiarities. The true connoisseur is also familiar with the many different elements within a stylistic school. Followers of the great Burne Hogarth include artists such as Steve Ditko, whose best-known work is the first thirty-eight issues of *Spider Man*, or John Buscema, who displays an elegant, strong, dynamic style similar to his master. Artists like Gil Kane and Russ Manning came from the art school run by Burne Hogarth.

Milton Caniff, one of the all-time greats of the comic strip, has many imitators. The rapid, superbly volatile brush-strokes of Frank Robbins (*Johnny Hazard*) are very reminiscent of *Terry and the Pirates* and *Steve Canyon*. Of course Alfred Andriola, who worked as an assistant to Caniff in *Terry and the Pirates*, was also influenced by him. He applied what he had learned in his own strip *Charlie Chan* from 1938 on and later in *Kerry Drake*. But many comic book artists such as Lee Elias (*Black Canary*) remind us of Milton Caniff rather too clearly.

Most of the artists do not rely only on their powers of imagination and willingly make use of other sources. Good reference material is often half the battle. That is why many artists have a comprehensive 'morgue' (archive) in which they have collected photos from magazines ready for any suitable occasion. *National Geographic* magazine is the most frequently used source for comics stories that take place in distant lands. Burne Hogarth also drew inspiration from this magazine, but only using it as a source of ideas which he then adapted to the universe of his own imagination. The shape of a chair or a coffee pot could inspire an oriental temple, the houses of a lost culture.[13]

233

This blow-up from *Tarzan* shows clearly how Russ Manning, a faithful follower of Burroughs, skilfully used cast shadows and screens to suggest a dense atmospheric night.
© 1969 United Feature Syndicate/UPI

To give their figures the right facial expression the artists merely have to glance in the mirror. Relatively few work with live models, and if they do you find the closer members of their family and circle of friends appearing in the strip. Milton Caniff is well known for this technique, and the work of Alex Raymond also contains many portraits of people familiar to him. Leonard Starr (*Mary Perkins on Stage*) further heightens the extreme realism of his strips by taking people he knows as models and portraying them exactly. He also takes care that the shapes of the heads of the characters in each individual episode do not resemble each other and that they all have different hair styles.

Deadlines determine the whole work process—unless, as in the case of *Peanuts*, the artist's style allows him to complete the whole week's programme in a space of three or four days. In the case of realistic strips it is practically impossible to execute both the Sunday page and the daily strips without assistance (Frank Robbins is an exception). Burne Hogarth and Hal Foster could make their *Tarzan* strip so well-balanced and give it such artistic effects only because the daily strip was drawn by Rex Maxon. For his realistic *Buz Sawyer* strip Roy Crane has three collaborators, although he is not nearly as fanatical about the tiny details of the military equipment as he was at the beginning and has handed over the whole of the Sunday page to a comedy strip featuring *Rosco Sweeney*, the friend of Buz Sawyer.[14]

If necessary yet another artist can help out. Phillip 'Tex' Blaisdell, for instance, was a landscape specialist, and collaborated wherever necessary on many different strips before taking over Harold Gray's *Little Orphan Annie* after Gray's

Mary Perkins On Stage by Leonard Starr (detail). Through his use of night scenes and lurid searchlights the artist manages to create an atmosphere of suspense, even though he is working in black and white on the Sunday page which is mainly in colour.
© 1967 Chicago Tribune—New York News Syndicate

death. Stan Drake, who draws *Juliet Jones*, tells[15] how for lack of time he hit upon the idea of simply replacing the background with xeroxed snapshots of towns which he then went over in ink and corrected. If time presses or if he does not feel like it, the artist can always show a face in close-up instead.

Comics and Pop art

In 1959 the critics could still without prejudice deny comics any artistic claims. Kenneth E. Eble wrote at the time: 'The comics fail badly as art despite their pretension to seriousness—or perhaps because of it. They have about the same relationship to serious art that a tract like *Pierce Pennilesse* has to *Paradise Lost*. At worst, they have as much artistic value as Campbell Soup

labels.'[16] A few years later Andy Warhol was to use Campbell Soup tins to make 'art' in the esoteric sense of the word highly questionable.

The reproductive technique of comics seemed to preclude any artistic claims; naturally only the original drawings were hung in museums and galleries. But this obstacle was surmounted when Pop artists made multiple reproductions of paintings such as the *Mona Lisa*, using a silk screen, and then offered this product to the art-loving public.

Lawrence Alloway, to whom the introduction of the term 'Pop art' is ascribed in 1954–5 first used it as a synonym for the mass media (popular culture) in order to counter the accusation that the mass media were an *ersatz* culture aimed at a public incapable of appreciating the value of genuine culture. So from the very

235

Lichtenstein's expressive picture of a hand holding a smoking colt revolver was used on the cover of the issue of *Time* magazine devoted to arms and violence in America. The colour screen used in comics has been turned into a stylistic technique by Lichtenstein. Cover portrait courtesy TIME Magazine.
© 1968 Time Inc.

beginning Pop art was the expression of a view of art which did not start by excluding mass culture but took it as seriously as 'fine art', in order to come to terms with it.

Commercial products were now accepted as subject matter for art and the antagonism between commerce and art was abolished by the technique of Pop art. If Warhol first painted his *Campbell's Soup Cans* in oils, the logical next step was to print them, to come closer and closer to the genuine object, in this way confirming that the production methods of commercial art were a form of artistic expression. Finally his *Brillo Boxes* are identical to the object. Once the step from handicraft to technical reproduction had been taken, the place of the individual artist was finally taken by the 'factory', Warhol's factory.

In the work of Roy Lichtenstein, too, comics represent the mass culture. He re-submitted comics to pictorial, artistic criteria, made them into 'museum art', in order to throw light upon the nature of the object of reference by distancing it. By the use of deliberate abstraction Roy Lichtenstein removes the existing 'commercial image' of comics, detaching the individual picture from its series, blowing it up and thus imbuing it with a timeless quality. Similarly, in the reproduction of comics for exhibitions and galleries, the desired artistic effect is usually only achieved by blow-ups.

From *c.* 1951 Roy Lichtenstein, inspired by the work of early painters of Westerns such as Remington and Charles Wilson Peel, had done cowboys, Indians and villains in cubist style; then in 1957 he began to paint anthropomorphic animals from comics such as *Bugs Bunny*, *Donald Duck*, *Mickey Mouse* and *Krazy Kat*, in mural size. Only after a period of abstract expressionism did Lichtenstein again return to comics as his subject matter. The emblematic function of the connection between picture and speech balloon was retained in these 'paintings'. By using a projector Lichtenstein obtained a large pictorial model, a blow-up several feet in size, which he did not then copy exactly, instead reducing it to even stricter lines. This heightened the expressive force of the comics style even further. Lichtenstein also took over the comics' screen of dots, the Ben Day Dots with which the Sunday page strips and comics were coloured. Lichtenstein applied the Ben Day Dots by means of a perforated screen and in his paintings they serve as point of reference to the mass printing technique of comics.

The pictures Lichtenstein chose as models for his paintings are typical examples of the whole genrre to which they belong. Lichtenstein himself calls them archetypal situations. In nearly every case he selects a climax in the action. In romances this is often the moment when the tears flow, the bitterest hour of love's

'WHAAM!' (1963) by Roy Lichtenstein. In most of his paintings, including those based on scenes in war comics, Lichtenstein concentrates on the climax of the action, the moment of firing.
© The Tate Gallery, London

torments, as in *Hopeless*, 1963. Lichtenstein chose his 'Nurses' because the doctor theme is usually the source of the greatest melodrama. His other favourite motifs—besides Westerns (*Draw*, 1963)—come from the war theme—war at sea, on land and in the air: again he chooses the climax, the moment of firing, as in *Whaam!*, 1963, *OK, Hot Shot, Okay! I'm Pouring!* 1963, or *As I opened Fire* 1964.

In spite of the opportunities it offered for criticizing society, by distorting familiar features of the everyday world and blowing them up to enormous proportions, Pop art was in the final analysis no more than an excursion of fine art into the field of mass culture and it was analysed to death. Whenever fine art has exhausted its forms of expression it turns to new things, in order to be able to match up to developments in the world around it more adequately. So Pop art can be seen as a period that took over from the abstract expressionism that preceded it, when the ambiguity and subjectivity of the latter no longer seemed in tune with the times.

Pop art aims to confront the observer with the pressures in his environment. Comics are representative examples of this commercial, pictorial world and this is why they played an important role in English and American Pop art from the very beginning, and not only under Roy Lichtenstein. The celebrated exhibition 'This is tomorrow' took place in London in 1956 and contributed a great deal to the breakthrough of English Pop art. The collage from the exhibition catalogue, *Just what is it, that makes today's homes so different, so appealing?* by Richard Hamilton, since reproduced again and again, is an inventory of mass culture. The collage includes a mural representing a title page from *Young Romance*. This comic book typifying the worst melodrama in any medium was to become a particular favourite with Roy Lichtenstein. In America in 1954 and 1955 Robert Rauschenberg used comic strip pages from the newspapers as background to his 'paintings', which were still in the abstract expressionist style at that time; for example *Satellite* 1955. Jasper Johns, one of the pioneers of American Pop art, painted over *Alley Oop* in 1958 and Andy Warhol used comic strip figures as models for his 'paintings' from 1959 on. His *Dick Tracy* of 1960 is particularly famous.

237

11 Trends and developments

Heroes are humanized

Superman, the *non plus ultra* in super-heroes for over thirty years, was given a new image. Symbolically, the title page picture of issue 233 (January 1971: 'A new year—a new start'), showed him bursting out of chains of kryptonite, the substance which had been his Achilles' heel until then. 'Kryptonite Nevermore!' blazed the title at the foot of the page. And the title of the issue actually announced 'The Amazing NEW Adventures of SUPERMAN'. What had happened?

In the issue concerned a chemical experiment transforms all the kryptonite on earth into harmless iron. So Superman has become totally invincible. But no! From the sand into which Superman was thrown by the explosion that freed him from kryptonite there rises a figure. While Superman is flying over it for the first time he has an inexplicable feeling of weakness. A new peril, greater than ever before, confronts the brazen hero: his duplicate, formed of sand, who robs him of his energies and power and threatens the earth. Superman's adventures are again full of the suspense they had long since lost. Of course it was not possible to make a complete break with the old tradition, but a change was possible. Superman's adventures no longer have a beginning and an end; instead they are a biography in the style of the Marvel comics, linked from issue to issue by the subplots. This new policy was continued even after Superman's double had disappeared again.

And so complications immediately await Superman—and Clark Kent. He no longer works as a newspaper reporter. Morgan Edge, the president of Galaxy Broadcasting System, a television company that has bought up the *Daily Planet* (a reference to the concentration of the press), employs Clark as a television reporter with his own overground car. But the familiar 'Great Caesar's Ghost!' of chief editor Perry White seems somehow to be missing. Clark Kent always steals the scene and is by now pleased at any job that allows him to fulfil his duties as Superman rapidly.

For the rest Superman is more conscious than before of being an outsider, a man from another planet who is tolerated on earth only because he helps humanity and in the end is treated as a human only in his Clark Kent identity. Moreover it is the Anti-

Superman. Title picture by Neal Adams. In 1971 Superman had a new start: from now on he was no longer vulnerable to kryptonite. © 1971 National Periodical Publications Inc.

Lois Lane by Werner Roth and Vince Colletta. Social commitment in comics. As a good journalist Lois Lane follows the example of John Howard Griffin in his book *Black Like Me* (1959) and of Grace Halsell in *Soul Sister* (1969). She changes the colour of her skin temporarily so that she can report on the slums. From *Lois Lane* No. 106.
© 1970 National Periodical Publications Inc.

Superman who underlines the schizophrenia latent in Superman more strongly than his former dual identity ever could. It was necessary for DC to bring even their best draughthorse down from the pedestal of hero worship in order to make him seem credible again.

Superman no longer comes forward as the untiring machine that can give help anywhere in the world. Either his efforts fail because of ownership relations that give a legal hold against his helpful intervention or he realizes that his action would rob men of any initiative of their own. From 1970 Superman did indeed go into the slums, but since his interference there would only bring about a forced solution, he is increasingly impelled to challenge humans to take action again themselves, to become fully aware of their duties and rights as citizens and to stop being passive and apolitical. Superman was not, however, the first super-hero to be humanized so that he could become more active socially.

As early as 1961, with his *Fantastic Four* and *Spider-Man*, Stan Lee had prepared the path which Superman was to tread in 1971 and on which almost all super-heroes had embarked by this time if they wanted to survive or at least continue to corner part of the market for a little while longer. The motto was no longer 'mindless distraction' but 'entertainment with a kick!'

At first even the Marvel heroes had no more to offer than the fact of their humanity. And in the long run humanity in itself is not enough to fascinate readers. However, even the small problems of private life have social references. So, gradually at first, social evils, treated realistically, began to appear in comics incidentally and almost unnoticed. When Peter (Spider-Man) Parker and Dick (Robin) Grayson went to college they suddenly found themselves in the thick of the protest against social evils and were involved in riots, sit-ins, demonstrations and protest meetings. This opened the door to revolutionary ideas in comic books.

Heroines such as Wonder Woman and Super Girl endowed with superior powers were robbed of these powers because powerless heroines seem more human and closer to reality than all-powerful creatures capable of everything. In some stories this produced direct links with the Womens' Liberation Movement. So lines like 'male chauvinist pigs' began to run through comics too. Even Lois Lane, Superman's girlfriend, has become very conscious of her rights and speaks of discrimination against women when she fails to obtain a reporting job. She has also become more self-assured towards Superman now that her rival Lana Lang has finally given him up. One issue of *Lois Lane* also

Terry and the Pirates. Topical events, even in conservative strips. Young anarchists have destroyed a private army museum and this gives the hero an opportunity to introduce himself and his attitudes.

Big Ben Bolt by John Cullen Murphy. Comics had always portrayed topical events, but controversial subjects such as the protection of the environment remained taboo in comic strips longer than in any other entertainment medium.
© 1970 King Features/Bulls

featured the first appearance of a new neurotic heroine in *Rose and the Thorn*. On the violent death of her policeman father Rose experiences such a shock that it awakens a subconscious desire for vengeance against the mafioso Band of 100 that is the source of all corruption. Every night she becomes the sleepwalking Thorn, engaging in a dangerous battle with the underworld of which she has not the slightest notion during her daily life as Rose. Heroines, who were becoming rare around 1955, are on the way up again. The growing number of super-heroines (some of them old revivals) such as *Black Canary, Black Widow, Medusa* and *Bat Girl* is leading to a more equal distribution of the sexes in comics.

Tired of interminable fighting, the heroes and heroines now discuss the same problems that can be heard daily on the news and read in the papers. Even invaders from other planets no longer desire to enslave the earth; instead they want to exterminate humans by encouraging their propensity to pollute and contaminate the environment. And once such external dangers

have been overcome, the view of smoking factory chimneys makes the heroes wonder just how long they have saved this world from destruction.[1] But there is no need of invaders from outer space to draw attention to the problems of pollution. The element in *Sub-Mariner*, the sea, gradually became so polluted and clouded as to be a serious threat to the survival of its inhabitants, the Atlantides. Now Sub-Mariner had real reason to continue waging battle against the detested land-dwellers. One of those responsible, the big industrialist Tony Stark, also super-hero of *The Invincible Iron Man*, had second thoughts and tried to make other polluters of the environment aware of the dangers brought on mankind by thoughtless production. The answer was: 'That will all sort itself out!—We have lots of time!'[2] Probably no other hero of a series has ever had to swallow such a defeat since the invention of comic books. In the context of the increasing number of references to reality 'The Amazing Ecology Man' no longer seems inconceivable.

Pogo by Walt Kelly. Man's greatest enemy is man himself.
© 1970 Walt Kelly

Legal proceedings in the 'new style' also provided a source for a number of 'adventures'. For instance Marvel's *Daredevil* fought for the life of three alleged bomb assassins in an extreme right-wing mock trial.[3] Green Lantern and Green Arrow even had to submit to a court that put no value on their evidence and brought them into court bound and gagged.[4] Ironically the jury were shown as rusty superannuated robots and after the last-minute self-liberation of the accused the 'judge' proved to be a power-crazed mechanic who had had to wait on the robots in the intergalactic court. This issue was alluding to the danger threatening any constitutional state that allows unqualified or corrupt forces to attain positions of power.

In fact Green Arrow and Green Lantern had had their first socially relevant adventures some issues before this 'trial'. In Issue 76, which is generally recognized as a milestone in the development of realistic super-heroes, Green Lantern came to realize while in the slums that rich, decent businessmen are not

always worth fighting for, even if outwardly they seem to be in the right. This caused the hero to reflect on his actions for the first time and not only to judge by appearances. And he had to confess with shame that throughout his long career he had dealt with all kinds of extra-terrestrial problems but had not once helped his black fellow-citizens on earth.

What can have moved the producers of comic books to rob their super-heroes of their powers, to conceive them in a more liberal and radical mould, thus opening their comic books to social questions? In the case of *Green Lantern* there were only two roads open in view of the falling circulation: either to cease publication altogether or to go forward and risk taking up relevant themes. *Aquaman*, for instance, could not take this road and the comic ceased publication.

The editors of DC had been dissatisfied with the old formula stories *à la* Superman for some time now and wanted something new. They wanted to get away from the aseptic style of their firm

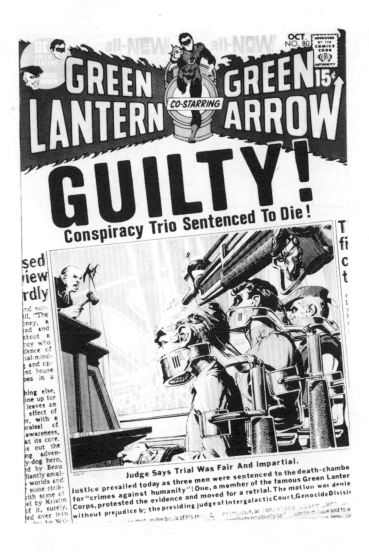

Green Lantern by Neal Adams. The super-hero at a turning point.
Green Lantern No. 76 marked a milestone in the social commitment
expressed in comic books.
© 1970 National Periodical Publications Inc.

Green Lantern. Title picture by Neal Adams. The super-heroes are
put on trial and this allows the comics to attack the weaknesses and
abuses of the System.
© 1970 National Periodical Publications Inc.

which was gradually threatening to lose ground to Marvel. So it
was decided in 1967 to let artists take over editing the issues and to
appoint Carmine Infantino, the star artist of the firm, editorial
director. This new and more visual approach proved to be justified and finally led to a greater social commitment, such as had
been current in Marvel for some time.

Ethnic minorities

Besides the more varied view of the world and the more three-
dimensional heroes it was above all by their increased reference to
social questions that comics were to recruit new readers; ac-
cordingly one of the major changes was a new attitude to black
Americans. Not that they had never featured before or only in
stereotyped roles. Even in the forties Will Eisner was trying to
include figures such as the black American Ebony in his comics,
and in the fifties there was actually a love comic for black

Americans. Ebony was, however, as stereotyped a figure as
Captain Marvel's little friend Steamboat Willie. But neither
Ebony nor the love comic achieved any success because they were
still trying to integrate black Americans as dark-skinned whites.
This is why all the ethnic minorities could identify only with white
heroes at that time.

When the racial problem began to penetrate the national consciousness with renewed force in the sixties, the time was ripe to
offer black Americans a place in comics corresponding to their
new appearance in films and on television. Comic books initiated
this trend. Now passers-by and policemen were no longer necessarily white. Next, dark-skinned subordinate figures were given
speech balloons like the white-skinned ones. Finally, in 1966,
the first black super-hero, *The Black Panther*, appeared in
Fantastic Four. The identity of his name with the Black Panther
organization was pure chance. The Black Panther stories were
kept fairly short for some years until Marvel decided in 1969 to
bring him into the limelight again, as a member of the combat

Wee Pals by Morrie Turner was the first comic strip to incorporate all the ethnic groups in America without prejudice.
© 1970 The Register and Tribune Syndicate Inc./UPI

group the Avengers. And in 1970 Captain America was partnered by a black hero he had trained, *The Falcon*, whose name now also appeared in large print in the title.

Although comic strips remained closed to social problems for a long time and featured black Americans only very rarely (the stereotyped sambo and servant roles having gradually disappeared again) the first integrated strips date back to 1964. That was the year the *Berkeley Post* began to print the comic strip *Wee Pals* by the black comic artist Morrie Turner. At first this series bridged the gap between black and white children only through its humour. But when the Register and Tribune Syndicate adopted *Wee Pals* in its programme in 1965 this strip had become a series in which all the important ethnic groups of American society were represented in the form of children. If any comic strip could shame its readers into greater insight and consideration, greater understanding of their fellowmen by means of humour, it was this one. But presumably the really inveterate, bigoted racists take great care not to read this series. As a result they also miss all the pleasure of Morrie Turner's *Black and White Coloring Book* that appeared in 1970 and features fifteen great and historically important black Americans in comic strip form with portraits.

Wee Pals belongs to the trend towards covering ethnic problems that also became apparent in other media at this time. In television the main example was the detective series *I Spy* in 1965, in which a black man and a white man played equally important roles for the first time. This led to a number of similar series. Hollywood also recognized these problems with films like *Guess Who's Coming to Dinner?* But this film, which was initially heralded as a great breakthrough because in it Hollywood's showpiece black American Sidney Poitier was allowed to marry a white woman, was soon declared to be a piece of disgraceful make-believe, since the action takes place at a VIP level very remote from the real problems of the racial question. Films such as *To Sir, With Love* and *In the Heat of the Night* were a little more honest. But there were no moves towards genuine realism until 1969–70, with films such as *Uptight* and *Cotton Comes to Harlem*.

While films and television generally had pressed forward with

Tomahawk by Neal Adams. Saving the members of an ethnic minority in a moment of crisis becomes, in both Westerns and war comics, a parable on the equality of races.
© 1970 National Periodical Publications Inc.

'socially relevant' themes much earlier, comics were more inclined to wait and see, although this medium had also recognized that attitudes were changing. Comic strips in particular remained rather conservative for a time, until in 1968 the theme of *I Spy* was taken up in the strip *Dateline: Danger*. As in the television series *Julia*, 1970 also saw the birth of a black comic strip heroine: *Friday Foster*. Unlike Julia, Friday does not live in an elegant middle-class apartment but in Harlem. However, her job as fashion photographer does upgrade her somewhat. As in *I Spy* there is of course a white counterpart in this series too, Friday's blond, blue-eyed boss, Shawn North.

The original inhabitants of America, the Indians, also found a place in comics and other media now. Since 1970 Marvel can even boast an Indian super-hero of today: *Red Wolf*. He follows in the line of *Pow Wow Smith*, *Strong Bow* and *Lone Eagle* who peopled the comic books of the fifties and can also trace his ancestry back to Little Sure Shot and Chief Jay Little Bear, who paved the way for him in the DC and Marvel war comics.

Drugs and the liberalization of the Code

In 1970 the Code Administrator said that in a medium like comics aimed primarily at children, scenes depicting drug addiction could inspire a curiosity to try drugs. Should this be the case, comics would soon become the object of widespread criticism.[5]

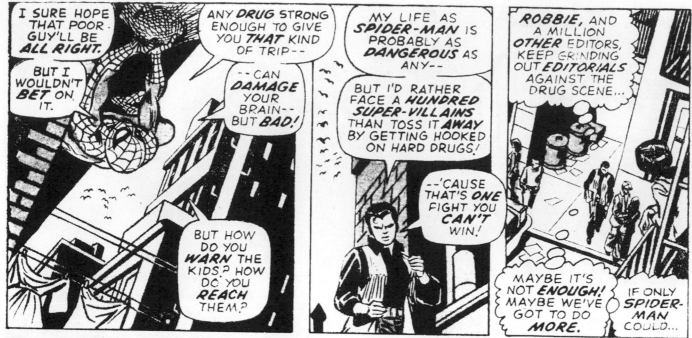

Spider-Man by Stan Lee. Artists Gil Kane and John Romita. Even in 1971 the Comics Code Authority was still against any mention of the drug problem in comic books, and so Spider-Man's warning about the abuse of drugs had to appear without the Code seal. From *Spider-Man* No. 96.
© 1971 Marvel Comics Group

The same year Stan Lee said: 'Self-censorship can be somewhat inhibiting.'[6] In an interview he also stated: 'I feel that comics could do much good as far as helping kids avoid the danger of drugs.'[7]

Since to take an anti-drug attitude was not possible under the Code, even though there was no explicit ruling, the only solution was to do without the seal of approval of the Comics Code. In any case the seal on the cover had recently become so small that it was hardly missed. *Spider-Man*, Issue 96 (May 1971), was the first issue by a firm that is a member of the Comics Magazine Association of America to appear without their approval. In this issue Spider-Man rescues a young black American who had imagined that he could fly and jumped from a skyscraper while under the influence of drugs. Later, in his Peter Parker identity, Spider-Man soliloquizes as follows: 'But I'd rather face a hundred super-villains than toss it [my life] away by getting hooked on hard drugs!—...'cause that's *one* fight you *can't* win!' The episode with the drug subplots ended with Issue 98. *Spider-Man* was given the Code seal again.

Carmine Infantino joined Stan Lee in urging an end to unconditional restrictions in the sphere of narcotics, since he was not in favour of hiding one's head in the sand. On the grounds of his position at DC Infantino is a member of the board of eight which represents the comics branch in the Code Authority and he had long considered the Code 'ridiculous'. Like Lee he was in favour of comics having more realistic relations with the world around them.[8] But even he did not manage to change the ruling on drugs at first.

Yet in January 1971 it proved possible to make the first changes to the Code, sixteen years after its introduction. Some restrictions were suspended. Thus it became possible to show criminal behaviour in a sympathetic light for social reasons. Even official corruption was admitted in the new catalogue of contents, as long as the guilty were punished. Under the same punishment condition, police officials could also be killed by criminals in the execution of their duty (*Rose and the Thorn* by DC is an early example).

Finally on 15 April 1971 the supervisory council of C.M.A.A. unanimously resolved to adopt a standard attitude, with the introduction: 'Narcotics addiction shall not be presented except as a vicious habit.' Although this ruling was decreed in binding terms, it was submitted to experts for examination as to whether the drugs passage could be formulated definitively after a six months' trial period. On the adoption of the new guidelines which had become necessary after Marvel's infraction, and because of the demands of some editors for a liberalization of the Code, Carmine Infantino said: 'I feel it's a great step forward for the industry. I think this can prove that the medium that was considered junk for one generation will be the jewel for the next. It can explore the social ills for the younger generation and help them decide how to direct their lives.'[9] The final draft of the drug provision of the Comics Code was adopted on 27 October 1971 by the board of the C.M.A.A.

Just as the American Film Code was gradually relaxed for commercial reasons and finally abolished, so too the Comics Code is in the process of becoming more lenient. In part it has adapted to current trends and been liberalized. For it became clear that comics were running the risk of losing their part of the market if they did not become more committed and more adult, as the other media had.

New directions

In the mid-sixties there was a dialectic reaction to the increasing concern with social evils, in the form of an alternative movement in the direction of sheer fantasy. This led to the Burroughs revival, the reissue of pulps such as *Conan*, *Doc Savage* and *The Shadow* (even in bibliophile get-up). The trend toward timeless 'Sword and Sorcery Sagas' even caught on in comics magazines of the Warren Publications type which, since 1965, had again been offering horror stories in the style of Poe, outside the Code, in magazine form and using the best artists in the business.

In 1968 *Spider-Man* also made two attempts to evade the Code, not in fact in order to embark on adventures of which the Code Authority would not have approved, but to pursue his traditional adventures in magazine format in half-tone drawings at 35 cents. In 1971 Marvel followed up these early attempts with a new magazine, *Savage Tales*, which relates the adventures of *Conan the Barbarian*, the wild *Ka-Zar* and the most beautiful 'Amazons' of all times in sixty-four pages of half-tone drawings. The magazine sold for 50 cents, thus anticipating the modern view that comics need a new image if they want to survive as something more than specialist and leisure publications. These magazines are superseding comics to an increasing extent because they offer the dealer a bigger profit margin and at the same time make less work than the innumerable comic books. Moreover there were already a lot of sixty-four page comic books on the market at 25 cents. So what was to prevent the reader from buying a few comics magazines with various series instead of a whole lot of different comics?

With the many different forms of comics, in principle everything is possible today. They can certainly no longer be regarded as a medium purely for children; in fact, they never really were in any case. The comic books aimed at children are mostly those produced by the industry and marked by the Code seal. Comic strips are addressed to all levels of society and all age groups. And issues in the style of the Warren Publications aim at a more adult public, if only because of their larger magazine format as distinct from the cheap comic books. The specialist comic books for intellectuals with a higher purchasing power are of a more 'private' nature, as are the underground comix, which again use the classification according to age group that was tossed back into the debate about the mass media in 1968. Underground comix, which since 1967–8 have been making a number of readers and officials unsure of their ground, are clearly marked 'For Adults Only'. While comics were critically elaborated in fan magazines, supercomics printed on fine art paper also appeared, like Wallace Wood's *Witzend*. With editions of five thousand copies *Witzend* will not make a fortune. But this magazine does provide a forum for comics of a special kind which are only censored by the ideas of their authors and artists. Magazines of this kind, like Gil Kane's *Savage*, whose first and only issue was torn up by a few critics, allow new experiments. Underground comix are more concerned with social or sexual statements made in a crude, hard-hitting style; but the super-comics explore the artistic possibilities of the medium. But not every contribution finally published without the Comics Code's seal of approval

Conan the Barbarian. Artist: Barry Smith. The Sword and Sorcery Saga is once again enjoying popularity. Comic books are reverting to the subjects of the pulps, and indeed at the end of the sixties Robert E. Howard's Conan celebrated a triumphant rebirth in books and comics. From *Conan the Barbarian* No. 3.
© 1970 Marvel Comics Group

proves that better things can be achieved when no holds are barred. The best sign that comic books have become more conscious of their opportunities today is the founding of the Academy of Comic Book Art in late 1970; like the film and television academies, it gives awards to the best achievements in the field and promotes scientific research. Like the National Cartoonist Society and the annual awards given by the Comic-Fans, the comic book industry now has its own Academy prize, the Shazam, which may encourage comics producers to become more interested than before in quality.

Stan Lee, co-founder and first president of the Academy, has found a slogan for the constant pursuit of better quality and new inspiration:

'Onward!'

Code of the Comics Magazine Association of America, Inc.

CODE OF THE COMICS MAGAZINE ASSOCIATION OF AMERICA, INC.

Adopted on October 26, 1954, the enforcement of this Code is the basis for the comic magazine industry's program of self-regulation.

CODE FOR EDITORIAL MATTER

General Standards   Part A

1) Crimes shall never be presented in such a way as to create sympathy for the criminal, to promote distrust of the forces of law and justice, or to inspire others with a desire to imitate criminals.
2) No comics shall explicitly present the unique details and methods of a crime.
3) Policemen, judges, government officials and respected institutions shall never be presented in such a way as to create disrespect for established authority.
4) If crime is depicted it shall be as a sordid and unpleasant activity.
5) Criminals shall not be presented so as to be rendered glamorous or to occupy a position which creates a desire for emulation.
6) In every instance good shall triumph over evil and the criminal punished for his misdeeds.
7) Scenes of excessive violence shall be prohibited. Scenes of brutal torture, excessive and unnecessary knife and gun play, physical agony, gory and gruesome crime shall be eliminated.
8) No unique or unusual methods of concealing weapons shall be shown.
9) Instances of law enforcement officers dying as a result of a criminal's activities should be discouraged.
10) The crime of kidnapping shall never be portrayed in any detail, nor shall any profit accrue to the abductor or kidnapper. The criminal or the kidnapper must be punished in every case.
11) The letters of the word "crime" on a comics magazine cover shall never be appreciably greater in dimension than the other words contained in the title. The word "crime" shall never appear alone on a cover.
12) Restraint in the use of the word "crime" in titles or sub-titles shall be exercised.

General Standards   Part B

1) No comic magazine shall use the word horror or terror in its title.
2) All scenes of horror, excessive bloodshed, gory or gruesome crimes, depravity, lust, sadism, masochism shall not be permitted.
3) All lurid, unsavory, gruesome illustrations shall be eliminated.
4) Inclusion of stories dealing with evil shall be used or shall be published only where the intent is to illustrate a moral issue and in no case shall evil be presented alluringly nor so as to injure the sensibilities of the reader.
5) Scenes dealing with, or instruments associated with walking dead, torture, vampires and vampirism, ghouls, cannibalism and werewolfism are prohibited.

General Standards   Part C

All elements or techniques not specifically mentioned herein, but which are contrary to the spirit and intent of the Code, and are considered violations of good taste or decency, shall be prohibited.

Dialogue

1) Profanity, obscenity, smut, vulgarity, or words or symbols which have acquired undesirable meanings are forbidden.
2) Special precautions to avoid references to physical afflictions or deformities shall be taken.
3) Although slang and colloquialisms are acceptable, excessive use should be discouraged and wherever possible good grammar shall be employed.

Religion

1) Ridicule or attack on any religious or racial group is never permissible.

Costume

1) Nudity in any form is prohibited, as is indecent or undue exposure.
2) Suggestive and salacious illustration or suggestive posture is unacceptable.
3) All characters shall be depicted in dress reasonably acceptable to society.
4) Females shall be drawn realistically without exaggeration of any physical qualities.

NOTE: It should be recognized that all prohibitions dealing with costume, dialogue or artwork applies as specifically to the cover of a comic magazine as they do to the contents.

Marriage and Sex

1) Divorce shall not be treated humorously nor represented as desirable.
2) Illicit sex relations are neither to be hinted at or portrayed. Violent love scenes as well as sexual abnormalities are unacceptable.
3) Respect for parents, the moral code, and for honorable behavior shall be fostered. A sympathetic understanding of the problems of love is not a license for morbid distortion.
4) The treatment of love-romance stories shall emphasize the value of the home and the sanctity of marriage.
5) Passion or romantic interest shall never be treated in such a way as to stimulate the lower and baser emotions.
6) Seduction and rape shall never be shown or suggested.
7) Sex perversion or any inference to same is strictly forbidden.

CODE FOR ADVERTISING MATTER

These regulations are applicable to all magazines published by members of the Comics Magazine Association of America, Inc. Good taste shall be the guiding principle in the acceptance of advertising.
1) Liquor and tobacco advertising is not acceptable.
2) Advertisement of sex or sex instruction books are unacceptable.
3) The sale of picture postcards, "pin-ups," "art studies," or any other reproduction of nude or semi-nude figures is prohibited.
4) Advertising for the sale of knives, concealable weapons, or realistic gun facsimiles is prohibited.
5) Advertising for the sale of fireworks is prohibited.
6) Advertising dealing with the sale of gambling equipment or printed matter dealing with gambling shall not be accepted.
7) Nudity with meretricious purpose and salacious postures shall not be permitted in the advertising of any product; clothed figures shall never be presented in such a way as to be offensive or contrary to good taste or morals.
8) To the best of his ability, each publisher shall ascertain that all statements made in advertisements conform to fact and avoid misrepresentation.
9) Advertisement of medical, health, or toiletry products of questionable nature are to be rejected. Advertisements for medical, health or toiletry products endorsed by the American Medical Association, or the American Dental Association, shall be deemed acceptable if they conform with all other conditions of the Advertising Code.

COMICS MAGAZINE ASSOCIATION OF AMERICA, INC.
300 PARK AVENUE SOUTH
NEW YORK, N. Y. 10010

Chronological table

giving a short history of comics: all entries refer to the USA unless otherwise stated.

1894 A cartoon by Richard Felton Outcault, composed of six coloured pictures, appeared in the *New York World*. It was called *The Origin of a New Species, or the Evolution of the Crocodile Explained*.

1895 Richard Felton Outcault's *Down Hogan's Alley* appeared in Pulitzer's *New York World*. William Randolph Hearst arrived in New York and took over the *Morning Journal* which was subsequently called the *New York Journal*; Hearst was just as successful with this paper as he had been with the *San Francisco Examiner* which he had taken over from his father.

1896 On 16 February the Yellow Kid became the main character in *Down Hogan's Alley*. On 18 February Hearst's *New York Journal* carried for the first time an eight-page colour supplement entitled *The American Humorist*; Hearst had persuaded almost the entire Sunday staff from the *New York World* to join the *New York Journal* so that he could bring out this supplement. Outcault moved several times from Pulitzer's papers to Hearst's papers and then back again, and this is why *The Yellow Kid* appeared in both the *New York Journal* and the *New York World*; when Outcault left the *New York World* the strip was continued by George Luks.

1897 On 12 December *The Katzenjammer Kids* (drawn by nineteen-year-old Rudolph Dirks) appeared for the first time in Hearst's *New York Journal*. The first real comic strip had been born.

1898 *The Yellow Kid* ceased to appear in *The American Humorist* because the readers were tired of the strip.

1899 Frederick Burr Opper made his debut in the *New York Journal* and, thanks to his strips *Happy Hooligan, And Her Name Was Maud* and *Alphonse and Gaston*, he soon became well known.

1902 In May the first instalments of Outcault's *Buster Brown* were published in James Gordon Bennett's *New York Herald*.

1903 *Sandy Highflyer* by Charles W. Kahles appeared in the *Philadelphia North American*: this strip was both a children's story and an adventure strip. *Herr Spiefelberger, the Amateur Cracksman* by Carl Anderson appeared in the *New York World*. George Herriman's first comic strip was *Lariat Pete*.

1904 The first daily comic strip appeared—in the *Chicago American*: it was *A. Piker Clerk* by Clare Briggs. The *New York World* featured George McManus' *The Newlyweds*.
Comic strips such as *The Katzenjammer Kids, Happy Hooligan, Alphonse and Gaston and their Friend Leon* appeared as comic books (40 pages, 10 × 15 in. 75 cents).

1905 COMIC STRIPS: Frederick Burr Opper's *And Her Name Was Maud*; James Swinnerton's *Little Jimmy*; Winsor McCay's *Little Nemo in Slumberland* which appeared from 1905 to 1911 and from 1924 to 1927; C. W. Kahles' *Mr. Buttin, Tim and Tom the Terrible Twins* and *Fun in the Zoo*. Between 1905 and 1910 George McManus created *Snoozer, The Merry Marceline, Nibsby the Newsboy in Funny Fairyland, Cheerful Charly, Panhandle Pete, Let George Do It* for Pulitzer's *Sunday World*.
EUROPE: Maurice Languereau and Jean-Pierre Pinchon began their picture stories about *Bécassine* in La Semaine de Suzette.

1906 Hearst bought Outcault, together with his strip *Buster Brown*, for the *American*; but at the same time the *New York Herald* featured its own version of this strip. The Sunday edition of the *Chicago Tribune* published four strips that had been drawn in Munich; two of these strips were by Lyonel Feininger: *The Kin-der-Kids* and *Wee Willie Winkie's World*. C. W. Kahles' *Hairbreadth Harry* appeared in the *Philadelphia Press*.
EUROPE: In October a translation of *Buster Brown* began to appear in the Danish weekly *Hjemmet*; it was called *Lille Svends Gavtyvestreger*.
FILM: The first cartoon film appeared; it was J. Stuart Blackton's *Humorous Phases of Funny Faces*.

1907 From 15 November Harry Conway ('Bud') Fisher's strip *Mr A. Mutt* appeared in the *San Francisco Chronicle*; it became a model for daily comic strips. (The title was changed to *Mutt and Jeff* in 1909.) Rube Goldberg became the cartoonist of the *New York Evening Mail*.

1908 EUROPE: The French magazine *L'Epatant* featured Louis Forton's *Les Pieds Nickelés*. Italy produced a children's weekly entitled *Corriere dei Piccoli*. And from No. 39 (dated 27 September) onwards the Danish *Hjemmet* featured *The Katzenjammer Kids* which was called *Knold Og Tot*.

1909 EUROPE: *Corriere dei Piccoli* published Antonio Rubino's picture series and Attilio Mussini's *Bilobul*.
OTHER MEDIA: *Gertie the Dinosaur*, drawn by Winsor McCay, was the first cartoon film with a story. McManus' strip *The Newlyweds and Their Baby* (Snookums) was turned into a musical comedy.

1910 On 26 July George Herriman added a small strip about a cat and a mouse underneath his main strip *The Family Upstairs* (originally called *Dingbat Family*). This later became an independent, successful strip, and since 1913 it has been called *Krazy Kat*. In this year Harry Hershfield also began to draw *Desperate Desmond*.

1911 Winsor McCay began to draw *Dreams of the Rarebit Fiend* for the *New York Herald*, under the pseudonym 'Silas'. The *Chicago American* issued collections of *Mutt and Jeff* in return for coupons (format 18 × 6 in.).

1912 COMIC STRIPS: *Bringing Up Father* by George McManus; *Polly and Her Pals* by Cliff Sterrett. H. H. Knerr took over *The Katzenjammer Kids* for the *Journal* while Rudolph Dirks continued to draw this strip in the *World*, using the title *The Captain and the Kids*.
OTHER MEDIA: Edgar Rice Burroughs' novel *Tarzan of the Apes* was published in *All Story Magazine*.

1914 King Features Syndicate evolved from Hearst's International Feature Service which had been founded in 1912. Harry Hershfield began the strip *Abie the Agent* which Arthur Brisbane has called 'the first adult comic strip in America'.

1916 Rube Goldberg encouraged the founding of the McNaught Syndicate.

1917 Joseph M. Patterson, founder of the *New York Daily News* invented *The Gumps*; the artist was Sidney Smith.

1918 COMIC STRIPS: *Toots and Casper* by Jimmy Murphy; *Boob McNutt* by Rube Goldberg.
OTHER MEDIA: The first Tarzan films were made, with Elmo Lincoln in the title role; they were *Tarzan of the Apes* and *The Romance of Tarzan*.

1919 COMIC STRIPS: *The Thimble Theatre* by Elzie Segar; *Barney Google* by Billy de Beck; *Gasoline Alley* by Frank King which began as a 'comics panel'.
EUROPE: Austen Bowen Payne created *Pip, Squeak and Wilfred* for the *Daily Mirror*.

1920 COMIC STRIPS: *Winnie Winkle* by Martin Branner, which appeared first as a gag strip and then as a continuous story strip.
EUROPE: *Rupert* by Mary Tourtel appeared in the *Daily Express*.
OTHER MEDIA: From 1920 to 1929 Paul Terry drew the first famous cartoon film series, *Aesop's Fables*.

1921 COMIC STRIPS: *Tillie the Toiler* by Russ Westover; *Just Kids* by Ad Carter. On 14 February *Gasoline Alley* featured Skeezix for the first time.
EUROPE: *Pop* by J. Millar Watt, which was the first strip to appear daily in Europe, appeared in England in the *Daily Sketch*.
OTHER MEDIA: Walt Disney's first cartoon film series *Laugh-O-Grams* was made in Kansas City. Tarzan appeared on the stage in England and the USA.

1922 COMIC STRIPS: *Smitty* by Walter Berndt; *Fritzi Ritz* by Meyer Marcus, drawn by Larry Whittington.

1923 COMIC STRIPS: *Moon Mullins* by Frank Willard; *Felix the Cat* by Pat Sullivan; (in May) *The Nebbs* by Texter Sol Hess, drawn by Wally A. Carlson. *The Nebbs* was inspired by Hess' dialogue for *The Gumps*.
EUROPE: *Totor* by Hergé appeared in *Le Boy-Scout Belge*.

1924 COMIC STRIPS: On 5 August Harold Gray's *Little Orphan Annie* began; Gray had already ghosted for *The Gumps*. Other new strips were: Chic Young's first successful strip *Dumb Dora*, Lyman Young's *The Kelly Kids* and Roy Crane's *Wash Tubbs*.

1925 COMIC STRIPS: *Ella Cinders* (a modern Cinderella) by Charlie Plumb; *Etta Kett* by Paul Robinson.
EUROPE: In France Alain Saint-Ogan drew the first French comic strip *Zig et Puce* for *Le Dimanche Illustré*; in the following year he added the famous mascot, the penguin Alfred.
OTHER MEDIA: Harold Ross started the journal *The New Yorker* which influenced American humour, although it was not a satirical magazine.

1926 OTHER MEDIA: John Alden Carpenter wrote a *Krazy Kat* ballet.

1927 COMIC STRIPS: *Little Annie Rooney* by Brandon Walsh, drawn by Darrell McClure continued the theme of the orphan which Gray had used so successfully. Lyman Young started *The Kid Sister*; later he created *Tim Tyler's Luck* which enjoyed a very long success.
EUROPE: *Witwe Knolle* by Rudolph Röse began in Germany.
OTHER MEDIA: *Tillie the Toiler* was turned into a film. The first *Felix the Cat* cartoon film with a sound track was produced.

1928 COMIC STRIPS: *Muggs and Skeeter* by Wally Bishop. Captain Easy was added to the cast of *Wash Tubbs*.
OTHER MEDIA: *Steamboat Willie*, Walt Disney's third Mickey Mouse cartoon film, drawn by Ub Iwerks, was a great success as a sound film, first in New York and eventually all over the world.

1929 COMIC STRIPS: Two new strips began on 7 January: *Tarzan* drawn by Hal Foster and *Buck Rogers* created by John F. Dille and drawn by R. W. Calkins. The sixty *Tarzan* instalments which appeared between 7 January and 16 March were so successful that from 17 June onwards the series became a regular feature; this was *The Return of Tarzan* drawn by Rex Maxon. Popeye was introduced into the *Thimble Theatre* series and he soon became the main character.
COMIC BOOKS: George T. Delacorte published *The Funnies*, a comic book in tabloid format, but it was discontinued after thirteen issues.
OTHER MEDIA: Walt Disney's first *Silly Symphonies* appeared in the cinemas.
EUROPE: *Tintin* by Hergé appeared in *Le Petit XXème*, the supplement of the Brussels daily newspaper *Le Vingtième Siècle*.

1930 COMIC STRIPS: Walt Disney's *Mickey Mouse*; John Terry's *Scorchy Smith* which Noel Sickles has been drawing since 1934; Ham Fisher's *Joe Palooka* which Fisher tried to sell to a syndicate for three years, without success. On 8 September *Blondie* by Chic Young.

1931 On 15 March *Tarzan* appeared for the first time on a Sunday and then on 27 September Hal Foster took over the Sunday sequences. On 4 October Chester Tracy's *Dick Tracy* started, as a Sunday strip, and then from 12 October it appeared daily. *Fu Manchu*, based on novels by Sax Rohmer, appeared as a comic strip.
OTHER MEDIA: issue no. 1 of the pulp series based on *The Shadow*; the publishers secured the copyright for the radio version of *The Shadow*.

1932 COMIC STRIPS: Milton Caniff's *Dickie Dare* and *The Gay Thirties*; Frank Godwin's *Connie*; Martha Orr's *Apple Mary*; *Pete the Tramp* by C. D. Russell who had previously ghosted Percy Crosby's *Skippy*; Carl Anderson's *Henry*. *Henry* was first published in the *Saturday Evening Post* and was then taken over by King Features in 1935. Al Smith became assistant to Bud Fisher on *Mutt and Jeff*. Roy Crane's *Wash Tubbs* was re-named *Captain Easy*.
OTHER MEDIA: First pre-recorded radio series of *Tarzan*. It had 364 instalments, each 15 minutes long. Jane was played by Burroughs' daughter and Tarzan was played by Jim Pierce, who also played Tarzan in the film made in 1926.

1933 COMIC STRIPS: *Smilin' Jack* by Zack Mosley; *Brick Bradford* by Texter Bill Ritt, drawn by Clarence Gray; (beginning on 7 August) *Alley Oop* by V. T. Hamlin.
OTHER MEDIA: Walt Disney received the Oscar for *The Three Little Pigs*; he was to receive nine more Oscars in the following ten years. Max Fleischer made his first cartoon film, *Popeye the Sailor*. On Monday 30 January 1933 George W. Trendle's radio series *The Lone Ranger* began. A pulp series based on *Doc Savage* also began.

1934 COMIC STRIPS: *Flash Gordon* by Alex Raymond; *Secret Agent X-9* by Dashiell Hammett, drawn by Alex Raymond; *Terry and the Pirates* by Milton Caniff; *Mandrake the Magician* by Lee Falk, drawn by Phil Davis; *They'll Do It Every Time* by Jimmy Hatlo; *Don Winslow of the Navy* by Frank Martinek; *Li'l Abner* by Al Capp; *The Little King* by Otto Soglow moved from the *New Yorker* magazine to *Puck the Comic Weekly*. The *New York Daily News* revealed how important comics were for the paper when it printed a special advertisement.
COMIC BOOKS: *Famous Funnies*, a comic book containing reprints of newspaper strips, was published.
EUROPE: In France the *Journal de Mickey* appeared; the form of

this weekly magazine had an influence on other magazines, such as *Robinson*. In Italy *L'Avventuroso* also influenced other magazines. In Germany *Vater und Sohn (Father and Son)* by Erich Ohser was published, under the pseudonym: e. o. plauen.

OTHER MEDIA: Donald Duck made his debut with a small part in the Disney cartoon film *The Orphan's Benefit*.

1935 COMIC STRIPS: Bill Holman began *Smokey Stover* and *Spooky the Cat*. Gus Edson took over *The Gumps* after Sidney Smith's death. Fred Lasswell became assistant on the strip *Barney Google and Snuffy Smith* and he finally took over the series in 1941.

COMIC BOOKS: Delacorte published M. C. Gaines's *Popular Comics*.

EUROPE: Mary Tourtel retired but her bear Rupert lived on.

OTHER MEDIA: Burroughs' Tarzan Enterprises produced the films *The New Adventures of Tarzan* and *Tarzan and the Green Goddess*, with Herman Brix as Tarzan. The *Hopalong Cassidy* film series began; Hopalong Cassidy later became very well known on television and in comics. Gene Autry began broadcasting.

1936 COMIC STRIPS: *Mickey Finn* by Lank Leonard; *Barney Baxter* by Lee Falk; on 17 February, *The Phantom* by Lee Falk. *The Phantom* was drawn by Ray Moore at first, then by Wilson McCoy and finally by Sy Barry.

OTHER MEDIA: Buster Crabbe played Flash Gordon in the Universal film series. Bugs Bunny made his film debut with the Warner Brothers.

1937 COMIC STRIPS: *Prince Valiant* by Hal Foster; *The Great Gusto*, drawn by Elmer Woggon and Texter Allen Saunders. *The Great Gusto* was later renamed *Chief Wahoo* and later still, when William Overgard was drawing it, it was renamed *Steve Roper*. On 5 May Burne Hogarth took over the *Tarzan* Sunday strip.

COMIC BOOKS: In March *Detective Comics*, the first 'real' comic book, appeared.

EUROPE: Opera Mundi launched *Robinson*, a magazine which introduced American series to the French. In England Stephen Dowling created the detective strip *Buck Ryan* for the *Daily Mirror*; it ran for twenty-five years.

OTHER MEDIA: Walt Disney's first full length feature film *Snow White and the Seven Dwarfs* quickly became one of Disney Production's greatest successes.

1938 COMIC STRIPS: *The Lone Ranger* by Charles Flanders; *Donald Duck* by Walt Disney. From 1938 to 1942 Vernon Green drew *The Shadow*. Martha Orr abandoned *Apple Mary* and Allen Saunders and Ken Ernst then changed the series to *Mary Worth*. Ernie Bushmiller took over *Fritzi Ritz* and gradually dropped the title figure in favour of Fritzi's niece Nancy. After Segar's death *Popeye* was continued by various artists—recently by Ralph Stein and Bud Sagendorf.

COMIC BOOKS: *Superman* appeared in issue no. 1 of *Action Comics*. Dell published the *Tarzan* booklets (up to no. 7) with Foster reprints.

EUROPE: In Belgium the magazine *Spirou* was started, on 21 April. The fascist regime in Italy banned all American comics.

OTHER MEDIA: Mickey Mouse appeared in the cartoon film version of the fairy-tale *The Brave Little Tailor*.

1939 COMIC STRIPS: Alex Raymond handed *Secret Agent X-9* over to Mel Graff and concentrated on *Flash Gordon* and *Jungle Jim*. Alfred Andriola started *Charlie Chan* and Jimmy Gary started *King of the Royal Mounted*. *Superman*, which had been very successful in comic books, now appeared as a comic strip.

COMIC BOOKS: The *Superman Quarterly Magazine* was published in the Spring. *Batman* appeared for the first time in issue no. 27 of Detective Comics. In November Timely Comics Group entered the super-hero business with *Marvel Comics* no. 1 (taken over from the pulps). *Sheena* and *Flash Comics* (featuring *Hawkman*) appeared.

OTHER MEDIA: Among the film series with heroes from comics were: *Tarzan, Charlie Chan, Blondie, The Thin Man, Hopalong Cassidy, Dr Kildare, The Cisco Kid, Torchy, Mr Moto, Sherlock Holmes* and *Topper*.

1940 COMIC STRIPS: *Brenda Starr* by Dale Messick.

COMIC BOOKS: There was an increase in the number of super-heroes: *Sub-Mariner* by Bill Everett, *Human Torch* by Carl Burgos, *Captain Marvel* by C. C. Beck. The first *Batman* comic book appeared in the spring. In April Robin became Batman's pal, in *Detective Comics* no. 38. In July *Green Lantern* first appeared. In *All Star Comics* Superman, Batman, Green Lantern, Spectre, Flash etc. joined together to form the *Justice Society of America*. From 1940 to 1945 comic books were used by the US army as instruction handbooks. The *Classics Illustrated* were started.

OTHER MEDIA: *Superman* was broadcast in a series starting on 12 February. Walt Disney's *Fantasia* and *Pinocchio* were shown in the cinemas.

1941 COMIC STRIPS: *Private Buck* drawn by Clyde Lewis, one of the first cartoons about army life. Will Eisner started *The Spirit*.

COMIC BOOKS: *Captain America* by Joe Simon and Jack Kirby; *Wonder Woman*.

EUROPE: From 29 January to 22 September the magazine *Tarzan* appeared in France, but then after no. 34 it was discontinued because of its alleged immorality and its American influence. Instead magazines such as *Le Téméraire*, *Sirocco* and *Fanfan la Tulipe* were published.

OTHER MEDIA: Walt Disney's *Dumbo* was shown in the cinemas. Between 1941 and 1943 Paramount produced eighteen *Superman* cartoon films, under the direction of Dave Fleischer. Walt Kelly left Disney Studios, where he had been working since 1935.

1942 COMIC STRIPS: *Barnaby* by Crockett Johnson; *Private Breger* by Dave Breger; *Hubert* by Dick Wingert; *Male Call* by Milton Caniff. The instalment of Caniff's *Terry and the Pirates* which appeared on 17 October was reprinted for several months and was mentioned in the Congressional Record.

COMIC BOOKS: In the first booklet of *Animal Comics* Walt Kelly drew *Albert the Alligator*, among others; an opossum called Pogo later appeared in this series. In the course of the next four years Pogo and Albert gradually assumed the characters which they have today in *Pogo*.

OTHER MEDIA: Walt Disney produced the cartoon film *Bambi*, based on the book by Felix Salten. The American Institute of Graphic Arts presented the first exhibition of comics.

1943 COMIC STRIPS: *Kerry Drake* by Alfred Andriola; *Rusty Riley* by Frank Godwin; *The Flop Family* by George Swanson; *Buz Sawyer* by Roy Crane. Crane's assistant Leslie Turner carried on the strip *Captain Easy*. In May a new series called *Vic Jordan*, by Paine and Wexler, started on the New York newspaper *PM*; in this series an American is helping a European underground movement.

EUROPE: In England *Garth* by Stephen Dowling, which featured the superman Garth, appeared in the *Daily Mirror*.

OTHER MEDIA: Columbia brought out the film series *Batman and Robin*.

1944 COMIC STRIPS: Frank Robbins started his *Johnny Hazard* strip about a pilot. *Krazy Kat* was discontinued when George Herriman died.

1945 COMIC STRIPS: Coulton Waugh's *Hank* ran from April to December in *PM*. The Publishers Syndicate came up with *Rex Morgan, M.D.*

EUROPE: Editions du Lombard were founded and they began by publishing *Tintin* albums.

1946 COMIC STRIPS: Alex Raymond started *Rip Kirby*, based on a story by Ward Greene. The National Cartoonist Society was founded.

COMIC BOOKS: *Albert and Pogo* no. 1 appeared as a one-shot issue and *Animal Comics* were discontinued. *Albert and Pogo* no. 2 did not appear until the following year.

EUROPE: In Belgium the magazine *Tintin* was published for the first time, on 26 September; before the end of the year the magazine was also published in Holland under the title *Kuifje*. In France the first post-war children's magazine appeared: it was called *Coq Hardi* and it was followed by *Vaillant*.

1947 COMIC STRIPS: Milton Caniff started *Steve Canyon* on 19 January. George Wunder took over *Terry and the Pirates*.
EUROPE: Morris (Maurice de Bévère) created *Lucky Luke* for *Spirou*. The Belgian government used advertisements containing comic strips in its fight against inflation.
OTHER MEDIA: *Tom and Jerry* films started.

1948 COMIC STRIPS: Walt Kelly's *Pogo* was published in the *New York Star*. Mac Raboy took over *Flash Gordon* in the spring.
EUROPE: A French edition of *Tintin* appeared.
OTHER MEDIA: Columbia's second *Batman* series reached the cinemas: *The New Adventures of Batman and Robin*. A series of *Superman* films also appeared. NBC brought out a very successful television series, which ran from 28 November 1948 to 30 December 1951, showing the old *Hopalong Cassidy* films.

1949 COMIC BOOKS: Dell revived the *Pogo Comics* after the demise of the *Star*. Syndicate President Robert Hall began to take an interest in *Pogo*. Issue no. 1 of *Superboy* appeared in March.
EUROPE: In France a law passed on 16 July established a commission to watch over the publication of children's periodicals. In Finland Tove Jansson started to draw *Mumintrollet*.
OTHER MEDIA: Terrytoon started a series of cartoon films called *Mighty Mouse*. Walt Disney brought out the cartoon film *Cinderella*.

1950 COMIC STRIPS: *Peanuts* by Charles M. Schulz; *Beetle Bailey* by Mort Walker; *Big Ben Bolt* by John Cullen Murphy and Elliott Caplin.
COMIC BOOKS: After the war series E.C. started the horror comics.
OTHER MEDIA: A new Columbia film series came out, called *Superman Vs. the Atom Man*. *Gunsmoke* started as a radio series.

1951 COMIC STRIPS: *Dennis the Menace* by Hank Ketcham; *The Cisco Kid* by José Luis Salinas and Rod Reed, based on O. Henry's novel. *Beetle Bailey* joins the army.
COMIC BOOKS: Nos. 4 to 8 of *Pogo Comics* achieve a circulation of two and a half million.
EUROPE: Issue no. 1 of *Micky Maus* appeared in Germany.
OTHER MEDIA: Another *Superman* film series and also another *Superman* television series went into production. Walt Disney made *Alice in Wonderland*. The first *Pogo* book was published.

1952 COMIC STRIPS: At the end of March Abner Yokum and Daisy Mae of *Li'l Abner* got married.
COMIC BOOKS: *MAD* was luanched.
EUROPE: Peyo started to work for *Spirou*; his first strip was *Johan*.

1953 COMIC STRIPS: *The Heart of Juliet Jones* by Stan Drake and Elliott Caplin.
EUROPE: In Germany *Till Eulenspiegel* turned into *Fix und Foxi*. From July onwards Lehning publishers imported Italian 'Piccolo' comic books. Mondial Publishing brought out *Tarzan*, *Pecos Bill*, *Der kleine Sheriff (The Little Sheriff)*. Phantom comic books appeared.
OTHER MEDIA: Walt Disney presented *Peter Pan*. Henry Hathaway's film *Prince Valiant* with Robert Wagner in the title role was the most successful film version of a comic strip made so far.

1954 COMIC STRIPS: *Hi and Lois* by Dik Browne and Mort Walker began. Al Smith took over *Mutt and Jeff* after the death of Bud Fisher. Vernon Greene took over *Bringing Up Father*, which George McManus had started, and Joe Musial took over *The Katzenjammer Kids* from Doc Winner.
COMIC BOOKS: Frederic Wertham attacked comics in his book *Seduction of the Innocent*. E.C. Comics stopped publishing altogether. *Jimmy Olsen* no. 1 appeared in September. On 26 October the statutes of the Comics Code Authority took effect.

EUROPE: Editions du Lombard started their own film section, called Belvision. Albert Weinberg created the series *Dan Cooper* for *Tintin*. *Jerry Spring* by Jijé (Joseph Gillain) appeared in *Spirou*.
OTHER MEDIA: The *Lone Ranger* radio series came to an end on 3 September, but the Lone Ranger was soon to appear on television and in the cinema; meanwhile the *Lone Ranger* comics continued.

1955 COMIC STRIPS: The Newspaper Comics Council was founded.
EUROPE: *Illustrierte Klassiker* were published in Germany.
OTHER MEDIA: On 10 September the television series *Gunsmoke* started. Walt Disney's cartoon film *The Lady and the Tramp* filled the cinemas, and his feature film *Davy Crockett* was equally successful.

1956 COMIC STRIPS: Bob Montana's *Archie* appeared as a comic strip, because the *Archie* comic books had been such a success. Jules Feiffer introduced psychoanalysis into comic strips.
COMIC BOOKS: Dell published television 'tie-ins' of series such as *Gunsmoke*.
EUROPE: Jean Graton's *Michel Vaillant* appeared in *Tintin*.
OTHER MEDIA: *The Lone Ranger* appeared in the cinemas. *Li'l Abner* became a successful Broadway musical and a few years later a film version was made.

1957 COMIC STRIPS: Among the new series *On Stage* by Leonard Starr was outstanding. *Moon Mullins* was carried on by Ferd Johnson after Frank Willard's death.
COMIC BOOKS: Comic books like *Captain America* were discontinued, because of declining interest among the readers.
OTHER MEDIA: William Hanna and Joseph Barbera left MGM and started their own firm which produced cartoon films for Screen Gems. They began their long series of television cartoon films with *Ruff and Reddy*, followed by *Huckleberry Hound*, *Yogi Bear*, *Quick Draw McGraw* and *The Flintstones*. The Hanna-Barbera team also made sure, as Walt Disney Productions had done, that all their ideas were taken up by comic books and comic strips.

1958 COMIC STRIPS: *B.C.* by Johnny Hart; *Rick O'Shay* by Stan Lynde; *Mr Abernathy* by Ralston Jones and Frank Ridgeway. Cliff Sterrett retired and his series *Polly and Her Pals* was discontinued after a run of forty-six years.
COMIC BOOKS: *Lois Lane* no. 1 appeared in April.
EUROPE: In France a decree was passed on 23 December strengthening the laws covering literature for juveniles. In Belgium *Les Schtroumpfs* appeared. In Germany *Felix* appeared.

1959 COMIC STRIPS: *Tillie the Toiler* and *The Gumps* were discontinued. Stephen Becker's book *Comic Art in America* was published.
EUROPE: In France the comics magazine *Pilote* was published and *Astérix* by René Goscinny and Albert Uderzo soon became its most popular strip.

1960 COMIC STRIPS: *Ponytail* by Lee Holley started.
EUROPE: Greg (Michel Regnier) started up *Zig et Puce* again, for *Tintin*. Europress Junio was formed; it was an association for European publishers of literature for young people.
OTHER MEDIA: Walt Disney's elaborately produced cartoon film *Sleeping Beauty* was ready after several years work.

1961 COMIC BOOKS: *Fantastic Four* and then *The Amazing Spider-Man* revolutionized the super-hero world. 'Fanzines' were magazines for fans; among them were *Alter Ego*, *Masquerader*, *Comics Heroes Revisited* and *The Comics Collector*.
OTHER MEDIA: The old *Popeye* films had been shown on television so often that they could no longer be used and so new television cartoon films were made.

1962 COMIC STRIPS: Alex Kotzky started *Apartment 3-G* and Ken Bald drew *Dr Kildare*.
COMIC BOOKS: Western Publishing Company separated from Dell and started publishing the Gold Key series. Gold Key started *Thriller* in October, a television 'tie-in' series for the Boris Karloff television series.

EUROPE: *Modesty Blaise* by Jim Holdaway appeared in the London *Evening News*. *Fu Manchu* appeared in the *Parisian Libéré* and *Barbarella* by Jean-Claude Forest appeared in the French magazine *V*. The first French comics club was founded. In Italy *Diabolik* by A. and L. Giussani ushered in the era of the *fumetti neri* (black comics).

OTHER MEDIA: *Little Annie Fanny* appeared in the October number of *Playboy*.

1963 EUROPE: Jean-Michel Giraud created the Western *Fort Navajo* for *Pilote*; it was drawn by Jean Giraud.

OTHER MEDIA: Television cartoon films based on *Krazy Kat*, *Snuffy Smith* and *Beetle Bailey*.

1964 COMIC STRIPS: The *Berkeley Post* started publishing Morris Turner's *Wee Pals*. Brant Parker and Johnny Hart started *Wizard of Id* on 9 November.

EUROPE: The French weekly magazine *Chouchou* presented new, experimental French comic strips, but ceased publication after thirteen issues. *Barbarella* was published as a book which was banned in France. The Société Civile d'Etudes et de Recherches des Littératures Dessinées (Society for Study and Research into Picture-literature) known as SOCERLID, was founded in Paris.

1965 COMIC STRIPS: Humorous strips: *Moose* by Bob Weber; *Tiger* by Bud Blake; *Eek & Meek* by Howie Schneider; *Tumbleweeds* by Tom K. Ryan. There was also *Tales of the Green Beret* by Joe Kubert, based on Robin Moore's novel.

MAGAZINES: *Creepy* and later *Eerie*, both devoted to the horror genre.

COMIC BOOKS: Gold Key started publishing the *Tarzan* novels adapted by Russ Manning. Jules Feiffer's book *The Great Comic Book Heroes* was published.

EUROPE: In April the first Tarzan books (translations of the Gold Key issues) were published in Germany. The first European Comics Congress took place in Bordighera. In Italy *Linus* was published; it was a magazine for comics fans with comic strips for adults. There was an exhibition in Göteborg entitled 'Die phantastische Welt der Comics' ('The Fantastic World of Comics') and the Svenska Serieakademien (Svenska Comics Academy) was founded.

OTHER MEDIA: Walt Disney's feature film *Mary Poppins* achieved record audiences. *I Spy* was shown on television with a white man and a black man playing equally important main parts.

1966 EUROPE: In Germany, Gold Key comic books like *Magnus* appeared from March onwards, Marvel comic books entitled *Hit Comics* appeared from August onwards, and in September *Superman* also appeared. Hermann (Hermann Huppen) drew *Bernard Prince* and *Jugurtha* for *Tintin*. In France *Jodelle* by Guy Peellaert and Pierre Bartier appeared. SOCERLID brought out the magazine *Phénix*. The second Comics Congress was held in Lucca, in Italy.

OTHER MEDIA: *Phoebe Zeit-Geist* appeared in the magazine *Evergreen Review*. A *Superman* musical came out. *Batman* and *Tarzan* series appeared on television. Walt Disney Productions continued to function after Walt Disney's death.

1967 COMIC STRIPS: *Redeye* by Gordon Bess.

EUROPE: In September the first issue of *Deutsches MAD* appeared. An exhibition entitled 'Bande Dessinée et Figuration Narrative' (Comic Strips and Narrative Drawings) was held in the Louvre, in Paris.

OTHER MEDIA: CBS launched a series on television based on *The Lone Ranger, Superman, Mighty Mouse, Space Ghost* etc. Walt Disney Productions brought out a cartoon film called *The Jungle Book*. A *Peanuts* musical came out. In France Belvision made a cartoon film of *Astérix le Gaulois*.

1968 COMIC STRIPS: *Boner's Ark* by Addison (Mort Walker) and *Dateline: Danger* by A. McWilliams and John Saunders. Russ Manning took over *Tarzan*. Tex Blaisdell continued *Little Orphan Annie* after Harold Gray's death. *Buck Rogers* was discontinued.

EUROPE: A few new strips appeared in Germany, among them *Perry* and *Tom Berry*. In Holland a comics club called Het Stripschaft was formed.

OTHER MEDIA: Robert Crumb joined the Underground with *Zap Comics*. Belvision finished work on the cartoon film *Astérix et Cleopatre* and started on *Le Temple du Soleil*.

1969 EUROPE: Germany imported new series from America, such as *Blitzmann* and *Grüne Laterne* but published also the pocket comics produced by Kaukaproduktion, which contained a number of imported Belgian strips.

1970 COMIC STRIPS: *Half Hitch* by Hank Ketcham; *Lancelot* by Penn and Coker, Jr.; *Friday Foster* by Jim Lawrence and Jorge Longaron.

COMIC BOOKS: Marvel published *Conan the Barbarian*. The Academy of Comic Book Art was founded.

1971 COMIC STRIPS: *Dark Shadows* drawn by K. Bruce, was the first comic strip based on a successful series of television (afternoon) programmes, of the gothic horror genre.

COMIC BOOKS: The Comics Code was relaxed and in January *Superman* No. 233 initiated a new era. *Spider Man* was published without the seal of the Code: this was because drugs were mentioned in the story. Marvel Comics produced *Savage Tales* and *M* (for 'mature readers').

Notes

Introduction
1 Jules Feiffer *The Great Comic Book Heroes* (New York 1965, London 1967) p. 186.

1 The characteristics of comics
1 This incident is always cited as an example of the importance of comics in American life.
2 Leo Bogart 'Comic Strips and Their Adult Readers', *The Funnies. An American Idiom* ed. David Manning White and Robert H. Abe (New York 1963) p. 244 f.
3 The first daily comic strip was Clare Brigg's *A. Piker Clerk* in the *Chicago American* (1904). However *Mutt* and *Jeff* was the first successful daily strip and the first to awaken interest.
4 Tabloid format is half the size of a newspaper page.
5 See Chapter 4 'Super-heroes'.
6 See Chapter 5 'Criticism and Censorship'.
7 *Cartoonist Profiles* No. 3, Summer 1969, 'The Al Williamson Story' p. 36.
8 See Chapter 8 'The European Comics Scene'.

2 Humour and everyday life
1 Such examples, of course, existed and still exist also in comic strips and comic books. Jerry Lewis started in DC booklets with Dean Martin as partner. One can find Stan Laurel and Oliver Hardy, Bud Abbott and Lou Costello or Bob Hope in comic books, whilst Charlie Chaplin appeared in a comic strip (*Charlie Chaplin's Comic Capers*). Mark Twain is represented in the *Classics Illustrated* and *Rowan and Martin's Laugh In* appears also as a gag strip in the comics section of newspapers.
2 In the introduction to the new edition of George W. Peck's *Peck's Bad Boy and His Pa* (New York 1958) Thomas Alva Edison and the Prince of Wales are mentioned as great practical jokers. Edison made Mark Twain get on to an apparatus which induced violent diarrhoea; the Prince of Wales served the German Kaiser with so-called roast wild boar, which was in fact a dog.
3 It is interesting to note that *Max and Moritz* appeared in America in 1870. A German equivalent of *Hennery the Bad Boy* would be *Mätzchen Mohr* from *Auerbachs deutscher Kinderkalender* (*Auerbach's German Children's Yearbook*).
4 In this Chic Young speaks for all artists drawing for the funnies.
5 Grobian Gans *Die Ducks. Psychogramm einer Sippe* (*The Duck Family. Psychogram of a Kinship*) (Munich 1970) may be of special interest in this context.
6 Robert Warshow 'Woofed with Dreams', *The Funnies. An American Idiom* ed. David Manning White and Robert H. Abel (New York 1963) p. 145.

7 Reuel Denney 'The Revolt Against Naturalism', *The Funnies. An American Idiom* ed. David Manning White and Robert H. Abel (New York 1963) p. 67.
8 The pseudonym has been abandoned in the interest of documentary exactness, not because there is any tie between the authors and the John Birch Society. Moreover Capp has changed his name, by law.
9 John Steinbeck, Introduction *The World of Li'l Abner* (New York 1952).
10 Al Capp, Foreword *The World of Li'l Abner* (New York 1952).
11 *From Dogpatch to Slobbovia—The Gasp!! World of Li'l Abner as Seen by David Manning White with Certain Illuminating Remarks by Al Capp* (Boston 1964) p. 90.
12 See Arthur J. Brodbeck and David Manning White 'How to Read Li'l Abner Intelligently', *The Funnies. An American Idiom* ed. David Manning White and Robert H. Abel (New York 1963). David Manning White is the greatest American expert on comics and he is also a friend of Al Capp.
13 This also throws a different light on Steinbeck's other favourite strip *Terry and The Pirates*.
14 *Playboy*, December 1965, p. 89 ff.

3 Adventure and melodrama
1 For the films Tarzan's victory cry has been made up from five different soundtracks: a camel's bleat; a hyena's howl; the growling of a dog; the note G played on a violin; and Johnny Weissmuller yodelling.
2 More about this in Chapter 10 'The Art of Comics'.
3 Robert M. Hodes *Tarzan* MS. (New York 1970) p. 11.
4 Edgar Rice Burroughs' novels about *John Carter of Mars* were adapted and drawn for comic strips by his son John Coleman Burroughs.
5 *Buck Rogers* was discontinued in 1968, when only twenty-eight papers were carrying the strip—compared to 287 at the peak of its popularity. Technical developments in the Apollo moon programme robbed the strip of its original appeal.
6 Ray Bradbury *Tomorrow Midnight* (New York 1966).
7 Gardner F. Fox has written 86 novels, including *Escape Across the Cosmos*, *Warrior of Llarn* and *The Borgia Blade*; his work comprises 'cloak and dagger' as well as science fiction tales.
8 See Chapter 5 'Criticism and Censorship'.
9 See also Chapter 11 'Trends and Developments' where she and Shawn North are mentioned.
10 Cf. Stephen Becker *Comic Art in America* (New York 1959) p. 195.
11 *Newsweek*, 24 April 1950.
12 The relationship between the various mass media is discussed in Chapter 7 'Inter-Media Dependencies'.

13 Fran Striker *The Lone Ranger and Tonto* (New York 1940) p. 6.

14 *Sheriff Klassiker* No. 166 (1971).

15 See for instance John D. Masters' unpublished Ph.D. thesis *Wyatt Earp's Virility and his Buntline Special* (Dodge City, Kansas).

4 Super-heroes

1 Jim Steranko *The Steranko History of Comics* vol. 1 (Reading, Pennsylvania 1970) p. 38 f.

2 Mxyzptlk is pronounced Mix-yes-pitelek.

3 Shazam: 'S' for Solomon's wisdom; 'H' for Hercules' strength; 'A' for Atlas' perseverance; 'Z' for Zeus' power; 'A' for Achilles' courage; 'M' for Mercury's speed.

4 Note how many people connected with Superman have the initials L.L. Lois Lane, Lana Lang, Lori Lemaris, Lex Luthor, Lyla Lerrol, etc.

5 MMMS: Merry Marvel Marching Society; later called Marvelmania.

6 See also Richard Kluger 'Sex and the Superman' *Partisan Review* vol. XIII (1966) p. 111 ff.

7 Leslie Fiedler 'The Middle Against Both Ends' (1955), *Mass Culture* ed. B. Rosenberg and D. White (New York 1957, London and New York 1965).

8 Before her *Amazona, The Mighty Woman* appeared in 1940—but only in a single issue of *Planet Comics*.

9 Kluger's suspicion that Wonder Woman may be a transvestite is absurd. See Richard Kluger 'Sex and the Superman' *Partisan Review* vol. XIII (1966).

10 Super-heroines like to wear glasses when they adopt their secret identity—even more so than their male colleagues do—although they are by no means short-sighted.

5 Criticism and censorship

1 Excerpts from the testimony of William M. Gaines, Publisher, Entertaining Comics Group, New York, N.Y., in US Congress, Senate Committee on the Judiciary: Subcommittee to Investigate Juvenile Delinquency, *Juvenile Delinquency (comic books)*; hearings pursuant to S. 190, April 21, 22 and June 4, 1954 (83:2, 1954), pp. 97–109.

2 Compare, for instance A. Bandura, Dorothea Ross and Sheila A. Ross 'Transmission of Aggression through Imitation of Aggressive Models', *J. Abnorm. Soc. Psychol.*, 63 (1961) pp. 575–82; L. Berkowitz 'Some Factors Affecting the Reduction of Overt Hostility' *J. Abnorm. Soc. Psychol.*, 60 (1960) pp. 14–22; S. Feshbach 'The Catharsis Hypothesis and some Consequences of Interaction with Aggressive and Neutral Play Objects' *J. Personality* 24 (1956) pp. 449–62; J. T. Klapper *The Effects of Mass Communication* (Glencoe, Ill. 1960).

3 For instance Arnold Arnold's *Violence and Your Child* (Award Books, New York 1969) where Wertham's accusations reappeared in 1969.

4 Gershom Legman *Love and Death. A Study in Censorship* (New York 1949).

5 Frederic Wertham, M.D. *Seduction of the Innocent* (New York 1954).

6 Benjamin Spock, M.D. *Dr. Spock talks about Problems of Parents* (Greenwich Conn. 1965) p. 210.

7 See Robert Warshow 'The Gangster as Tragic Hero' *The Immediate Experience* (New York 1970).

8 Marilyn Graalf 'Violence in Comic Books (Before Self-Regulation by the Comics Industry)', *Violence and the Mass Media* ed. Otto N. Larsen (New York and London 1968) p. 95.

9 See also Chapter 11 'Trends and Developments'.

6 Society as portrayed in comics

1 David Manning White and Robert H. Abel 'Comic Strips and American Culture', *The Funnies. An American Idiom* ed. Robert H. Abel and David Manning White (New York 1963) p. 10.

2 Cover Story to *Peanuts, Time,* 9 April 1965, p. 84.

3 *Giff Wiff* No. 20, May 1966, p. 30: 'pas question de faire ça'.

4 *Cartoonist Profiles* No. 3, Summer 1969, p. 29.

5 Cover story to *Peanuts, Time,* 9 April 1965, p. 84.

6 Compare *Time,* 2 November 1970, p. 37.

7 For details of the Code and the resulting changes in the content of comics see Chapter 11 'Trends and Developments'.

8 *Catalogue of Famous Artists and Writers* (King Features Syndicate 1949) p. 4.

9 Usually the following surveys are consulted:
E. J. Robinson and D. M. White 'Who Reads the Funnies—and Why?' (1963).
Francis E. Barcus 'The World of Sunday Comics' (1963).
Gerhart Saenger 'Male and Female Relations in the American Comic Strip' (1955).
Leo Bogart 'Comic Strips and Their Adult Readers' (1957).
All the essays in *The Funnies. An American Idiom* ed. David Manning White and Robert H. Abel (New York 1963).

10 The convention of making Tonto speak in broken English was taken from the radio series: Tonto's part was played by a former Shakespearean actor of Irish extraction who could only play a Red Indian by speaking in broken English.

11 Jules Feiffer 'The Great Comic Book Heroes', *Playboy*, October 1965, p. 80.

12 Frederic Wertham, M.D. *Seduction of the Innocent* (New York 1954) p. 40.

13 ibid. p. 34.

14 Leslie Fiedler 'The Middle Against Both Ends' (1955), *Mass Culture* ed. B. Rosenberg and D. White (New York 1957, London and New York 1965), p. 545.

15 Information given to the authors by a chief editor.

16 Information given to the authors by a chief editor.

17 Robert Warshow 'American Popular Culture' (1954), *The Immediate Experience* (New York 1970) p. 39.

18 Information given to the authors.

19 Figure arrived at after consulting the CMAA statistics, which show that 298,279,786 comic books were sold in America in 1968; an increase of 4% over the year 1967.

7 Inter-media dependencies

1 An author writing for the 'feuilleton' of a paper originally wrote day by day instalments.

2 Mary Noel *Villains Galore . . . The Heyday of the Popular Story Weekly* (New York 1954) p. 18.

3 Richard Lupoff *Edgar Rice Burroughs: Master of Adventure* (New York 1968).

4 Compare Chapter 3 'Adventure and Melodrama'.

5 Big Little Books were a combination of comic book and children's book. See Chapter 1 'The Characteristics of Comics'.

6 Compare the chapter on the pulps in Jim Steranko's *The Steranko History of Comics* vol. 1 (Reading, Pennsylvania 1970).

7 *True Comics* are an exception, because they have a different origin. See Chapter 5 'Criticism and Censorship'.

8 Today co-operation between television and publishing firms is genuinely desired.

9 At the same time as Orson Welles was speaking the Shadow's voice he gave his listeners a tremendous shock—in fact people still talk about it today—when he broadcast his version of H. G. Wells' *War of the Worlds* over the radio, on Halloween in 1938. Incidentally, a repeat of this broadcast, on Halloween in 1971, caused another scare in some parts of the USA.

10 Compare the chapter on the pulps in Jim Steranko's *The Steranko History of Comics* vol. 1 (Reading, Pennsylvania 1970) p. 14–33.

11 *Ellery Queen's Mystery Magazine* evolved from *Black Mask*, the best of the detective pulps which gave birth to a new style of writing

known as the 'Black Mask School of Writing'. Authors who adopted this style in the thirties and forties included Dashiell Hammett, Erle Stanley Gardner, Carroll John Daly, John D. MacDonald, Raymond Chandler and Frank Gruber. There are a large number of film and television adaptations of these authors' works. Radio and also comics to a certain extent, used some of their themes.

12 Compare Jim Steranko *The Steranko History of Comics* vol. 1 (Reading, Pennsylvania 1970) p. 47.

13 Comics based on Walt Disney feature films often change the titles and the main protagonists. See Chapter 2 'Humour and Everyday Life'.

8 The European comics scene

1 Compare 'Superman als Sozialist' ('Superman as Socialist') *Süddeutsche Zeitung* No. 295, 10 December 1969, p. 29.

2 The information about the America-image put forward in comics was given to the authors on enquiry.

3 Information received from Ehapa Verlag.

4 Information received from Bulls Pressedienst.

5 Example of readers' reaction to comics: the editors of the paper *Lübecker Nachrichten* asked readers in the spring of 1969 whether they wished the comic strip *Wurzel (Fred Basset)* to continue. 95% of the answers were in favour of the strip being retained, 5% were against it; of the latter, however, only 3·5% were against any kind of comic strip at all: the other 1·5% wanted a different strip. Roughly a third of those who wrote in wanted an additional strip.

6 Information given in answer to authors' questions.

7 More about this in Chapter 9 'Sex and Satire'.

8 SOCERLID—Société Civile d'Etudes et de Recherches des Littératures Dessinées (Society for Study and Research into Picture-literature) founded 4 November 1965.

9 'Fellini and Comics' *Film*, February 1966, p. 24–5. Fellini, an admirer of comics, visited Marvel Comics and wrote the introduction to Jim Steranko's book about comic books.

10 This is a constant feature in *Diabolik*, as conceived by A. Giussani one of its creators.

11 'Comics 1966: Kennen Sie Jena, das Höllenweib?', *Twen*, January 1967, p. 64.

12 Mary Ann Reese 'Andy Capp Is No 'andicap', *Stars and Stripes*, 24 January 1971, comics section pp. iv–v.

9 Sex and satire

1 Jules Feiffer 'The Great Comic Book Heroes', *Playboy*, October 1965, p. 81.

2 Jacob Brackman writes euphorically about comics in his article 'The International Comix Conspiracy', *Playboy*, December 1970, p. 195.

3 Compare, for instance *Wonder Wart-Hog, Captain Crud and Other Super Stuff* ed. Chuck Alverson (New York 1967). Comic artists Vaughn Bode and Hank Hinton, both represented in this book, moved over to the Establishment at a later date.

4 'X' rating means that a film is forbidden to anyone under eighteen years of age.

10 The art of comics

1 Opinion given in answer to authors' questions.

2 Opinion given in answer to authors' questions.

3 Mort Walker 'Look Ma! I'm an Artist', *Cartoonist Profiles* No. 4, Summer 1969, p. 46–7.

4 Milton Caniff was one of the first comics artists whose work was shown in museums. His drawings for *Terry and the Pirates* were in the Metropolitan Museum of Art in 1944 and his drawings for *Male Call* were exhibited in the Berkshire Museum in 1945.

5 In 1946, when Caniff had given up *Terry and the Pirates* and had started to draw *Steve Canyon* a 'picture biography' was published entitled *Milton Caniff: Rembrandt of the Comic Strip*. This metaphor was later taken up again; see *The Funnies*, Annual No. 1, ed. J. P. Adams (New York 1959) p. 30.

6 See Pierre Couperie, Maurice Horn and others *A History of the Comic Strip* (New York 1968) p. 219.

7 Famous Artists have a special course for pupils who want to become comics artists, and there are any number of correspondence courses on 'How to Draw Comics'.

8 The reader can still discover this pleasure, even today, in reprints of pages from old comics books, for instance in *The Great Super Heroes* by Jules Feiffer.

9 John Benson 'An Interview with Will Eisner', *Witzend* No. 6, p. 7.

10 'Recent Discovery! Bud Fisher Scrapbooks!', *Cartoonist Profiles* No. 3, Summer 1969, p. 47.

11 John Benson 'An Interview with Will Eisner', *Witzend* No. 6, p. 10.

12 Jim Steranko in *Artist Self Portraits* (Marvelmania International).

13 'Burne Hogarth interviewé par Eric Leguebe', *Phénix* No. 7, March 1968, p. 7 f.

14 Roy Crane enriched comics with many new techniques. The best known is the 'craftint' technique; the drawing is done on a specially prepared 'Craftint "doubletone" paper' and a developing fluid which produces different grades of light and shadow is then applied. It is a technique which requires great skill.

15 'The Heart of Juliet Jones by Stan Drake' *Cartoonist Profiles* No. 4, November 1969, pp. 4–13.

16 Kenneth E. Eble 'Our Serious Funnies' (1959), *The Funnies. An American Idiom* ed. David Manning White and Robert H. Abel (New York 1963) p. 109.

11 Trends and developments

1 Compare *Justice League of America* No. 79, March 1970.

2 *Iron Man* No. 25, May 1970.

3 Compare *Daredevil* No. 71, December 1970.

4 Compare *Green Lantern* No. 80, October 1970.

5 Code Administrator in conversation with the authors.

6 Stan Lee in conversation with the authors. He was not referring to any specific problem.

7 Lindsy Van Gelder and Lawrence Van Gelder 'The Radicalization of the Superheroes', *New York*, October 1970, p. 43.

8 Compare 'The Radicalization of the Superheroes', ibid.

9 Lawrence Van Gelder 'Comic-Book Industry to Allow Stories on Narcotics', *The New York Times*, 16 April 1971.

Bibliography

Chapter 1: The Characteristics of Comics

Anon. *Famous Artists and Writers of King Features Syndicate* (New York 1949)

Baumgärtner, Alfred C. *Die Welt der Comics* (Bochum 1965)

Becker, Stephen *Comic Art in America* (New York 1959)

Benayonn, Robert *Le Ballon dans la Bande Dessinée* (Paris 1968)

Couperie, Pierre, Maurice Horn and others *A History of the Comic Strip* (New York 1968)

McLuhan, Marshall *The Mechanical Bride, Folklore of Industrial Man* (Boston 1951, London 1967)

Newspaper Comics Council *Cavalcade of American Funnies. A History of Comic Strips from 1896* (New York 1970)

Perry, George and Alan Aldridge *The Penguin Book of Comics* (London 1971)

Riha, Karl *Zok roarr wumm. Zur Geschichte der Comics-Literatur* (Steinbach, Giessen 1970)

Rosenberg, Bernard and David Manning White (ed.) *Mass Culture. The Popular Arts in America.* (New York 1957, London and New York 1965)

Sternberg, Jaques, Michael Caen, Jaques Lob (ed.) *Les Chefs-d'Oeuvres de la Bande Dessinée* (Paris 1967)

Waugh, Coulton *The Comics* (New York 1947)

White, David Manning and Robert H. Abel (ed.) *The Funnies. An American Idiom* (New York 1963)

These books also study topics which are discussed in Chapter 2. The reader will also find the following magazines helpful: *Cartoonist Profiles* (Fairfield, Conn.); *Giff-Whiff* (Paris); *Linus* (Milan); *Phénix* (Paris); *Stripschrift* (Rijswijk, Holland).

Chapter 2: Humour and Everyday Life

Adams, John P. (ed.) *The Funnies, Annual No. 1* (New York 1959)

Brodbeck, Arthur J. and David Manning White 'How to Read Li'l Abner Intelligently', in *The Funnies* ed. White and Abel

Capp, Al *The World of Li'l Abner (With an Introduction by John Steinbeck)* (New York 1952)

Denney, Reuel 'The Revolt Against Naturalism; in *The Funnies* ed. White and Abel

From Dogpatch to Slobbovia—The Gasp!! World of Li'l Abner as Seen by David Manning White with Certain Illuminating Remarks by Al Capp (Boston 1964)

Gans, Grobian *Die Ducks. Psychogramm einer Sippe* (Munich 1970)

'Good Grief', cover story in *Time* 9 April 1965, p. 80 ff.

'Interview with Al Capp', in *Playboy* December 1965, p. 89 ff.

Kelly, Walt *Ten Ever-Loving' Blue-Eyed Years With Pogo* (New York 1959)

Loria, Jeffrey H. *What's It All About, Charlie Brown? Peanuts Kids Look at America Today* (New York 1968)

Short, Robert L. *The Gospel According to Peanuts* (New York 1964, London 1969)

'Speaking of Pictures: Pogofenokee Land', in *Life* 12 May 1952, pp. 12–14

'Special Al Capp', in *Giff-Whiff* No. 23, March 1967

Warshow, Robert 'Woofed with Dreams', in *The Funnies* ed. White and Abel

Chapter 3: Adventure and Melodrama

Burroughs, Edgar Rice and Burne Hogarth *Tarzan, Seigneur de la Jungle* (Paris 1967)

Dille, Robert C. (ed.) *The Collected Works of Buck Rogers in the 25th Century* (New York 1970)

'Dumas From Ohio', article about Milton Caniff in *Newsweek* 24 April 1950

'Hal Foster' in *Phénix Spécial* No. 9, 1969

Hodes, Robert M. *Tarzan, MS.* (New York 1970)

Lacassin, Francis 'Tarzan; mythe triomphant, mythe humilié', in *Bizarre Numéro spécial Tarzan* (Paris 1963)

Tarzan ou le Chevalier crispé (Paris 1971)

Lupoff, Richard A. *Edgar Rice Burroughs: Master of Adventure* (New York 1968)

'Tarzan' in *Phénix Spécial Couleur* No. 1, 1970

Raymond, Alex *Flash Gordon* (New York 1967)

Chapter 4: Super-heroes

Akademie der Künste (publisher) *Vom Geist der Superhelden* (Berlin 1971)

'Comic Book Editor for National' *Cartoonist Profiles* No. 6, May 1970

Feiffer, Jules *The Great Comic Book Heroes* (New York 1965, London 1967)

Feiffer, Jules 'The Great Comic Book Heroes', in *Playboy* October 1965, p. 75 ff.

Kluger, Richard 'Sex and the Superman', in *Partisan Review* January 1966, pp. 111–5

Lupoff Dick and Don Thompson (ed.) *All in Color for a Dime* (New York 1970)

Mark, Norman 'The New Superhero (Is a Pretty Kinky Guy)', in *Eye* February 1969, p. 40 ff

'Stan Lee and Marvel Comics' *Cartoonist Profiles* No. 4, Autumn 1969

Steranko, Jim *The Steranko History of Comics* vol. 1 (Reading, Pennsylvania 1970)

Chapter 5: Criticism and Censorship
Arnold, Arnold *Violence and Your Child* (New York 1969)

Larsen, Otto N. (ed.) *Violence and the Mass Media* (London and New York 1968)

Legman, Gershom *Love and Death, A Study in Censorship* (New York 1949)

Warshow, Robert 'Paul, the Horror Comics, and Dr Wertham', in *Mass Culture* ed. Rosenberg and White

Wertham, Frederic M.D. *A Sign for Cain* (New York 1966)

Wertham, Frederic M.D. *Seduction of the Innocent* (New York 1954)

Chapter 6: Society as Portrayed in Comics
Barcus, Francis E. 'The World of Sunday Comics', in *The Funnies* ed. White and Abel

Bogart, Leo 'Comic Strips and Their Adult Readers', in *The Funnies* ed. White and Abel

Fiedler, Leslie 'The Middle Against Both Ends', in *Mass Culture* ed. Rosenberg and White

Robinson, E. J. and David Manning White 'Who Reads the Funnies—and Why?', in *The Funnies* ed. White and Abel

Saenger, Gerhart 'Male and Female Relations in the American Comic Strip', in *The Funnies* ed. White and Abel

Warshow, Robert *The Immediate Experience* (New York 1970)

Chapter 7: Inter-Media Dependencies
Ackerman, Forrest J. *Boris Karloff, The Frankenscience Monster* (New York 1969)

Essoe, Gabe *Tarzan of the Movies* (New York 1968)

'Fellini and Comics', interview with Federico Fellini in *Film* February 1966, p. 24 ff.

Gasca, Luis *Los comics en la pantalla* (San Sebastian 1965)

Goodstone, Tony (ed.) *The Pulps* (New York 1970)

Gruber, Frank *The Pulp Jungle* (Los Angeles 1967)

Harmon, Jim *The Great Radio Heroes* (New York 1967)

Higby, Mary Jane *Tune in Tomorrow* (New York 1968)

Lacassin, Francis 'Tarzan; mythe triomphant, mythe humilié', in *Bizarre Numéro spécial Tarzan* (Paris 1963)

Lupoff, Richard A. *Edgar Rice Burroughs: Master of Adventure* (New York 1968)

Noel, Mary *Villains Galore . . . The Heyday of the Popular Story Weekly* (New York 1954)

Peterson, Theodore *Magazines in the Twentieth Century* (Urbana, Ill. 1964)

Schickel, Richard *Walt Disney* (London 1968): originally published as *The Disney Version* (New York 1968)

Shulman, Arthur and Roger Corman *How Sweet It Was. Television: A Pictorial Commentary* (New York 1966)

Steranko, Jim *The Steranko History of Comics* vol. 1 (Reading, Pennsylvania 1970)

Chapter 8: The European Comics Scene
Beccin, Leonardo *Il fumetto in Italia* (Florence 1971)

Ghiringhelli, Zeno *Erotismo & Fumetti* (Milan 1969)

Hamme, Jean Van *Introduction à la bande dessinée Belge* (Brussels 1968)

'Le dossier Hergé', in *Tintin* No. 1159, 14 January 1971

Metken, Günter *Comics* (Frankfurt am Main 1970)

Pforte, Dieter 'Deutschsprachige Comics', in *Comic Strips. Geschichte, Struktur, Wirkung und Verbreitung der Bildergeschichte*, exhibition catalogue of the Akademie der Künste (Berlin 1970)

Pohl, Ulrich *Von Max und Moritz bis Fix und Foxi* (Munich 1970)

Chapter 9: Sex and Satire
Brackman, Jacob 'The International Comix Conspiracy', in *Playboy* December 1970, p. 195 ff.

Flagler, J. M. 'The *MAD* Miracle', in *Look* 19 March 1968, p. 46 ff.

Gilmore, Donald H. *Sex and Censorship in the Visual Arts* (San Diego 1970)

Horn, Maurice 'Introduction: What is Comic Art?', in *75 Years of the Comics* ed. The New York Cultural Center (Boston and New York 1971)

Sadoul, Jacques *L'enfer des bulles* (Paris 1968)

Winick, Charles 'Teenagers, Satire, and *MAD*', in *People, Society and Mass Communications* ed. Lewis Anthony Dexter and David Manning White (London and New York 1964)

Chapter 10: The Art of Comics
Benson, Jones 'An Interview with Will Eisner', in *Witzend* No. 6, p. 9 ff.

Lippard, Lucy R. *Pop Art* (New York 1966, London 1967)

'Pop Art et Comic Books', interview with Roy Lichtenstein, in *Giff-Wiff* No. 20, May 1966, pp. 6–15

Rublowsky, John *Pop Art* (New York 1965)

Willette, Allen (ed.) *Top Cartoonists Tell How They Create America's Favorite Comics* (Fort Lauderdale, Florida 1964)

Chapter 11: Trends and Developments
Benson, John 'An Interview with Will Eisner', in *Witzend* No. 6, p. 9 ff.

Braun, Saul 'Shazam! Here comes Captain Relevant', in *New York Times Magazine* 2 May 1971, pp. 32–55

Gelder, Lindsy Van and Lawrence Van Gelder 'The Radicalization of the Superheroes', in *New York* October 1970, pp. 36–43

Acknowledgements

We should like to express our gratitude to all who have helped to make this book a success.

We are particularly indebted to:

Stan Lee of Marvel Comics Group, New York, for his inspiration and encouragement, and for admitting us into the select circle of the FFFers.

Maria-M. Lamm of Bulls Pressedienst, Frankfurt, and Harold Schneider of King Features Syndicate, New York, for supplying valuable information and for generously making available to us the archives of Bulls and King Features Syndicate.

Jack L. Hees and George H. Pipal of United Press International/ United Features Syndicate, Frankfurt/New York, for supplying picture material and for giving us important advice.

The following people kindly provided us with information and material:

Leonard Darvin, Administrator of the Comics Code Authority, New York

Walt Kelly, New York

Jules Feiffer, New York

Wallace Wood, Woodmere/New York

Woody Gelman, New York

Charles M. Schulz, Sebastopol/California

David Goldin, Archives of Radio Yesteryear, New York

Deena Stevens, Gilberton Company, New York

Birgit C. Liesching, Western Publishing Company, London

Sal Gentile, Charlton Comics Group, Derby/Connecticut

Ulrich Pohl, Kauka Verlag, Munich, Germany

Ernim Heimberger and Dieter Rex, Bildschriftenverlag, Aachen, Germany

Carmine Infantino and Bernard Kashdan, National Periodical Publications, New York

Irmhild Günther, Ehapa Verlag, Stuttgart, Germany

The following people gave us friendly help:

Henry Raduta, Chicago Tribune—New York News Syndicate, New York

Michael Chinigo, International Feature Enterprises, Rome

Joseph D. McGraw, Publishers—Hall Syndicate, New York

John Sanders, International Publishing Corporation, London

Viviane Rousie, Editions du Lombard, Brussels

Louis Ollivier, Dargaud S.A. Editeur, Neuilly-sur-Seine, France

Sergio Bonelli, Edizioni Araldo, Milan, Italy

Piero Dami, Eurostudio, Milan, Italy

A. Giussani, Casa Editrice 'Astorina' Milan, Italy

Michael I. Silberkleit, Archie Comic Publications, New York

George A. Pflaum, Jr, George A. Pflaum Publisher, Dayton/ Ohio, USA

Wallace B. Black, T. S. Denison Co./Treasure Chest

James Warren, Warren Publishing Company, New York

Jay Lynch, Bijou Publishing Empire, Chicago, USA

Horst Koblischek, Walt Disney Productions, Frankfurt, Germany

Phil Sammeth, Walt Disney Productions, Burbank, California, USA

Gigi Spina, Valentina Verlag, Bad Honnef, Germany

Fred Mahlstedt, Columbia Broadcasting System, New York

Arnold Lewis, Licensing Corporation of America, New York

A. Tarbard, Associated Newspapers, Ltd., London

Peter Knight, London Express News & Feature Services, London

Paul Eisler, Syndication International, London

The following people kindly gave us permission to reprint:

Edizioni Erregi, Milan, Italy

Editoriale Corno, Milan, Italy

S.E.P.I.M. Milan, Italy

Stern, Hamburg, Germany

20th Century Fox Films, Frankfurt, Germany

Publicness, Paris

Editions Aventures et Voyages, Paris

Verlag H.M. Hieronimi, Bonn, Germany

Carl Schünemann Verlag, Bremen, Germany

Viking Press, New York

März Verlag, Frankfurt, Germany

Grove Press, New York

Konkret Buchverlag, Hamburg, Germany

Above all we should like to thank Professor Dr Friedrich G. Friedmann of the Amerika-Institut of Munich University for his kind help and encouragement.

Index

(Figures in italics refer to illustrations. All entries refer to American comics unless stated otherwise.)